ITEM NO: 2019654

KT-452-162

DOING QUALITATIVE RESEARCH

DAVID SILVERMAN
DOING QUALITATIVE RESEARCH
A PRACTICAL HANDBOOK
THIRD EDITION

Los Angeles | London | New Delhi
Singapore | Washington DC

Third edition © David Silverman 2010

Chapter 14, third edition © Clive Seale 2010

First edition published 2000; second edition published 2005
Reprinted 2000, 2001, 2002, 2003, 2004, 2010 and 2011

Apart from any fair dealing for the purposes of research or
private study, or criticism or review, as permitted under the
Copyright, Designs and Patents Act, 1988, this publication may
be reproduced, stored or transmitted in any form, or by
any means, only with the prior permission in writing of the
publishers, or in the case of reprographic reproduction, in
accordance with the terms of licences issued by the Copyright
Licensing Agency. Enquiries concerning reproduction outside
those terms should be sent to the publishers.

SAGE Publications Ltd
1 Oliver's Yard
55 City Road
London EC1Y 1SP

SAGE Publications Inc.
2455 Teller Road
Thousand Oaks, California 91320

SAGE Publications India Pvt Ltd
B 1/I 1 Mohan Cooperative Industrial Area
Mathura Road
New Delhi 110 044

SAGE Publications Asia-Pacific Pte Ltd
33 Pekin Street #02-01
Far East Square
Singapore 048763

British Library Cataloguing in Publication data

A catalogue record for this book is available from the
British Library

ISBN 978-1-84860-033-1
ISBN 978-1-84860-034-8 (pbk)

Library of Congress Control Number: 2008941909

Typeset by C&M Digitals (P) Ltd, Chennai, India
Printed in Great Britain by TJ International, Padstow, Cornwall
Printed on paper from sustainable resources

For my students

If this stone won't budge at present and is wedged in, move some of the other stones round it first.

All we want to do is to straighten you up on the track if your coach is crooked on the rails. Driving it afterwards we shall leave to you. (Wittgenstein, 1980: 39e)

Contents

Preface to the Third Edition

This edition of *Doing Qualitative Research* is substantially updated and revised. It includes two new chapters on collecting qualitative data and on ethical issues in student research. In addition, much more attention has been given to visual data and to consideration of how theoretical models inform qualitative research. The remaining chapters have all been revised and updated.

Perhaps the most striking change is a new problem-based format which makes extensive use of comments and queries by recent research students. Additional study features include tips and links to websites throughout the text, and an expanded index and glossary. I have also tried to make this edition even more responsive to the needs of the range of students from different disciplines who are involved with qualitative research projects.

I am very excited by the new companion website for this book. This website provides free access to over 50 recent journal articles relevant to the material found here. It also offers further student advice and exercises.

This third edition underlines my aim to offer a basic primer for research students, combining 'hands-on' guidance on completing a good qualitative research project with practical advice on the criteria used in oral examinations and in publication. I have also attempted to make the book useful and accessible to the many MA and BA students who now prepare qualitative research dissertations. Although such students will normally be expected to complete their research in months rather than years, they face the same problems of research design, execution and writing up discussed in this book. Even if they do not face an oral examination on their research, the best MA students should be thinking about publishing their work, and both BA and MA students should be interested in how higher-level work is evaluated and the significance of 'originality'.

The content of this book derives from my experience of supervising many MA dissertations and around 30 successful PhDs. Supervision and course teaching have convinced me that the only way to learn the craft skills of qualitative research is to apply classroom knowledge about different methodologies to actual data (found here in the case studies and exercises provided in each chapter).

During the past 10 years, I have taught workshops for research students in a range of disciplines from sociology to management and community medicine in the UK, France, Finland, Norway, Sweden, Denmark, Sri Lanka and Tanzania. I have been struck by the energy and originality that a new generation of students is bringing to our field. This book draws upon the lessons I have learned from that experience, including thinking through whether qualitative research is properly fitted to your research problem (see Chapter 2) and understanding the ways in which doing qualitative research is always a theoretically driven undertaking (Chapter 7).

Qualitative research is a contested terrain in which very different models and methods compete for attention. My own biases have been made explicit in my recent book *A Very Short, Fairly Interesting, Reasonably Cheap Book about Qualitative Research* (Sage, 2007). By contrast, in this book, while I do not claim neutrality, I have tried to be reasonably even-handed and, thereby, to reach out to a wide range of readers.

My focus here on completing a research project complements the discussion of the uses and limitations of different qualitative research methods in *Interpreting Qualitative Data* (third edition, Sage, 2006). Both are supplemented by the readings in my edited collection *Qualitative Research* (second edition, Sage, 2004) and by the authoritative texts on different disciplines and a range of research methods published in my Sage series 'Introducing Qualitative Methods'.

Chapter 14 of this book on computer-assisted qualitative data analysis was written (and updated) by Clive Seale. I am most grateful for his skilful exposition of the subject. I also want to thank Amir Marvasti for his generous permission to allow me to use some of the material that he prepared for a North American version of this book. Amir, Clive Seale and Linnie Price have also made helpful comments on parts of an early draft and I thank them for their help. Celia Kitzinger, Jonathan Potter, Jay Gubrium and Clive Seale kindly advised me on finding relevant journal articles for my website. Anne Ryen made available some of her unpublished data and Anne Murcott allowed me to quote from her unpublished paper on writing a student dissertation. I also want to thank Moira Kelly, Sally Hunt, Simon Allistone, Seta Waller, Kay Fensom and Vicki Taylor for allowing me to quote from their research diaries. The Economic and Social Research Council (ESRC) kindly gave me permission to reproduce their guidance on research ethics in Chapter 10.

Many students in four continents have allowed me to quote from their workshop papers and others have written short pieces about their work which are included here. I thank them all and hope I have followed their wishes in terms of providing or concealing their identity. I am also most grateful to Jonathan Potter, Jay Gubrium, Paul Luff, Amir Marvasti and Gary Wickham for helping me find such material from their own students.

I could not have wished for a better Sage editor than Patrick Brindle. His suggestions have invariably been stimulating and useful. I also wish to thank two other Sage staff: Emily Jenner who came up with some very helpful suggestions from previous users of this book, and Ian Antcliff for efficiently organizing the production of this book. Finally, thanks are due once again to Sara Cordell for keeping my back in working order.

Companion Website

Visit the companion website at www.sagepub.co.uk/silverman to find links to relevant Sage journal articles as well as further tips and exercises.

Part One
Introduction

Contents

Part One provides a context for thinking about doing qualitative research. A brief introduction to the themes of this book and how best to use it is provided in Chapter 1. Chapter 2 compares qualitative and quantitative research and raises questions about how to decide whether qualitative methods are appropriate for your research topic. Chapters 3 and 4 offer examples of early and late stages of research students' work and show what you can learn from their experiences and ideas. Finally, in Chapter 5, I address (and seek to demystify) the troubling concept of 'originality' in research.

1

How To Use This Book

This is the fifth textbook on methodology which I have written or edited since 1985. Everyone knows that research methods texts often sell well but that is hardly an excuse to write yet another one. So you may properly ask: what has this book to offer?

The brief answer is that, in my view, research students still lack a singly authored, 'hands-on', practical guide to the business of doing qualitative research, writing it up and making use of it. This is what this book sets out to do. Much more than other methodology texts, it aims to teach the skills of qualitative research in the context of the practical problems that face the novice researcher. To this end, it combines telling examples of students' experiences 'in the field', case studies of relevant qualitative research, summaries of key skills and exercises to test your knowledge.

In this short chapter, I outline the structure of this book and provide some suggestions about how to make optimum use of it.

Part One is aimed at the beginning research student. Part Two assumes that you have overcome your initial doubts and now need to deal with the nitty-gritty issues that arise when you start to design a research study. Chapter 6 discusses how to select a topic. Chapters 7 and 8 deal with using theories and choosing a methodology. The tricky question of selecting some case(s) (and then wondering about how representative it is) to study is discussed in Chapter 9. Ethical issues are becoming much more to the fore in all research and are discussed at length in Chapter 10. The final chapter in Part Two considers how to write a research proposal.

Part Three focuses upon the period when you have begun to gather and analyse data. In Chapter 12, I discuss what is involved in collecting qualitative data. The next chapter outlines what is to be gained by working early with datasets and shows you how to develop your early analysis. The next two chapters consider the use of computer-aided qualitative data analysis and validity and reliability. Chapter 16 shows you how to apply what you have learned in Part Three to evaluate qualitative research.

Pertti Alasuutari describes writing a thesis as rather like learning to ride a bicycle through gradually adjusting your balance:

> **Writing is first and foremost analyzing, revising and polishing the text. The idea that one can produce ready-made text right away is just about as senseless as the cyclist who has never had to restore his or her balance. (1995: 178)**

Following Alasuutari, Part Four is concerned with the 'writing-up' stage of research. Its five chapters address the following topics: how to begin your research report;

how to write effective literature review and methodology chapters; how to structure your data chapters; and how to produce a lively concluding chapter.

In Part Five, I examine how you can get support during your research. Its two chapters discuss making good use of your supervisor and how to get feedback about your research from other people. Part Six has one chapter which provides a discussion of effective qualitative research and, thereby, offers an overview of the main themes of this book.

The four chapters in Part Seven consider the aftermath of a finished piece of research. Depending on the level of your work, this may involve an oral or viva. This is often shrouded in mystery, like some weird Masonic ritual! Chapter 25 attempts to demystify the PhD examination. Whether or not you face an oral examination, in the aftermath of submitting your dissertation, you are likely to come face to face with three other issues: getting published (discussed in Chapter 26), conveying your findings to non-academic audiences (Chapter 27) and getting a job (Chapter 28).

From Part Two onwards, the order of this book very roughly follows the likely chronological sequence of doing a piece of research. However, I recognize that textbooks are not usually read in the same way as novels. For instance, although you may want to resist the temptation to skip to the final chapter of a whodunnit, no such prohibitions are sensible when using a textbook. So, for example, you may want to consult Chapter 22 on making good use of your supervisor quite early on. Or, if you want a quick summary of the story this book offers, you may turn at once to Chapter 24. Each chapter is more or less self-contained and so there should be no problems in zigzagging through the book in this way, using the glossary provided where appropriate.

Zigzagging also makes sense because qualitative research rarely follows a smooth trajectory from hypothesis to findings. As we shall see, this is less a drawback than a chance to refocus your work as new ideas and opportunities arise in the field. Consequently, most readers will want to move backwards and forwards through the book as the occasion arises. Alternatively, you may find it useful to skim read the book in advance and then work through certain chapters in greater detail to correspond with different stages of your research.

The examples and exercises in this book are designed to allow the novice to emerge with practical skills rather than simply the ability to write good examination answers. The exercises mostly rely upon the stage of your research coinciding with the chapters where they are found. So when you are zigzagging through the book or skimming it, it will usually make sense to return to the exercises at a relevant stage of your work, using your supervisor for feedback and advice. When you finish each chapter, please take advantage of the additional readings and exercises available on the website for this book: www.sagepub.co.uk/silverman.

Ultimately, of course, no book can or should provide for how it will be read. Complete anarchy is nonetheless rarely very useful to anybody. In this spirit, the structure I have provided tries to give you an initial orientation. From then on, it is up to you. As the philosopher Ludwig Wittgenstein wrote:

> All we want to do is to straighten you up on the track if your coach is crooked on the rails. Driving it afterwards we shall leave to you. (1980: 39e)

2

What You Can (and Can't) Do with Qualitative Research

Chapter Objectives

By the end of this chapter you will be able to:

- Recognize that there is no simple distinction between 'qualitative' and 'quantitative' research.

- Understand the uses and limitations of both forms of research.

- Work out whether qualitative methods are appropriate to your research topic.

Introduction

2.1 This chapter offers practical help in answering four very concrete questions that you should consider before you think of beginning a qualitative research study. These are:

- Why do students start to use qualitative methods?

- Are qualitative methods always the best?

- Is qualitative research appropriate to the topic in which you are interested?

- If so, how should it influence the way you define your research problem?

In a way, this book as a whole is dedicated to answer these kinds of questions. However, some initial answers will help to give you a good sense of the issues involved. As in the rest of the book, I will set out my argument through examples of actual student research.

2.2 Chance factors related to your biography can sometimes count for more than logically defined choices. We see this in Michelle Day-Miller's story about realizing that the subjects had all but disappeared in the survey research she conducted prior to her PhD.

STUDENT EXAMPLES

Finding Your 'Home'

Like many students, I began my graduate training being socialized within a positivist paradigm. I was learning my statistics and how to conduct surveys and develop quasi-experimental designs. But one day I experienced a transforming moment in graduate school. Donna, one of the participants in a survey-based study I conducted, was reading a manuscript I had written reporting the findings of this study when she exclaimed, 'Where is the depth? Where is the feeling? Where am *I* in all of these words?'

'Well,' I responded, 'right there on page 17!'

'I know that I'm the *subject*,' Donna went on, 'and I know that you are the *researcher*. But … uhmmm … I really don't get a sense of either one of us in the paper.'

She was absolutely right! Donna, along with the other participants, provided a unique voice during the collection of the data, yet that voice was ultimately muted by the deadening 'thud' of an aggregate statistic. In my research report she was nowhere to be found.

This experience occurred only a few months before I took my first qualitative research methods course. In that course I found my home. While my education to that point was focused on teaching me to collect information and understand social behaviour, I wasn't getting at the *understanding human experience* part of my aspiration. I realized that to truly capture experience I needed to embrace the subjective and, along with it, the humanity of social science. [Michelle Day-Miller, USA]

Michelle's emphasis on 'voice' and 'subjectivity' shows how an interest in subjectivity and the authenticity of human experience is a strong feature of qualitative research. As I show shortly, this kind of **emotionalist** model is one of the dominant paradigms within qualitative research.

In my own case, the places I studied and the people who supervised me had a key influence on how I did my graduate research. My undergraduate work was at the London School of Economics (LSE) where my only experience of research methods was an excellent introductory course in survey methods taught by Claus Moser. Although not particularly numerate, I was enticed by Moser's use of risqué examples drawn from topics like dating behaviour, guaranteed to fascinate a young man of 18!

After completing an MA in the USA, I returned to LSE to do my PhD. I then discovered that one of my undergraduate teachers (Robert McKenzie, a political sociologist) expected that I would be supervised by him on a topic close to McKenzie's own interests (e.g. voting behaviour). However, by this time, my interests had shifted away from political sociology and towards social class and status. Influenced by my survey course and by sociologists of the 1960s (like C. Wright Mills and David Lockwood), I planned to conduct an interview study of white collar workers at four different kinds of workplace, focusing on their lifestyles and aspirations. Not wishing to upset my undergraduate tutor (McKenzie), I chose him as supervisor together with an industrial relations specialist, Ben Roberts.

Without any real research training, I began my research interviews and, after two years, published a short note on my initial findings in the *British Journal of Sociology* (Silverman, 1967). As I shall argue in Chapter 13, this shows the value of beginning data analysis at an early stage rather than allowing the data to accumulate.

Early data analysis has a further advantage: it allows you to reconsider the direction in which your research is heading. In my case, such reconsideration had quite a drastic result:

- I started to worry about the reliability of data gathered from semi-structured interviews. How far did my respondents' answers to my prepared questions actually reflect their own experiences? Moreover, didn't my own assumptions come into play when I interpreted their answers to some open-ended questions?

- I now had a junior post at Goldsmiths College where I unexpectedly found myself teaching a course on the sociology of organizations. As a result, I published a paper on organization theory in *Sociology* (Silverman, 1968). Was this a better topic for my PhD?

My joint supervisor, Ben Roberts, settled the matter. Having read my published paper, he suggested that it might make sense to develop it in the form of a library-based, theoretical PhD. Seeing how quickly such a dissertation could be written, given my reading for his teaching work, I switched topics. This example shows what you can gain by discussing the direction of your research with your supervisor.

Two years later, I was awarded my PhD at about the same time as my dissertation was published as a book (Silverman, 1970). So, as a result of chance factors and my own research experience, my research topic was totally redefined.

Through biographical events, I moved out of quantitative research towards a purely theoretical PhD. By 1970, I had a vague curiosity about qualitative research but no real understanding of it. So, while the final chapter of my book twitters on about the importance of understanding people's 'meanings', the only method it refers to is a purely quantitative method of 'measuring' meaning deriving from the positivist psychologist Charles Osgood.

While the context today is very different, I have no doubt that biographical factors continue to play an important part in how students plan their research. Here is a recent example from an American graduate student.

STUDENT EXAMPLES

The 'Proper' place for Qualitative Research

As I was going through graduate school, there was an ongoing debate over the centrality of one form of social science research over another. Specifically, some very difficult and contentious debates revolved around the 'proper place' for qualitative research in the social sciences as opposed to quantitative. My master's degree was directed by an individual who was working at the margins of both qualitative and quantitative methodologies. The underlying idea was to take qualitative data and quantify them. I was enthralled by the concept and accepted the orientation readily. As I moved to my doctoral institution, the old debates were still lingering and it was easy to identify those oriented to qualitative research as opposed to quantitative. In fact, there were no classes offered that were positioned to an in-depth study of qualitative research. Moreover, a form of implicit pressure was brought to bear on doing quantitative research: 'clean and easy' was the catchphrase. Nonetheless, for my dissertation I chose to follow a mixed methods approach. My decision was based on the realization that while quantitative methods provide very interesting data about how much or how many questions, they missed some of the 'story.' The analogy I used was that of people in poverty. A determination can be made as to how many, where, when, and the like, but what was missing, from my perspective, was a very simple and compelling question: what is it like to be in poverty? So, when it came to my topic, employee loyalty, it was a matter not simply of determining who might have been loyal or not, but also of what underlying interpersonal dynamics were at play, how they factored into loyalty, and what conditions had to be met for loyalty to exist. [John Linn, USA]

John's story, like Michelle's, shows how, as with myself several decades earlier, the experience of doing research can lead you to question some of the received wisdom you have been taught. It also reveals that, rather than one methodology being intrinsically superior to another, it might be wiser to think of quantitative and qualitative approaches as complementary parts of the systematic, empirical search for knowledge.

LINK

In 2003, the UK government set up a working party to report on how to judge the quality of qualitative research. For its findings go to:

http://www.gsr.gov.uk/downloads/evaluating_policy/qqe_rep.pdf

Are Qualitative Methods Always the Best?

2.3 'Qualitative research' seems to promise that we will avoid or downplay statistical techniques as well as the mechanics of the quantitative methods used in, say, survey research or epidemiology. Indeed, the qualitative/quantitative distinction seems to assume a fixed preference or predefined evaluation of what is 'good' or at least 'appropriate' (i.e. qualitative) and 'bad' or 'inappropriate' (i.e. quantitative) research when, as we all know, methods are only more or less appropriate to particular research questions.

It is worth repeating the truism that research methods should be chosen based on the specific task at hand. Amir Marvasti's personal experience with a study of juvenile offenders who were charged with adult criminal offences is a good illustration of this point. In 1999, Amir was working as a graduate research assistant on a project which used quantitative methods to isolate the factors that cause legal authorities to recommend a minor for adult judicial processing. This is how he describes his intellectual journey.

STUDENT EXAMPLES

Pushing Quantitative Research to the limits

The data [I was working with] came from two official sources. One was a statewide database called Client Information System (CIS). The CIS data contained numerically coded information on thousands of offenders from around the state. This information came to the researchers in the form of magnetic cartridge tapes that had to be mounted on a mainframe computer before they could be accessed and analysed. The other source of data for the project was local court records, which contained arrest reports, indictments, sentencing reports, and a host of other documents about the cases. Summarizing and analysing the numerical data was relatively easy. Once the data tapes were mounted on the mainframe, I used statistical programs like SAS or SPSS to read the data. With amazing speed, the computer programs could peruse thousands of records and extract just what was needed for analysis. For example, if I wanted to know the average age of offenders who had committed a violent crime like robbery, I would write a few lines of computer syntax, submit the request, and have the report, or output, back in seconds.

However, the work was much more challenging where the local court files were concerned. To transform these documents into data suitable for statistical analysis, the researchers put together a lengthy data collection instrument. After making an appointment at the appropriate courthouse, which could be hundreds of miles away, I myself or one of my colleagues would drive to the location and peruse the dossiers in search of information that corresponded to the hundreds of variables on the data collection instrument. For example, if the minor offender had used a firearm during an offence, that would be coded as 1; a blunt weapon, such as a baseball bat, would be coded as 2; etc.

As the project proceeded, the principal investigators and I had to add more variables to capture the nuances of each case. For example, I came across a few cases that started in one jurisdiction and were transferred to another. This required the inclusion of new variables to the data collection instrument. All of us soon realized that no matter how many variables were added, many details of the case simply did not fit a precoded, standardized format. Additionally, we were faced with the problem of overlapping categories. For instance, I had difficulty recording a case in which the offender began beating his victim with a baseball bat as a 1 or 2.

(Continued)

(Continued)

To remedy these problems, we had to supplement the numerical data about a case with a qualitative narrative or a case history to capture additional nuances. These case histories were written on a blank sheet of paper that was provided on the back of the data collection form. For example, I would write that offender X lost his father to cancer at the age of 12, and was placed in a foster home after his mother refused to care for him, and so on. Finally, the principal investigators for this project added more depth to their data by conducting in-depth interviews with a small sample of offenders. They would go to prisons, halfway houses, or other venues and interview the juvenile offenders face to face. [Amir Marvasti, USA]

As you can see from this example, methods should be our servants, not our rulers. Methods are properly used as tools when they are needed. So it would have been silly for Amir and his colleagues to turn away from the case study method because it seemed 'too qualitative'. It would have been equally unreasonable to exclude the statewide (CIS) data from the research because they were 'too quantitative'.

> **TIP**
>
> **You can become much more effective as a researcher if you reject arbitrary, self-imposed categories and instead systematically pursue knowledge about a topic wherever the data might take you.**

Any good researcher knows that your choice of method should not be predetermined. Rather you should choose a method that is appropriate to what you are trying to find out (see K. Punch, 1998: 244). For instance, if you want to discover how people intend to vote, then a quantitative method, like a **social survey**, may be the most appropriate choice. On the other hand, if you are concerned with exploring people's life histories or everyday behaviour, then qualitative methods may be favoured. An insistence that any research worth its salt should follow a purely quantitative logic would simply rule out the study of many interesting phenomena relating to what people actually do in their day-to-day lives, whether in homes, offices or other public and private places. This suggests a purely pragmatic argument ('horses for courses'), according to which our research problem defines the most appropriate method.

> **TIP**
>
> **Never assume that qualitative methods are intrinsically superior. Indeed, a quantitative approach may sometimes be more appropriate to the research problem in which you are interested. So, in choosing a method, everything depends upon what you are trying to find out. No method of research, quantitative or qualitative, is intrinsically better than any other.**

As we shall see later, research problems are not neutral. How we frame a research problem will, as we saw in Michelle's story, inevitably reflect a commitment (explicit or implicit) to a particular **model** of how the world works. And, in qualitative research, there are multiple, competing models (see Chapter 7).

■ Attempt Exercise 2.1

What does all this mean in practice? In the final substantive section of this chapter, using some more student accounts, I look at the sort of questions you should ask yourself before embarking on a qualitative research project.

Should You Use Qualitative Methods?

2.4

An obvious question for this book would be: why do some students choose qualitative research? In the United States, quantitative research tends to be more prevalent. In most sociology departments, the majority of the faculty use quantitative methods in their research, and most journals publish a disproportionate number of quantitative papers. The so-called 'norm', at least for now, is quantitative. What then attracts some to qualitative research? Here are some answers directly from the researchers.

While there is a general sense among some researchers that qualitative data are inherently more 'interesting' than numbers, there are less aesthetically oriented and more analytically astute reasons for choosing qualitative methods. In the example below, Karyn McKinney suggests that qualitative research was a better fit for the type of questions she was asking.

STUDENT EXAMPLES

'How?' or 'How Many?'

I've always found qualitative data more interesting than quantitative data. Beyond that I believe that qualitative data are often more suited to provide me with the answers to questions I'm interested in. I find that my interests usually lie in 'how' questions rather than in 'how many' questions. In my dissertation, I was interested in *how* whiteness is created and sustained in everyday life. The question of how many whites live in the United States or how much money whites make compared to other groups could have easily been answered using census data. [Karyn McKinney, USA]

Similarly, Sara Crawley states that in her research on lesbian identities, quantitative measures seemed inadequate.

STUDENT EXAMPLES

When Should 'Identities' Be Counted?

My substantive interests were related to identity and sexuality. The notion that anyone could describe such intimate matters with a 6 or some quantitative measure seemed atheoretical and, frankly, ludicrous. I am not suggesting that nothing is measurable or that attempts to measure are less useful for some topics. But with a topic that is so intimate and constantly forming as sexuality and identity, it seemed extremely important to highlight individual narrators' ideas and concepts with some detail. As it turns out, I became very interested in talk and how people narrate their identities and realities. The good stuff was in their descriptions and ideas. It fascinated me every day. [Sara Crawley, USA]

Sara's reference to 'the good stuff' is telling. As she notes, she does not wish to deny the possibility of measurement. Rather, sometimes qualitative research is just a good fit for the question. As Darin Weinberg states, there is nothing inherently superior about qualitative research and its practitioners. Selecting qualitative methodology could be mostly a practical matter of deciding what works best.

STUDENT EXAMPLES

Choosing What Works (for You)

I would say my choice to do a qualitative dissertation was a product of both personal taste and a sense that the themes in which I was interested could be best explored through qualitative approaches. I was never committed to keeping the study strictly qualitative. As it turned out, my use of quantitative data was fairly minimal, but this was more a product of contingency and how the foci of the project evolved than it was one of *a priori* commitments. Had I come across quantitative materials that could have helped me flesh out my analysis, I would have had no hesitation to use them. [Darin Weinberg, USA]

These stories show the diversity of qualitative research. The features that attract researchers to this methodology are many and so are the ways this methodology is practised. Table 2.1 summarizes many of these issues.

Table 2.1 shows that qualitative research is not always appropriate to every research problem. You need to think through exactly what you are trying to achieve rather than be guided by some fashion or trivial preference (perhaps you are not comfortable doing statistical calculations). So, following item 2 of Table 2.1,

TABLE 2.1 Should I use qualitative research?

1 What exactly am I trying to find out? Different questions require different methods to answer them
2 What kind of focus on my topic do I want to achieve? Do I want to study this phenomenon or situation in detail? Or am I mainly interested in making standardized and systematic comparisons and in accounting for variance?
3 How have other researchers dealt with this topic? To what extent do I wish to align my project with this literature?
4 What practical considerations should sway my choice? For instance, how long might my study take and do I have the resources to study it this way? Can I get access to the single case I want to study in depth? Are quantitative samples and data readily available?
5 Will I learn more about this topic using quantitative or qualitative methods? What will be the knowledge payoff of each method?
6 What seems to work best for me? Am I committed to a particular research model which implies a particular methodology? Do I have a gut feeling about what a good piece of research looks like?

Source: adapted from K. Punch,1998: 244–5

if you are mainly interested in making systematic comparisons in order to account for the variance in some phenomenon (e.g. crime or suicide rates), then quantitative research is indicated. Equally, as a rule of thumb, if it turns out that published research on your topic is largely quantitative (item 3), does it pay to swim against the tide? As I stress several times in this book, if you can align your work with a previous, classic study, this makes a lot of sense. The last thing you want to do is to try to reinvent the wheel!

Of course, we should not overplay the opposition between qualitative and quantitative methods. If resources allow, many research questions can be thoroughly addressed by combining different methods, using qualitative research to document the detail of, say, how people interact in one situation and using quantitative methods to identify variance (see Chapter 8). The fact that simple quantitative measures are a feature of some good qualitative research shows that the whole 'qualitative/quantitative' dichotomy is open to question. In the context of this book, I view many such dichotomies or polarities in social science as highly dangerous. At best, they are pedagogic devices for students to obtain a first grip on a difficult field: they help us to learn the jargon. At worst, they are excuses for not thinking, which assemble groups of researchers into 'armed camps', unwilling to learn from one another.

Of course, as Table 2.1 (item 6) suggests, such armchair debates are of less relevance than the simple test used by Darin Weinberg in his earlier story: 'what works for me'. Howard Becker comments about his use of qualitative data: 'It's the kind of research I've done, but that represents a practical rather than an ideological choice. It's what I knew how to do, and found personal enjoyment in, so I kept on doing it' (1998: 6).

However, Becker adds that his 'choice' has not blinded him to the value of quantitative approaches:

I've always been alive to the possibilities of other methods (so long as they weren't pressed on me as matters of religious conviction) and have found it particularly useful to think about what I did in terms that come from such other ways of working as survey research or mathematical modeling. (1998: 6)

Not only does it sometimes pay to think of qualitative research, as Becker suggests, in terms of quantitative frameworks, it can also be helpful occasionally to combine qualitative and quantitative methods. As I show in Chapter 15, simple tabulations can be a useful tool for identifying **deviant cases**.

In this section, I have used students' accounts to show the importance of thinking through one's research problem before committing yourself to a choice of method. But, as I have already hinted, the situation is rather more complicated than this. In Chapter 7, we will see how theoretically defined models enter into your research strategy.

 ■ **Attempt Exercise 2.2**

Concluding Remarks

2.5 There is considerable overlap between the themes discussed in this chapter. For example, as we noted, data collection, analysis and writing are virtually inseparable in qualitative research. Thus these categories are not intended to be treated as mutually exclusive; their main purpose is to show you the diversity of research experiences. If, in selecting your topic, you are pushed and pulled by different forces, you are not unique. Doing qualitative research is in many respects no different than doing everyday life: it is complex and sometimes downright chaotic. The point of this book and other advice and mentorship you receive is to help you manage this chaos and direct it into a coherent research project.

Ultimately, everything depends on the research problem you are seeking to analyse. I conclude this chapter, therefore, with a statement which shows the absurdity of pushing too far the qualitative/quantitative distinction:

We are not faced, then, with a stark choice between words and numbers, or even between precise and imprecise data; but rather with a range from more to less precise data. Furthermore, our decisions about what level of precision is appropriate in relation to any particular claim should depend on the nature of what we are trying to describe, on the likely accuracy of our descriptions, on our purposes, and on the resources available to us; not on ideological commitment to one methodological paradigm or another. (Hammersley, 1992: 163)

| KEY POINTS |

- 'Qualitative' research involves a variety of quite different approaches.

- Although some 'quantitative' research can be properly criticized or found insufficient, the same may be said about some 'qualitative' research.

- In these circumstances it is sensible to make pragmatic choices between research methodologies according to your research problem and model.

- Doing 'qualitative' research should offer no protection from the rigorous, critical standards that should be applied to any enterprise concerned to sort 'fact' from 'fancy'.

■ ■ Further Reading ■

In my recent book *A Very Short, Fairly Interesting, Reasonably Cheap Book about Qualitative Research* (Sage, 2007: 11–36), I outline the sort of topics that I believe qualitative research is best placed to answer. Other short introductions are 'Inside qualitative research', the introduction to Seale, Gobo, Gubrium and Silverman's edited book *Qualitative Research Practice* (Sage, 2004: 1–11); and my book *Interpreting Qualitative Data: Methods for Analysing Talk, Text and Interaction* (third edition, Sage, 2006), especially Chapter 2.

The most useful introductory texts are Alan Bryman's *Quantity and Quality in Social Research* (Unwin Hyman, 1988); Nigel Gilbert's (ed.) *Researching Social Life* (third edition, Sage, 2008); Clive Seale's (ed.) *Researching Society and Culture* (Sage, 2004); and Keith Punch's *Introduction to Social Research* (second edition, Sage, 2005). More advanced sources are Miles and Huberman's *Qualitative Data Analysis* (second edition, Sage, 1994); Hammersley and Atkinson's *Ethnography: Principles in Practice* (third edition, Tavistock, 2007); and Denzin and Lincoln's (eds) *Handbook of Qualitative Research* (third edition, Sage, 2005).

■ Exercise 2.1

Review any research study with which you are familiar. Then answer the following questions:

- To what extent are its methods of research (qualitative, quantitative or a combination of both) appropriate to the nature of the research question(s) being asked?

- How far does its use of these methods meet the criticisms of both qualitative and quantitative research discussed in this chapter?

- In your view, how could this study have been improved methodologically and conceptually?

■ **Exercise 2.2**

In relation to your own possible research topics:

- Explain why you think a qualitative approach is appropriate.

- Would quantitative methods be more appropriate? If not, why not?

- Would it make sense to combine qualitative and quantitative methods? Explain your answer.

3

The Research Experience I

|‾‾‾| **Chapter Objectives** |‾‾‾

By the end of this chapter you will be able to:

- **Understand the basic issues involved in developing a research project from initial ideas to data analysis.**

- **Appreciate the crucial links between theory and method.**

- **See how student researchers can work rigorously with data while following a consistent analytical approach.**

- **Understand how you can analyse your own impact on the field.**

- **Recognize the importance of keeping a research diary to note how your ideas change in response to the contingent factors that inevitably arise.**

Introduction

3.1 Switch on your television and graze through the channels. You will undoubtedly come across a chat show in which people are talking about their rise and fall from grace. Or maybe you will find a sports channel where, more often than not, you will see not a game but interviews with players about their hopes and feelings.

We live in a world in which our yearning for people's 'experiences' is more than satisfied by the popular media. Indeed, very often this pursuit of the 'personal' becomes repetitive and we should resist it (see Atkinson and Silverman, 1997).

However, this is not always the case. Any book which sets out to offer information and advice about doing a piece of research without telling a few personal 'stories' would be in danger of being received as empty and unhelpful. If we can draw out appropriate implications from these stories, moving from the personal to the practical, then we will have achieved something more substantial than merely providing some kind of experiental comfort blanket.

In this spirit, this chapter is devoted to telling the stories of three of my research students. The three students have much in common apart from the fact that I supervised them for a PhD in sociology. Moira Kelly and Sally Hunt began their research many years after their first degrees. Simon Allistone began his PhD at the age of 29. All three were products of the MA in qualitative research at Goldsmiths College and had been supervised by myself on their MA dissertations.

Moira and Sally held down demanding jobs while doing their research. Moira was, in turn, a research nurse, a health promotion research manager and then a health researcher; Sally was a lecturer in nursing. Unlike Moira and Sally, Simon was able to work on his doctorate on a full-time basis thanks to a three-year grant from the British Economic and Social Research Council (ESRC).

Their work spans a broad range of qualitative methodologies. Moira analysed interviews which she had conducted. Sally carried out an organizational **ethnography** and Simon studied interactions at a school meeting. While all three were registered for a PhD in sociology, their substantive interests crossed into other disciplines: health studies and nursing (Moira and Sally), organization studies (Sally and Simon) and media studies and education (Simon).

However, while the three of them worked with audio-recorded data, their analytic perspectives were rather different. Sally drew on Erving Goffman's (1974) concept of **frame** in her study of decision making by a mental health team (MHT) caring for homeless people. Simon based his study of a parent–teacher evening on concepts of turn-taking derived from **conversation analysis (CA)**. In her research on interviews with surviving partners of people who had died of cancer, Moira combined CA with an approach familiar to researchers who analyse interview accounts as **narratives**.

I realize that many of my readers will have different interests and backgrounds. Let me assure you at once that you will not need any special knowledge to under-stand what follows. The approach that my students used is, for my present purposes, of far less significance than the trajectory of their projects. Moreover, as I argue below, there are lessons here to be drawn for anybody who is contemplating writing a research dissertation for both MA and PhD.

Perhaps more relevant than their common theoretical perspective was the different amount of time that their research took. Working full-time, Simon completed his PhD in four years. Reflecting the pressures of demanding jobs, Moira took seven years and Sally finished in 10. As already suggested, these different timespans were strongly associated with practical contingencies, more or less unrelated to techni-cal issues of research design.

In what follows, the three tell their stories largely in their own words drawn from their research diaries. I have limited myself merely to adding some headings and asides. After each story, I suggest some more general implications. The chapter concludes with a summary in the form of a 15-point guide to completing a successful research study.

3.2 Moira's Research Diary

Beginnings

3.2.1

The research process began when I [Moira] took up post as research associate on a study of hospice and hospital care of people with terminal cancer. The aim of that project was to compare hospice and hospital care for people who had died from cancer and their spouses. The project was carried out between October 1994 and September 1995 and was directed by Clive Seale at Goldsmiths College. The main research project included the collection of quantitative and qualitative interview data. I had worked as a research nurse at St Christopher's Hospice (which funded the project) for four years before starting this project. I wanted both to use some of the qualitative data from the project for a PhD and to apply a theoretical approach I had learned during my MA.

I was drawn to the way **ethnomethodology** made it possible to identify the skills and practices ordinary people use to produce social action. The micro-analysis of social interaction seemed to me to be a valuable way of understanding some of the health issues and problems I had encountered in my experience working in clinical health settings as a psychiatric nurse and as a research nurse. Many of these problems appeared to hinge on the interactive practices and skills of the various parties involved (professional and laypeople).

In my post as hospice research nurse, I worked on a range of different topics. In one study I recruited breathless patients to a randomized controlled trial. It was this that got me interested in the (mismatched) relationship between methods of measurement used in research and the actual practices of the people being researched.

In the research trial, breathlessness was treated as a subjective symptom. However, in practice I found that nurses and doctors produced their own assessments of the patient's breathlessness, which sometimes did not correspond, either with each other or with the subjective assessment of patients themselves. This problem formed the basis for my MA dissertation in which I applied Goffman's frame analysis (1974) to patient case note data. This study highlighted the importance of looking at *how* people do things, rather than what they say they do. However, it only went so far in examining **members'** practices.

Theoretical orientations

3.2.2

The experience of doing my MA research, together with my experience as a practitioner, policy maker and sociologist, led me to believe that social research driven by theoretical concerns (rather than by a defined social problem) can contribute to policy and practice. It can do this through developing knowledge about social issues such as experience of healthcare but without setting up a rigid definition of the problem at the beginning. This ties in with my experience as a health researcher and practitioner up to that point, where I had observed that problems often appeared to arise around attempts to measure states of health and disease through imposing particular definitions and categorizations.

There seemed to me to be value in taking a step back to get a closer look at the phenomenon. More useful outcomes may be achieved if theoretical imperatives drive the research in a direction which can offer new perspectives on social problems [see Chapter 16 of this book]. Theoretical concerns should steer the analytic conception of the research problem, otherwise there is a danger of taking the research problem at face value, and of providing policy makers and practitioners with the answers they require, in *their* terms.

The study data

3.2.3 In the study directed by Clive Seale, 70 interviews were undertaken with bereaved spouses in South London. There were 35 interviews with spouses whose husband or wife had died in hospice, and 35 interviews with spouses matched by age and sex whose husband or wife had died in hospital. The sample was drawn from death certificates of all those who had died from cancer approximately six to nine months beforehand. These were kept at local departments of public health, and ethical committee approval was obtained from the three health authorities covered.

Each interviewee received a letter asking them to take part in the study. I called round to their house a couple of days after the letter had been sent and asked to interview them. Written informed consent was gained prior to all the interviews. The main findings from the study were written up, with Clive Seale, for *Palliative Medicine* in 1997.

Sixty-five interviews were tape-recorded with the consent of the respondents. The interviews started with an open-ended request, 'tell me the story of what happened'. The intention was that, for this part of the interview, there would be minimal interruption by the interviewer (MK), allowing the respondents to structure their own accounts. The response to this request, the initial 'story', constitutes the data for my PhD study. The rest of the interview followed a semi-structured format involving a series of questions.

Many qualitative research studies set out clear aims and objectives at the start of a project. These may often refer to collecting and analysing data on a particular topic, such as describing the views of patients about a particular type of illness experience. The aims of ethnomethodological studies such as this one tend to be quite general, centring on the examination of some data. When analysis starts, this form of analysis throws up a whole range of possible research problems that could be examined in detail. Decisions therefore need to be made about objectives for particular pieces of analysis at each stage. Eventual objectives can be quite specific but this will follow a more general exploratory analysis to see what members are doing in the talk under examination (e.g. making assessments). Objectives therefore tend to evolve over the course of the research.

The importance of being flexible about objectives is demonstrated in the way in which the specific topics of 'cancer' and 'bereavement' were not treated as central concerns by the interviewees. I had initially used these labels in early descriptions of the study, and in presentations. However, although these accounts are about cancer, in that the 'story of the death' requested is about cancer, the interviewees do not topicalize cancer. In a similar way, as a researcher I had been referring to the data as 'accounts of bereaved spouses', giving the impression to myself and others that the analysis is about bereavement. However, the interviewees did not make bereavement relevant to their descriptions, i.e. they did not talk about their personal experience of being bereaved. This supports the need to consider the relevance of the local context in the production of meanings.

My initial intention was to explore the character of the moral accounting work members do. This contrasts with most interview studies in which the information provided by the interviewee is usually treated as data about the events and experiences described.

Ethnomethodologists view this as problematic and regard interviews as an unreliable source of information about what actually happens in the situations described. A description of healthcare produced in an interview cannot be treated as a straightforward report of that care. Treating the data as a primary source in this way can be potentially misleading even if one were to take account of such conventional issues as error and bias.

The emphasis in the first instance was on investigating *how* the interviewees (surviving spouses) are saying what they say (as members of a social world), rather than focusing on *what* they are saying, such as 'bereavement talk'. In other words this was a study not of bereaved spouses, but of social interaction. Following Baker's (2002) theoretical direction, my analysis was concerned with what kind of social world the speakers make happen in their talk and what kind of social world speakers assume so that they can speak in the way they do.

Getting into the data: doing being reasonable

3.2.4 I began the analysis by reading and rereading the five interview accounts I had initially transcribed, looking for a starting point for my analysis. At this point my main interest was in the talk of the interviewees, partly because they did most of the talking. I followed Sacks's call to examine some (interview) data in terms of 'how it is that the thing comes off' (1992, Vol. 1: 11) but, as so much goes on in talk, a decision needed to be made as to what the 'thing' would be. Several interesting issues regarding the activities interviewees were doing in their accounts arose and appeared to warrant further exploration. These included: producing a 'reasonable' account, the use of time to locate events, the constitution of lay and medical competences, criticism, gender and emotion.

Given that there were several possible directions for the data analysis, a decision had to be made about what to look at first. In line with the (ethnomethodological) principle adopted by Baruch (1981), that a feature of all accounts is a display of moral adequacy, a key characteristic of these accounts seemed to be the way in which the interviewees construct their behaviour and that of others as reasonable or unreasonable in their descriptions. This seemed like a productive place to start. I again read and reread all the transcripts, this time extracting sections in which the spouses appeared to be presenting their behaviour and that of others as reasonable or unreasonable, systematically going through the data extracts identifying the use of pairs like husband and wife, and other categories, as well as looking for the description of activities which implied particular categories (see Silverman, 1998).

The research process: criticism, assessments and the interview

3.2.5 I reread the transcriptions of the first five interview accounts, identifying instances where criticism of health professionals were made. The health professionals referred to specifically were doctors and nurses. Identification of criticism in the accounts was not generally clear-cut. Considerable identity work was carried out around criticisms. A number of different 'types' of criticism were distinguished, ranging from 'very cautious' to 'direct'. Ambiguity was used by the account-giver, with the interviewer being drawn into the production of the description as criticism. Even when the interviewee identifies their action as criticism, considerable moral work goes on regarding the roles and responsibilities of those involved, including the interviewee and interviewer.

I had initially intended to undertake separate analyses of instances of criticisms of self (by the interviewee) and of the dead spouse in the accounts also. However, having undertaken the analysis of criticism of health professionals, and following the ethnomethodological principles I had adopted, I decided a more constructive tack would be to conduct a closer analysis of members' practices in producing the accounts. So I took a step back in order to take a closer look.

I had identified criticism as an activity in the talk in a similar way to more traditional qualitative studies, and gone some way to describing how it was produced by interviewees through categorization work. I now wished to examine in more depth how activities such as criticism are constructed in the interview talk. This meant refocusing my analysis to look more closely at how assessment work was carried out by both parties and how the interview accounts were cooperatively produced as 'stories'.

Sampling data

3.2.6 I refer to the data analysed here as interviews, though the analysis is based on the first part of the interview only, up to the end of the story. These stories would constitute my data.

The detailed level of analysis involved in examining participants' practices in the talk has meant that the empirical analyses of criticism of health professionals and assessment work drew on the first five interviews only. Later analysis of the construction of the talk using CA drew on 25 interviews, with additional interviews (to the five initially analysed) being selected on the basis of emerging theory.

Decisions about the selection of the sample were not pre-set, but have been conceptually driven by the theoretical framework underpinning the research from the start (cf. Curtis et al., 2000). In order to undertake analysis that addresses the adequacy of the underlying theory described by Mitchell (1983), decisions about the **sampling** of data have been made during the research. This has been influenced by the two different ethnomethodological research methods which have been applied to the interview data. Analysis of communicative practices (in the interview accounts) can only be discerned in 'the fine grained detail of talk-in-interaction' (Drew, 2001: 267). I have set out to undertake the fine grained analysis recommended by Drew and also to make comparisons across cases, using both intensive and extensive analysis where appropriate to my research problem.

Practical relevance

3.2.7 This research study set out to contribute to a body of institutional knowledge, the sociology of health and illness. The examination of how the interviews are produced has highlighted a number of analytic points regarding the status attributed to the accounts by the interviewees. They are set up as 'assessments of healthcare experience'. Setting up the accounts to be heard in this way has implications for the sociology of health and illness, and healthcare policy, in particular regarding how 'lay' or 'consumer' evaluations of healthcare experience are produced.

The increasing emphasis on the consumer in British government policy has led to a search for the best ways to find out about both what consumers want from health services, and how satisfied they are with the services they receive. A great deal of this research is quantitative, but there are frustrations with consumer satisfaction questionnaires and scales, as they tend to show uniformly high levels of satisfaction (Avis et al., 1997). There has consequently been a search for different ways of evaluating satisfaction with healthcare, and an increase in qualitative research. It has been suggested that increased interest in qualitative research has, in part, been fuelled by the growing demand for research that gives consumers a voice in developing services. My study takes up the issues raised above through an ethnomethodological analysis of data initially collected as a form of lay or consumer evaluation.

Concluding remarks

3.2.8 I have worked as a health researcher for a number of years, and this study has been the first time I have not set out with at least a fairly well-defined problem that needed a solution. This includes qualitative studies in which the goal may be to describe something about which little is known. Even in such studies, however, you do know broadly what you are required to describe.

In this instance, however, I was attempting to describe something that I knew was going on but could not see at the start.

The need to refrain from introducing my own categorizations *before* producing the description of members' practices that I was aiming for has not been easy. However, I believe that the fine grained analysis of the practices engaged in by interview participants has enabled me to contribute the new insights to the sociology of health and illness that I had hoped for at the start. What attracted me to ethnomethodology is how, in its suspension of interest in both external structural factors and assumed 'subjective' states, the skills of participants in producing social action through talk are demonstrated. This is made possible through its focus on 'describing members' viewpoints and definitions as the basis for rational actions, and for their participation in the sites of social life (Drew, 2001: 267).

Implications of Moira's story

3.2.9 The beginning of Moira's story (Sections 3.2.1, 3.2.2) shows the value of basing a PhD thesis on a substantive area with which you are already familiar. Both her work experience and her MA research were in the health area and it made sense to stay in this familiar realm when choosing a topic for her PhD.

Her MA had shown her the uses and limitations of a particular way of conceptualizing healthcare interactions (3.2.1) and now she wanted to shift slightly her analytic focus (3.2.2). But she was never in doubt of the need for such a focus in order to make sense of the data. For Moira, theory was not a piece of window-dressing to make research respectable. Instead, 'theory' represented the very practical ways in which she made sense of her data.

Moira had gathered her interview data as part of another study with different objectives (3.2.3). Drawing on the fortunate fact that these interviews had been audio-recorded, she was able to retranscribe them in order to address her new analytic concerns. Note that this did not mean that the previous transcripts were 'faulty'. Transcripts, like other methods of recording data (e.g. **fieldnotes**, diaries, memos), can only be judged in relation to a specific research problem and theoretical orientation.

The instant availability of her data meant that Moira, unlike many other PhD students, could begin her data analysis on day one of her research! As I argue in Chapter 13, such secondary analysis of existing data can offer a marvellous short cut to completing a PhD, freeing you from the need to collect data – providing that you are not looking for excuses for delay and/or sloppy analysis.

Like many qualitative researchers, Moira worked inductively, avoiding too early categorizations of her data and setting research problems and objectives as she explored (analytically) her transcripts (3.2.4). As she puts it, the idea is to 'step back in order to take a closer look' (3.2.5). So, for instance, given her analytic orientation, it was not enough simply to report 'criticisms' of the treatment of a spouse. Instead, she wanted to understand how apparently critical comments were contexted in the co-production of 'assessments' and 'stories'.

Clearly, Moira's approach required very careful listening to the details of verbal interaction. So she focused mainly on just five out of her 65 interviews. However, this did not mean that her other interviews were completely neglected. A much larger sample of interviews was used in her chapters based on CA. In this way, her study combined intensive and extensive analysis (3.2.6).

Moira's approach reveals that there need be no simple polarity between qualitative and quantitative research (see Chapter 2). Unlike much quantitative research, our research problems often require much more detailed analyses of small bodies of data. However, by combining intensive and extensive analysis, we can achieve understanding of a relatively large dataset and test emerging hypotheses with a fair degree of credibility.

Finally, Moira's story shows that theoretically driven research is far from incompatible with practical relevance. Quite the contrary! It is precisely those many, apparently atheoretical studies which have little to contribute to practical matters, simply because their authors do not have the time or the ability to stand back from their data and to think laterally. As Moira implies, her own work makes a substantial contribution to current debates regarding lay or consumer evaluation of healthcare (3.2.7). It also complements more 'structural' approaches in the study of health and illness with an understanding of the skills of participants involved in healthcare interactions (3.2.8).

3.3 Sally's Research Diary
Gaining access

3.3.1
When I [Sally] began this case study, I had little idea of how I might go about it. I had vague notions of exploring how diagnoses are constructed by health professionals. This was based on my past experience of having a psychiatric liaison role in a unit linked with an accident and emergency department. Looking at patient admission sheets, I was struck by the number of times I read 'schizo/affective disorder' as the reason for admission to hospital. I concluded that such a cautious descriptor could 'cover' both patient *and* doctor for almost any clinical or legal eventuality. I also had a long-standing interest in the concept of 'illness careers'.

I anticipated that access to the field would be difficult because of the particularly sensitive ethical nature of mental health practice. I made an initial attempt at negotiating access to an inpatient area but this was not successful. A further difficulty was matching the demands of full-time teaching to the constraints of organizational shift patterns.

As with Silverman's (1987) experience of gaining access to the field of paediatric cardiology, my entry to mental health casework was a chance happening. I met up with a former colleague in a local supermarket. After I recounted my difficulty in negotiating access to an inpatient area, he invited me to meet the community team with whom he worked. I was both pleased and relieved to have been given this opportunity but I did not recognize it as advocacy at the time. Upon reflection many years later, I now appreciate that this was indeed the case.

Following two separate meetings with the team's psychiatric consultant and with the team leader (a community psychiatric nurse), I was eventually given permission to audio-record the team's weekly case meetings on the understanding that I destroy the tapes when the study concluded.

The choice of team meetings was a deliberate one. These were 'scheduled events', so I would not waste time waiting to see whether or not relevant data would appear but rather would have them to hand [see Chapter 13 of this book]. Having successfully negotiated access to the field I then became a **participant-observer**.

To undertake a case study of 'single homelessness' in the context of full-time employment makes heavy demands on the researcher in terms of personal resources and operational constraints. The field is so vast and the nature of subjects' lives so dispersed that I elected to observe professional caseworkers rather than service users. For practical reasons, then, I became a participant-observer at the mental health team's (MHT's) weekly case conferences.

Keeping a record

3.3.2 Once I had achieved access to mental health casework, my starting point was to observe and record what members were saying and doing in their meetings about clients. I audio-recorded meetings and made handwritten fieldnotes of my observations whilst the tape was recording. This enabled me to record visual data that might otherwise be lost or unavailable to me if I relied on the audiotape alone.

A total of 15 meetings lasting approximately 75 minutes each were recorded over eight months. The first meeting was 'lost' due to problems with the tape-recorder. Forty-five client stories were available overall. Of these, 13 were fully transcribed and four were partially transcribed. The shortest transcript was only three pages long. This later turned out to be a deviant case. The longest ran to 18 pages. One hour of recorded team interaction took an average of 10 hours to transcribe.

A total of 45 hours was spent on data collection overall. This included 20 hours of recording and 25 hours of participant observation. No selection process as such was involved in the transcribing of complete accounts. Accounts were transcribed in chronological order which equated with the time frame of the fieldwork.

I chose to collect data in the way that I did because this was/is appropriate to the study of situated action. Audiotapes provide detailed recorded talk which fieldnotes alone cannot provide, while preparing transcripts is itself a research activity.

The act of producing the transcripts was not a straightforward matter. In the main, they were constructed according to my own common-sense reasoning as I had no precedent for the process of transcribing. Because of this, transcripts do not always conform to accepted conventions. However, there is no perfect transcript and those I have capture sufficient detail of the MHT team's practice for the kind of analysis I carried out.

The practicalities of audio-recording multiple voices in a less-than-soundproof environment exerted certain constraints. It was not possible to denote overlapping voices, for example. Neither was it possible to decipher the simultaneous secondary interactions which frequently occurred alongside the main action. I tried to transcribe what I heard as faithfully as possible using standard spelling and punctuation so that members' accounts would not appear 'unnecessarily odd' to the reader. I did not attempt to represent accented talk, and lengths of pauses were not timed exactly.

Fieldwork observation demonstrated that the talk was generally unhurried, even 'leisurely', and that it was frequently punctuated by laughter. I approximated the duration of pauses as being in the range of one second for the shortest, 'um', to almost four seconds for the longest (long pause).

With hindsight, I might use more conventional transcription devices if I were to do the transcripts again. This would save the 'creative' work of devising my own. However, as I lacked the quality of recording more commonly associated with CA, it remains a matter of debate as to whether this could have been a practical option. From a methodological perspective, I did not need the fine detail required by those working with the CA method.

Analysing my data

3.3.3
At the outset I made my own broad descriptive headings for each case account. These were based on the member's introduction to the case which invoked both age and gender. An example of such a heading was: 'Fifty-year-old woman who has just been accepted by a hostel in the local area'.

I tried to make the description as 'flat' as possible, but found on later inspection that in many instances I had provided my own summary of the opening presentation. The heading was intended to be an identification device for differentiating the transcripts and for matching them to the accompanying fieldnotes. This demonstrates quite clearly that even in the role of note taker, my recording skills as a fieldworker are influenced by my practitioner past.

I had other surprises. One heading read: 'Surveillance of a 29-year-old man in a hostel who is preoccupied with religious tapes'.

Listening to the recording again and rereading fieldnotes at a later date demonstrated that the word 'surveillance' was not actually used by the narrator of that account. The heading represents my own, broad, descriptive category.

I attempted to transcribe as much as I could of what was said and to record in fieldnotes the setting in which this social activity took place. After transcribing a total of six accounts in full, I began to identify recurring instances in the raw data. These broad, analytic categories are listed, crudely, as follows:

- client vulnerability
- deviancy and common-sense reasoning
- character work

- distancing of other professionals and agencies

- bending the rules

- interchangeable roles.

'Client vulnerability' and 'deviancy' appeared to be topics of concern for MHT members. The remainder of the list was generated after noting instances of the first two categories when they emerged in the transcripts. No computer software package was used in this process. This had advantages as well as disadvantages in that the initial categories remained very flexible. For example, the last category was set aside as it served no immediate analytic purpose.

I had audiotapes, transcripts and fieldnotes which gave me limitless opportunities to return to my original data and redefine the categories as the analysis progressed. Through such means, I was able to test out emerging hypotheses about members' common-sense reasoning generated by fieldwork. It was at this point that I attempted to construct a model which I later rejected because it was too rigid to explain the complexity of members' social action.

I was also able to consider instances in the data which contradicted the emerging **hypotheses** [see Chapter 15 of this book]. One such instance was an account in which the client was not directly taken on by the team.

Statistical measures were not used in the analysis overall. However, counting the number of times 'family history' was invoked in members' accounts threw new light on gender as an interpretive frame. Hammersley and Atkinson (1983) suggest that with the help of the discriminate use of numbers, quantification can be used as an aid to precision [see Chapter 15 of this book]. In *this* study, counting was used to examine a hunch.

My focus on **members**' activities generated initial questions about what they had to know to do their work. It also built on my original interest in diagnostic construction. It was only after the first two phases of fieldwork were complete, and I had constructed the broad categories upon which my preliminary analysis was based, that I began to examine extracts rather than whole transcripts. In this sense, my work differed from research which appears to be based on the use of 'favourable' extracts only.

Generating a research problem analytically

3.3.4 By using extracts in this way, I attempted to find 'the sense' of what members were saying, and what was *made* of what they were saying. I then shifted my emphasis to the **discourse**-based question: 'How do participants *do* things?' My desire to pose such a question derived from my reading of other **ethnographic** work as I strove to define my research problem.

While my early observations provided a descriptive background for my research, I still needed to focus on clear questions to ask about my data and to use these questions to shape the very act of data collection itself.

The earliest influence on my study was Goffman's *Frame Analysis* (1974). It explores the relational dimension of meaning. For Goffman, a **frame** is defined by its *use* rather than by its content. Events are seen in terms of 'primary frameworks'. The particular frame used provides a means of interpreting the event to which it is applied. For Goffman, frames are both structural *and* flexible as they are susceptible to change by interacting participants. Indeed, they are highly vulnerable, being continually subject to dispute. In the event, much of my study used Goffman's concept of frame to demonstrate how understandings emerged among the MHT.

Data analysis and reading are mutually informing. In a sense, there is no end to updating one's knowledge. In this research, the literature was used as a continuing opportunity to make connections with the MHT data. For instance, halfway through the research the analysis began to lose focus. Reading Holstein's (1992) work on descriptive practice and Loseke's (1989) study of a shelter for battered women provided new knowledge about the accomplishment of social problems work. Similarly, towards the end of my research, fresh material from Kitzinger and Wilkinson (1997) helped me construct a chapter on 'gender' which arose from my reading of Holstein (1992).

Reflections on participant observation

3.3.5 I was now a participant-observer in a field where members were healthcare professionals like myself. Although I no longer practise directly, what effect this might have on the data is an important issue.

To suppose that *any* researcher enters a field without past experience or some pre-existing ideas is unrealistic. To suppose that their presence will not exert an influence on the data is equally unrealistic (cf. Strong, 1979: 229). In my own case, I accepted that my presence in the field would influence what I saw, but I could not predict 'how' or to what extent. In this sense, data produced by the team were a mutual production which also involved myself as researcher (cf. Emerson et al., 1995: 106).

Unlike Strong's (1979) experience of researching in paediatric settings, I cannot admit to being treated 'as part of the furniture' (1979: 229) by the team members I was observing – possibly because of my practitioner background. However, I *was* aware of feeling more accepted as the fieldwork progressed.

I was initially incorporated into the MHT's practical frame. Members were intolerant of my chosen position at the side of the room during fieldwork and 'ordered' rather than invited me to sit with them in their discussion circle even though I maintained a non-speaking role.

In the team leader's words, this was to 'close the circle'. As Peräkylä surmises about his own role as researcher, maybe this was the best way of collecting data and relating to members in the field (1989: 131). Certainly it was of practical use in that I knew the tape was recording data so I was left free to observe and write notes (cf. Silverman, 1993: 38). However, as Hammersley warns: 'When a setting is familiar the danger of misunderstanding is especially great' (1990: 8).

I was aware that I might become too 'comfortable' with the team, but upon reflection this did not happen. Speculatively speaking, constructing a democratic atmosphere was possibly also functional to the team in that it positioned me where I could be involved and seen.

Nonetheless, the danger of 'over-rapport' with members of the team was a continuing issue for me. Despite my similar professional background to team members, I had to treat their perspectives as problematic.

Ethical considerations

3.3.6 Gaining ethical approval for the study was in no sense 'plain sailing'. In the early months of 1992, I put forward my proposal to the ethical committee of the trust hospital to which the team was attached. Apart from stressing the qualitative nature of my research intentions and the fact that staff, rather than clients, would be my proposed subjects, I could only state with certainty that I wished to audio-record the team's weekly case conference.

In addition, I found the form I was required to complete somewhat problematic. It conformed to the standard type for purely *clinical* research involving human subjects rather than to any proposed sociological research. Predictably, it was very 'physically' oriented.

One question asked for 'potential hazards' and the precautions I might take to meet them. The possible contravening of confidentiality was my written response to this enquiry. I undertook to use pseudonyms for the names of staff, clients and care areas throughout the research to preserve anonymity and to safeguard confidentiality.

In the event, even references to months or seasons of the year in the transcripts were changed as the work got under way. Dates of legislation were retained as were dates of fieldwork and any reference to clients' ages, as such data were necessary to the analysis. In addition, I undertook to write a report on the progress of the study for the ethical committee, should this be required at any stage of the work. I was not given permission to interview clients or to access their case records.

I guaranteed to keep all audiotapes at home under lock and key and to do all my own transcribing rather than eliciting secretarial assistance. I also promised to destroy the tapes at the end of the study. I did not expect to see or interview clients. Finally, I undertook not to proceed without the permission of all team members following a full explanation of what I proposed to do [see Chapter 10 of this book].

Several months later, I received written consent to proceed with my project from the chairman of the ethics committee. I also discussed my proposal with the chairman of the trust's mental health board, a practising consultant psychiatrist. He voiced no objection in principle and recommended that I contact the team's consultant and team leader to seek their individual permission, which I did.

However, being a participant-observer raises a number of ethical issues which extend beyond formal consent to the research. Before the research began, I decided that the best way to carry out participant observation, both morally and practically, was to be as open as possible with the team.

My rationale for making this decision was that this would permit me to be free to ask questions as the fieldwork progressed without creating too much suspicion. Being open would also permit audio-recording of data. To a certain extent this strategy worked, although my insider knowledge of professional practice always made me conscious that what I was being offered of the team's world would be partially restricted.

I was aware that my presence in the field might affect the behaviour of those being observed, especially as the team was aware of my health professional background. I entered the field in the knowledge that a certain amount of professional self-consciousness would be inevitable, but I accepted this as a necessary 'tradeoff' in terms of access. It was a tacit assumption on my part and possibly on theirs, but on the basis of it, both I and they were able to proceed.

In this sense, my past experience as a practitioner was in no way disadvantageous to my present role as researcher. As a case study researcher, it became useful to me as a source of data.

For example, there were almost certainly times in this study when members responded to my presence in terms of what might be called 'ethical correctness'. I sensed that there were some occasions when members overtly displayed their moral adequacy as a consequence of being observed. My general *impression* was that members responded to me as a more senior member of staff, i.e. as an older, experienced professional now working in higher education. I felt that the team's display of moral adequacy in my presence was particularly marked, especially where ethical dilemmas were prominent.

Some implications of Sally's story

3.3.7 Research problems rarely come out of the blue. Sometimes, we may be the more or less fortunate recipient of a topic 'given' to us by a supervisor. In Sally's case, her own work experience combined with previous academic study to suggest an interesting topic. Her previous job as a nurse had underlined what she had read about illness 'careers' and the functions for staff of labelling patients and the intended and unintended consequences of such labels once applied (Section 3.3.1).

Now Sally needed a setting in which to explore this issue. She made use of a chance encounter to gain access to a relevant healthcare context (3.3.1). The demands of her full-time work now influenced the data she sought from this setting. Like many part-time researchers, she avoided a time-consuming ethnography of everything that the MHT did, in favour of a focus upon scheduled meetings. This meant that her focus was necessarily on one side of the coin: not on how staff and clients perceived each other, but on how staff categorized their homeless clients in order to make decisions about whether (and how) to help them (3.3.1).

Three points emerge for beginning researchers. First, a research study can offer an opportunity to pursue a topic that intrigues you personally. Where your own experience seems to support an approach or a study that you have come across, a good research problem may be lying on your lap.

Second, where access to a setting is difficult, draw upon your own contacts and experience as Sally did.

Third, as I argue in Chapter 6, research topics and data generally need to be narrowed down in order to be workable. Sometimes, this narrowing down will arise for quite mundane, practical reasons – for example, as in Sally's case, the amount of time you have available. Providing that you thoroughly analyse the data you have, this need not be a problem. Indeed, it can be an advantage by giving your research a direction.

As Sally argues, it was a great advantage to have audiotapes as her core data to complement her fieldnotes (3.3.2). Indeed, on one occasion, listening to a tape revealed a crucial error in a note (3.3.3).

She was satisfied that her way of transcribing her tapes was appropriate to her research topic. However, on reflection, she realized that it might have been simpler to have used an existing transcription method, like CA notation, rather than to have started from scratch (3.3.2).

This illustrates a general point to which I return several times in this book. When you are faced with a new task (e.g. finding data, coming up with a research-able problem, transcribing your data), look around for some already existing model. Nothing is gained (and a lot lost) by wasting time reinventing the wheel!

When she began to analyse her data, Sally, like Moira, worked inductively. She identified recurring instances of some activity in one meeting and then extended her search to several cases 'to examine a hunch' (3.3.3). Crucially, she sought contrary as well as confirming evidence to test out her hunches (3.3.3).

Throughout her research, Sally was aware that even the most inductive approach depends upon some theoretical orientation. In her case, Goffman's account of 'framing' gave direction to her research (3.3.4). However, she kept on reading other work as she analysed her data and showed a welcome readiness to modify direction as she came up with new findings and concepts (3.3.4).

Finally, Sally's diary discusses familiar issues in participant observation: how your own preconceptions may enter into your research; how being observed may affect people's behaviour (towards you and in relation to their own normally routine activities); and ethical issues in relation to obtaining informed consent and to what you reveal to the people you are studying (3.3.5, 3.3.6). As Sally shows, it is wise to reflect on these issues but also to treat them as valuable data. Indeed, she was able to use her core concept of 'frame' to depict the MHT's categorization of herself – and thereby to understand more about how it dealt with others.

3.4 Simon's Research Diary

Beginnings

3.4.1
My [Simon's] first degree was a BSc in sociology and media studies, chosen partly on account of some spurious advice I had received

concerning the 'higher status' of a joint honours degree. I also felt that the media studies component meant that the course would necessarily focus on those cultural products invested with meaning by, and therefore relevant to, most people on a day-to-day basis. It is not necessary to go into explicit detail regarding the development of my thought during this time, for the purposes of this brief biographical outline. However, it is important to note that, by the end of my period of undergraduate study, I was greatly vexed by issues surrounding the tendency within the various schools of sociology towards using **social structure** too loosely as a way of accounting for data.

The basis for this concern can be broadly represented by examining the focus of my final-year project at City University, which took as a general theme the role of the media as 'moral entrepreneurs' (cf. Becker, 1963; also Cohen and Young, 1973; Cohen, 1980) in the creation and imposition of labels and stereotypes on a societal level. The project consisted of a comparative study of the reporting, by two contemporaneous newspapers, of two similar crime stories from the 1950s and the 1990s. Unfortunately, my experience of travelling to The British Library's Newspaper Library and reading the various original newspaper sources archived there left me with a sense of detachment from the materials I was studying. I had serious doubts as to the veracity of my own reading of the print and claims made regarding it, based mainly on the realization that I had little idea how contemporary readers may or may not have engaged with the texts.

It was in this frame of mind that I decided to broaden my knowledge of research methodologies, and gain some practical research experience in the meantime, by undertaking an MA in sociology with special reference to qualitative research at Goldsmiths College, University of London, in 1997.

Learning about CA

3.4.2 Whilst the course acquainted me with a wide range of research methodologies, it was my introduction to **conversation analysis** (CA) during this period that most caught my imagination. As the course began to contextualize more clearly my previous misgivings as part of the ongoing debate within sociology regarding the 'theory relative' activity of defining social structure (cf. Silverman, 2001), I was taken by ten Have's statement that 'CA refuses to use available "theories" of human conduct to ground or organize its arguments, or even to construct a "theory" of its own' (1998: 27).

In setting forward 'a different conception of how to theorize about social life', CA also moves away from invoking 'obvious' social structural factors when explaining social phenomena. While the concept of social structure is an important element in sociological inquiry in general, 'the problem becomes one of not allowing it to take on an analytic life of its own' (Boden and Zimmerman, 1991: 5). The way in which many sociological analyses allow social structure to 'take on a life of its own' is memorably summed up by Sacks in his analogy of society being viewed by the social sciences as a piece of machinery where much of what takes place is random, and it is worth quoting at length:

> Such a view suggests that there are a few places where, if we can find them, we will be able to attack the problem of order. If we do not find them, we will not. So we can have an image of a machine with a couple of holes in the front. It spews out some nice stuff from those holes, and at the back it spews out garbage. There is, then, a concern among social scientists for finding 'good problems', that is, those data generated by the machine which *are* orderly, and then attempt to construct the apparatus necessary to give those results. (1984b: 21–2)

The search for 'good problems' not only is carried out mainly in terms of reference to 'big issues' regarding large-scale institutions, but also necessarily imposes order on the phenomena being studied. Rather than search for an order based on the analyst's conception of what this order might be, CA proposes an examination of how individuals orient to (and therefore display) that order themselves: 'whatever humans can do can be examined to discover some way they do it, and that way will be stably describable. That is, we may alternatively take it that there is order at all points' (Sacks, 1984b: 22).

Not only did I find the movement away from fruitless theoretical debates between opposing theories refreshing, I was also impressed by the methodological focus that CA afforded. In focusing on the order found at all points within 'what humans do', CA delineated its field of study, since as Sacks pointed out, it is possible that 'detailed study of small phenomena may give an enormous understanding of the way humans do things and the kinds of objects they use to construct and order their affairs' (1984b: 24). Indeed, this focus meant that the question of social structure took on a new relevance for me, since in examining the ways in which interactional parties display their identities relative to one another, *and* how it matters to them, CA necessarily deals with the 'senses of "who they are" that connect directly to what is ordinarily meant by "social structure"' (Schegloff, 1991: 48).

Hoping to be relevant

3.4.3 Although the need for some theoretical formulation of what should be studied was no longer an overriding consideration, I still inclined towards research that could be said to be of practical relevance. On one level, this was due to my own lack of confidence in my ability to add anything of worth or interest to the cumulative fund of interactional knowledge that ten Have has typified as the aim of 'pure CA' (1998: 8). But it was equally due to a reaction against the ongoing dismissive view within the British media towards sociological research, claiming it is irrelevant and badly conducted.[1] Fortunately, I found that both concerns were addressed within CA.

Not only does the primacy of mundane conversation provide the 'richest available research domain' (Heritage, 1984: 240), it also 'uses the practices found in ordinary conversation as a baseline from which to analyse institutional talk' (Silverman, 2001: 172). Added to this, Silverman (1993), in his discussion of the contribution social science could make to wider society, highlights CA's role in offering a new perspective to participants within institutional settings. He states that 'researchers ought *not* to begin from normative standards of "good" and "bad" communication' (1993: 192), but should focus instead upon understanding 'the *skills* that participants deploy and the *functions* of the communication patterns that are discovered' (1993: 192, original emphasis).

Finding a topic

3.4.4 It was with these issues in mind that I happened across the parents' evening data [at a local school]. At the time my partner was a relatively new primary school teacher, and her exposure to the realities of parents' evening led to her assertion that such meetings had not been directly addressed within her teacher-training course. This difficulty with parents' evening from the teacher's perspective chimed with further anecdotal information from my own parents, whose experience of such meetings tallied with the 'public relations exercise' view outlined by Baker and Keogh:

> [Parents' evenings] are understood and talked about as ritual or ceremonial encounters, in which teachers go through routine expressions of interest and academic diagnosis, and which parents attend in order to show their 'interest' in their children's schooling. (1995: 264)

Part of this characterization involves the view that parents' evening meetings are events in which 'nothing much was accomplished' (cf. Baker and Keogh, 1995, and above) which, as Baker and Keogh point out, 'is an invitation, if not provocation, to ethnomethodological inquiry' (1995: 265). It should equally be remembered, however, that Baker and Keogh's characterization of such meetings stems from their understanding of 'educational folklore' (1995: 264). Indeed, some parents find these occasions very helpful opportunities to review their child's academic progress. But this in itself provides further justification for examining the meetings.

Handy and Aitken, in their study of the organization of the primary school, point out that whilst there exists for all schools 'a bond between them and the families and communities they serve' (1994: 246), in practice the situation is not that simple. As they note:

> Some parents are over-anxious and expect more from the school for their child than is realistic. But sadly too many other parents abdicate once their child is at school. Teachers know that the parents whom they really want to see, to know, and to help are often the ones who never come to school. (1994: 246)

Given both this variation in parental attitudes to their children's schooling in general, and teachers' views of parents' evening meetings in particular, it is perhaps unsurprising that the assorted sections of the school community, be they teachers, parents, or children, regard parents' evening in such different ways. With the question of what parents' evening 'means' being such a contentious one, the need to examine what goes on during them seemed to me to be particularly relevant.

Obtaining access

3.4.5 Having had these meetings drawn to my attention in this way, I began to consider their use as the basis for my dissertation. My ongoing unofficial pastoral role at my partner's school meant that I had already built up a rapport with the head teacher, so approaching him with a proposal to record some parents' evening meetings was straightforward enough. Once the process of the research was explained and agreed upon, he was happy for the recording to take place, with one stipulation: my access was restricted to the recording of only one teacher in the school, namely my partner. Not wanting to risk what rights to conduct the research I had already gained, I decided not to make any representations regarding the recording of any of the other Year 6 teachers. This did not unduly worry me at the time, since this restriction sat well with the time frame within which I could gather, transcribe and analyse the data for my MA dissertation. As it transpired, I only used a single meeting for the dissertation, leaving me (so I thought) with a surfeit of data.

Worrying about sample size

3.4.6 Focusing upon a single teacher has certain limitations in terms of generalizing the findings of this research to a wider population. It can be argued that the conversational techniques utilized by the teacher in this research are unique to her, and therefore not easily extrapolated to the parents' evening practice of other teachers. Equally, the fact that the teacher in the data was a class teacher rather than a set teacher could have been an important influential factor. Perhaps set teachers do things differently in such meetings by dint of the fact that they are dealing with the specificities of their curriculum area. Furthermore, the entire format of the meetings might have been different at another stage of the academic year, even if carried out by the same teacher studied in this research. In short, various permutations in the actual accomplishment of parents' evening could be hidden by the fact that the data sample consists of a single teacher on a single parents' evening.

How, then, should this research be seen in terms of both **sampling** variety and external **validity**? Indeed, given the tension between the specific difficulties associated with the gathering of the data and the ideal research design outlined above, can this study say anything useful about the phenomenon that has been studied?

I believe the answer lies in seeing this research not as an attempt to provide categorical 'truths' about all parents' evenings in general, but as an attempt to raise questions about such meetings by looking at a single case in detail [see Chapter 9 of this book]. To some extent, raising questions in this way relies upon the perspective within CA that '*social practices that are possible*, that is, *possibilities of language use*, are the central objects of all conversation analytic case studies on interaction institutional settings' (Peräkylä, 2004: 297, original emphasis).

This element of *possibility* can be taken too far in terms of ascribing a certain level of universality to the findings of studies into conversational and interactional phenomena, but as Seale points out, 'readers must always make their own judgements about the relevance of findings for their own situations' (1999: 108). The corrective, he suggests, is simple: 'threats to such transferability are dealt with most adequately if details, or "thick" descriptions of the "sending" context (or the "sample"), are provided' (1999: 108). This study can therefore be seen as being *exploratory* rather than *definitive*, examining the achievement of routine by a single individual in a specific setting in such a way that further analytical possibilities are opened up.

Narrowing down my research problem

3.4.7 Although I subsequently came to realize the deficiencies in my MA thesis, and sought to correct them during my doctoral research, the findings of the MA (such as they were) formed the basis for my research proposal to a major British research council (the ESRC). Although the majority of the proposal focused upon CA's methodological relevance to my funding agency's thematic area of communication and learning, it did include the following research problem:

> Whilst these meetings would seem to fall distinctly into the category of professional–lay interactions, with the attendant problems associated with the differential exercise of power by the interactants, in this situation both the parents and the teacher can claim a level of 'expert' knowledge with regard to the subject of the interaction, namely the child. The research problem to be addressed is that of what impact this dual claim to competency has upon the joint construction of context by the parents and teacher as the two most powerful interactants.

Aside from some of the more obvious difficulties related to the unproblematic application of concepts such as 'power' and 'claims to expert knowledge', this research proposal conflicted with CA's stated aim that analysis should always begin with what Psathas (1990: 45) has called 'unmotivated looking' [see Moira's discussion in Section 3.2]. This is summed up by Sacks's assertion that 'when we start out with a piece of data, the question of what we are going to end up with, what kind of findings it will give, should not be a consideration' (1984b: 27). So, despite the stated aims (however limited) of the research proposal, at the start of the MPhil/PhD course I struggled to come to the data 'anew', without the constraint of wondering where I was going to 'end up'.

Of course, the central issue of this struggle is one of discipline, not only in terms of focusing on one or two analytic concepts at a time, but also with regard to allowing the details of the talk to go where they will. As Sacks has pointed out, 'it ought never to be a matter of concern to anybody who's doing a piece of description which way it comes out, as long as it comes out some way' (1992, Vol. 1: 472).

Discipline was imposed by moving away from the consideration of individually interesting features, framing them instead with regard to the overall structural organization of the meetings. CA deals with and explicates 'patterns of stable, recurrent structural features' (Heritage, 1984: 241, and above) within talk. Through examination of the trajectory of the reportings on the child, fitted to both the search for parental response by the teacher, and how the form of the response shaped the unfolding trajectory, a framework for the research began to become clearer.

Some implications of Simon's story

3.4.8 The experience of writing an undergraduate dissertation had given Simon an understanding of the uses and limits of a key concept: 'social structure' (Section 3.4.1). Once again, this underlines the point that true understanding comes by applying ideas one has learned in the library to new topics.

However, being aware of the deficiencies of a concept is not sufficient. One also needs to learn an analytic approach to data and then discover how to use it. Conversation analysis (CA) turned out to be Simon's key to the social world (3.4.2). Of course, ultimately such approaches cannot be true or false but only more or less useful (see my discussion of **models** in Chapter 7). For Simon, the usefulness of CA seemed to be twofold. First, it gave him a clear idea of what kind of data he wanted and of how to analyse them. Second, it made personal sense to him by according with his previous research experience and also, perhaps, by being aesthetically pleasing.

Yet the appeal of theory can be double-edged. Aesthetic satisfaction can sometimes mean that you never can extricate yourself from the charms of the library to confront the external world (see my discussion of 'grand theory' in Chapter 6). Simon was aware of this danger from the outset and was determined to combine his theoretical 'narrowness' with a concern for practical relevance (3.4.3).

At this point, like Sally, Simon had a lucky break. His partner was a primary school teacher prepared to give him access to her work. A parent–teacher evening was looming and this appeared to be a setting which was problematic to its participants and under-researched (3.4.4). Needing to tape his data (a requirement of CA), Simon drew upon his own fortuitous association with the school and received permission from the head teacher (3.4.5).

However, achieving access brought its own worry. Simon was now troubled about the small size of his sample. While studying one teacher's work seemed to be enough for his MA thesis, would it be sufficient for a PhD? As it turned out,

Simon came to the conclusion that a small sample will do if you have thought through its limitations (3.4.6) and if the quality of the analysis is sufficient.

Indeed, when it came to the stage of data analysis, Simon was confronted by multiple, emergent research problems. This created an initial tension between the inductive approach he was using and his funding body's demand for an initial hypothesis. For a while, he could not see the wood for the trees. Fortunately, in time, an overall unifying theme became clearer as his various observations revealed a sequential structure to the parents' meetings (3.4.7). So Simon's thesis became organized around the trajectory of reportings of 'news' to parents by their class teacher.

 ■ **Attempt Exercise 3.1** ■■■■■■■■■■■■■■

Concluding Remarks

3.5
Obviously, there are many different stories that research students can tell about their experience and I do not pretend that what you have read was typical or representative. Nonetheless, there are several clear messages in these stories that are worth listening to.

I set these out below as a *fifteen-point guide*. Obviously, like any recipe, you will need to apply it to your own circumstances. Nevertheless, I believe the points below apply to *all levels* of student research from BA and MA dissertations through to the PhD.

1   *Begin in familiar territory*. If you can, work with data that are close to hand and readily accessible. For instance, if, as in Moira's case, you have data from another study which you can (re)analyse, grab the opportunity. There are no 'brownie points' to be obtained for gathering your data in difficult circumstances. Make it easy on yourself at this stage so that you can concentrate your energies on the infinitely more important task of data analysis.

2   *Find a settled theoretical orientation*. As I stress throughout this book, research is never just about techniques. All three stories refer to finding a theoretical approach which made sense to the students and then could provide a settled basis for inference and data analysis.

3   *Narrow down your topic*. Strive to find a topic that is appropriate to your theory and data and is workable (this issue is discussed at length in Chapter 6). Later, if you wish, like Moira, Sally and Simon, you can use your research to make contributions to a substantive area (e.g. health and illness, education) and to a methodology (e.g. interview research, ethnography, CA), and to reflect upon issues of social policy.

4   *Don't try to reinvent the wheel*. In Chapter 5 I discuss what 'originality' might mean in research. For the moment, it is worth recalling that Moira used an earlier study as a model for her research and that both she and Simon used a well-established method of transcribing their audiotapes. So, at the outset, look at previous successful dissertations in your university library or departmental files and, where possible, focus on work directed by your supervisor.

5   *Keep writing.* Commit your ideas to paper. Don't worry how short or draft your papers are. Indeed, in some ways it makes more sense, initially at least, to submit 500-word pieces so that you can be guided in the right direction before you have expended too much time and effort.

6   *Begin data analysis early.* Don't be deflected away from early data analysis by literature reviews and the exigencies of data gathering. If you haven't got any data yourself at an early stage, try analysing someone else's data – published data, your supervisor's data, etc. (see Chapter 13).

7   *Think critically about data.* When you start to identify a pattern in your data, don't rush to conclusions. See how robust this pattern is by working comparatively with different parts of your data (as Moira did) and by trying to identify deviant cases (like Sally).

8   *Use your supervisor.* Make use of your supervisor to test out your ideas and give you confidence (see Chapter 22).

9   *Use other resources and opportunities.* Graduate students should take every opportunity to attend relevant conferences and, better still, to give conference papers, and to take appropriate training courses. Find out if there are study groups of research students working on similar topics. If not, try to establish such a group.

10 *Do not expect a steady learning curve.* Be prepared for the sequence of highs and lows that will inevitably happen. For instance, Sally found that her early ideas about how her MHT made decisions were too simplistic, and Simon puzzled over how to integrate his apparently diverse findings. Treat setbacks as opportunities: Sally came up with a better explanatory model and Simon eventually saw an overall pattern.

11 *Keep a research diary.* Moira, Sally and Simon kept a file of their current ideas, hopes and worries. This file is an invaluable resource which, as I suggest in Chapter 19, can be used in edited form in your methodology chapter.

12 *Earmark blocks of working time.*[2] If you are researching part-time, it is crucial to find blocks of time in which you can focus solely on your research. Use this time for intensive data analysis and writing.

13 *Do not reproach yourself.* If you experience a setback, it may be best to take some time out to relax before you return to your research.

14 *Treat field relations as data.* How others treat you in the field is never just a technical matter. Like Moira and Sally, reflect upon how your interaction with your subjects is shaping your data.

15 *Understand that there is no 'perfect' model of research design.* Practical contingencies (e.g. access or the lack of it; the time you have available) are always going to affect any piece of research. Don't be afraid of working with what data you happen to have. Your examiners will not be comparing your research with some 'perfect' model, but they will expect you to have thought through the limitations of your data and your analysis (see Chapter 5).

KEY POINTS

- It helps to begin your research in familiar territory.

- Find a settled theoretical orientation that works for you.

- Once you get a feel of your field, narrow down your topic as soon as you can.

- Don't try to reinvent the wheel; find what has worked for others and follow them.

- Keep writing.

- Begin data analysis immediately.

- Think critically about your data; don't rush to conclusions.

- Test out your ideas with your supervisor; don't worry if, in the early stages, you are often wide of the mark.

- Use other resources and opportunities inside and outside your own department.

- Do not expect a steady learning curve; no research study is without some disasters.

- Keep a research diary.

- Earmark blocks of working time to complete different activities.

- Do not reproach yourself about setbacks.

- Treat your relations within the field as data.

- Understand that there is no perfect model of research design.

Notes

1 Although many examples could be cited, this brief quotation from an article by Will Buckley in *The Observer* newspaper of 30 May 1999 serves as a case in point: 'Here we go again. Yet more supposed research (this time from the sociology department at Edinburgh University) claiming that men are lousy parents, incapable of spending more than 15 minutes a day with their children … Crap dads are back on the agenda because yet another bored sociologist has made a few phone calls and cobbled together some stats.'
2 Items 12 and 13 were suggested by Vicki Taylor after reading an earlier draft of this chapter.

■ ■ Further Reading ■

The best place to look for similar research histories is in the writings of students at your own university. BA students should seek to obtain past successful undergraduate dissertations from their department. Graduate students should study MA and PhD theses in the library, focusing particularly on the work of people having your supervisor. If the methodology chapter does not include an autobiographical account, try to contact the author and discuss what lessons they drew from their experience.

Two recent books offer useful practical advice on managing a student research project: Renata Phelps, Kath Fisher and Allan Ellis's *Organizing and Managing Your Research: A Practical Guide for Postgraduates* (Sage, 2007) and Harriet Churchill and

Teela Sanders's *Getting Your PhD: A Practical Insider's Guide* (Sage, 2007). Judith Bell's *Doing Your Research Project* (fourth edition, Open University Press, 2005) is a good introduction to research at the undergraduate or MA level. Estelle Phillips and Derek Pugh's *How To Get a PhD* (fourth edition, Open University Press, 2005) is the best British account of the practical issues involved in writing a PhD.

 ■ Exercise 3.1

Keep a research diary for a given period (one month for an undergraduate dissertation, three months for an MA project, at least six months for a PhD). Record:

- changes in your ideas about topic, data, theory and method

- new ideas from the literature or from lectures and talk

- meetings with your supervisor and their consequences

- life events and their consequences for your work.

At the end of your chosen period, reread your research diary and assess:

- what you have achieved in that period

- what would be required for you to do better in future

- your achievement targets for the next equivalent period.

4

The Research Experience II

```
┌─── Chapter Objectives ┌─────────────────────────────────────┐

By the end of this chapter you will be able to:

• Think about the theoretical basis of your research.

• Understand what data and methods are relevant to your research topic.

• Grasp the elements of qualitative data analysis.

• See what is involved in designing a practical, achievable research study.
```

Introduction

4.1 In this part of the book, I have been attempting to set out the context in which qualitative research dissertations are written. We began with a brief overview of qualitative research. Then, in Chapter 3, we considered the lessons that could be drawn from three completed research dissertations.

Yet, for many readers of this book, their own completed graduate or undergraduate dissertation is a distant, desired object. So, in this chapter, we draw upon the accounts of research students at an early stage of their research. Through these accounts, we examine the analytical, methodological and practical problems that confront the beginning researcher.

In some senses, the beginning researcher has far less to prove than established scholars. If you imagine a sliding scale of levels of achievement, then journal articles, as the stock in trade of established scholars, are (or should be) the pinnacle of scholarly accomplishment. Somewhat surprisingly, books are a little further down the scale since they do not depend on the same degree of independent review. Further down the scale are also completed research dissertations which, I suggest, are properly viewed as displays of successful apprenticeship.

However, my sense of a sliding scale in research is intended simply to mark a stage of a research career; it is not a moral category. Although it is 40 years since I was at that stage, I do not look down upon the work of first-year research students. Indeed, frankly, I sometimes come across more exciting ideas in a first-year graduate seminar than in many journal articles!

What follows is by no means a representative survey of qualitative research at its early stages. Instead, the material below has been drawn from research students in my own department and in various social science and humanities departments of Finnish universities.[1]

While the range of research covered below is limited, I hope you will eventually agree that it is not narrow. In other words, I hope and expect that readers will find at least some echo of their own ideas and interests represented below.

In collating these presentations for this chapter, I had to decide upon an organizing principle. In particular, I had to choose whether to organize the material by topic, theory or methodology. I reasoned that grouping by topic would be lively but might appear to exclude readers working on different topics. By contrast, a theory grouping might be too abstract and, perhaps, confusing for an audience coming from a disparate range of disciplines. By taking a methodological perspective, I hope to be more inclusive by encompassing many of the methods used (and contemplated) by qualitative researchers.

The discussion below is thus organized by method, with sections on interview studies, **ethnographies**, textual analysis, work with videotapes and audiotapes, and multiple methods. However, such a focus on method is not narrowly technical. As I make clear below, methods only acquire meaning and vitality by their embeddedness in particular theoretical perspectives.

As in Chapter 3, I will proceed case by case, offering some comments with each example and then summarizing the points that emerge from each methodology. The chapter concludes with some suggestions about managing the early stages of research. After each topic title, I have noted the social science discipline in which the student is working as well as the student's name.

4.2 Interviews
Living and coping in a community of elderly people

4.2.1 (Information studies/sociology) [Tippi] Tippi writes about her joint research: 'We wanted to ask how the inhabitants feel about living in the community where they have lived for many years.' Her study is based upon thematic interviews with a random sample of eight elderly people from the community. As she puts it, the aim of this study 'is to [clarify] ... the basic meaning of living [in this community]'.

This is how she describes her interviews: 'The elderly people were asked about their daily schedules, their attitudes to relatives, services, neighbourhood and environment, their interests and their opinions about society today compared with their earlier life experiences.'

Preliminary findings suggest two things. First, members of the community told the same kinds of life stories. Second, such people described themselves as more independent than she had thought. They described 'coping' by attempting to keep control of four issues: financial, social, health related and security.

An analytic issue potentially arises in such studies where interviews are used to elicit respondents' perceptions. How far is it appropriate to think that people attach a single meaning to their experiences? In this case, may not there be multiple meanings of living in the community, represented by what people say to the researcher, to each other, to carers and so on (Gubrium, 1997)?

This raises the important methodological issue of whether interview responses are to be treated as giving direct access to 'experience' or as actively constructed **narratives** (Gubrium and Holstein, 2009; Riessman, 2008). Both positions are entirely legitimate but the position taken will need to be justified and explained.

Students' views of evaluation and feedback

4.2.2 (Behavioural sciences) [Laura] Laura is examining students' responses to the assessment of their distance education essays. Her research question is: 'Does it deliver the feedback that is needed and when it is needed?' Her data are derived from thematic interviews with 11 students chosen from four different localities. Her preliminary findings suggest that students want more detailed, critical feedback on their essays so that they can know what are the gaps in their knowledge and what they can do about them.

Laura describes the theoretical basis of her research as 'a **hermeneutic** method based on how researcher and subjects interpret the world and attempt to merge their horizons of meaning'. This is ambitious and its value will need to be demonstrated in the data analysis. Indeed, it might be simpler to settle on presenting her research as a descriptive study based upon a clear social problem. Either way, the issues about the status of interview data, also raised in Tippi's project, will need to be engaged.

Football and masculinity

4.2.3 (Sociology) [Steven] Steven's approach is based upon theories of masculinity within the general area of gender studies. More specifically, his work is concerned with football supporters and masculinity. He is particularly interested in understanding the experience of football supporters as opposed to the way in which their behaviour is represented (for instance in the media).

Care needs to be taken in how such appeals to 'experience' are described. This is one way of 'slicing the cake' and other approaches (e.g. studies of media representations of sport), using other forms of data, are not directly competitive.

The data he is using derive from interviews with football supporters. As Steven acknowledges, he still needs to sort out tricky methodological issues relating to his sampling procedure, his involvement with his interviewees and how he analyses his data. A possible resource is Jocelyn Cornwell's (1981) study of health, gender and poverty, *Hard Earned Lives* – an interview study which shares some of his ambitions.

It is always sensible, in this situation, to familiarize yourself more deeply with the methodological literature on analysing interview data. Even if you choose to take a position opposed to such texts, you will need to be able to justify it. Without doing this, you are in danger of trying to reinvent the wheel.

Text processing in foreign-language classrooms

4.2.4 (English) [Pia] In Finland, foreign languages are primarily taught through textbooks. Yet textbook-based learning is often defined as monotonous or boring by students. Pia's topic is whether there are different ways of talking about foreign-language teaching and whether there is a conflict between them. Her broader concern is with what hinders change in classroom practices.

Her data consist of 12 interviews (half with teachers and half with students). She also has five 'think aloud' sessions in which students were asked to do an exercise from a text and think aloud at the same time. This is an interesting idea because it attempts to relate what people say to a particular task they are doing – although it has to cope with the likelihood that people's practical skills are far more complicated than they could tell you in so many words (Garfinkel, 1967).

Pia describes her analytical approach as **discourse analysis** (DA). This implies that she is more interested in identifying different ways of *talking* about foreign-language reading than in addressing the actual experiences of learning a foreign language through a textbook. Given that the latter can be seen as a social problem, there may be a mismatch between DA, which assumes that issues of social definition are paramount, and a direct address of social problems. This might suggest either dropping DA or reconceptualizing the problem.

If we are interested in what happens in the classroom, there is a further issue about the appropriateness of interview data. Shouldn't we observe what people do there instead of asking them what they think about it? Is how we talk about schooling directly related to what happens in schooling?

The family grief and recovery process as narratives

4.2.5 (Psychiatry) [Katarin] Katarin is analysing interviews with couples after the loss of their baby. She is interested in how family members construct stories about their grief and recovery processes after such a loss. She has identified three **discourses** at work here:

- a religious discourse ('everything is clear ... I think my faith is strengthened')

- a medical discourse ('our baby did not have a chance to live, this is better, the lungs were undeveloped')

- a protest discourse ('who can decide who is allowed to live and who isn't?').

Katarin calls her work **narrative analysis**. By treating her respondents' accounts as skilfully structured stories, she gets a lively, theoretically informed grip on her data.

Only two cautions are appropriate here. First, the mere identification of different discourses in respondents' talk can lead to a simple, reductive list. At some stage, it is analytically productive to move beyond such a list in order to attempt to map the skilful way in which such discourses are laminated on one another (see Silverman, 2006: 223–37).

Second, the assembly of narratives in interviews (or conversations) is always a two-way process. Therefore, we must treat the interviewer's questions not as (possibly distorted) gateways to the authentic account but as part of the process through which a narrative is collectively assembled (see Gubrium and Holstein, 2009: 41–53; Rapley, 2004).

Narratives by bereaved relatives

4.2.6 (Sociology) [Moira] We first came across Moira's research in Chapter 3. Here I describe her early thoughts on her project in a presentation at a graduate workshop. Using interview data drawn from an earlier study, Moira, like Katarin, is concerned with how bereaved relatives organize their initial stories of their bereavement. Moira's approach is drawn from **ethnomethodology's** concern with how people demonstrate the rationality and moral accountability of their talk. In their stories, people show that they hear (and pre-emptively manage) possible charges against them. By doing this, the analysis can fully show how people are not 'judgemental dopes' but rather display a lively concern for the maintenance and repair of the moral order.

Her method derives from Sacks's **membership categorization analysis**, using Baruch's (1981) work on the 'moral tales' of mothers of handicapped children as an example. As we saw in the previous chapter, basing your work on an earlier study deriving from a clear-cut theoretical approach can be a short cut to a successful research dissertation (see also Chapter 6).

In her presentation, Moira showed how she had started to analyse five data extracts using this method. At a later point, in line with her theoretical approach, the analysis can be deepened by working more intensively with small pieces of data to delineate precisely how particular descriptions serve to support particular activities like 'doing a complaint', 'excusing oneself' and so on. In this way, like Katarin, she can avoid the temptation simply to *list* different categories.

Interviews: summary

4.2.7 Common themes have emerged from our six interview studies which I summarize below. For the sake of simplicity, I present this summary in the form of a list of questions that you need to think about if you are planning to do an interview study.

It should be apparent that here, as elsewhere, I am concerned with data *analysis* rather than the mechanics of data gathering (the latter is discussed in Chapter 12).

What status do you attach to your data?

Many interview studies are used to elicit respondents' perceptions. How far is it appropriate to think that people attach a single meaning to their experiences? May not there be multiple meanings of a situation (e.g. living in a community home) or of an activity (e.g. being a male football fan) represented by what people say to the researcher, to each other, to carers and so on (Gubrium, 1997)?

As mentioned earlier, this raises the important methodological issue of whether interview responses are to be treated as giving direct access to 'experience' or as actively constructed 'narratives' involving activities which themselves demand analysis (Silverman, 2006: 109–52; Gubrium and Holstein, 2009; Riessman, 2008). Both positions are entirely legitimate but the position you take will need to be justified and explained.

Is your analytic position appropriate to your practical concerns?

Some ambitious analytic positions (e.g. hermeneutics, discourse analysis) may actually cloud the issue if your aim is simply to respond to a given social problem (e.g. living and coping in a community of elderly people; students' views of evaluation and feedback). If so, it might be simpler to acknowledge that there are more complex ways of addressing your data but to settle on presenting your research as a *descriptive* study based upon a clear social problem.

Do interview data really help in addressing your topic?

If you are interested in, say, what happens in school classrooms, should you be using interviews as your major source of data? Think about exactly why you have settled on an interview study. Certainly, it can be relatively quick to gather interview data but not as quick as, say, extracting data from texts and documents. How far are you being influenced by the prominence of interviews in the media (see Atkinson and Silverman, 1997)?

In the case of the classroom, couldn't you observe what people *do* there instead of asking them what they *think* about it? Or gather documents that routinely arise in schools, e.g. pupils' reports, mission statements, and so on?

Of course, you may still want to do an interview study. But whatever your method you will need to justify it and show you have thought through the practical and analytical issues involved in your choice.

━━━━━━━━━━━━━━━━ LINK ━━━━━━━━━━━━━━━━

If you plan to do qualitative interviews, a useful website is:

http://www.andrle.org.uk

Are you making too large claims about your research?

It always helps to make limited claims about your own research. Grandiose claims about originality, scope or applicability to social problems are all hostages to fortune. Be careful in how you specify the claims of your approach. Show that you understand that it constitutes one way of 'slicing the cake' and that other approaches, using other forms of data, may not be directly competitive.

Proper analysis goes beyond a list

Identifying the main elements in your data according to some theoretical scheme should only be the first stage of your data analysis. By examining how these elements are linked together, you can bring out the active work of both interviewer and interviewee and, like them, say something lively and original.

We now turn to **ethnographic** studies that involve some element of observation. As we shall see, these kinds of studies also raise complex methodological and analytic issues.

4.3 Ethnographies

Ethnographies are based on observational work in particular settings. The initial thrust in favour of ethnography was anthropological. Anthropologists argue that, if one is really to understand a group of people, one must engage in an extended period of observation. Anthropological fieldwork routinely involves immersion in a **culture** over a period of years, based on learning the language and participating in social events with the people.

By contrast, non-anthropologists are more likely to study particular milieux or **subcultures** in their own society. We will see examples of this latter approach in the studies discussed below where activities in classrooms and hospitals and on the Internet become objects of research observation.

The analysis of communicative functions of peer interaction during small group learning

4.3.1 (Education) [Caroline] Working in small groups has become a common feature of modern education. The exact nature of such 'learning' presents a clear and apparently under-researched topic tied to a recognizable social problem. As Caroline remarks: 'The ways in which knowledge is constructed in children's verbal interactions during small group work learning without direct teacher control has not yet been fully researched.'

Caroline has gathered data from children aged from 10 to 12 in small classroom groups working on mathematics, science and language. Her focus is on 'the socio-cognitive and interpersonal dynamics of peer interaction' using categories 'based on the communicative functions identified in the interactions'.

This is a theoretically defined topic which nonetheless might have a clear practical input. It uses a clearly defined method derived from certain forms of **discourse analysis**. However, Caroline's study also raises a more general issue about how a researcher goes about identifying features in her data.

Caroline's use of the passive voice in her reference to 'the communicative functions *identified* in the interactions' draws attention to a neglected issue in social research: namely, how does the analyst go about 'identifying features' in her data? One common answer is to claim to follow proper procedural rules. For instance, coders of data are usually trained in procedures with the aim of ensuring a uniform approach.

This is a tried and trusted method designed to improve the reliability of a research method. However, it is sensible to be conscious that **coding** is not the preserve of research scientists. In some sense, these students, like all of us, 'code' what they hear and see in the world around them. Moreover, this 'coding' has been shown to be mutual and interactive (Sacks, 1992; Silverman,1998).

Of course, as I said earlier, the research 'cake' can be legitimately sliced in many ways. So I am *not* suggesting that the vast mass of researchers who treat 'coding' as purely an analyst's problem abandon their work. Instead, my minimalist suggestion is that they mention and respond to this well-established critique (for an example, see Clavarino et al., 1995).

Analysing how radiologists work

4.3.2 (Information processing science) [Julia] Radiology, like many health professions, has recently experienced a sea change of technologies with the conventional X-ray image being complemented by computer-based, digitalized images. As Julia points out, any new technology creates new constraints as well as new possibilities. Her focus is on such technologically mediated interaction in workplace settings.

Using videotapes, observation and interviews, Julia has gathered data about radiological image interpretation conferences. By examining actual workplace interaction she hopes to contribute to the growing body of knowledge about human–computer interaction and to inform future technological design (see Suchman, 1987; Heath, 2004).

I hope you will agree with me that this is an exciting combination of a theoretically defined approach with clear practical relevance. However, Julia writes that she is concerned about what is *missing* from both her interviews and her videos. As she puts it:

> Thus far in my research it has become clear that there are aspects of work which I can't 'reach' through interviews (people can't readily articulate aspects that are so familiar to them as to be unremarkable) or through observation and interactional analysis of video-recordings (those aspects of work that are not evident in what people can actually be seen to do).

In a sophisticated way, Julia raises a problem that often troubles research students: the necessarily 'partial' character of any data source. I believe this problem is potentially huge yet, in a practical sense, easily resolved. One simply avoids trying to find the 'whole picture'. Instead, one analyses different kinds of data separately, aware that all data are partial.

So make do with what you have and understand that there are multiple phenomena available in any research setting. If you must go beyond any particular dataset, save that until you have completed smaller-scale analyses. Worrying about the 'whole picture' at the outset is, in my view, a recipe for stalling your research (see Silverman and Gubrium, 1994).

Newsgroups on the Internet _____

4.3.3 (Sociology) [Danny] Danny's topic is the Internet. He is concerned with how people assemble themselves as a community via the net, without recourse to speech inflections or body language. Broader issues relate to how the net is regulated, how it developed and what is exchanged on it. He proposes to focus on newsgroups on the net since their messages are publicly available and offer an interesting way to look at how a 'community' is assembled and develops.

Danny's approach derives from his interest in the Internet as a possible new locus of power and, to this end, he plans to draw upon the German critical theorist Jurgen Habermas's conception of distorted communication. In this way, he will compare how people actually communicate with Habermas's **normative** theory.

Danny's study shows the implications of making theoretical choices. Using Habermas's concept of 'distorted communication' will give a particular thrust to his study that is very different from other kinds of theory.

Even if you decide to eschew such grand theories, that itself is a theoretical choice! In this sense, there is no escape (nor should there be) from theory. At the same time, however, there is nothing wrong with a descriptive study providing that the researcher is conscious about the choice that is being made.

Ethnographies: summary _____

4.3.4 Once more, I have been concerned with how you analyse your data. I deal below with three issues that have arisen above.

What is involved in coding data?

As we have seen, coders of data are usually trained in procedures with the aim of ensuring a uniform approach. Later in this book, we examine how computer-aided qualitative data analysis can help in such coding (see Chapter 14).

However, as I pointed out, it is sensible to be conscious that 'coding' is not the preserve of research scientists. All of us 'code' what we hear and see in the world around us.

One response is to make this everyday 'coding' (or 'interpretive practice') the object of inquiry. Alternatively, we can proceed in a more conventional manner but mention and respond to this well-established critique.

Are my data 'partial'?

Of course they are. But this is not a problem – unless you make the impossible claim to give 'the whole picture'. So celebrate the partiality of your data and delight in the particular phenomena that they allow you to inspect (hopefully in detail).

Is my theory appropriate?

Your theory must be appropriate to the research questions in which you are interested. Indeed, rather than being a constraint, a theory should generate a series of directions for your research.

────────── LINK ──────────

For readings relevant to ethnography, visit:

http://www.sagepub.co.uk/gobo/

Texts

4.4 To introduce a separate section on 'texts' can look a little artificial. After all, aren't people on the Internet constructing texts? Again, if we treat an interview as a narrative, this can mean looking for the same textual features as researchers working with printed material. Indeed, the mere act of transcription of an interview turns it into a written text.

In this section, I use 'text' as a heuristic device to identify data consisting of words and images which have become recorded without the intervention of a researcher (e.g. through an interview). Below I examine five studies of texts.

Analysing classroom religious textbooks

4.4.1 (Teacher education) [Pertti] Since 1985 Finnish schools have had a religious instruction syllabus mainly based on three textbooks deriving from the Finnish Lutheran Church. Pertti's approach treats such textbooks as a form of literary genre (see Silverman, 2001: 198–200) which filters certain values into the school. He is examining such features as tables of contents in order to ask, 'How is otherness constructed in these texts through particular methods of classification?' His analysis derives from Michel Foucault's (1977; 1979) discussion of the construction of subjects and disciplines.

This study benefits from a manageable body of data: three textbooks are more than enough to carry out the analysis Pertti proposes. The analysis derives from a clearly defined theoretical approach, although it may be uneconomical to work with both Foucauldian ideas and writers on literary genre. In particular, from a Foucauldian position, one would want to study education in its own right, not in terms of ideas developed to study literature.

The form of Japanese 'modernity'

4.4.2 (Sociology) [Yoji] Yoji is interested in how far Japanese modernity depends upon concepts and practices deriving from the West (e.g. the assumption that history involves 'progress') and how far it is a feature of Western colonialization. His data will be drawn from representations of urban space in Tokyo. Although a major focus will be on the family, Yoji is also interested in other institutions including prisons, the police, the hospital, the school and the factory.

Yoji's approach derives from Foucault's (1977) account of the micropolitics of space. From this perspective, he is concerned with how space is racialized, colonized and gendered. It also leads to a concern with how space constructs 'modern' subjects (e.g. 'us' and 'them') and the 'inside' and 'outside' (for instance, the inner city, the ghetto, etc.).

Like Pertti, Yoji is working with a clear analytic approach. However, he might learn from Pertti's limited database by focusing on one archive or body of data. He is currently working with historical data from around the Meiji Restoration and it may be fruitful just to focus on one such period and/or to limit the material to visual images or certain texts.

The medicalization of the middle-aged female body in the twentieth century

4.4.3 (Sociology) [Greta] Greta is interested in the way in which middle-aged women have become a topic for medicine and the 'psy' sciences. Like Pertti and Yoji, Greta's analysis is based upon a Foucauldian discourse analytic approach, concerned with the construction of subjects within various forms of power/knowledge. Using this approach, she is able to chart how the medical gaze has moved from a biomedical model to medico-psy models and, most recently, a medico-psycho-social model.

Her data derive from the *British Medical Journal*, medical textbooks and a history of menopause clinics in the 1970s. Simple keyword analysis has proved fruitful in the early stages of her research, illustrating for instance how the clinical type of 'the chronic pelvic woman' emerged into discourse.

As Greta's research develops, like Katarin's and Moira's interview studies (discussed above), she will want to map how different discourses are laminated on each other. She will also have to decide whether to look for yet more sources of data (e.g. articles and letters on advice pages in women's magazines) or to narrow down the amount of data she has already collected.

The representation of 'crime' in local newspapers _____

4.4.4 (Sociology) [Kay] Analysis of newspapers in the UK has usually focused on the mass circulation press and has used theoretical models deriving from either Marxism or literary studies. Kay's work is distinctive in that it uses data drawn from small, local newspapers and capitalizes on the small corpus of newspaper studies using Sacks's **membership categorization analysis** (see Silverman, 1998: Chs 5 and 7). The research incorporates a nice comparative perspective as the two newspapers Kay is studying derive from different geographical locations: suburban London and a Northern Ireland city. The value of this comparison can be explored by examining the local categories that the newspapers use in their descriptions of crime (e.g. national and local boundaries).

Like Pertti, Kay has a manageable body of data. By limiting her data simply to two newspapers' headlines on 'crime' stories she is in a good position to say 'a lot about a little'. Like Greta, her clear analytic approach will pay off when used as more than a simple listing device in order to reveal the precise sets of relationships locally constructed in her data.

'Enterprise discourse' in higher education _____

4.4.5 (Sociology) [Neil] Neil's research is concerned with strategic development documents from a higher education college arising from recent changes in the tertiary sector. He is focusing on what he calls 'enterprise discourse' and how it constitutes the professional's conception of identity.

Like Kay, Neil's original approach derives from ethnomethodology and was based on Sacks's membership categorization analysis. However, Neil acknowledges the attraction of the Foucauldian approach and aims to recast his concerns in terms of Foucault's conception of the 'architecture of the text'.

Neil's problem is that Foucault provides no clear methodology (but see Kendall and Wickham, 1998). He is attempting to find a usable method from the 'critical linguistics' of Norman Fairclough and from semiotics' concern with **syntagmatic and paradigmatic** relations (see Silverman, 2006: 249–54). Using these approaches, the aim is to analyse whole texts rather than a few extracts. The value of these approaches will be clearer when Neil presents an extensive piece of data analysis.

However, I feel there is less to worry about in relation to Neil's concerns that working on a single case might mean that he has too few data. As Mitchell (1983) shows, the validity of qualitative analysis depends more on the quality of the analysis than on the size of the sample. Moreover, the comparative method can be used on a single case by isolating and comparing different elements (Flyvbjerg, 2004).

Texts: summary _____

Limit your data

4.4.6 Like many other qualitative approaches, textual analysis depends upon very detailed data analysis. To make such analysis effective, it is imperative to have a limited body of data with which to work. So, while it may be useful initially to explore different kinds of data (e.g. newspaper reports, scientific textbooks, magazine advice pages), this should usually only be done to establish the dataset with which you can most effectively work. Having chosen your dataset, you should limit your material further by only taking a few texts or parts of texts (e.g. headlines).

Have a clear analytic approach

All the textual studies discussed above have recognized the value of working with a clearly defined approach. Even Neil, who was unsure which approach to use, was convinced that such a choice is crucial. Having chosen your approach (e.g. Foucauldian discourse analysis, Saussurian **semiotics**, Sacks's analysis of membership categorization), treat it as a 'toolbox' providing a set of concepts and methods to select your data and to illuminate your analysis.

Recognize that proper analysis goes beyond a list

I make no apology for repeating a point that I made above in my discussion of interview studies. It seems to me that the distinctive contribution qualitative research can make is to utilize its theoretical resources in the deep analysis of small bodies of publicly shareable data. This means that, unlike much quantitative research, we are not satisfied with a simple coding of data. Instead, we have to show how the (theoretically defined) elements identified are assembled or mutually laminated.

LINK

For a useful set of links to sites which discuss document analysis, go to:

http://www.cs.jcu.edu.au/~michael/document_sites.html

Audio Data _____

4.5 The three types of qualitative data discussed so far all end up in the form of some kind of text. For instance, in interviews the researchers usually work with written transcripts, and in ethnographies one often records and analyses written fieldnotes.

In the same way, audiotapes of **naturally occurring** interaction are usually transcribed prior to (and as part of) the analysis. The two main social science traditions which inform the analysis of transcripts of tapes are **conversation analysis** (CA) and discourse analysis (DA). For an introduction to CA, see ten Have (1998); for DA, see Potter and Wetherell (1987) and Potter (2004). Both examples below involve the use of CA (a further example is found in Simon's research, discussed in Chapter 3).

Team meetings at a hospice

4.5.1 (Sociology) [Anthony] While studying for his MA, Anthony started to do voluntary work at a hospice in a London suburb. Staff at the hospice were later happy to grant him access to tape-record some of their work. He chose team meetings for two reasons. First, focusing on such data meant that he did not need to trouble patients. Second, team meetings in which patients were discussed were scheduled events, so Anthony did not have to waste time waiting for 'relevant' data to appear. Moreover, another researcher had already tape-recorded some team meetings at the hospice and was happy to lend him her good quality tapes.

Anthony had used conversation analytic methods for his MA dissertation and applied the Jeffersonian CA transcription method to his new data (see the Appendix to this book). He then inspected his transcripts, informed by CA's focus on the sequential organization of talk. After an initial series of discrete observations, he selected a number of sequences in which disagreements emerged and were resolved by team members. The management of agreements and disagreements has been extensively analysed within CA through the concept of **preference organization** (Heritage, 1984: 265–9). However, Anthony now realizes that his data allowed a new twist to be given to such analyses by looking at how 'third parties' manage disagreements by others. This looks likely to be both analytically interesting and practically relevant to medical staff concerned with effective decision making.

Asymmetry in interactions between native and non-native speakers of English

4.5.2 (English) [Marla] Marla is working with taped naturally occurring conversations in English between native speakers of English and Finnish (both informal conversations and professional/client encounters). As she notes: 'Research in pragmatics and sociolinguistics has shown that various forms of communicative trouble may arise where the linguistic and sociocultural resources of the participants are not shared.' However, she is taking a different approach. Rather than treat asymmetries as a 'trouble', her initial idea is to examine how the participants 'use emerging asymmetries as a resource through which they can renegotiate the current context of discourse and their interpersonal relationship'.

Like much good research, this is based on a nicely counter-intuitive idea which derives from a clear theoretical perspective (CA suggests that participants can treat apparent troubles as local resources). As in Anthony's case, Marla's data, method and analytical approach are elegantly intertwined.

Audio data: summary

Choose a single concept or problem

4.5.3 Choosing a clear analytic approach is a help but is not everything. The danger is that you seek to apply too many findings or concepts deriving from that approach. This can make your analysis both confused and thin or a naive listing of observations consonant with each of these concepts. By narrowing down to a single issue (e.g. preference organization or troubles as a local resource), you may begin to make novel observations.

Give a problem a new twist

As the data analysis proceeds, you should aim to give your chosen concept or issue a new twist. In the studies above, we have seen this done by pursuing a counter-intuitive idea and by noting an additional feature little addressed in the literature.

Make data collection as easy as possible

There are no 'brownie points' given by most disciplines for having gathered your own data – perhaps with the exception of anthropology's expectation that most researchers will have spent their statutory year with their 'tribe'. Indeed, by choosing 'difficult' situations to gather data (because nothing 'relevant' may happen, or even because background noise may mean you have a poor quality tape), you may condemn yourself to have less time to engage in the much more important activity of data analysis.

Marla and Anthony found practical ways of efficiently gathering data. Both chose to study scheduled encounters and Anthony was able to supplement his own data with tapes collected by somebody else. As I pointed out in the previous chapter, secondary analysis of other people's data is to be commended rather than condemned.

LINK

For information on CA, go to:

http://www.paultenhave.nl/

For information on discourse analysis (DA), visit:

http://www.lboro.ac.uk/research/mmethods/resources/links/da.html

---

4.6

When people interact face to face, they do not use merely verbal cues – except if they are on the telephone. Researchers who work with videos have access to many of these cues. However, as we shall see, complicated data can often mean complicated analysis!

Talk, text and visual communication in desktop video-conferencing environments

4.6.1

(English) [Erkki] Erkki is studying a one-month teaching experiment in which a university course was given on the Internet in two places in Finland and Sweden. Ideas and papers were regularly exchanged and weekly presentations and feedback sessions were held through video conferencing (Internet seminars). Recordings of the video-mediated sessions between the two centres were obtained and transcribed (see Heath, 2004).

Erkki is combining CA with ideas from Erving Goffman (1974) about 'participation frameworks' adopted in particular settings. This setting is, of course, pretty unusual in that participants' sharing of time and space is technologically mediated. In some sessions, the camera positions were fixed. In others, the camera zoomed in and out on the participants. This is allowing Erkki to get a hold on how different use of video-conferencing technology affects interaction.

Erkki's work combines a manageable body of data and a clear theoretical approach ('participation frameworks') with a likely practical input for systems design. As she recognizes, however, it is very complex to work with video data since both transcription and analysis are more complex than is the case with audio data. Fortunately, there is a growing body of CA-inspired work on technologically mediated interaction which Erkki can use as a model (see Heath, 2004; Heath and Luff, 2000).

The early interaction between a mother and a baby aged under one

4.6.2

(Finnish) [Suzanne] This is a study of interaction between Suzanne's own baby, Sara, and others based on 9.5 hours of videos of 22 episodes up till Sara's first birthday. Suzanne's initial interest was at what age a baby begins to imitate other people. Consequently, she is attempting to describe what (and how) she says to her baby at different ages and what linguistic elements begin to emerge in the baby's vocalizations.

Like Erkki, she is using transcription methods and analytic ideas from CA. Based on this approach, she is treating mother–baby talk as interactional, e.g. how the mother interprets the baby's utterances and behaviour in concrete situations and how she acts in response to them.

At the time of her presentation, Suzanne submitted a set of written questions which I set out below with my answers:

- *Is one baby (my own) enough data?* For qualitative work, one case study is sufficient. Obviously, there are issues to be thought through when you are yourself a principal actor. However, from a CA point of view, the complexity of what all of us do is so great that we are unable to grasp it or indeed to change it significantly at the time.

- *Is one video camera enough, particularly as you don't always see mother and baby together?* This is not a major objection. Once you recognize that there can be no 'perfect' recording of interaction, it is always a case of making do with what you have.

- *How far can you reconstruct all aspects of the interaction between a baby and her family from 10 hours of videotape?* Never attempt to reconstruct *everything* about an interaction! Not only is this an impossible task, but it is likely to deflect you from establishing a clear focus on one manageable topic.

- *Does an analysis of interactional situations give any hints as to how the baby reciprocally interprets her mother's actions?* Who knows what baby (and mother) are thinking? CA instructs us to look at what each party does without speculating about what they are thinking.

- *Should imitations associated with gestures and expressions be analysed separately from vocal imitations?* No! Use your rich video data to examine the inter-weaving of talk, gesture and expression.

- *Should more approaches be used (e.g. **hermeneutics**)?* Don't even think about it! Once you have found an approach which suits you, stick with it. Using multiple approaches is uneconomical and likely to delay completion of your research.

- *How do we distinguish 'imitation' from other activities such as 'repetition'?* Look at how the baby's utterances are treated by the mother, e.g. praise. But be prepared to change topic. 'Imitation' may give you an early hold on to the topic but detailed description may lead in different directions.

The construction of ethnic identity among Spanish immigrants in London

4.6.3 (Sociology) [Viviana] Viviana's work focuses on styles of cultural consumption in relation to intergenerational differences within families of first- and second-generation immigrants. She has moved from an interview-based study to one based largely on observation and videotaping of Spanish families watching television together.

Viviana's research involves two overlapping areas: media studies and nationality. It is important for her to think through whether her main focus is on media reception or, as I think, on national identity, using the media as a case study. Again, although video data are potentially exciting material, they are notoriously difficult to analyse. Even though the analysis of interview data has all kinds of difficulties attached to it (see above), it may be more suited to her focus on ethnic identity. With a video, you have to infer identities. Through interviews, you can ask people to speak about their identity.

Viviana's work is situated in the expanding area of 'audience studies' (see Morley, 1992). Practical guidance on the methodological issues involved in studying audiences is available in Rose (2007: Ch. 9).

How 'female experience' is presented and problematized on TV

4.6.4 (Sociology) [Nora] Nora's research is concerned with 'confessional' television as represented by Oprah Winfrey and other 'chat' shows. She has a particular interest in how 'psychological health' is invoked in such programmes.

She argues that most existing research focuses on audience participation in terms of issues relating to democracy and resistance. As she points out, the problem with such studies is that they simply posit general structures of power, class and gender. Instead, Nora, following Foucault, wants to problematize subjectivity. In particular, she is interested in the productivity of power in relation to what it means to be a woman; the kind of ethical agent who might adopt this subject position; and the forms of knowledge that have helped to construct it.

By its focus on media products from a Foucauldian perspective, her research promises to break new ground. Her major difficulty is the lack of any detailed direction for empirical work on media products within Foucault's work. Help on this issue is provided by Kendall and Wickham (1998). Alternatively, she could review methodologies deriving from other traditions to see if there are any useful points to be derived. In particular, CA offers a detailed way of transcribing video material and is beginning to address issues of **validity** and **reliability** in relation to single case studies (see Perakyla, 2004). Ultimately, however, she should choose the approach with which she feels most confident.

Visual data: summary

4.6.5 All the points made above about audio data apply here, so I limit myself to a few additional observations arising from our four video studies.

Beware of complexity

Although video data are very attractive, they are very complex to work with since both transcription and analysis are more difficult than is the case with audio data. So think very carefully about whether you need video data for your research. For instance, unlike CA, neither Foucault nor theories of identity provide a clear template for video analysis.

Keep it simple

You are not making a feature film! One video camera is fine for most purposes. When you have your data, maintain a clear focus. Never attempt to reconstruct all aspects of the interaction from the videotape.

Think about the many kinds of visual data

Working with visual data does not necessarily mean shooting your own videos. Nora's research analyses recordings of TV programmes. Other researchers have analysed paintings and photographs or used visual cues such as family photographs as a topic for interviews (see Rose, 2007: Ch. 11).

Stick with one approach

By all means test out different ways of analysing your data, but always settle on one clear analytic approach. Draw on other approaches only for particular technical skills (e.g. in transcribing video data).

LINK

For several papers on analysing visual data, visit:

http://www.qualitative-research.net/index.php/fqs/issue/view/11

Multiple Methods

4.7
Researchers are often tempted to use multiple methods. For instance, ethnographers often seek to combine observation with the interviewing of 'key informants'. In this section, I consider four examples of ethnographic work involving methods additional to observation.

How texts are reconstructed

4.7.1
(Sociology) [Anne] Anne's research is concerned with how a text changes as it moves from a book to television or radio. She is also concerned with the effects of mediation on performance.

Her approach derives from an extensive literature on theories of mediation dealing with literary products, film, sound/music and art. This seems to form a good basis for her research, although perhaps more work needs to be done on distinguishing these theories from our everyday assumption that something is 'lost' when books are turned into mass media products.

Anne intends to study media practices during the process of production as well as to interview translators, scriptwriters and actors to try to understand the principles that inform mediators. This looks like an interesting project working with accessible data, but I wonder if her data analysis might be simplified by focusing on media practice and products and leaving out any reference to the 'intentions' of those involved in the process and/or by just following through the transformation of one text.

Botswana women in public life (from 1800)

4.7.2 (Sociology) [Mercy] This study is a development of Mercy's earlier research. It centres around questions of women, power and politics in the context of Botswana society and culture. Her research derives from a feminist focus on the factors limiting women's political influence in Botswana. This means concentrating on forms of patriarchy as expressed in the *kgotla* system and in women's fragile citizenship rights. The research questions that flow from this concern women's changing experiences, the limits to women's participation in political life and the role of outside influences.

To answer these questions, Mercy proposes to use three methods: interviews, **focus groups** and the analysis of archive material, perhaps using ideas from Foucault. However, she may be limited by the need to obtain government approval for her research.

This is an ambitious project which may be made more manageable by considering using only *one* dataset and not pursuing her reading of Foucault unless she decides to make the textual data her primary focus. However, as in all field research, it makes sense to treat her dealings with official authorities as data rather than as a technical difficulty prior to data gathering (see Chapter 12).

American 'concert dance' in the post-war era

4.7.3 (Sociology) [Rita] Rita's background is in dance studies and, more recently, sociology. Rita has found that after World War II the US government was building a new relationship with the dance community through sending out cultural 'ambassadors'. The period also coincided with the development of an American dance 'style' eschewing expressionism in favour of formalism.

Rita wants to explain both the politics of US support for dance and the emergence of a style which avoided seeking to express the 'self' or 'inner emotions'. She will focus on two groups of dance companies, as well as examining perform- ances and texts by dance theorists.

Rita describes her approach as deriving from the work of Pierre Bourdieu, drawing upon his account of the body as a site in which agents struggle for domination. Bourdieu's work should help her achieve her ambitious aim to bring together history and social theory.

It remains to be seen whether it will be possible effectively to combine data deriving from different methods. Not only does this increase the scope of the research but it raises complicated issues about how to 'map' one set of data upon another (see my critique of **triangulation** in Chapter 15).

How women experience depression

4.7.4 (Sociology) [Philippa] Philippa's research is concerned with how women, as user communities of psychiatry, experience depression, self and identity. Her interest in this topic arose partly from family and work experience and partly because of her curiosity about the statistics which seem to show that women are twice as likely as men to be diagnosed as 'depressives'.

Her approach derives from Foucauldian **genealogical** analysis and hence leads to a focus on how 'depression' is discursively constituted. This approach differs from feminist concerns with patriarchy and misogyny and from an interactionist focus on labelling by psychiatrists. The research questions that arise for her from this approach are: how do women speak of themselves as subjects who are 'depressed'? How do such women position and speak about themselves compared to 'normal' gendered subjects? And how far do we find traces of a 'pharmacological culture' in how depression is constituted and treated?

Her data are drawn from women whom she meets through her work as a counsellor. Unusually, given her approach, Philippa has opted initially at least for a questionnaire (partly this reflects her lack of confidence in interviewing women she also counsels). A pilot of this questionnaire showed a high rate of non-response. She is currently revising her questionnaire as well as planning to do some archive analysis.

Philippa is aware that there might be more fruitful research designs. In particular, the use of focus groups or of open-ended interviews based on a single request (such as, 'tell me your story') might overcome the problem of using leading or incomprehensible questions. Nonetheless, her project is ambitious and she might consider working entirely with available archives in the usual Foucauldian manner.

Multiple methods: summary

Keep it simple I

4.7.5 Like videotapes, multiple methods are tempting because they seem to give you a fuller picture. However, you need to be aware that multiple sources of data mean that you will have to learn many more data analysis skills. You will need to avoid the temptation to move to another dataset when you are having difficulties in analysing one set of material.

Keep it simple II

Often the desire to use multiple methods arises because you want to get at many different aspects of a phenomenon. However, this may mean that you have not yet sufficiently narrowed down your topic. Sometimes a better approach is to treat the analysis of different kinds of data as a 'dry run' for your main study. As such, it is a useful test of the kind of data which you can most easily gather and analyse.

Keep it simple III

'Mapping' one set of data upon another is a more or less complicated task depending on your analytic framework. In particular, if you treat social reality as constructed in different ways in different contexts, then you cannot appeal to a single 'phenomenon' which all your data apparently represent.

Research design should involve careful thought rather than seeking the most immediately attractive option. However, none of the points above exclude the possibility of using multiple means of gathering data. Ultimately, everything will depend on the quality of your data analysis rather than upon the quality of your data.

■ **Attempt Exercise 4.1**

Concluding Remarks

4.8

In this chapter, we have examined the early stage of student research projects. The following suggestions have been made:

- Define your research problem analytically.
- Limit your data.
- Demonstrate that your data analysis goes beyond a list.
- Limit the claims you make about your study.
- Think about the relevance of your research for other scholars and for 'society'.

These points are explained below.

Define your problem

1 Research 'problems' do not arise out of a clear blue sky! Sometimes, their source is a scholarly debate; sometimes a pressing social problem. In any event, you will need to think through the *analytic basis* of your way of defining your research

problem. Having chosen an approach, treat it as a 'toolbox' providing a set of concepts and methods to select your data and to illuminate your analysis.

2   Your approach must be appropriate to the research questions in which you are interested. Indeed, rather than being a constraint, a theory should generate a series of directions for your research (see Chapter 7). It will influence what status you attach to your data – for instance, as a true or false representation of reality – and how you code them.

Limit your data

1   Decide which data to use by asking yourself which data are most appropriate to your research problem. For instance, are you more interested in what people are thinking or feeling or in what they are doing?

2   To make your analysis effective, it is imperative to have a limited body of data with which to work. So, while it may be useful initially to explore different kinds of data, this should usually only be done to establish the dataset with which you can most effectively work (see my discussion of multiple methods in Chapter 8).

3   Make data collection as easy as possible. There are no 'brownie points' given by most disciplines for having gathered your own data. Indeed, by choosing 'difficult' situations to gather data (because nothing 'relevant' may happen, or even because background noise may mean you have a poor quality tape), you may condomn yourself to have less time to engage in the much more important activity of data analysis.

4   Beware of complexity. For instance, as we have seen, although video data are very attractive, they are very complex to work with. So keep data gathering simple. Go for material that is easy to collect. Do not worry if it only gives you one 'angle' on your problem. That is a gain as well as a loss!

Data analysis goes beyond a list

1   Choosing a clear analytic approach is a help but is not everything. The danger is that you seek to apply too many findings or concepts deriving from that approach. This can make your analysis both confused and thin or a naive listing of observations consonant with each of these concepts. By narrowing down to a single issue, you may begin to make novel observations.

2   Identifying the main elements in your data according to some theoretical scheme should only be the first stage of your data analysis. Go on to examine how these elements are linked together (see Chapter 13).

3   As your data analysis proceeds, you should aim to give your chosen concept or issue a new twist, perhaps by pursuing a counter-intuitive idea or by noting an additional feature little addressed in the literature.

Limit the claims you make about your research

It always helps to make limited claims about your own research. Grandiose claims about originality, scope or applicability to social problems are all hostages to fortune. Be careful in how you specify the claims of your approach. Show that you understand that it constitutes one way of 'slicing the cake' and that other approaches, using other forms of data, may not be directly competitive.

Issues of relevance

1 When you have finished, reflect upon the contribution that your research makes to contemporary scholarly debates. How does it add to knowledge or change our sense of the role of particular methods or concepts (see Chapter 21)?

2 Is your analytic position appropriate to any practical concerns you have? For instance, many contemporary social theories look at the world quite differently from respondents, policy makers or practitioners. If you use such an approach, you will need to think carefully about what you can offer such groups – although it may well turn out that you can offer them more interesting findings than rather more conventional research (see Chapter 27).

LINK

For specialist texts on qualitative research in management (Eriksson and Kovalainen, 2008), marketing (Moisander and Valtonen, 2006), education (Freebody, 2003), health (Green and Thorogood, 2009), information systems (Myers and Avison, 2002), social work (Shaw and Gould, 2002), gender (Jarviluoma et al., 2004), cultural studies (Saukko, 2003) and criminology (Noaks and Wincup, 2004), go to: www.sagepub.co.uk/textbooks

All are in my series 'Introducing Qualitative Methods'.

KEY POINTS

In this chapter, we have examined the early stage of student research projects. The following suggestions have been made:

• Define your research problem analytically.

• Limit your data.

• Demonstrate that your data analysis goes beyond a list.

• Limit the claims you make about your study.

• Think about the relevance of your research for other scholars and for 'society'.

Note

1   These research ideas derive from presentations during graduate workshops I coordinated at Goldsmiths College and at Oulu University, Finland. In the Finnish material, I have been able to draw upon research abstracts written by the students prior to the workshop. I was dependent upon my contemporary notes for the Goldsmiths' material and apologize for any inaccuracies present. In any event, it should be borne in mind that this is an account of the early stages of research studies which, no doubt, have developed and changed. For this reason, students' names have been anonymized.

■ ■ Further Reading ■

An excellent practical guide to the business of writing a dissertation is Pat Cryer's *The Research Student's Guide to Success* (third edition, Open University Press, 2006). Judith Bell's *Doing Your Research Project* (fourth edition, Open University Press, 2005) is a much more basic treatment, mainly aimed at undergraduate dissertations.

 ■ Exercise 4.1

The following exercise is meant to help you think through the issues raised in this chapter about the value and implications of different ways of gathering and analysing qualitative data. Please go through the following steps, ideally with another student:

1   Define your research topic in no more than two sentences.

2   Explain which method you propose to use to gather data. Why that method?

3   Why would other methods not be possible or appropriate?

4   How big a data sample do you intend to collect? Could you manage with fewer data? Might you need more?

5   What theoretical approach do you favour? How will it help or hinder you in the analysis of your data?

6   What other approaches might be appropriate/inappropriate? Why?

7   Is there anything about your theory/method/data that could be simplified to make a more effective study?

5

What Counts as 'Originality'?

Chapter Objectives

By the end of this chapter, you will be able to:

- Know what is involved in being a professional researcher.

- Understand the basics of independent critical thought.

- Be more confident in pursuing originality.

Introduction

5.1 All students speculate about the standards through which they will be assessed. Many students beginning a research study crave to be 'original'. Whether the research is for a PhD, an MA or only a humble BA dissertation, 'originality' is, for many, both a goal and a perceived critical standard which will be used by your examiners to beat you with!

Such fears are associated with a lack of knowledge about what is expected at a new, 'higher' level of your education. In this respect, we are talking about a common experience when we reach the next step on any ladder.

Many social transitions are associated with rites of passage, and educational careers are no exception. In English secondary schools, after the age of 16, one enters the sixth form where one is expected to specialize narrowly and to become more self-reliant and less spoonfed. At my own school, boys just out of short trousers suddenly found themselves addressed by their sixth-form teacher as 'gentlemen'. We looked round the room but, weirdly, the appellation was directed at us.

The process is repeated in some form all over the world when you begin a BA at a university. Now, it seems, you are truly on your own, having to meet strange new criteria of achievement without any obvious means of support. Your time tends to be much more your own and you have to decide how much time to allocate to the library, the computer centre or – at British universities – the students' union bar.

How much worse, then, when you register to do an MA or a PhD. Suddenly, everything you could count on in the past now seems to amount to nothing. You are no longer the outstanding undergraduate but just one of many students all of whom, presumably, achieved good first degrees. In the past, university examinations were mysteries that you had cracked. Now, although some further written examinations may await, you know that this is not how you are going to be mainly judged.

To some extent, this transition to graduate status is eased by the provision of taught courses for first-year research students, many of whom will have already taken an MA. However, a nagging doubt is still likely to torment many beginning graduate students. Are you 'up to it'? Above all, do you have the capacity to be 'original'? Or is 'originality', like so many things these days, something you can learn?

Originality

Original: not derived, copied, imitated or translated from anything else; novel; creative; independent in invention. (*Chambers English Dictionary*, 1990)

5.2 Consulting a dictionary about 'originality' brings mixed blessings. You are not planning to plagiarize anybody else and so should have no problem in meeting the 'negative' definition of 'originality' given above: your dissertation is unlikely to be 'derived, copied, imitated or translated from anything else'.

But how about the 'positive' components of 'originality'? Can you be 'novel; creative; independent in invention'? Moreover, since 'imaginativeness' is linked to 'originality' by Roget's *Thesaurus*, have you the talent to be 'imaginative'?

However you answer these questions, you are going to be in trouble! Obviously, if you don't feel that your intellect is especially 'novel', 'creative', 'inventive' and 'imaginative', then you are going to worry yourself sick about whether you are up to doing a worthwhile piece of research. Conversely, if you are full of confidence about these matters, it is very likely that you are underestimating what is required to be granted these epithets.

If you doubt me, scan the book review pages in a journal in your field. My guess is that you will not find such words thrown around freely. And, remember, many of the books reviewed will be authored by established scholars, well past their own PhDs.

If the work of established scholars is not regularly judged to be 'novel', 'creative', 'inventive' or 'imaginative', what chance do you have? The answer is surprising: you have no problem.

Such epithets are rarely used by the examiners of successful PhD dissertations. Most dissertations are no more than solid and workmanlike. Indeed, it would cheapen the currency of academic description to use the vocabulary of 'originality' too frequently. Even Nobel Prize laureates never fail to cast doubt on their own supposed 'genius'. Instead, they regularly refer to the support of their research teams and to the old metaphor: 'one per cent inspiration, ninety-nine per cent perspiration' (see Mulkay, 1984).

As Phillips and Pugh point out, in the context of a PhD, 'an original contribution to knowledge' is a very shaded term: 'it does not mean an enormous breakthrough which has the subject rocking on its foundations' (1994: 34). Following Kuhn (1970), PhD research is unlikely to involve a **paradigm** shift in your discipline. Instead, Phillips and Pugh suggest, it demonstrates that you have a good grasp of how research is normally done in your field (i.e. that you can do what Kuhn calls 'normal science'). What does this mean in practice?

Among other things, it can mean:

> **making a synthesis that hasn't been made before; using already known material but with a new interpretation, bringing new evidence to bear on an old issue ... [and] adding to knowledge in a way that hasn't been done before. (Phillips and Pugh, 1994: 61–2)**

So Phillips and Pugh suggest that a PhD is less to do with 'originality' and is more about displaying that you are 'a fully professional researcher' (1994: 19). In turn, this means showing:

- that you have something to say to which your peers will want to listen
- that you are 'aware of what is being discovered, argued about, written and published by your academic community across the world' (1994: 19).

The upshot of this is that a PhD is best viewed as an apprenticeship prior to admission to a community of scholars. This implies that:

> **you are not doing research in order to do research; you are doing research in order to demonstrate that you have learned *how* to do research to fully professional standards. (1994: 20)**

██████████████████████████ LINK ██████████████████████████

For a lively paper on originality, entitled 'It's a PhD not a Nobel Prize', go to:

http://www.griffithuni.net/rhd/pdf/mullins_kiley_02_Article.pdf

---

Being a Professional

5.3
'Originality' is only one of four criteria upon which examiners of the University of London PhD must report. To get a London PhD, the examiners must report:

- that the thesis is genuinely the work of the candidate

- that the thesis forms a distinct contribution to the knowledge of the subject, and affords evidence of originality by *the discovery of new facts* and/or *the exercise of independent critical power* (my emphasis)

- that the thesis is satisfactory as regards literary presentation

- that the thesis is suitable for publication ... as submitted or in abridged or modified form.

Despite the passing reference to 'originality' in the second item, all these criteria are really about professionality. We only need to concern ourselves about the second criterion: the discovery of new facts and the exercise of independent critical thought.

Considered on its own, 'the discovery of new facts' is rarely an important or even a challenging criterion in most of the social sciences. In the natural sciences, perhaps, a PhD researcher may discover a new substance or process and be applauded. But, in my experience, it is much rarer for qualitative social science PhDs to argue that they have found new 'facts'. Indeed, if they did so, they would most likely be greeted with the riposte: 'So what?'

For example, say such a dissertation claims that it has discovered that a particular group has beliefs or displays behaviours that were previously unknown. Any examiner worth their salt would then want to ask: 'Why, on earth, should it matter that this is the case?' In other words, what analytical or practical significance are we being asked to attach to this 'finding'?

Such a line of questioning is *not* a case of the examiner being difficult. As I argue in Chapter 7, any scientific finding is always to be assessed in relation to the theoretical perspective from which it derives and to which it may contribute.

This means that, while 'facts' are never unimportant, they derive their relevance from the theoretical perspectives from which they stem and to which they contribute. The clear implication is that 'the exercise of independent critical thought' is the major criterion through which your dissertation will be assessed.

How can you satisfy this criterion? If professionality consists in the display of independent critical thought, what is the secret of being independent, critical and professional?

Independent Critical Thought

5.4 In fact, as is the usual case in research, there is no secret or magic process to be revealed. In Chapter 3, we saw how Moira, Sally and Simon went about their research as solid craftspersons. Although occasionally they may have jumped out of their bath shouting 'eureka', most of their time they just plodded along, building a workmanlike analysis in the face of setbacks and opportunities.

Using their experience and the work of other students I have supervised, I outline below four procedures which contribute to the successful display of 'independent critical thought':

- developing a concept and/or a methodology

- thinking critically about your approach

- building on an existing study

- being prepared to change direction.

Develop a concept and/or a methodology _____

5.4.1 In 1997 Paul Acourt completed a theoretical dissertation, under my supervision, on the emergence and apparent disappearance of discussion of 'progress' in the social science literature. Armed with a well-supported argument about the analytical and practical relevance of such a concept, he was able to convince his examiners of his 'independent critical thought'.

Many social science dissertations have a more empirical content. Sally used Erving Goffman's (1974) concept of **frames** to understand how a mental health team made decisions about what services to offer to homeless people. Moira and Simon employed the concepts and methodology that the sociologist Harvey Sacks used to study the descriptive process.

Moira applied **membership categorization device analysis** (MCDA) and **conversation analysis** (CA) to interviews with the partners of people who had recently died in hospital. Simon used CA to study the sequential organization of talk at parent–teacher meetings.

Twenty years earlier, Geoffrey Baruch (1981) had used one of these approaches (MCDA) to analyse transcripts of interviews with parents of handicapped children. Like Moira and Simon, he showed the ability to work with and to advance Sacks's specialist approach. Indeed, Moira used Baruch's thesis as a baseline for her own research and showed how his analysis of interviews as 'moral tales' could be developed.

In the normal way, Moira, Simon and Geoffrey were influenced by the interests and skills of their supervisor. In my case, I had a long-standing interest in making Sacks's work more widely known (see Silverman, 1998) and four of my other successful PhD students have used the concepts and methodology of the subdiscipline Sacks founded.

Of course, social science has a broad and rich stream of concepts and methodologies and my students' work has expressed this breadth while reflecting my interests in processes of language and representation. So Kobena Mercer (1990) used some ideas from the French tradition of semiotics in his research on the speeches of an English politician, Enoch Powell. The related concepts of Foucauldian **discourse analysis** were used by Mary Fraser in her study of representations of children in a British nursing journal.

In all these cases, because the approach was theoretically informed, the dissertation could justifiably argue that it had contributed to conceptual development.

Think critically about your approach

5.4.2 As we saw in Chapter 3, your prior experience usually has an important bearing on how you approach your data. For instance, Sally was constantly aware of how her own nursing experience might be influencing how her health professionals related to her and how she might be taking for granted certain aspects of their behaviour.

Sometimes, doubts about an overall approach can have far-reaching consequences for how you think about your data. So Moira became dissatisfied with the conventional version of open-ended interviews as a potential window into people's experiences. Instead of using brief extracts from her interviews to illustrate particular categories, she started to analyse the sequential mechanisms through which her interviewees told recognizable 'stories'. Similarly, Simon was determined not to treat his parents' evenings as mere 'products' of familiar social structural **variables** (e.g. class and ethnicity of the parents, measured ability of the child).

Fifteen years earlier, another of my students, Gill Chapman (1987), had devised an unusual way of demonstrating her independent critical thought. Having discussed a range of possible ways of analysing her audiotapes of nurses' meetings, she decided to experiment with a wide range of concepts and methodologies. Each of the empirical chapters of her dissertation is thus both an analysis of her data and a critical evaluation of the approach used.

Build on an existing study

5.4.3 Don't try to reinvent the wheel! Try to find a previous study that, in some respect, mirrors your own interests and topic. Then model your own research on that study and develop some aspect of it.

Of course, with limited resources, you are unlikely to be able to offer a complete 'test' of the findings of that study. But by careful analysis of your limited data, you can reflect on its approach and conclusions in an informed way.

Sometimes a more realistic model is a previous PhD thesis. It is worth recalling that Moira used an earlier PhD that I had supervised as a model for her research. So, at the outset, look at earlier dissertations in your university library and, where possible, focus on work directed by your supervisor.

Be prepared to change direction

5.4.4 Both MA and PhD students tend to believe that what matters most is showing that their research has followed a logical sequence. Based on how research is sometimes reported, this structure seems to display the following sequence:

- research problem
- hypothesis
- data analysis
- conclusion.

However, anyone who has ever done any research knows that such a rigid sequence is rarely followed. Moreover, it sometimes makes sense to divert from an expected path if you come across new data or a new concept or if your data suggest a different focus (see Chapter 13 for a discussion of how I changed paths in my research on a paediatric cardiology clinic).

So, as I argue in Chapter 25, although your examiners will look for evidence of a logical structure to your research, they will also want to see that you have been prepared to be flexible and to change direction when appropriate. After all, originality is not consonant with always following a predetermined plan.

 ■ **Attempt Exercise 5.1**

Concluding Remarks

5.5 The message of this chapter is that a successful dissertation does not require genius. Once one defines the task of the research student in terms of the display of professional competence, then one can abandon those sessions in front of the mirror wondering whether you really look like Einstein, Keynes or Marie Curie!

In any event, you are likely to discover these things after a while through the response of your supervisor to your work. As Phillips and Pugh (1994) point out, worrying about the originality of your thought tends to be a concern only during the first few months. After then, this problem tends to disappear.

The case of a PhD examination many years ago makes this point very nicely. The thesis of the philosopher Ludwig Wittgenstein was being examined by two famous professors, Bertrand Russell and G.E. Moore. While these two had no doubt about its merits, there is some evidence that both examiners found Wittgenstein's thesis somewhat beyond them. In their report, Russell and Moore make clear that getting a PhD is different from being a genius. As they put it:

This is a work of genius. It is also up to the standard required for a Cambridge PhD.

KEY POINTS

Students at all levels desire to be original. However, BA and MA students can comfort themselves that even PhDs are rarely awarded for originality. In the context of a research degree, 'originality' is largely about your ability to display 'independent critical thought'. In turn, such thought can be shown by:

- developing a concept or a methodology

- thinking critically about your approach

- building on an existing study

- being prepared to change direction.

■ ■ Further Reading ■

PhD students should turn to Estelle Phillips and Derek Pugh's *How To Get a PhD* (fourth edition, Open University Press, 2005) which gives a realistic, supportive account of what is required to achieve a PhD. A helpful account of what counts as 'originality' in any student research is Pat Cryer's *The Research Student's Guide to Success* (third edition, Open University Press, 2006).

■ Exercise 5.1 ■

Pat Cryer has suggested that we can understand originality in research through an analogy with a travel expedition: 'the research student is the explorer and the expedition is the research programme' (1996: 145). Cryer uses the expedition analogy to suggest different senses of 'original research'.

Review each kind of originality below in terms of what you think your research might contribute and decide which kind is most likely to be applicable to your work:

- originality in tools, techniques and procedures

- originality in exploring the unknown

- originality in exploring the unanticipated

- originality in use of data

- originality in outcomes

- originality in byproducts (1996: 146–8).

You might return to this exercise at regular intervals to review any changes in how you view your research.

Part Two
Starting Out

Contents

6

Selecting a Topic

Chapter Objectives

By the end of this chapter you will be able to:

- **Understand why you need a clear research topic.**

- **Recognize the main problems which stop you narrowing down your topic.**

- **Find solutions to these problems.**

Introduction

6.1 In this chapter, I discuss the problems that you may find in defining your research topic. I then suggest some strategies you can use to overcome these problems.

However, this can suggest that finding a research topic is a purely logical activity conducted inside one's own head. By contrast, in the student stories that follow, in many cases the researchers come across a topic by chance, or begin studying a topic because the data or the research site were conveniently available.

Using the self as a starting point

6.1.1 For some, direct personal experience becomes the starting point of their research. Amir Marvasti's experience of being an immigrant to the USA led him to look at homeless people. In some ways, for Amir, homelessness became a metaphor for the immigration experience and the struggle for belonging. Similarly, Michael Arter speaks of how being an undercover police officer became an impetus for his study of policing.

STUDENT EXAMPLES

Researching Familiar Territory

I returned to graduate school after many years in the military and law enforcement. As I became acclimatized to the academic setting and my background became known to the faculty and other students, I noticed there was a lot of emphasis placed upon and interest in my time spent as an undercover officer. Along with much misinformation that was held by many regarding such assignments, there was an unspoken mystique and subtle respect that was accorded to me for the work I had done. I realized at that time that most individuals lacked actual knowledge about such assignments and relied on media presentations and sensationalized examples for their understanding about the undercover function. At the same time I was very aware of the impact undercover assignments had in my life and the lives of others with whom I had worked. While considering a topic for a research methods class, I conducted a literature search to assess research available relating to stress in policing and discovered there was a distinct gap in this body of literature. I decided to adopt this topic for the research class and, as I began to research the available literature, I became more entrenched in this topic as a viable venue for my dissertation. [Michael Arter, USA]

Like Michael, Sally Hunt decided to use her occupational experience to study nurses working in a mental health team. Sally's own nursing background made access to the team somewhat easier but, as we saw in Chapter 3, also influenced the team's behaviour when she was present. Similarly, Simon Allistone took advantage of his own (and his partner's) work in a school to gain access for his study of parents' evenings.

Social obligations

6.1.2 For some graduate students, selecting a topic derives from a sense of social obligation. For example, Karyn McKinney's research on how white college students construct their racial identity was motivated by her desire to expose the system of racial hierarchy in the United States. In a sense, she was morally driven to select this topic, or as she puts it, 'I was interested in the topic out of thinking about what *I should do* to effectively change the status quo.' Karyn was committed to studying race relations, and settling on a specific area within that field was a fortunate coincidence.

STUDENT EXAMPLES

Pursuing What Matters to You

Eventually, my real excitement about *data* was what decided me on my topic. I was teaching a class in race and ethnicity, and had asked students, as their main project for the class, to write what I referred to as a 'racial/ethnic autobiography'. In my assignment for the course, students were to go chronologically through their lives, telling their stories, focusing on situations and incidents that made them more aware of their own or other people's race or ethnicity. Basically, these papers would be first-person analyses of the development of racial and/or ethnic identity. When I got the students' papers back, I was mesmerized by reading them. I literally could not put them down. All of the students told stories that showed how racial and ethnic identity is a process, not a static characteristic. They were fascinating, to me at least. Most of my students were white, and I began to think about the new area I'd been reading in, 'whiteness studies'. [Karyn McKinney, USA]

Karyn's research agenda was not entirely planned in advance. She was simply assigning a project for a course and happened to realize the importance of the data that were pouring in: the data 'mesmerized' her. Note that her social obligations did not dictate her research entirely. To a large extent it was her fascination with the data that focused her interests.

Curiosity

6.1.3 Other researchers cite general curiosity as the main reason for selecting a particular topic. Essentially, they are intrigued by a facet of social life and want to learn more about it. Michelle Miller-Day's story is illustrative of this approach.

STUDENT EXAMPLES

Prying with Purpose

There is a quote from Zora Neale Hurston that, for me, captures what I hope to achieve with qualitative research. She said:

> Research is formalized curiosity.
> It is poking and prying with purpose. It is a seeking that he who wishes may know
> the secrets of the world and they that dwell therein.

I have always been curious. Choosing a career as a social science researcher, I assumed I could make a living asking questions and seeking answers. (In my more noble moments) I also believed that this career would enable me to make real contributions to the understanding of social behaviour and the human experience. [Michelle Miller-Day, USA]

In Michelle's story, social obligations are not necessarily at the forefront of her work. A general sense of curiosity coupled with the 'noble' desire to understand others dictated her research choices. This sense of wonder about the world guided her questions and her observations.

6.1.4 As we saw in Chapter 3, Moira Kelly's interviews with bereaved relatives emerged directly out of her employment on a funded study directed by Clive Seale. Such employment fortuitously can provide access to respondents and several possible topics. This was also true in Greg Bolystein's case below.

STUDENT EXAMPLES

Finding a Topic from your Job

I accepted a job as a research assistant (RA) at the local Veterans Administration Medical Center. Initially I did home interviews with veterans who recently had had a stroke. Through time I became more intimately involved in the project, helping construct the initial theoretical framework with the principal investigator and my dissertation chair who was a consultant on the study. Since I was a member of the research team on this large project it became natural for me to use the first phase of data as a basis for my dissertation research. I did not have any particular interest or knowledge in stroke recovery prior to this RA position … Rather than being isolated in my dissertation research, I actually became integrated into a large investigative centre focused on stroke rehabilitation, with my dissertation making up one component of disseminating our initial findings. [Greg Bolystein, USA]

For other researchers who received less restrictive, individual grants, the funding simply provided them with the time and resources to pursue topics of personal interest. Consider, for example, Nikitah Imani's case.

STUDENT EXAMPLES

Being Involved in a Scene

I actually did not *per se* select my topic for the dissertation. I received a grant from the National Science Foundation to participate in a summer qualitative methods workshop. Part of the responsibilities associated with successful completion of that workshop was the completion of a qualitative research project … We were given the run of the local social theatre to choose as sites and given the convenience of the university setting itself and some issues it resolved in advance (like securing primary access). I became engaged by a grant-funded psychotherapy programme the university was running. It targeted presumably 'dysfunctional' African-American families. Initially, without a topic, I sought merely to use ethnographic tools to describe to those external to the programme what was 'taking place'. It was not long after embarking on this quest that my pursuits turned far away from merely 'test-driving' the methodology to looking at

---

critical questions of how 'dysfunctionality', which I had taken for granted in the programmatic definitions, was being articulated, defined, redefined, and reified in the implementation phase. So it would be fair to say that the 'scene' and the associated circumstances gave me my topic which, given the methodology I had chosen, seemed an appropriate line of inquiry to follow. [Nikitah Imani, USA]

As we can see in Nikitah's example, selecting a research topic is often a complex process where personal interests, financial resources, and access to data converge to shape the ideal research question.

The factors listed here, like those that will follow, often coexist and overlap in the same project. What is noteworthy here is not the distinct pattern that a particular researcher follows, but the fact that the process as a whole – that is, the practice of qualitative research – does not follow an exact, uniform model. Essentially, the lesson with selecting a topic is always to keep an eye out for researchable issues, to take advantage of opportunities when they present themselves, and to be flexible.

However, although chance factors are often relevant in your choice of a topic, this does not mean that anything will do. As I show in the next section, whatever your inspiration, you will need soon to develop a well-defined and workable research question.

LINK

For articles on the qualitative–quantitative debate:

www.qualitative-research.net/fqs/fqs-e/inhalt1-01-e.htm

Workable Research Questions

6.2 People are often impressed when they find out that you are 'doing research'. They may even want to know more. If you have ever been in this situation, you will know how embarrassing it can be if you are unable to explain clearly exactly what you intend to study. Such embarrassment can be multiplied a thousandfold if your interrogator is, say, a smart professor you have never met before. How are you to respond?

The answer to this question becomes easier if you recognize that there are practical as well as social reasons for having a clear research topic. Above all, such clarity can give your research focus, as shown in Table 6.1.

The undergraduate training you have received may not help much in finding a *workable* research question. Some social science programmes reward passive knowledge rather than the ability to use ideas for yourself. They often leave students better able to leap the hurdles to pass their assessments than to use their knowledge to formulate a workable research topic.

TABLE 6.1   The role of research questions

1 They organize the project and give it direction and coherence
2 They delimit the project, showing its boundaries
3 They keep the researcher focused
4 They provide a framework when you write up your research
5 They point to the methods and data that will be needed

Source: adapted from K. Punch, 1998: 38

In qualitative methodology courses, this phenomenon is seen when courses encourage rote learning of critiques of quantitative research and offer minimal practice of alternative methods. By contrast, in quantitative methods courses, one tends to learn by rote recipe knowledge which *is* of practical use in drafting a research proposal (e.g. defining variables and measures).

In this context, selecting a research topic to be studied through qualitative methods is a very risky activity. This is because it involves committing yourself to a particular course of action rather than reiterating spoonfed 'critiques'.

Faced with this risk, students often try to play safe by opting for one of three apparently 'low-risk' strategies:

- simplistic inductivism

- the 'kitchen sink' gambit

- grand theory.

I briefly discuss each strategy below before offering some more satisfactory solutions.

Simplistic Inductivism

6.3
In many social sciences, the qualitative tradition was initially characterized by its opposition to the strict research designs demanded in most quantitative work. So anthropologists would select their tribe, take up residence, learn the language and do no more than keep a field diary. Similarly, sociological **ethnographers** would identify an activity, an institution or a subculture and just 'hang out'. In both cases, the idea was to grasp 'reality' in its daily accomplishment.

The hope was that somehow meaning would 'emerge' by itself from such 'in-depth' exposure to the field. It was believed that any prior definitions of topics or concepts would only stand in the way of a sensitive understanding of the slice of the cultural world to which one was being exposed.

In the 1960s, this belief was apparently supported by Glaser and Strauss's (1967) famous idea of theory 'grounded' in data rather than presumed at the outset of a research study. Ironically, but understandably, the idea of qualitative research as unstructured 'exposure' to the world was also supported by quantitative researchers. So we learn in one quantitative text that:

> Field research is essentially a matter of immersing oneself in a naturally occurring ... set of events in order to gain firsthand knowledge of the situation. (Singleton *et al.*, 1988: 11)

In common with crude inductivists, Singleton et al. refer to 'the situation' as if 'reality' were a single, static object awaiting observation. Like such qualitative researchers, they emphasize 'immersion' which they implicitly contrast with later, more focused, research. This is underlined in their subsequent identification of qualitative or field research with 'exploration' and 'description' (1988: 296) and their approval of the use of field research 'when one knows relatively little about the subject under investigation' (1988: 298–9).

This apparent unanimity at both ends of the research spectrum is noted by the authors of one qualitative methodology text: 'The conventional image of field research is one that keeps prestructuring and tight designs to a minimum' (Miles and Huberman, 1984: 27). Miles and Huberman note two objections to this position and the cosy consensus that supports it: the omnipresence of theory and the need for a research design. I will briefly consider each in turn.

First, 'any researcher, no matter how unstructured or inductive, comes to fieldwork with *some* orienting ideas, foci and tools' (1984: 27). As Gubrium and Holstein note, the apparently atheoretical position of some ethnographers itself derives from a theory: 'The directive to "minimize presuppositions" in order to witness subjects' worlds on their own terms is a key to *naturalistic* inquiry' (1997: 34, my emphasis).

| **TIP**

The idea of just 'hanging out' with the aim of 'faithfully representing subjects' worlds' is a convenient myth derived from a theory that Gubrium and Holstein (1997) term naturalism. Without some conceptual orientation, you would not recognize the field you are studying. So, many closet naturalists fail to come clean about the theory dependence of their research (see Chapter 7).

A second objection to simply going out into the field and inducing observations is that it can be an excuse for sloppy, unfocused research. Mason (1996: 6) rejects the suggestion that qualitative research can just 'describe' or 'explore' the social world. As Miles and Huberman point out, such unfocused research can be a recipe for disaster:

> the looser the initial design, the less selective the collection of data; *everything* looks important at the outset to someone waiting for the key constructs or regularities to emerge from the site, and that wait can be a long one. (1984: 28)

Moreover, such a purely **inductive** approach can be blind to the need to build cumulative bodies of knowledge. If this is not an intentionally anti-scientific ploy, it can be just naive. In the 1920s and 1930s, research students in Chicago, following Robert Park's injunction to get out of their armchairs into the virgin territory of urban streetlife (see Bulmer, 1984), could justify their inductivist aims. By the 1960s, however, even Glaser and Strauss (1967) were requiring that field researchers think about the **formal theories** that might be developed out of apparently isolated substantive, inductive studies.

As we move further into the twenty-first century, qualitative research would indeed be in a sorry state if it had not developed such theories and related cumulative bodies of knowledge. As I commented more than a decade ago:

> we no longer need to regard qualitative research as provisional or never based on initial hypotheses. This is because qualitative studies have already assembled a usable, cumulative body of knowledge. (Silverman, 1997: 1)

Sometimes, the previous literature or (for experienced researchers) one's own work will suggest a **hypothesis** crying out to be tested, or a finding ripe for retesting. Where this happens, particularly where the earlier study derived from a theoretical approach to which you are sympathetic, an attempt to strike out afresh would be in danger of reinventing the wheel.

Of course, as Chapter 3 shows, this does not mean that you should necessarily be stuck with your original ideas. The beauty of qualitative research is that its rich data can offer the opportunity to change focus as the ongoing analysis suggests. But such changes of direction, like the original research proposal, do not come out of the blue but reflect the subtle interplay between theory, concepts and data.

The 'Kitchen Sink' Gambit

6.4 Like any piece of advice, you can take too far the suggestion that you should avoid simplistic inductivism. In drafting your first research proposal, it is tempting to select a very broad topic. By including every aspect of a problem that you can think of, you hope to show the breadth of your knowledge and to impress potential supervisors.

Unfortunately, this 'kitchen sink' approach is a recipe for disaster. Unless you have the resources for a big team of researchers, depth rather than breadth is what characterizes a good research proposal. If you define your topic very widely, you will usually be unable to say anything at great depth about it.

TIP

As I tell my students, your aim should be to say 'a lot about a little (problem)'. This means avoiding the temptation to say 'a little about a lot'. Indeed, the latter path can be something of a 'cop-out'. Precisely because the topic is so wide ranging, one can flit from one aspect to another without being forced to refine and test each piece of analysis.

The case study below illustrates how one research student worked to refine and narrow down her problem. Over time, Seta Waller moved from quite a broad psychological interest in the 'alcoholic' to a quite narrow but workable concern with the narrative structure of patients' accounts.

'Narrowing Down' a Topic

My interest in developing a research study in the field of alcoholism came about naturally as I had been working in this field for many years. My research experience and training however had been exclusively in quantitative socio-medical studies on alcoholism.

Following training in social policy and administration, I joined the alcohol treatment unit (ATU) of a psychiatric hospital. At the ATU I was involved in a set of quantitative studies designed to measure treatment outcome in alcoholic patients.

When I decided to develop a PhD study, my initial interest was to find out what patients thought of their drink problem – how they conceptualized it. This would have been a quantitative study but quite different from the usual measurement of outcome studies. I therefore began designing a quantitative study enquiring into alcoholic patients' concepts of alcoholism. The sample was to be drawn from groups of alcoholics admitted to a four-week inpatient treatment programme in the alcohol treatment unit where I was employed.

Having developed some rating scales on concepts of alcoholism, following interviews with patients, I carried out a pilot study on a small sample. Patients were asked to complete five-point rating scales consisting of statements, by indicating whether they agreed or not with each statement; responses ranged from 'agree strongly' to 'disagree strongly'.

This whole process took about eight months. However, I was feeling uncomfortable with the results of my pilot study as I tried to make sense of the data. I felt very uncertain about the attitudes and beliefs expressed in the scales; I began to question how one could consider that all patients who, for instance, stated 'agree strongly' on the rating scales, meant the same thing.

I started thinking of a new study with a qualitative methodology which I was introduced to on my MA course in sociology at Goldsmiths College. On this course, I became aware of the relevance of the status of interview data, how **naturally occurring data** or unstructured interview data can be treated as analysable texts which do not need to be considered as being true or false.

As my main interest in my work had been alcoholism for many years, I decided to look at alcoholic patients' accounts of their experiences by means of open-ended interviews rather than the traditional structured methods. I therefore asked the patients to tell me about their drinking, allowing them to talk with a non-directive approach. I tape-recorded some interviews in the beginning and, when I looked at my transcripts, I knew this was what I ought to do. The qualitative data resulting from this kind of approach were so rich and rewarding that I decided to proceed in this way and carried out 40 interviews.

I realized that my interest lay in how patients were formulating and presenting their drinking problem and then in attempting to look at 'why' they were presenting in these particular ways. Adopting a qualitative approach, I was able to look at the narrative structure of patients' accounts to see how the texts were accomplished and organized. The structure of the accounts seemed to have a common chronologically organized pattern. Examination of the narratives made me realize that patients were showing their skills in presenting themselves as morally adequate individuals, as Baruch (1981) had found in his sample of parents of children with congenital illness. I also found that patients were displaying considerable insights into their problems and were emerging as well-informed individuals.

(Continued)

(Continued)

My current approach is therefore not simply an analytical shift, but another way of looking at interview data to see how they can help our understanding of alcoholic patients' versions and presentations of their problems. [Seta Waller, Sociology, Goldsmiths]

The case study above illustrates how ideas derived from methodology and theory can help in specifying a research topic. However, some people are more comfortable working solely at theoretical level and seek to substitute theoretical syntheses or critiques for data analysis. Following Mills (1959), I call this approach grand theory.

The Grand Theorist

6.5 While the kitchen-sinker flits about trying this and that, the grand theorist is kept busy building theoretical empires. Stuck firmly in their armchairs, such theorists need never trifle with mere 'facts'. Instead, they may sometimes spin out cobwebs of verbiage which, as C. Wright Mills (1959) shows, can be reduced to a few sentences.

Nonetheless, a situation in which you can obtain a research degree without ever leaving your familiar university library is not to be despised. Indeed, I should be the last to criticize grand theory since my own PhD was obtained by this very method!

However, it is usually wise to assume that every 'solution' contains seeds of further problems. In the case of grand theory, these problems include:

- Can you ever get out of the library in order to write your thesis? One book will surely have a list of further 'crucial' references and so on, *ad infinitum*. Anybody who thinks a library PhD is a 'quick fix' would be well advised to ponder whether they have the willpower to stop reading. They would also be wise to consult a short story called 'The Library of Babel' by the Argentinian writer Borges. This tells a chastening tale of scholars who believe that, if they only keep on looking, all knowledge will finally be revealed by yet another book.

- Theoretical fashions change – nowhere more so than in the social sciences. If you commit yourself to a theoretical topic, you must always be looking over your shoulder at the prospect of some change in direction in the theoretical wind from, say, Paris to an obscure location with a school of thought of which you are totally unfamiliar.

If you do grand theory, you may spend so much time constructing elegant accounts of the world that you never touch base with the ground upon which the world rests. Kafka's (1961) wonderful short story 'Investigations of a Dog' creates a marvellous image of 'Airdogs' (*Lufthunde*) who float on cushions above the ground, surveying the world from on high, yet cut off from any contact with it (so cut off that Kafka's doggy investigator wonders how they manage to reproduce). However, readers of this book will be more interested in solutions than in critiques. In response to this, I set out below some practical strategies that may be of use to potential 'simplistic inductivists', 'kitchen-sinkers' and 'grand theorists'.

Strategies for Simplistic Inductivists

6.6 If your previous education has equipped you with few research ideas of your own, comfort yourself that your predicament is not unusual and can be resolved.

I outline below three strategies that you can use if you find yourself in this boat. Each seeks to encourage you to use the knowledge you have already gained as a resource in generating a researchable problem. The three strategies I discuss are:

- using concepts as sensitizing resources
- following up findings from other studies
- introducing a third variable.

Using concepts

6.6.1 Treating the knowledge you have learned as a resource involves thinking about how it can sensitize you to various researchable issues. In an earlier book (Silverman, 2006: 16–18), I sought to distinguish three types of sensitivity: historical, political and contextual.

Most of this is self-explanatory. Historical sensitivity means that, wherever possible, one should examine the relevant historical evidence when setting up a topic to research. Political sensitivity shows the vested interests behind current media 'scares' and reveals that this way of determining our research topics is just as fallible as designing research in accordance with administrative or managerial interests.

Contextual sensitivity is the least self-explanatory and most contentious category in the present list. A longer explanation is therefore warranted. By 'contextual' sensitivity, I mean two things:

- the recognition that apparently uniform institutions like 'the family', 'a tribe' or 'science' take on a variety of meanings in different contexts
- the understanding that participants in social life actively produce a context for what they do and that social researchers should not simply import their own assumptions about what context is relevant in any situation.

Such contextual sensitivity implies that it is worthwhile to distance yourself a little from the prevailing vocabulary in the setting you want to study. For example, in medicine there is a vocabulary of 'good communication' with patients. This vocabulary is emphasized in medical education including in-service training for physicians.

Undoubtedly, this discussion of communication is important in the study of many medical settings. However, in working out your research problem, it is worth keeping a little critical distance from it. As shown in Geraldine Leydon's study of oncology consultations, it is usually helpful to treat participants' vocabulary as a *topic* rather than as a *resource*.

STUDENT EXAMPLES

What Is 'Good Communication'?

Discussions of 'good' and 'bad' communication are common in the health literature in general and continue to be reported in the academic literature. In the field of oncology, *good* is routinely described as equal, facilitative, open ended, supportive, and patient centred, and these concepts frequent policy documents and other studies in the field.

I found the opacity of what [concepts] like these refer to in interactional and practice terms frustrating. What, for example, might 'active listening', 'frequent clarifying' and 'paraphrasing' sound or look like in practice? Where is the demonstration that these particular skills have positive interactional consequences? Moreover, the patients seemed to be 'missing'.

Reading conversation analytic work helped me to decide how I might distance myself from work like that above and what approach I might fruitfully take, time and data permitting. The opportunity to examine that which already occurs and, as far as possible, without thinking too much about what I or anyone else might consider to be good or bad, offered a more satisfying alternative and provided good reason for a parting of the 'methodological' ways.

Eventually, with all of these issues in mind, my PhD came to be concerned with the following: how is it that the outpatient oncology treatment consultation 'comes off', and how do participants offer and receive 'information' about cancer?

This large question fuelled early analysis and, following my repeated listening and reading, the study became concerned with particular sets of practices that occur at separate moments in the consultation trajectory. These include an examination of the work that goes into:

1 the establishment of what each participant knows of the other during early history taking, including the journey to the here and now of the consultation

2 the naming/topicalization of cancer during later history taking moments and clarification that patients own their cancer diagnosis

3 the delivery of further diagnostic news once cancer is established as the diagnosis; The provision of evidence that prepares the way for talk about treatment, radiotherapy or chemotherapy

4 the negotiated meaning and delivery and receipt of different types of news (good and bad) and their relation to an (accomplished) omni-relevant context of uncertainty and positivity. [Geraldine Leydon, Sociology, Goldsmiths]

Geraldine's focus on what actually happens in certain kinds of medical consultation made use of contextual sensitivity. Rather than assume that 'medical communication' defined a single object, she preferred to study how communication worked out in a particular medical setting.

One final point. The three kinds of sensitivity we have been considering offer different, sometimes contradictory, ways of generating research topics. I am not suggesting that all should be used at the beginning of any research study. However, if we are not sensitive to *any* of these issues, then we run the danger of lapsing into a commonsensical way of defining our research topics. This is a topic to which I shall return, particularly in Chapter 7.

Following up other findings

6.6.2 Phillips and Pugh (1994: 49–52) suggest that one aid for the sluggish research imagination is to begin with previously proposed generalizations and then try to find their limits by postulating new conditions.

Since most undergraduate social science teaching places a great deal of emphasis on the 'classical' literature, you can sometimes mobilize your knowledge of 'classical' work in order to generate a research problem. In an earlier book (Silverman, 1985: 10–11), I gave two sociological examples of postulating a new condition for a classical generalization:

- Alvin Gouldner (1954) observed that Max Weber's 'ideal type' of bureaucracy was largely based on studies of government bureaucracies. This meant that Weber stressed the role of democratically defined formal rules in obtaining consent. By studying rule following in the private sector, Gouldner was able to identify varying levels and bases of consent by staff to rules.

- Lipset et al. (1962) noted that Robert Michels's 'Iron Law of Oligarchy' had encouraged a focus on the factors that make organizations undemocratic. By studying a highly democratic organization, Lipset et al. identified both anti-democratic and democratic pressures in how organizations operate. By doing so, they were able to question the inevitability of this iron law.

More recently, I became interested in the conditions under which clients were likely to demonstrate uptake of the advice that they were given in interviews with health professionals. In a study of interviews between British health visitors and first-time mothers, Heritage and Sefi (1992) had found that mothers were more likely to acknowledge the relevance of advice which was related to their expressed concerns.

In my own study of HIV-test counselling (Silverman, 1997), I began with Heritage and Sefi's findings as my initial research focus. However, I observed that time constraints in many counselling centres meant that it was very difficult for counsellors to adopt such an apparently 'client-centred' approach. My research question now changed to considering how both parties acted to prevent open disagreements while giving or receiving potentially irrelevant advice (1997: 154–81).

Introducing a third variable

6.6.3 As described by Rudestam and Newton (1992: 12–16), introducing a third variable involves adding a focusing factor to your area of research interest. These authors give the example of a student interested in how young people view the elderly. You can make this topic less general, more researchable and more interesting by introducing a third variable. For instance, you can ask: does living with a grandparent influence views? Alternatively, you can focus on the effect on young people of media representations of the elderly. Further, using 'contextual sensitivity', as described above, you can limit your focus even more by asking how, when and where young people generate descriptions of elderly people.

 ■ Attempt Exercise 6.1 ▬▬▬▬

If you have a tendency to be a 'simplistic inductivist', you should now attempt Exercise 6.1.

Strategies for 'Kitchen-Sinkers'_____

Do less, more thoroughly. (Wolcott, 1990: 62)

6.7
Wolcott's advice is sound. Narrowing down is often the most crucial task when drafting a research proposal. Kitchen-sinkers have so many ideas buzzing around in their heads that getting down to a focused piece of research is entirely beyond them.

Every issue seems so fascinating. Each aspect seems interconnected, and each piece of reading that you do only adds further ideas (and suggests further readings). So, while you can grasp the value of making a lot out of a little, it is easier said than done. The question remains: how do you go about narrowing down your ideas?

I set out below three practical techniques which help to answer this question:

- Draw a flow chart
- Find a puzzle
- Look through a zoom lens.

The flow chart _____

6.7.1
Dealing with data means moving from passive reading to active analysis. If you have failed to use the early stages of your research to narrow down your topic, data analysis is going to be very difficult because:

> having a large number of research questions makes it harder to see emergent links across different parts of the data base and to achieve successful integration of findings. (Miles and Huberman, 1984: 36)

To help you narrow down, it can make sense to do an early flow chart setting out your key concepts and how they might relate. Following Miles and Huberman:

> Conceptual frameworks are best done graphically, rather than in text. Having to get the entire framework on a single page is salutary. (1984: 33)

The single-page flow chart is a useful technique in writing books as well as in doing research. For instance, as I write these words, I regularly move to a second document which houses the outline of this book. This outline was continually revised as I did my preliminary reading. It is still being revised as I write each chapter.

Several attempts will usually be needed to get your flow chart into a state that will be useful to you. Miles and Huberman recommend experimenting with different ways of specifying your research focus. But their basic advice is to 'begin with a foggy research question and then try to defog it' (1984: 35).

Find a puzzle

6.7.2 One way to break out of the vicious circle of unending facts and theories is to put your books on one side and to ask yourself: what am I really trying to find out? More specifically, what *puzzle* am I trying to solve?

Think of research as one of many kinds of puzzle solving among a set of activities like doing jigsaws, completing crosswords or solving crimes. Each activity will be associated with its own set of more or less unique activities (but see Alasuutari, 1995 on the parallel between the qualitative researcher and Sherlock Holmes). Jennifer Mason has argued that 'all qualitative research should be formulated around an intellectual puzzle' (1996: 6). She distinguishes three kinds of question that may generate the type of intellectual puzzle which qualitative researchers would recognize, namely:

- How or why did X develop? (a developmental puzzle)
- How does X work? (a mechanical puzzle)
- What causes X or what influence does X have on Y? (a causal puzzle) (1996: 14)

Let us consider how, following Mason, you might find a puzzle. Say you have a general interest in 'child abuse'. You might narrow down your topic by choosing among the following questions:

- How or why was 'child abuse' first recognized? (a developmental puzzle)
- How (and by whom) is 'child abuse' identified? (a mechanical puzzle)
- What are the characteristics of child abusers and abused children? What effect does child abuse have on each group? (a causal puzzle)

Once you make a list of this kind, you should see that it is impossible to solve satisfactorily all these puzzles. So which puzzle do you choose? Below are some further questions that are worth asking:

- Which puzzle most interests me?
- Which puzzle might most interest my supervisor/funding body?

- Which puzzle most relates to issues on which I already have some theoretical, substantive or practical background?
- Which puzzle would generate questions that could be answered using my own resources and with readily available data?

The zoom lens

6.7.3 Wolcott (1990) gives the example of one PhD student who never finished his study of classroom behaviour. The true 'kitchen-sinker', this poor student was always reading more or gathering yet more data.

Wolcott uses the analogy of a zoom lens to suggest a practical solution. Say you want to take some photographs of a holiday resort. You could find some suitably high place, say a nearby hill, and try to take a picture of the whole resort. Then as Wolcott points out: 'If you want to take in more of the picture, you must sacrifice closeness of detail' (1990: 63).

Alternatively, you can zoom in on one small image. What you lose in breadth, you may well gain in telling detail – say a particular dish that you enjoyed or the interaction between two local people.

Now apply the zoom lens analogy to defining your own research task. Wolcott suggests 'taking some manageable "unit of one" as a focus' (1990: 69). So if, like his student, you are interested in classroom behaviour, focus on one student, one day, one lesson or one critical event.

The beauty of this narrowing of focus is that it will produce a manageable and achievable research task. Moreover, you are not locked forever in this close-up picture. Just like the photographer, you can:

> zoom in progressively closer and closer until your descriptive task is manageable, then zoom back out again to regain perspective. (1990: 69)

Following Wolcott, later on you can always attempt to broaden your generalizations through more data at different levels of 'reality'. But your initial 'zooming in' will have got you going – out of the library and into dealing with data.

 ■ **Attempt Exercise 6.2**

If you have a tendency to be a 'kitchen-sinker', you should now attempt Exercise 6.2.

A caution: avoid reductionism

6.7.4 One of the advantages of introducing a third variable is that it guards against the tendency to try to explain complex social processes in terms of a single cause. Such reductionism is regularly demanded in both legal cross-examinations ('answer yes or no'!) and in media interviews (where the demand for simplification sometimes makes research scientists seem like incoherent babblers).

So my diagnosis of 'kitchen-sinking' and my recommendations for specifying a research problem should not be confused with attempts to reduce the complexities of the social world to a single variable. Just as doctors talk about meeting patients who make their hearts sink, there is nothing worse than when a detailed seminar on one's research is greeted by some bright spark with a version of: 'That's all very interesting. But surely what you've described is all to do with power/ gender/postmodernity etc.' What a nice, simple world it would be if everything reduced to one factor! For the moment, however, we should leave the pursuit of this kind of simplicity to bigots and to those theoretical physicists who valiantly seek a single theory of matter.

So narrowing down a research problem should not be confused with this kind of reductionism. I can only echo the arguments of the authors of a qualitative methodology textbook:

> Such reductive arguments are always distressing, given the variety and complex organization of social worlds. They reflect mentalities that cannot cope with the uncertainties and ambiguities of social research. (Coffey and Atkinson, 1996: 15)

Strategies for Grand Theorists

6.8 Reducing 'reality' to ungrounded sets of categories is an obvious potential failing of grand theorists. However, the minority of readers who feel they have the flair and temperament for theorizing will not, I suspect, be dissuaded by anything I might write. Indeed sometimes, as I have already remarked, library-based work can be a quick way to write an acceptable thesis.

In this situation, all I can usefully do is wish you luck and offer you a couple of suggestions to speed you on your way. First, try to ignore fashions. Second, think about how some data may actually help you to theorize better. I set out these suggestions below.

Ignore fashions

6.8.1 Having found the corner of the intellectual garden which suits you, stick with it. Don't worry about those smart-alecs who have always read a 'crucial' book by some new author: nine times out of ten, it will just distract you. Guided by your supervisor, work out the set of readings that will be your central material and stay with them. When you have written most of your thesis, you may then have the luxury of reading more widely and using that reading to reflect on the implications and limitations of your position – perhaps for your final chapter. Till then, don't be distracted.

Find some data

6.8.2 Even the most active minds can become a little stilted when confined to their armchairs. So think about examining some empirical materials of some kind. Even though these may not be central to your thesis, they may work as an aid to the sluggish imagination.

Take the case of two students in my own department who wrote 'theoretical' PhDs. Nick was interested in what he calls 'the refusal of work' which he linked to theoretical ideas about 'the ontology of desire'. Despite this highly complex theory, Nick still felt it worthwhile to gather material on the history of Autonomia – an Italian movement to refuse work – and the organization of unemployment benefit in the UK.

Jake was interested in a critique of existing theories of the community. In this context, he attempted what he described as largely a philosophical exercise. Nonetheless, to aid his thinking, he observed and interviewed homeless people, beggars and the mainstream community. Attempting what he called 'a situated phenomenology of the moral encounter', his data were intended to be only illustrative.

Strategies for all Researchers

6.9 Whether you tend to be this kind of a grand theorist or you are a kitchen-sinker or a simplistic inductivist, there are certain general issues that apply to everybody who wants to select a research topic. I call these issues:

- finding a workable (not just narrow) research topic
- recognizing 'feedback loops' between topic(s) and data analysis
- understanding that your categories (or variables) are always theoretically saturated.

I deal with each issue below.

Find a workable research topic

6.9.1 'Narrowing down' is necessary but not sufficient for a good research project. It is possible to have a narrowly defined, clear and unambiguous research topic (using concepts which clearly connect to data indicators) which is simply not workable.

For instance, there may be no way you could obtain appropriate data, or the topic may simply not be very interesting or important. Table 6.2 lists three features of workable research questions.

Recognize feedback loops

6.9.2 Good research rarely moves smoothly from A (research topic) to B (findings). As Seta's case (discussed above) shows, alert researchers are

TABLE 6.2 Workable research questions

1 *Answerability*: we can see what data are required to answer the questions, and how the data will be obtained
2 *Interconnectedness*: the questions are related to each other in some meaningful way, rather than being unconnected
3 *Substantively relevant*: the questions are interesting and worthwhile, so justifying the investment of research effort

Source: adapted from K. Punch, 1998: 49

always prepared to change their focus as they learn new things from others and from their own data.

David Wield has called this to and fro between data and topic a 'feedback loop' (2002: 42). This is how he addresses the issue of research focus in the context of such feedback:

> Each stage of the research work will result in challenging a project's focus and lead to some re-evaluation. At all times, you will find that you have to maintain a careful balancing act between the desirable and the practical. Too strong a focus early on may lead to you ignoring what actually are more important issues than the ones you have chosen. Too weak a focus results in following up each side issue as it emerges and not getting anywhere! So focus needs to remain an issue as the research progresses in order to avoid the pitfall of these extremes. (2002: 42)

Recognize the theoretical saturation of categories _____

6.9.3 Seta's case, above, nicely illustrates that the categories we use to formulate our research problem are not neutral but, inevitably, theoretically saturated. In her case, the issue revolved around the status which she should attach to her interviewees' accounts. To take two extreme formulations: were these the raw experiences of alcoholics, or provoked narratives in which a drinking story was constructed?

These kinds of issues have already been discussed in Chapter 4 when I examined several interview studies, and will be discussed further in Chapter 13. The interdependence between research design and such analytical issues is examined in the next chapter.

Concluding Remarks _____

6.10 Like most dispositions, whether you tend to be a simplistic inductivist, a kitchen-sinker or a grand theorist is likely to arise from a combination of temperament and experience. As such, you are unlikely to be deflected by anything I write. So this chapter will have succeeded not by converting you, but if it helps you to speed along your ordained path.

On the other hand, it may be over-reductionist to view these three tendencies as personal dispositions. Jay Gubrium (personal correspondence) has suggested to me that simplistic inductivism, kitchen-sinkism and grand theory are occupational hazards of all social science inquiry. In this sense, they are tendencies present in all of us and we need to be constantly wary of them if our enterprise is going to be theoretically informed *and* empirically grounded.

 ■ **Attempt Exercise 6.3**

| **KEY POINTS** |

Selecting a research topic can be made easier if you resist three temptations:

1 *Simplistic inductivism* assumes that we need make no assumptions in studying the world. Instead, hypotheses will somehow emerge if we just 'hang out' with the aim of 'faithfully representing subjects' worlds'. Simplistic inductivism is at best a convenient myth which ignores the theory-saturated nature of any observation and can be an excuse for sloppy, unfocused research. It is best countered by:

   • using concepts as sensitizing resources

   • using other people's generalizations

   • introducing a third variable.

2 *The kitchen sink gambit* seeks to include every aspect of a problem that you can think of in order to show the breadth of your knowledge and to impress potential supervisors. However, if you define your topic very widely, you will usually be unable to say anything at great depth about it. Depth rather than breadth is what characterizes a good research proposal. It can be countered by:

   • drawing a flow chart

   • finding a puzzle

   • looking through a zoom lens.

3 *Grand theorists* build theoretical empires. Stuck firmly in their armchairs, such theorists need never trifle with mere 'facts'. The consequence may not be enlightenment but merely cobwebs of verbiage. This tendency can be countered by:

   • ignoring the latest fashions

   • finding some data.

■ ■ **Further Reading** ■

To help you think some more about defining your research, I recommend three basic texts: Amanda Coffey and Paul Atkinson's *Making Sense of Qualitative Data* (Sage,

1996: Ch. 1); Jennifer Mason's *Qualitative Researching* (second edition, Sage, 2002: Ch. 1 and 2); and David Silverman's *Interpreting Qualitative Data: Methods for Analysing Talk, Text and Interaction* (Sage, 2006: Ch. 1). Useful but more specialist texts are: Pertti Alasuutari's *Researching Culture* (Sage, 1995: Ch. 13); Martyn Hammersley and Paul Atkinson's *Ethnography: Principles in Practice* (third edition, Tavistock, 2007); and Anselm Strauss and Juliet Corbin's *Basics of Qualitative Research* (third edition, Sage, 2008: Chs 1–4). Specific guidance on narrowing down a research problem is offered by Harriet Churchill and Teela Sanders's *Getting Your PhD* (Sage, 2007: 22–32).

 ■ Exercise 6.1 ▬▬▬▬▬▬▬▬▬▬▬▬

Strategies for 'Simplistic Inductivists'

1 Attempt to relate your research ideas to one or all of the types of 'sensitivity' discussed above:

- historical

- political

- contextual.

How might this lead you to reformulate your research interest?

2 Review any theoretical or research study with which you are familiar. Try to postulate new conditions which might allow you to develop a new but related research topic.

3 Try adding a few extra variables into your area of research interest. Now work out which of these variables would add most depth to your project and/or be most simply researched (e.g. is the data available and can it be relatively easily gathered?).

 ■ Exercise 6.2 ▬▬▬▬▬▬▬▬▬▬▬▬

Strategies for 'Kitchen-Sinkers'

1 Draw a flow chart of no more than one page setting out your key concepts and how they relate.

2 Review your area of research interest in terms of the following questions and formulate your research problem in terms of one kind of puzzle:

- How or why did X develop? (a developmental puzzle)

- How does X work? (a mechanical puzzle)

- What causes X or what influence does X have on Y? (a causal puzzle) (Mason, 1996: 14)

3 Use the zoom lens technique to focus in on some manageable 'unit of one' which might serve as an initial dataset to resolve your puzzle.

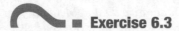 ■ **Exercise 6.3**

A trick from Howard Becker

Howard Becker is the author of a very useful book for research students called *Tricks of the Trade* (1998). One trick he mentions suggests the following exercise:

1   Ask your supervisor (or a fellow student who knows your work reasonably well) to offer a snap characterization of what you are trying to find out.

2   Now respond to this characterization of your work (e.g. by denying it or modifying it).

This exercise, says Becker, should help you to get a better understanding of what you *are* trying to do.

7

Using Theories

| **Chapter Objectives** |

By the end of this chapter you will be able to:

- **Know what a theory is.**
- **Distinguish between a theory, a model and a concept.**
- **Understand the ways in which models shape your research problem.**

Introduction

7.1

As we saw in Chapter 6, refining your research topic is never a purely technical activity. How we think about our research is always shaped by our assumptions about:

- the nature of social phenomena
- the proper ways to investigate such phenomena.

When I run workshops for beginning research students, such assumptions are highly visible. Let me show you what I mean by looking at how they describe their research. Their topics include:

- What are the factors associated with the effective classroom teaching of mathematics (education researcher, Tanzania)?
- The effectiveness of entrepreneurial education, using educational and psychological indicators (management student, France).
- Factors, processes and sources of inequalities in women's careers in connection with the transformation of Czech society after the fall of communism (sociology and geography student, Norway).

Before you read on, I would like you to work out why it might be problematic to develop a viable qualitative methodology to study these topics.

Now here is my answer. First, we can note certain common features in these topics:

- Each begins with a 'social problem' of the kind you might read about in an intelligent newspaper or magazine.

- Each uses a language of 'variables' ('factors', 'indicators').

- Each is seeking to correlate variables.

- Each seems to be assuming that such variables ('effectiveness', 'transformation') can be defined at the outset and, in this sense, are non-problematic.

- None of these statements implies that we might study how, in various contexts and situations, things like 'effectiveness' and 'transformation' come to be represented or defined.

This leads me to my second observation. The common features in these statements of research topics derive from a model of science commonly used in quantitative research. This model, known as **positivism**, treats 'social facts' as existing independently of the activities of both participants and researchers. Please note, however, I am not trying to criticize these topics or the students who defined them. I sincerely believe each addresses a genuine social problem. Indeed, I should also add that the students concerned are aware of many of the problems of incompatibility between their research topic and a qualitative approach and have sought my advice on how to transform their topic to make it accessible by such an approach.

 ■ **Attempt Exercise 7.1**

We should not assume that all research students begin with a problem which is so clearly linked to a particular research model. Many times, we will begin with an apparently 'neutral' setting and simply seek to discover some information about it. For example, Eric Livingston (1987) asks us to imagine that we have been told to carry out some social research on city streets. Where should we begin? Some alternatives are set out in Table 7.1.

Believe it or not, once we have got to the stage of thinking about such possible data, we have moved deep into theoretical issues. For, as Livingston points out,

TABLE 7.1   Viewing a street: data possibilities

1 Official statistics (traffic flow, accidents)
2 Interviews (how people cope with rush hours)
3 Observation from a tower (viewing geometric shapes)
4 Observation/video at street level (how people queue or organize their movements)

Source: adapted from Eric Livingston, 1987: 21–7

each of these different ways of looking involves basic theoretical as well as methodological decisions. Very crudely, if we are attached to social theories which see the world in terms of correlations between social facts (think of demography or macroeconomics), we are most likely to consider gathering official statistics (option 1 in Table 7.1). By contrast, if we think that social meanings or perceptions are important (as in certain varieties of sociology and psychology), we may be tempted by the interview study (option 2). Or if we are anthropologists or those kinds of sociologists who want to observe and/or record what people actually do, *in situ*, we might elect options 3 or 4. But note the very different views of people's behaviour we get from looking from on high (option 3), where people seem like ants forming geometrical shapes like wedges, or from street level (option 4), where behaviour seems much more complex.

⌐ TIP ⌐

None of the possible datasets discussed by Livingston are more real or more true than the others. For instance, people are not really more like ants or complex actors. So, in designing your research, reflect upon how your theoretical assumptions about the social world are shaping the methodology you favour.

So methodologies and research questions are inevitably theoretically informed. Even down-to-earth policy-oriented research designed to evaluate some social service will, as Livingston implies, embed itself in theoretical issues as soon as it selects a particular evaluation method (see my discussion of HIV counselling research in Chapter 8).

So we *do* need social theories to help us to address even quite basic issues in social research. Howard Becker quotes a famous American social psychologist of the past to make just this point:

> One can see the empirical world only through some scheme or image of it. The *entire* act of scientific study is oriented and shaped by the underlying picture of the empirical world that is used. This picture sets the selection and formulation of problems, the determination of what are data, the kinds of relations sought between data, and the forms in which propositions are cast. (Blumer, 1969: 24–5)

However, these student topics and Livingston's example of viewing a city street only take us so far.

How Theoretical Models Shape Research _____

7.2

Keith Punch asks us: 'Are we committed to a particular research model, which implies a particular methodology? Do [you] have a gut feeling about what a good piece of research looks like?' (1998: 245). Models provide an overall framework for viewing reality. They inform the concepts we use to define our research problem.

For instance, in the three student topics I noted earlier, the problem was defined in terms of the relation between 'variables' apparently to be defined by the researcher. Now, although positivism is the most common model used in quantitative research (i.e. the default option), it sits uneasily within most qualitative research designs. This is why I had difficulties in using qualitative methodology to study the student topics with which this chapter began.

Qualitative research designs tend to work with a relatively small number of cases. Generally speaking, qualitative researchers are prepared to sacrifice scope for detail. Moreover, even what counts as detail tends to vary between qualitative and quantitative researchers. The latter typically seek detail in certain aspects of correlations between variables. By contrast, for qualitative researchers, detail is found in the precise particulars of such matters as people's understandings and interactions. This is because qualitative researchers tend to use a non-positivist model of reality.

However, 'non-positivism' is a negative term which does not tell us directly about how qualitative researchers reason. As we shall now see, qualitative research is an intellectually diverse field in which researchers use many different models. In some sense, they speak different languages.

The Different Languages of Qualitative Research

7.3 A thorough discussion of differences in method and theory among qualitative researchers is found in Gubrium and Holstein's *The New Language of Qualitative Method* (1997). This book classifies qualitative research in terms of various orientations towards the empirical data under analysis. In particular, Gubrium and Holstein focus on how each qualitative approach uses a particular analytical language to emphasize a particular facet of social reality. As the authors put it:

> Our strategy for understanding the diversity of qualitative research is to treat each variant as an enterprise that develops, and is conducted in, a language or idiom of its own. Accordingly, each idiom represents a distinctive reality, virtually constituting its empirical horizon. (1997: 5)

At the heart of this classification system is the division between substance and process, or between *what* is being studied and *how* it is constructed. Take the topic of nudity, for example. A qualitative researcher might ask the following: *what* are the deviant traits that characterize nudists and *what* practices are associated with a nudist? Another researcher studying the same topic could examine *how* nudity could be made normal or routine. In 'The nudist management of respectability', Martin Weinberg (1994) explores how nudist colonies achieve the 'respectability' of the unclothed body through a set of locally defined and enforced norms like 'no body contact' and 'no accentuation of the body' (e.g. sitting with one's legs open). Weinberg's goal is to answer the question, 'How can they see their behavior as morally appropriate?' (1994: 392).

With this distinction between *how* (process of constructing reality) and *what* (reality as substantive truth), let us now look at the four models of qualitative research discussed in Gubrium and Holstein's book:

- naturalism

- emotionalism

- ethnomethodology

- postmodernism.

Naturalism

7.3.1 As a model of qualitative research, **naturalism** focuses on the factual characteristics of the object under study. Gubrium and Holstein cite William Whyte's *Street Corner Society* as a classic example of naturalism. In this urban ethnography from the 1940s, Whyte's goal is to describe what life is really like in an inner-city Italian neighbourhood located in Boston. The observations and analysis are intended to objectively reflect *what* Whyte saw and heard in this real world of poverty. Naturalism's strength is its representational simplicity. A naturalistic ethnography is almost formulaically built around the following tasks:

- entering the setting

- establishing rapport

- recording observations with an eye toward social scientific concepts (e.g. social status and group dynamics)

- presenting the findings.

The major shortcoming of naturalists, according to Gubrium and Holstein, is this:

> Because they view the border [between the topic of study and the way in which it is socially constructed] as a mere *technical* hurdle that can be overcome through methodological skill and rigor, they lose sight of the border as a region where reality is constituted within representation. (1997: 106)

This criticism suggests that naturalists overlook *how* people create meaning in their lives. Respondents are treated as mere sources of data without any interpretive capacity of their own. In a naturalistic framework, the participants' 'interpretive practice' (Gubrium and Holstein, 1997), or how they make sense of their own world, is irrelevant.

Emotionalism _____

7.3.2 Like naturalism, **emotionalism** takes for granted the reality of the topic under study. The difference between the two is that where naturalism searches for objective reality in physical places, emotionalism locates the real in the emotional life of the researcher and the respondents; or as Gubrium and Holstein put it, an emotionalist 'virtually takes naturalism to heart' (1997: 59).

Emotionalists are especially concerned with authenticity, which for our purposes can be defined as 'deeper truths about the self'. For emotionalists, alternative writing techniques can be used in qualitative research to better represent 'true feelings'. In the following extract, for example, Laurel Richardson describes why she chose poetry to represent her interview data:

> Writing poetry is emotionally preoccupying; it opens up unexpected, shadow places in my self. As a kind of time-saving/snaring-two-birds-with-one-net strategy I decided to fashion material from an unmarried mother interview into a poem. (1992: 131)

For Richardson, transforming interview data into poetry enables the researcher to preserve the authenticity and breadth of her respondent's story – information that she feels would otherwise be lost in a traditional style of writing and analysis. As she puts it, 'For sociological readers, the poem may seem to omit "data" that they want to know. But this is Louisa May's [her interview respondent's] story, not the sociologist's' (1992: 126).

The problem with emotionalism, as Gubrium and Holstein note, is that 'by peering so intently into subjects' interior lives and inner realms, emotionalists can blind themselves to the ways that subjects shape these spheres by way of their own interpretive actions' (1997: 108). Under emotionalists' exclusive focus on inner feelings and self-reflective confessions, all substantive inquiries about social reality dissolve into self-explorative texts.

Ethnomethodology _____

7.3.3 The third qualitative approach reviewed by Gubrium and Holstein is **ethnomethodology**, which could roughly be translated into the study of people's methods of constructing reality in everyday life. Unlike the other two approaches, ethnomethodology is very much concerned with *how* social reality is constructed in everyday interaction. Ethnomethodologists' primary aim is to understand how people go about doing things in their everyday lives by creating meaningful categories for themselves and others. Thus, for example, an ethnomethodologist might ask seemingly curious questions like: what does it mean to be a 'man'? The researcher would then *bracket* any prior knowledge about the topic (i.e. keep preconceived understandings from entering the analysis). In essence, bracketing means ontological detachment from the topic. Therefore, in representing the analysis, the word *man*, for example, would be placed in quotation marks to indicate its bracketed usage for the purpose of the study.

Harold Garfinkel, one of the founders of ethnomethodology, offers numerous examples of this qualitative approach in *Studies in Ethnomethodology* (1967). Some of the studies cited in this book are labelled 'breaching experiments', or small research projects deliberately designed to violate taken-for-granted social order in order to reveal the process of its construction. In one such study, college students were asked to 'engage an acquaintance or a friend in an ordinary conversation and, without indicating that what the experimenter was asking was in any way unusual, to insist that the person clarify the sense of his commonplace remarks' (1967: 42). The goal of the study was to reveal 'seen but unnoticed' (1967: 42) norms used in everyday conversations. Here is an extract from the study:

> Extract 7.1 [S = subject, E = experimenter]
>
> [S waves his hand cheerily]
>
> S: How are you?
> E: How am I in regard to what? My health, my finances, my school work, my peace of mind, my …?
> S: [Red in the face and suddenly out of control.] Look! I was just trying to be polite. Frankly, I don't give a damn how you are. (1967: 44)

In this case, by problematizing conversational norms, the experimenter reveals how the question 'How are you?' is used to achieve 'politeness' in everyday encounters. For Gubrium and Holstein, although analytically powerful, the problem with ethnomethodology is that it risks losing sight of the topic of analysis in the name of focusing on the process of its creation. As they put it:

> As the substantively meaningful aspects of local culture are shunted aside in order to concentrate on constitutive interactional activity, the content of lived experience becomes almost incidental. (1997: 107)

While ethnomethodology's analytical rigour can free us of trite or stereotypic understandings of a research problem, it does, on the other hand, impose restrictions on substantive interests. For example, one cannot study poverty ethnomethodologically without bracketing its meaning, or placing it in quotation marks (i.e. 'poverty'). In this way, poverty loses its significance as a global social problem and becomes a particular achievement at a particular place and time. As a whole, a strict ethnomethodological analysis appears to trade the substance of everyday life for a rigorous understanding of the activities that define it.

Postmodernism

7.3.4 Although **postmodernism** refers to a vast body of literature, for the sake of simplicity and flow of discussion, let us assume the term encapsulates an analytical orientation that questions all the achievements of modernity (e.g. humanism, rationality, reason, science and so on). One of the key contributions of postmodernism to qualitative analysis is its critique of the representational authority of the written text. In particular, postmodernists ask: who owns the knowledge embedded in the text and what power or authority supports it? Gubrium and Holstein assert that the common theme of postmodernism is how and through what cultural forces we come to understand and accept certain representations of reality as being 'true', 'legitimate' or 'acceptable'. Whereas ethnomethodologists study the processes through which members construct their reality, postmodernists question the power relations and the political rhetoric embedded in the representations and constructions of social reality. While some postmodernists call for experimenting with alternative modes of representing social reality, others fundamentally question all forms of representation to the point of nihilism by arguing that nothing can be known as 'true' or 'good' (for a discussion of the different branches of postmodernism, see Pauline Rosenau, 1992). Gubrium and Holstein's critique of postmodernism is best illustrated by these ominous words:

> Postmodernism in the guise of qualitative inquiry is very risky business. Rhetorical ubiquity notwithstanding, at the lived border, reality is always on the verge of collapsing into representation, taking with it the substantively distinct parameters of experience whose 'qualities' are qualitative method's unique subject matter. Trying to capture that which is not there, or to describe the inexpressible, using mere rhetoric that begs its own deconstruction, is hazardous indeed. Qualitative inquiry is surely in peril as it gambles with empirical nihilism. (1997: 109)

Thus, while raising very important questions about the content of social reality and the methods of its production, in its extreme forms, postmodernism threatens the very need for scientific investigation and analysis. If, according to some postmodernists, we cannot and should not separate fact from fiction or truth from falsehood, then there is no point in spending precious resources to study and analyse social reality; we could just as well write poems or a novel about our experiences (see Silverman, 2007: 132–9).

Nonetheless, it is possible to learn from the important insights of ethnomethodology and postmodernism without drowning in a whirlpool of intellectual nihilism. The most important of these insights is an emphasis on the rhetorical and constructive aspects of knowledge: that is, the realization that facts (like the three students' research topics at the beginning of this chapter) are socially constructed in particular contexts. In some respects, this defines the **constructionist** model, concerned with questions of 'what?' and 'how?', which informs so much qualitative research (see Holstein and Gubrium, 2008).

By now, this whole debate may have left you thoroughly confused. As a beginning researcher, you may rightly feel that the last thing you need is to sink into an intractable debate between warring camps. However, it helps if we treat this less as a war and more as a clarion call to be clear about the issues that animate our work and help define our research problem. As I argued in Chapter 6, purely theoretical debates are often less than helpful if we want to carry out effective

TABLE 7.2 Basic research terms

Term	Meaning	Relevance
Model	An overall framework for looking at reality (e.g. positivism, constructionism)	Usefulness
Concept	An idea deriving from a given model (e.g. 'stimulus–response', 'the social construction of reality')	Usefulness
Theory	A set of concepts used to define and/or explain some phenomenon	Usefulness
Hypothesis	A testable proposition	Validity
Methodology	A general approach to studying research topics	Usefulness
Method	A specific research technique (e.g. interview, focus group)	Good fit with model, theory, hypothesis and methodology

Source: Silverman, 2006: 13

research. The point is to work with a model that makes sense to you. The strengths and weaknesses of any model will only be revealed in what you can do with it.

Theories, Models and Hypotheses

7.4 In this section, we shall be discussing models, concepts, theories, hypotheses, methods and methodologies. In Table 7.2, I set out how each term will be used.

As we see from Table 7.2, *models* provide an overall framework for how we look at reality. In short, they tell us what reality is like, the basic elements it contains ('ontology') and what is the nature and status of knowledge ('epistemology'). In this sense, models roughly correspond to what are more grandly referred to as **paradigms** (see Guba and Lincoln, 1994).

Concepts are clearly specified ideas deriving from a particular model. Examples of concepts are 'social function' (deriving from functionalism), 'stimulus/response' (behaviouralism), 'definition of the situation' (interactionism) and 'the documentary method of interpretation' (ethnomethodology). Concepts offer ways of looking at the world which are essential in defining a research problem.

Theories arrange sets of concepts to define and explain some phenomenon. As Strauss and Corbin put it: 'Theory consists of plausible relationships produced among concepts and sets of concepts' (1994: 278).

━━━━━━━━━━━━━━━━━━━━━━━━━ LINK ━━━━━━━━━━━━━━━━━━━━━━━━━

For more information on the grounded theory recommended by Strauss and Corbin, visit:

www.groundedtheory.com

Without a theory, such phenomena as 'death', 'tribes' and 'families' cannot be understood. In this sense, without a theory there is nothing to research. So theory provides a footing for considering the world, separate from, yet about, that world. In this way, theory provides both a framework for critically understanding phenomena and a basis for considering how what is unknown might be organized (Gubrium, personal correspondence).

By provoking ideas about the presently unknown, theories provide the impetus for research. As living entities, they are also developed and modified by good research. However, as used here, models, concepts and theories are self-confirming in the sense that they instruct us to look at phenomena in particular ways. This means that they can never be disproved but only found to be more or less useful.

This last feature distinguishes theories from *hypotheses*. Unlike theories, hypotheses are tested in research. Examples of hypotheses, discussed in Silverman (2006), are:

- How we receive advice is linked to how advice is given.

- Responses to an illegal drug depend upon what one learns from others.

- Voting in union elections is related to non-work links between union members.

In many qualitative research studies, there is no specific hypothesis at the outset. Instead, hypotheses are produced (or induced) during the early stages of research. In any event, unlike theories, hypotheses can and should be tested. Therefore, we assess a hypothesis by its validity or truth.

A *methodology* refers to the choices we make about cases to study, methods of data gathering, forms of data analysis etc. in planning and executing a research study. So our methodology defines how one will go about studying any phenomenon. In social research, methodologies may be defined very broadly (e.g. qualitative or quantitative) or more narrowly (e.g. **grounded theory** or **conversation analysis**). Like theories, methodologies cannot be true or false, only more or less useful.

Finally, *methods* are specific research techniques. These include quantitative techniques like statistical correlations, as well as techniques like observation, interviewing and audio-recording. Once again, in themselves, techniques are not true or false. They are more or less useful, depending on their fit with the theories and methodologies being used and the hypothesis being tested and/or the research topic that is selected. So, for instance, positivists may favour quantitative methods and constructionists often prefer to gather their data by observation. But, depending upon the hypothesis being tested, positivists may sometimes use qualitative methods – for instance in the exploratory stage of research. Equally, constructionists may sometimes use simple quantitative methods, particularly when they want to find an overall pattern in their data.

Models

↓

Concepts

↓

Theories

↓

Hypotheses ←

↓

Methodology

↓

Method

↓

Findings ─

FIGURE 7.1
Levels of analysis

The relation between models, concepts, theories, hypotheses, methodology and methods can be set out schematically as in Figure 7.1.

Reading Figure 7.1 downwards, each term reflects a lower level of generality and abstraction. The arrow from 'findings' to 'hypotheses' indicates a feedback mechanism through which hypotheses are modified in the light of findings.

Examples

7.5
Let me now try to put flesh on the skeleton set out in Figure 7.1 through the use of some concrete examples. Imagine that we have a general interest in the gloomy topic of 'death' in society. How are we to research this topic?

Before we can even define a research problem, let alone develop a hypothesis, we need to think through some very basic issues. Assume that we are the kind of social scientist that prefers to see the world in terms of how **social structures** determine behaviour, following the sociologist Emile Durkheim's (1951) injunction to treat social facts as real 'things'. Such a positivist model of social life will suggest concepts that we can use in our research on death. Using such a model, we will tend to see death in terms of statistics relating to rates of death (or 'mortality'). And we will want to explain such statistics in terms of other social facts such as age or social class.

Armed with our concepts, we might then construct a theory about one or other aspect of our topic. For instance, working with our assumption that death is a social fact, determined by other social facts, we might develop a theory that the rate of early death among children, or 'infant mortality', is related to some social fact about their parents, say their social class. From this theory, it is a quick step to the hypothesis that the higher the social class of its parents, the lower the likelihood of a child dying within the first year of its life. This hypothesis is sometimes expressed as saying that there is an 'inverse' relationship between social class and infant mortality.

As already implied, a model concerned with social facts will tend to favour a quantitative methodology, using methods such as the analysis of official statistics or the use of large-scale social surveys based on apparently reliable fixed-choice questionnaires. In interpreting the findings of such research, one will need to ensure that due account is taken of factors that may be concealed in simple correlations. For instance, social class may be associated with quality of housing, and the latter factor (here called an **intervening variable**) may be the real cause of variations in the rates of infant mortality.

This overall approach to death is set out schematically in Figure 7.2.

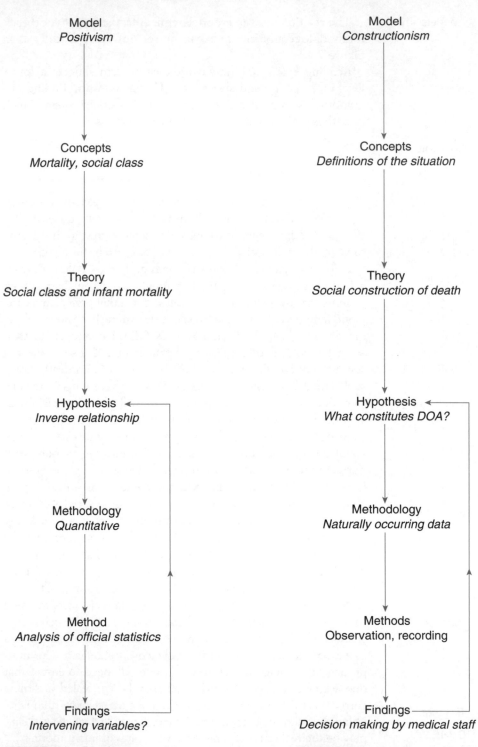

Model
Positivism

↓

Concepts
Mortality, social class

↓

Theory
Social class and infant mortality

↓

Hypothesis ←
Inverse relationship

↓

Methodology
Quantitative

↓

Method
Analysis of official statistics

↓

Findings —
Intervening variables?

FIGURE 7.2 Death as a social fact

Model
Constructionism

↓

Concepts
Definitions of the situation

↓

Theory
Social construction of death

↓

Hypothesis ←
What constitutes DOA?

↓

Methodology
Naturally occurring data

↓

Methods
Observation, recording

↓

Findings —
Decision making by medical staff

FIGURE 7.3 Death as a social construction

But this is a very different way of conceiving death as a possible research topic. For constructionists, social institutions are created and/or stabilized by the actions of participants. A central idea of this model is that how we label phenomena defines their character. This, in turn, is associated with the concept of 'definitions of the situation' which tells us to look for social phenomena in how meaning gets defined by people in different contexts. The overall message of this approach is that 'death' should be put in inverted commas, and hence leads to a theory in which 'death' is treated as a social construct.

Of course, this is very different from the 'social fact' model and, therefore, nicely illustrates the importance of theories in defining research problems. Its immediate drawback, however, may be that it appears to be counter-intuitive. After all, you may feel, death is surely an obvious fact. We are either dead or not dead – and, this being so, where does this leave constructionism?

Let me cite two cases which put the counter-argument. First, in 1963, after President Kennedy was shot, he was taken to a Dallas hospital with, according to contemporary accounts, half of his head shot away. My hunch is that if you or I were to arrive in a casualty department in this state, we would be given a cursory examination and then recorded as 'dead on arrival' (DOA). Precisely because they were dealing with a president, the staff had to do more than this. So they worked on Kennedy for almost an hour, demonstrating thereby that they had done their best for such an important patient (cf. Sudnow, 1968a).

Now think of contemporary debates about whether or when severely injured people should have life-support systems turned off. Once again, acts of definition constitute whether somebody is alive or dead. And note that such definitions have real effects.

Of course, such a way of looking at how death is socially constructed is just one way of theorizing this phenomenon, not intrinsically better or worse than the 'social fact' approach. But, once we adopt one or another model, it starts to have a big influence upon how our research proceeds. For instance, as we have seen, if 'dead on arrival' can be a label applied in different ways to different people, we might develop a hypothesis about how the label 'dead on arrival' is applied to different hospital patients.

Because of our model, we would then probably try to collect research data that arose in such **naturally occurring** (or non-research-generated) contexts as actual hospitals, using methods like observation and/or audio- or video-recording. Note, however, that this would not rule out the collection of quantitative data (say from hospital records). Rather, it would mean that our main body of data would probably be qualitative. Following earlier research (e.g. Jeffery, 1979; Dingwall and Murray, 1983), our findings might show how age and presumed moral status are relevant to such medical decision making as well as social class. In turn, as shown in Figure 7.3, these findings would help us to refine our initial hypothesis.

A student example on a related topic will nicely illustrate the logic of such a constructionist model. Gunhild Tøndel studied how office staff in Norwegian local authorities compiled health statistics. Here is her account.

Managing Health by Numbers

My project is a qualitative study of statistical practices in municipal health services. I focus on micro-level processes and take a constructivist and interactionist perspective on how statistics are constructed and produced in someone's everyday settings; how their production affects service providers who supply the data; how they are interpreted by service users, local administrators, and politicians; and not least, what distortions thereby make their way into data during this collection, reporting, and transportation chain, and how they are accounted for when data are put to use. In other words: how statistics function as a tool of governance in these services. First and foremost I will use one statistical tool as a case – IPLOS – which is designed to measure clients' function levels and so map their needs for assistance.

  I will use texts as public documents and incentive reports to gain an overview of the structural context and background framework(s) surrounding local practice. Hopefully, I will gain access to observe actors' situated production of numbers and statistical indicators within the municipalities' health service units and also the interaction between these units and the administrative bureaucracy. I will conduct interviews with data reporters (mostly health professionals) about this process and their interpretations of e.g. how this affects the 'counted ones'. [Gunhild Tøndel, Sociology, Trondheim, Norway]

Note that Gunhild's focus is on how these health statistics are put together in a particular context. For her, as a constructionist, the issue is not whether such statistics are accurate or inaccurate but rather the social processes of their production and the effects of those processes on the people who are counted.

Concluding Remarks

7.6 The philosopher of science Thomas Kuhn (1970) has described some social sciences as lacking a single, agreed set of concepts. In Kuhn's terms, this makes social research 'pre-paradigmatic' or at least in a state of competing paradigms. As I have already implied, the problem is that this has generated a whole series of social science courses which pose different social science approaches in terms of either/or questions.

Such courses are much appreciated by some students. They learn about the paradigmatic oppositions in question, choose A rather than B and report back, parrot fashion, all the advantages of A and the drawbacks of B. It is hardly surprising that such courses produce very little evidence that such students have ever thought about anything; even their choice of A is likely to be based on their teacher's implicit or explicit preferences. This may, in part, explain why so many undergraduate social science courses actually provide a learned incapacity to go out and do research.

Learning about rival 'armed camps' in no way allows you to confront research data. In the field, material is much more messy than the different camps would suggest. Perhaps there is something to be learned from both sides; or, more constructively, perhaps we start to ask interesting questions when we reject the polarities that such a course markets.

Even when we decide to use qualitative and/or quantitative methods, we involve ourselves in theoretical as well as methodological decisions. These decisions relate not only to how we conceptualize the world but also to our theory of how our research subjects think about things.

But theory only becomes worthwhile when it is used to explain something. Howard Becker (1998: 1) reports that the great founder of the Chicago School, Everett Hughes, responded grumpily when students asked what he thought about theory. 'Theory of what?', he would reply. For Hughes, as for me, theory without some observation to work upon is like a tractor without a field.

Theory, then, should be neither a status symbol nor an optional extra in a research study. Without theory, research is impossibly narrow. Without research, theory is mere armchair contemplation.

 ■ **Attempt Exercise 7.2** ▬▬▬▬▬▬▬▬▬▬▬

KEY POINTS

- Research questions are inevitably theoretically informed. So we *do* need social theories to help us to address even quite basic issues in social research. But theories need to be distinguished from models and concepts.

- *Models* provide an overall framework for how we look at reality.

- *Concepts* are clearly specified ideas deriving from a particular model.

- *Theories* arrange sets of concepts to define and explain some phenomenon.

- *Methodologies* define how one will go about studying any phenomenon.

- *Methods* are specific research techniques.

■ ■ **Further Reading** ■

Seale, Gobo, Gubrium and Silverman's edited book *Qualitative Research Practice* (Sage, 2004) contains seven chapters which show the relevance of seven contemporary theories to qualitative research (Part 2, 'Analytic Frameworks', pp. 107–213). Becker's book *Tricks of the Trade* (University of Chicago Press, 1998) contains two chapters which are highly relevant to learning how to theorize about your data (Chapter Two on 'Imagery' and

Chapter Four on 'Concepts'). Jaber Gubrium and James Holstein's text *The New Language of Qualitative Method* (Oxford University Press, 1997) is an invaluable, thought-provoking guide to the vocabularies, investigatory styles and ways of writing of different theoretical 'idioms', while the same authors' edited *Handbook of Constructionist Research* (Holstein and Gubrium, Guilford Press, 2008) is a vital guide for anyone considering doing a constructionist-style research project. Martyn Hammersley's *Questioning Qualitative Inquiry: Critical Essays* (Sage, 2008) provides a lively discussion of the assumptions underlying qualitative research.

■ Exercise 7.1

Later in this chapter, I shall offer my own ideas about how we can transform these topics into a problem that may be treated by qualitative methods. Using one or more of these topics, what would you suggest?

■ Exercise 7.2

Howard Becker reports that his colleague Bernard Beck responded to students seeking to theorize about their data by instructing them: 'Tell me what you've found out, but without using any of the identifying characteristics of the actual case' (1998: 126).

Becker gives the example of his own research on Chicago teachers which seemed to show that these teachers seeked to improve their situation by moving to different schools rather than trying to get promoted in their present school. Using his data but forbidden to talk about 'teachers' or 'schools', how might Becker have generated an account of his research that would have satisfied Beck?

8

Choosing a Methodology

Chapter Objectives

By the end of this chapter you will be able to:

- Understand how to choose a method appropriate to your research topic and analytic model.

- Make a rational choice about whether you want to stick to naturally occurring data.

- Decide whether you want to use multiple methods.

Introduction

8.1 As we saw in Chapter 7, decisions about **methodology** are always theoretically loaded. In this chapter, I provide more specific advice about the role of methodological issues in the way you design your research study. First, I use a number of student accounts which address the issue of why one might choose a qualitative methodology. Then I introduce the concept of 'research strategy', illustrated by an extended case study. Next I discuss the contentious topic of whether **naturally occurring data** have a special place in qualitative research design. Finally, I examine whether it makes sense to use multiple research methods.

Qualitative or Quantitative?

8.2 An obvious question for this book would be: why do some students choose qualitative research? As we saw in Chapter 2, some students say they want to do qualitative research but their research topic is much more suited to quantitative methods. So the solution is either to change their methodology or to redefine their research problem.

In Chapter 2, examples were drawn from students in Western Europe, where qualitative research can be the norm in many social science departments. By contrast, in universities in the United States, quantitative research is often the name of the game. In most sociology departments, the majority of the faculty use quantitative methods in their research, and most journals publish a disproportionate number of quantitative papers.

What then attracts students to go against the norm and prefer qualitative research? Here are some answers directly from the research students.

Because the other approach is limited

8.2.1 Although there is a general sense among some researchers that qualitative data are inherently more 'interesting' than numbers, there are less aesthetically oriented and more analytically astute reasons for choosing qualitative methods. In her dissertation, Karyn was interested in *how* whiteness is created and sustained in everyday life. The question of how many whites live in the United States or how much money whites make compared to other groups could have easily been answered using the census data. But Karyn decided that qualitative research was a better fit for the types of questions she was asking.

> **STUDENT EXAMPLES**
>
> ### 'How?' Rather Than 'How Many?'
>
> I've always found qualitative data more interesting than quantitative data. Beyond that, I believe that qualitative data are often more suited to provide me with the answers to questions I'm interested in. I find that my interests usually lie in 'how' questions rather than in 'how many' questions. [Karyn McKinney, USA]

Like Karyn, Sara Crawley states that quantitative measures seemed inadequate for her research on lesbian identities.

> **STUDENT EXAMPLES**
>
> ### Finding the 'Good Stuff'
>
> My substantive interests were related to identity and sexuality. The notion that anyone could describe such intimate matters with a 6 or some quantitative measure seemed atheoretical and, frankly, ludicrous. I am not suggesting that nothing is measurable or that attempts to measure are less useful for some topics. But with a topic that is so intimate and constantly forming as sexuality and identity, it seemed extremely important to highlight individual narrators' ideas and concepts with some detail. As it turns out, I became very interested in talk and how people narrate their identities and realities. The good stuff was in their descriptions and ideas. It fascinated me every day. [Sara Crawley, USA]

A related limitation of quantitative research is highlighted in Michelle Miller-Day's story about realizing that individual people had all but disappeared in her survey research.

STUDENT EXAMPLES

Where Is the Depth?

Like many students, I began my graduate training being socialized within a positivist paradigm. I was learning my statistics and how to conduct surveys and develop quasi-experimental designs. But one day I experienced a transforming moment in graduate school. Donna, one of the participants in a survey-based study I conducted, was reading a manuscript I had written reporting the findings of this study when she exclaimed, 'Where is the depth? Where is the feeling? Where am *I* in all of these words?'

This experience occurred only a few months before I took my first qualitative research methods course. In that course I found my home. While my education to that point was focused on teaching me to collect information and understand social behaviour, I wasn't getting at the *understanding human experience* part of my aspiration. I realized that to truly capture experience I needed to embrace the subjective and, along with it, the humanity of social science. [Michelle Miller-Day, USA]

Michelle's emphasis on the 'subjective' and 'understanding human experience' is a strong feature of some qualitative research. As we saw in Chapter 7, such concepts resonate with an emotionalist model.

Doing what we already like

8.2.2 For Sylvia Ansay and her dissertation on house arrest, doing qualitative research was not an epiphanic shift in her thinking, but rather a natural extension of what she 'already liked doing'.

STUDENT EXAMPLES

Listening to Stories

As a former elementary teacher and guardian *ad litem* [a volunteer worker who functions as an advocate for abused children in the US courts], I have years of experience listening to stories in context and analysing situations and needs. For me, qualitative research merely formalized what I already did well and what I loved doing. Having chosen the dissertation

(Continued)

(Continued)

topic based on a close friend's experience, I was already aware of the storied nature of his accounts, how his personality, alcoholism and ongoing feud with a local underground were all part of the story of his house arrest as well as his criminal offence. I knew that his circumstances, such as being a small-business owner, gave him privileges that someone unemployed or on an 8-to-5 schedule wouldn't have. I had heard his descriptions of good officers and 'pricks'. Everyday life on house arrest was a story within stories, and I felt that perspective was necessary for understanding the *why*s and *how*s of the intensive supervision experience. [Sylvia Ansay, USA]

Bridging the social distance

8.2.3 Yet another student researcher, John Talmage, found qualitative methodology to be an ideal way of bridging 'the social distance' in his study of 'the social world' of the homeless.

STUDENT EXAMPLES

Understanding Another Social World

While survey research is clearly an appropriate methodology for many research questions, I did not believe that it covered the depth of meaning that seemed to be so important in understanding the social world. I did a qualitative dissertation to understand the social world from the perspective of the homeless population, and to that end it seemed helpful to get closer to the data. This I eventually did by spending time with the homeless in public places, in their hobo camps and cat holes, in shelters, and in meetings with my 'research team' [a group of homeless research informants]. These were ways to reduce the social distance between myself and those homeless persons with whom I worked and spoke. [John Talmage, USA]

Here we can see that John relies on ethnographic methods as a way of bridging the status gap between him and a marginal impoverished population.

Doing what is practical

8.2.4 Finally, sometimes qualitative research is just a good fit for the question. As Darin Weinberg states, there is nothing inherently superior about qualitative research and its practitioners. Selecting qualitative methodology could be mostly a practical matter of deciding what works best.

What Works Best

I would say my choice to do a qualitative dissertation was a product of both personal taste and a sense that the themes in which I was interested could be best explored through qualitative approaches. I was never committed to keeping the study strictly qualitative. As it turned out, my use of quantitative data was fairly minimal, but this was more a product of contingency and how the foci of the project evolved than it was one of *a priori* commitments. Had I come across quantitative materials that could have helped me flesh out my analysis, I would have had no hesitation to use them. [Darin Weinberg, USA]

These stories reiterate the points made in Chapter 2 about the diversity of qualitative research. Qualitative research is more than one thing. The features that attract researchers to this methodology are many, and so are the ways this methodology is practised.

Your Research Strategy

8.3 In Chapter 7, I defined 'methodology' as 'a general approach to studying research topics'. In this sense, your choice of method should reflect an 'overall research strategy' (Mason, 1996: 19) as your methodology shapes which methods are used and how each method is used.

Four issues arise when you decide that strategy:

- Making an early decision about which methods to use.

- Understanding the link between methods, methodologies and society.

- Appreciating how **models** shape the meaning and use of different methods.

- Choosing method(s) appropriate to your research topic.

An early decision

Knowing what you want to find out leads inexorably to the question of *how* you will get that information. (Miles and Huberman, 1984: 42)

8.3.1 In quantitative research, it is expected that you begin by establishing a set of variables and methods (often using already existing, proven measures). However, when you are at the start of a piece of qualitative research, how far are you forced to choose between different methods?

This question is raised by Miles and Huberman (1984) who suggest that qualitative researchers have a range of options in how far they use what the authors call 'prior instrumentation' (i.e. predefined methods and measures):

- *No prior instrumentation*: fieldwork must be open to unsuspected phenomena which may be concealed by prior instrumentation; all you really need are 'some orienting questions, some headings for observations [and] a rough and ready document analysis form' (1984: 42).

- *Considerable prior instrumentation*: if the research is not focused, you will gather superfluous data; using measures from earlier studies allows for comparability.

- *An open question*: exploratory studies need to be far less structured than confirmatory studies; if your sample size is very small then cross-case comparison will be more limited and, therefore, the need for standardized research instruments will be less.

Miles and Huberman show that, although prior structuring of a research design is more common in quantitative studies, such structuring is worth considering in more qualitative work. For instance, in my study of HIV-test counselling (Silverman, 1997), I was able to begin with a prior hypothesis about the consequences of different kinds of advice-giving based on a recent research study which also applied CA to audio-recorded data (Heritage and Sefi, 1992).

If, as in this case, there is a previous study upon which you can base your research, a qualitative study can be highly structured. So what Miles and Huberman call 'no prior instrumentation' should not be regarded as the default option for non-quantitative research. An early decision about your preferred methods is often preferable.

Methods are linked to methodologies and to society

8.3.2 Most research methods can be used in research based on either qualitative or quantitative methodologies. This is shown in Table 8.1. The table underlines my earlier point that methods are techniques which take on a specific meaning according to the methodology in which they are used. All this means that we need to resist treating research methods as mere *techniques*.

To take just one example, although quantitative researchers have tried to establish quantifiable, standardized observation schedules, observation is not generally seen as a very important method of data collection in quantitative research. This is because it is difficult to conduct observational studies on large samples. Quantitative researchers also argue that observation is not a very reliable data collection method because different observers may record different observations. If used at all, observation is held to be only appropriate at a preliminary or 'exploratory' stage of research.

Conversely, observational studies have been fundamental to much qualitative research. Beginning with the pioneering case studies of non-Western societies by early anthropologists (Malinowski, 1922; Radcliffe-Brown, 1948) and continuing with the

TABLE 8.1 Different uses for four methods

| Method | Methodology | |
	Quantitative research	Qualitative research
Observation	Preliminary work, e.g. prior to framing questionnaire	Fundamental to understanding another culture
Textual analysis	Content analysis, i.e. counting in terms of researchers' categories	Understanding participants' categories
Interviews	'Survey research': mainly fixed-choice questions to random samples	'Open-ended' questions to small samples
Transcripts	Used infrequently to check the accuracy of interview records	Used to understand how participants organize their talk and body movements

Source: Silverman, 2006: 19

work by sociologists in Chicago prior to the Second World War (Hughes, 1984), the observational method has often been the chosen method to understand another **culture** or **subculture**.

But there is a broader, societal context in which methods are located and deployed. As a crude example, texts depended upon the invention of the printing press or, in the case of television or audio-recordings, upon modern communication technologies.

Moreover, such activities as observation and interviewing are not unique to social researchers. For instance, as Foucault (1977) has noted, the observation of the prisoner has been at the heart of modern prison reform, while the method of questioning used in the interview reproduces many of the features of the Catholic confessional or the psychoanalytic consultation. Its pervasiveness is reflected by the centrality of the interview study in so much contemporary social research. Think, for instance, of how much interviews are a central (and popular) feature of mass media products, from 'talk shows' to 'celebrity interviews'. Perhaps we all live in what might be called an **interview society** in which interviews seem central to making sense of our lives (see Atkinson and Silverman, 1997).

This broader societal context may explain qualitative researchers' temptation to use methods such as the interview. Of course, such a link between culture and method should be an opportunity to question ourselves about our methodological preferences. However, such self-questioning (sometimes, mistakenly I think, referred to as **reflexivity**) does not itself provide a warrant for the choices we make. As I argue in Chapters 15 and 16, such a warrant depends on the robustness and credibility of our research design.

Models shape the meaning of methods

8.3.3 Most qualitative researchers believe that they can provide a 'deeper' understanding of social phenomena than would be obtained from

TABLE 8.2 Methods and models of qualitative research

Method	Model I	Model II
Observation	'Background' material	Understanding of 'subcultures'
Texts and documents	'Background' material	Understanding of language and other sign systems
Interviews	Understanding 'experience'	Narrative construction
Audio- and video-recording	Little used	Understanding how interaction is organized

purely quantitative data. However, such purportedly 'deep' understanding arises in qualitative researchers' claims to have entered and mapped very different territories such as 'inner experiences', 'language', 'narratives', 'sign systems' or 'forms of social interaction'. Some of these claims associated with different qualitative models are set out in Table 8.2.

Each activity shown in Table 8.2 is not neutral but depends upon an implied model of how social reality works. In this table, I have simplified different approaches into just two models. However, in terms of Gubrium and Holstein's (1997) four **idioms** discussed in Chapter 7, **naturalists** give priority to understanding 'subcultures', **emotionalists** favour understanding 'experience' and focus on the open-ended interview, **ethnomethodologists** prefer to understand 'interaction' and **postmoderns** prioritize sign systems.

Such idioms or models are a necessary but not sufficient warrant for a claim that any given research method has been properly used. So a purely theoretical warrant does not guarantee that a method will be appropriately used in a particular data analysis.

Choosing an appropriate method

8.3.4 There are no right or wrong methods. There are only methods that are appropriate to your research topic and the model with which you are working.

Let us take two contrasting examples from Chapter 4. Tippi was interested in the experience of living in a community of elderly people. Her concept of 'experience' clearly derives from an emotionalist model. This makes her choice of open-ended interviews entirely appropriate. By contrast, if she were interested instead in how people *behave* in such a community, this naturalist topic might have suggested that she should use observational methods.

Anne's research was concerned with how a narrative changes as it is moved from book to television or radio. Her intention to observe what happens during the process of production sounds like a highly appropriate method for this topic. However, she also wanted to interview the participants to understand their motivation.

The problem here is the potential conflict within her research design between emotionalist and naturalist models. If she primarily wants to understand behaviours, then the naturalist stress on observation makes most sense. By contrast, if 'experience' and 'motivation' are really her thing, then she should stick with the interview method. This argument is developed in my discussion of 'multiple methods' below.

| **TIP**

Sometimes it makes sense to think laterally and to combine methods and models. But the safest option for most apprentice researchers is to keep it simple and to have a straightforward fit between your topic, method and model.

8.4 Choosing a Methodology: a Case Study

What follows next is an extended discussion of one case. It shows how I encountered these issues in designing my study of HIV-test counselling (Silverman, 1997).

8.4.1 Studying counselling

The counselling study discussed here emerged out of my work as a medical sociologist. Between 1979 and 1985, I worked on data from British outpatient consultations which involved parents and children. At the same time, I also conducted a small study of adult oncology clinics, comparing National Health Service (NHS) and private consultations conducted by the same doctor. This research was reported in a number of papers (Silverman, 1981; 1983; 1984; Silverman and Bloor, 1989) and brought together in a book (Silverman, 1987). In that book, I focused on how apparently 'patient-centred' medicine can work in many different directions.

In 1987, I was given permission to sit in at a weekly clinic held at the genito-urinary department of an English inner-city hospital (Silverman, 1989). The clinic's purpose was to monitor the progress of HIV-positive patients who were taking the drug AZT (Retrovir). AZT, which seems able to slow down the rate at which the virus reproduces itself, was then at an experimental stage of its development.

Like any observational study, the aim was to gather first-hand information about social processes in a **naturally occurring** context. No attempt was made to interview the individuals concerned because the focus was upon what they actually did in the clinic rather than upon what they thought about what they did. The researcher was present in the consulting room at a side angle to both doctors and patient.

Patients' consent for the researcher's presence was obtained by the senior doctor. Given the presumed sensitivity of the occasion, tape-recording was not attempted. Instead, detailed handwritten notes were kept, using a separate sheet for each consultation. The sample was small (15 male patients seen in 37 consultations over seven clinic sessions) and no claims were made about its representativeness. Because observational methods were rare in this area, the study was essentially exploratory.

However, as we shall see, an attempt was made to link the findings to other social research about doctor–patient relations.

As Sontag (1979) has noted, illness is often taken as a moral or psychological metaphor. The major finding of this early study was the moral baggage attached to being HIV-positive. For instance, many patients used a buzzer to remind them to take their medication during the night. As one commented, 'It's a dead giveaway. Everybody knows what you've got.'

However, despite the social climate in which HIV infection is viewed, there was considerable variation in how people presented themselves to the medical team. Four styles of 'self-presentation' (Goffman, 1959) were identified which I called 'cool', 'anxious', 'objective' and 'theatrical' (Silverman, 1989). But there was no simple correspondence between each patient and a particular 'style' of self-presentation. Rather each way of presenting oneself was available to each patient within any one consultation, where it might have a particular social function. So the focus was on social processes rather than on psychological states.

Along the way, I also discovered how an ethos of 'positive thinking' was central to many patients' accounts and how doctors systematically concentrated on the 'bodies' rather than the 'minds' of their patients. This led on to some practical questions about the division of labour between doctors and counsellors.

About the time I was writing up this research, Kaye Wellings, who then was working for the publicly funded Health Education Authority (HEA), approached me about the possibility of extending my research to HIV counselling. Until that time, the HEA had been funding research on the effectiveness of 'safer sex' messages carried in the mass media. In the light of the explosion in the number of HIV tests in the UK in the late 1980s, Kaye thought it might be useful to take a longer look at the effectiveness of the health promotion messages being delivered in counselling people around the HIV antibody test.

I was interested in such a study for two reasons. First, it was the logical development of my study of medical interviews with AIDS patients. Second, it offered the opportunity to pursue my interest in looking at how communication between professionals and their clients worked out in practice – as opposed to the injunctions of textbooks and training manuals. Consequently, I submitted a research proposal and received funding from the HEA for 30 months beginning in late 1988.

The quantitative bias

8.4.2 John McLeod has reminded us that 'almost all counselling and psychotherapy research has been carried out from the discipline of psychology' (1994: 190). One consequence has been a focus on quantitative studies concerned with the attributes of individuals. This has meant that linguistic and sociological issues, such as language use and social context, have been downplayed (see Heaton, 1979).

Such a psychological focus has also had an impact on research design, leading to the dominance of experimental and/or statistical methods favoured in psychology. Of course, no research method is intrinsically better than any other; everything

TABLE 8.3   Three familiar methodologies for counselling research

1   Measuring clients' response to counselling by means of research interviews which elicit their knowledge and reported behaviour. This would involve a longitudinal study, following a cohort of patients. The study could have either an experimental or a non-experimental design
2   Measuring clients' response to counselling by means of objective behavioural indicators. This also would involve a longitudinal study, following a cohort of patients
3   Measuring the degree of fit between actual counselling practice and certain agreed **normative** standards of 'good counselling'

Source: Silverman, 1997: 16

will depend upon one's research objectives. So it is only a question of restoring a balance between different ways of conceiving counselling research.

In designing my research proposal, I therefore needed to balance two competing objectives:

• my desire to examine how HIV counselling worked in actual counsellor–client interviews

• having to adjust to a context in which most counselling research had been informed either by a quantitative methodology or by **normative** assumptions about what constitutes 'good' counselling.

Designing a methodology: three familiar options

8.4.3 Quantitative or normative approaches suggest three obvious ways of researching counselling, all of which appear to take seriously the demands of **validity** and **reliability**. These three methodologies are set out in Table 8.3.

In order to underline the methodological options that arise in the early stages of research design, I review each strategy below. As I do so, we will see that each raises both methodological and analytic questions. I shall suggest that, in terms of either or both of these groups of questions, none of these three strategies is entirely satisfactory.

The research interview

As already noted, this might have either an experimental or a non-experimental design.

In the experimental design, we might randomly assign clients to two groups. In group 1 the clients are counselled, while in group 2, the control group, no counselling is provided. Both groups are then interviewed about their knowledge of AIDS and how they intend to protect themselves against the disease. This interview is followed up, some months later, with a further interview examining their present behaviour compared to their reported behaviour prior to the experiment.

In the non-experimental design, existing counselling procedures are evaluated by a cohort of patients. Again, we might follow up a cohort some time later.

The advantage of such research designs is that they permit large-scale studies which generate apparently 'hard' data, seemingly based on unequivocal measures. However, a number of difficulties present themselves. Of course, I know that these problems are recognized by researchers who use such research instruments. In turn, they have ingenious methods for dealing with them. Let me list a few:

1   How seriously are we to take patients' accounts of their behaviour? Isn't it likely that clients will tend to provide answers which they think the counsellors and researchers will want to hear (see McLeod, 1994: 124–6)?

2   Doesn't the experimental design ignore the *organizational* context in which healthcare is delivered (e.g. relations between physicians and other staff, tacit theories of 'good counselling', resources available, staff turnover, etc.)? Such contexts may shape the nature and effectiveness of counselling in non-laboratory situations.

3   Even if we can overcome the practical and ethical problems of not providing, say, pre-test counselling to a control group, may not the experience of being allocated to a control group affect the reliability of our measures and the validity of our findings (see McLeod, 1994: 124)?

4   Don't both studies treat subjects as 'an aggregation of disparate individuals' who have no social interaction with one another (Bryman, 1988: 39)? As such, they give us little hold on how counselling is organized as a local, step-by-step social process and, consequently, we may suspect that we are little wiser about how counselling works in practice.

The non-experimental study may have either a quantitative or a qualitative design. In the latter case, we might expect to carry out a relatively small number of open-ended interviews in order 'to enter, in an empathic way, the lived experience of the person or group being studied' (McLeod, 1994: 89).

This pursuit of 'lived experience' means that many qualitative researchers favour the open-ended interview (see Chapter 16). Unfortunately, both the 'in-depth' accounts apparently provided by the 'open-ended' interview and the apparently unequivocal measures of information retention, attitude and behaviour that we obtain via laboratory or questionnaire methods have a tenuous basis in what people may be saying and doing in their everyday lives. Moreover, if our interest is in the relation of counselling to health-related behaviour, do such studies tell us how people actually talk with professionals and with each other as opposed to via responses to researchers' questions?

An example makes the point very well. At a meeting I attended in the 1990s of social scientists working on AIDS, much concern was expressed about the difficulty of recruiting a sample of the population prepared to answer researchers' questions about their sexual behaviour. As a result, it was suggested that a subsequent meeting should be convened at which we could swap tips about how to recruit such a sample.

Now, of course, this issue of recruiting a sample is basic to survey research. And, for potentially 'delicate' matters, like the elicitation of accounts of sexual behaviour, survey researchers are quite properly concerned about finding willing respondents.

At the same time, it is generally acknowledged that the best chance of limiting the spread of HIV may be by encouraging people to discuss their sexual practices with their partners. This implies something about the limits of interview-based research in this area. Such research necessarily focuses on finding people prepared to talk about their sexuality in an interview. However, it can say nothing about how talk about sexuality is organized in 'naturally occurring' environments such as talk between partners or, indeed, talk about sexuality in the context of real-time counselling interviews.

Behavioural indicators

This method seeks to elicit behavioural measures which reliably report the effectiveness of counselling. Its advantage is that, unlike the research interview, it does not depend upon potentially unreliable client perceptions and self-reports of behaviour and behavioural change. Moreover, by eliminating a concern with the information that clients may acquire from counselling, it takes on board the research that shows that acquired knowledge does not have any direct link with behavioural change.

In relation to HIV-test counselling, it was suggested to me by a senior physician at an AIDS unit in Sweden that an appropriate behavioural indicator is seroconversion (developing antibodies to the HIV virus). Presumably, then, we would need to study a cohort of patients who test seronegative and are counselled. We could then retest them after a further period, say 12 months, to establish what proportions from different counselling centres and with different counsellors have seroconverted. In this way, it would be claimed, we could measure the effectiveness of counselling in relation to promoting safer behaviour.

As already noted, the advantage of this approach is that it generates quantitative measures of behaviour which are apparently objective. However, like the research interview, its reliability also has serious shortcomings:

1 How do we know that the counselling alone is the variable that has produced the reported behaviour? Although we may be able to **control** for some gross **intervening variables** (like gender, age, sexual preference, drug use, etc.), it is likely that some non-measured variables may be associated with the reported behaviour (e.g. access to other sources of information, availability of condoms or clean injecting equipment, etc.).

2 *Ad hoc* decisions are often made about which part of a counselling interview should be assessed. The scope extends from one whole interview (or even several interviews with the same client) down to a micro-segment of one interview. The latter approach gains precision but with a loss of context. Such context is provided by studying whole interviews but at a likely loss of precision.

3 Even if such measures are reliable and precise, the result 'assesses only the presence or absence of a mode, and not the skilfulness with which it is delivered' (McLeod, 1994: 151).

Normative standards and outcomes

Such problems in attempts to use internal, normative standards of evaluation look even worse when viewed in the context of studies which seek to relate such measures to particular outcomes. As McLeod (1994) notes, one such study (Hill et al., 1988) found that only 1 per cent of variance in client responses was related to observed measures of counsellor behaviour!

The methodology chosen

8.4.4 It is now time to lay my cards on the table and to offer the alternative approach on which my research was based: **conversation analysis** (henceforth CA). CA, as we saw in the studies discussed in Chapters 3 and 4, is centrally concerned with the organization of talk, although its concern with social organization leads it to describe its subject matter as 'talk-in-interaction'.

Equally, counsellors, by definition, treat talk as a non-trivial matter. However, even if we concede the centrality of talk to social life, why should counselling researchers give priority to recording and transcribing talk? Given the usefulness of other kinds of data derived, say, from observations of behavioural change or interviews with clients, what is the special value of transcripts of tape-recordings of conversation?

One way to start to discuss this question is to think about how research based upon data which arise in subjects' day-to-day activities can seek to preserve the 'phenomenon' of interactions like counselling interviews. Although such **naturally occurring data** are never uncontaminated (for instance, they may need to be recorded and transcribed), they usually give us a very good clue about what participants do outside a research setting.

Conversely, in research interviews, as Heritage puts it: 'the verbal formulations of subjects are treated as an appropriate substitute for the observation of actual behaviour' (1984: 236). The temptation here is to treat respondents' formulations as reflections of some pre-existing social or psychological world.

However, even when counselling researchers contemplate tape-recording actual interactions, they sometimes become easily deflected away from the counselling session itself. For instance, although McLeod calls for a study of 'the interior of therapy', he also cites favourably attempts at 'interpersonal process recall' where participants are played back the tape 'to restimulate the actual experience the person had during the session' (1994: 147). Thus, in common with many qualitative researchers, what matters for McLeod is what people think and feel rather than what they do.

However, if we follow this temptation in designing a study of counselling, then we deny something that all counsellors recognize: namely, that talk is itself an activity. Although this is recognized in many normative versions of counselling, to base our research on such versions would be to narrow our focus to those activities which we already know about.

An alternative is to investigate how counselling interviews actually proceed without being shackled by normative standards of 'good' communication. In this way, we might discover previously unnoticed skills of both counsellors and clients as well as the communicational 'functions' of apparently 'dysfunctional' counsellor behaviour.

Summary and implications

8.4.5 In this section, I have used the case of a study of HIV counselling to illustrate several options that are available in designing a qualitative study. I did not want to imply that a CA study of counselling interviews is the 'one right method'. Instead, I wanted to demonstrate that choosing a particular method always has more implications than you might think. I have shown here how those implications encompass preferred analytical models, questions of reliability and validity and, in this particular case, relevance for professional practice.

 ■ **Attempt Exercise 8.1** ▬▬▬▬▬▬▬▬▬▬▬▬

To follow up this point, you should attempt Exercise 8.1 now.

In developing my research design in this study, I took a position on two issues that need further discussion: I chose to study behaviour *in situ* (i.e. naturally occurring data), and I rejected combining multiple methods. This reflected my own preferences. Since other choices can (rightfully) be made by others, it is worth reviewing both issues.

Naturally Occurring Data?

8.5 Some qualitative researchers prefer to avoid creating data through setting up particular 'artificial' research environments like interviews, experiments, **focus groups** or survey questionnaires. They argue that, since so many data occur 'naturally' (i.e. without the intervention of a researcher), why not study those data and, thereby, access what people are routinely up to without, say, being asked by a researcher? To those who argue that such access can be difficult, the answer is that lateral thinking can move you into areas which *are* accessible.

For instance, to use an example raised by someone at a recent talk I gave, we might think that how couples negotiate the consequences of their different sleeping patterns can only be elicited by interviewing those involved. However, if indeed this is a real problem to members of society, it should crop up say in the advice or letters pages of certain magazines. Why not try looking for actual instances first, before resorting to interviews?

Moreover, the problem with methods like interviews and (to some extent) focus groups is that the researcher has to set things up by asking questions of respondents. By contrast, the beauty of naturally occurring data is that they may show us things we could never imagine. As Harvey Sacks once put it: 'Thus we can start with things that are not currently imaginable, by showing that they happened' (1992, Vol. 2: 420).

Although I am highly sympathetic to this argument, it also has limitations (see Speer, 2002). For instance:

- Data cannot be intrinsically unsatisfactory; it all depends on what you want to do with them.

- No data can be 'untouched by human hands' (e.g. recording equipment is sometimes present and this has to be positioned by a researcher).

- The difference between what is 'natural' and 'non-natural' should be investigated rather than used as a tacit research resource.

These are powerful arguments. However, rather than abandon my preference, I prefer to take a non-dogmatic position. This involves the following two elements:

- Everything depends on your research topic. So, as Speer notes, if you want to study how counselling gets done, it may not make sense to seek retrospective accounts from clients and practitioners or to use a laboratory study.

- We need to consider how far any research setting is *consequential* for our research topic. For instance in one lab study, limitations were placed on who could speak. This made the experimental setting consequential for its topic (of 'self-repair') and undercut its conclusions (Schegloff, 1991: 54). Without such limitations, the study would have been sound.

To conclude: choosing any method, based on any kind of data, can never be intrinsically right or wrong. However, as a non-emotionalist, I am sympathetic to Jonathan Potter's argument that, given the (unthought?) dominance of open-ended interviews in qualitative research:

> the justificatory boot might be better placed on the other foot. The question is not why should we study natural materials, but why should we not? (2002: 540)

Multiple Methods?

8.6 So far I have been assuming that you will always want to choose just one method. However, the methods presented in Table 8.2 are often combined. For instance, many qualitative case-studies combine observation with interviewing. This may be because you have several research questions or 'because you want to use different methods or sources to corroborate each other so that you are using some form of methodological triangulation' (Mason, 1996: 25).

For instance, Miles and Huberman (1984: 42) give the example of research on how police suspects are arrested and booked. You might think here of combining several methods, e.g.

- interviews (with suspects, police and lawyers)

- observation (of arrests and bookings)

- collecting documents (produced by this process)

- recording (of arrests and bookings).

If you are a pure **empiricist**, uninterested in the theoretical bases of research design, multiple methods may look like a good idea. By having a cumulative view of data drawn from different contexts, we may, as in trigonometry, be able to **triangulate** the 'true' state of affairs by examining where the different data intersect. In this way, some qualitative researchers believe that triangulation may improve the reliability of a single method. Take the following example of a well-designed student research project which uses multiple methods.

STUDENT EXAMPLES

Citizenship in a Multicultural Society

My PhD project is focusing on citizenship and feminism, and asks how feminism, ethnic identity and religion are brought together in the policies of women's movements and in the daily lives of women. [I will use three sets of data:]

- qualitative interviews with members of selected minority and majority women's organizations in Norway

- interviews with civil servants/bureaucrats in national government departments and representatives from national political parties

- analysis of relevant policy documents: selected periodic reports to the UN, government action plans, green and white papers on gender equality and discrimination policy and violence against women.

By combining the interviews and the document analysis, my aim is to explore whether ethnic minority women's demands have been rejected and resisted or embraced and accepted by the majority women's organizations, and how the political opportunity structure works in regard to their influence on the government's policy making. [Cecilie Thun, Sociology and Women's Studies, Oslo]

Cecilie's multi-method study is likely to provide rich data on private and public perceptions of gender and ethnicity. However, before you consider using multiple methods, I should sound two warning notes:

- Have you got the time and resources to gather and to analyse multiple datasets? Isn't there a danger that one or other of your datasets will be under-analysed?

- Have you thought through the issues involved in trying to establish the 'true' state of affairs by comparing data from different sources? In Cecilie's case, may not both the documents and the interviews with organizational leaders tell you more about the *rhetoric* of women's rights than about the reality?

As I remarked in Chapter 4, 'mapping' one set of data upon another is a more or less complicated task depending on your analytic framework. In particular, if you treat social reality as constructed in different ways in different contexts, then you cannot appeal to a single 'phenomenon' which all your data apparently represent (see Chapter 15).

Mason (1996: 27) gives the example of the mistaken attempt to combine (say) interview data on individuals' perceptions with **discourse analysis** (DA) of particular texts. The mistake arises because DA treats all accounts as socially constructed and, therefore, cannot treat interview accounts as providing a definitive version of reality.

Such triangulation of data seeks to overcome the context boundedness of our materials at the cost of analysing their sense in context. For the purposes of certain kinds of social research, particularly that based on a **constructionist** model, it is simply not useful to conceive of an overarching reality to which data, gathered in different contexts, approximate.

At the very least, we need to note Fielding and Fielding's (1986) suggestion that the use of triangulation should operate according to ground rules:

- Always begin from a theoretical perspective or model.

- Choose methods and data which will give you an account of structure and meaning from within that perspective (e.g. by showing the structural contexts of the interactions studied).

Many theoretical perspectives in sociology and elsewhere suggest we cannot simply aggregate data in order to arrive at an overall 'truth'. This implies that we should receive with caution the clarion calls for multiple methods in areas like nursing, family medicine and elsewhere. As Hammersley and Atkinson point out: 'One should not adopt a naively "optimistic" view that the aggregation of data from different sources will unproblematically add up to produce a more complete picture' (1983: 199).

As already noted in Chapter 4, multiple methods are often adopted in the mistaken hope that they will reveal 'the whole picture'. But this 'whole picture' is an illusion which speedily leads to scrappy research based on under-analysed data and an imprecise or theoretically indigestible research problem. For instance, multiple methods may tempt novice researchers to move to another dataset when they are having difficulties in analysing one set of material. It is usually far better to celebrate the partiality of your data and delight in the particular phenomena that it allows you to inspect (hopefully in detail).

■ LINK ■

Giampietro Gobo's book *Doing Ethnography* (2008: Ch. 5) is an excellent treatment of designing qualitative research. For the website connected to this chapter look up Chapter 5 on:

http://www.sagepub.co.uk/gobo/resources

Concluding Remarks

8.7
The debate about multiple methods and naturally occurring data illustrates the theoretically laden environment in which we make methodological choices. It underlines the fact that many apparently technical choices are saturated with theoretical import.

Of course, to some extent this complicates the picture when you are attempting to design a research study. However, a concern at this stage with theoretical issues also helps in at least two ways. First, it may allow you to simplify your research design as you realize that it is often misleading to attempt to research 'the whole picture'. Second, thereby, it may add theoretical consistency and even some elegance to the research design. As I remarked in Part One, often the best research says 'a lot about a little'.

KEY POINTS

- Your choice of method should reflect both your research topic and your overall research strategy as your methodology shapes which methods are used and how each method is used.

- Although most research methods can be used in either qualitative or quantitative studies, research methods are more than mere *techniques*. Different theoretical idioms or models provide different justifications for using particular research methods.

- Methods do not just belong to social researchers. Before choosing a method, you should reflect upon the broader societal context in which this method is located and deployed.

- Think carefully before you generate data through research instruments like interviews and focus groups. Sometimes such methods may indeed be appropriate to your topic and model. Sometimes, however, you may be neglecting to study illuminating, naturally occurring data.

- Think carefully before adopting multiple methods. Many models suggest that we cannot simply aggregate data in order to arrive at an overall 'truth'. Choose simplicity and rigour rather than the often illusory search for the 'full picture'.

My recent book *A Very Short, Fairly Interesting, Reasonably Cheap Book about Qualitative Research* (Sage, 2007) discusses many of the key issues in methodology. Many of these topics are given a different twist in Martyn Hammersley's *Questioning Qualitative Inquiry* (Sage, 2008). David Silverman's edited *Qualitative Research: Theory, Method and Practice* (second edition, Sage, 2004) provides state-of-the-art accounts by leading scholars of the uses of interviews, observations, texts, Internet data, and audio and visual data. Other useful books on methodology are: Amanda Coffey and Paul Atkinson's *Making Sense of Qualitative Data* (Sage, 1996); Jennifer Mason's *Qualitative Researching* (second edition, Sage, 2002); Pertti Alasuutari's *Researching Culture* (Sage, 1995); and David Silverman's *Interpreting Qualitative Data: Methods for Analysing Talk, Text and Interaction* (third edition, Sage, 2006).

■ **Exercise 8.1**

Mason (1996: 19) notes that your choice of a methodology is likely to reflect your own biography and the knowledge and training your education has given you. As she comments: 'Whilst practical issues to do with training and skill are ... relevant in your choice of method ... they should not govern your choice' (1996: 19). She suggests instead making a list of possible research methods and data source options and thinking through why you are accepting or rejecting each one.

1 Follow Mason's suggestion about making a list of possible research methods and data source options. Explain why you are accepting or rejecting each one.

2 Answer the following questions (adapted from Mason, 1996: 20–1):

- What data sources and methods of data generation are potentially available or appropriate?

- What can these methods and sources feasibly tell me?

- Which phenomena and components or properties of social 'reality' might these data sources and methods potentially help me to address?

- Which of my research questions could they help me to address?

9

Selecting a Case

Chapter Objectives

By the end of this chapter, you will be able to:

- **Understand what a case study is.**

- **Know the main types of case study.**

- **Understand how to generalize from a single case.**

Introduction

9.1 I concluded the previous chapter with my favourite research maxim: 'make a lot out of a little'. If you take me seriously, you will have every chance of producing a thorough, analytically interesting research study. However, at least three nagging doubts may well remain. I list them below together with some soothing words about each.

- *My case may not be important.* Here you are worried that the case you are studying may be seen by others as 'trivial' or 'not a real problem'. The famous ethnographer Howard Becker (1998) remarks that such criticisms have been made of his own work on several occasions. As he puts it: 'Just as some people think tragedy is more important than comedy … some problems are seen as inherently serious and worthy of grownup attention, others as trivial, flyspecks on the wallpaper of life … mere exotica' (1998: 92). There is a very good response to this kind of complaint, namely: what seems to be important is usually governed by little more than current fashions; who knows what might become important? Apparently trivial cases may, through, good analysis, turn out to have far-reaching implications.

- *I can only study the (part of the) case to which I have access.* This is a more serious issue. When we are studying an organization, we are dependent on the whims of gatekeepers. Such people will usually seek to limit what we can study, assuring us that, if we need to know more, they can tell us about it (1998: 90). How do we get round this problem? Becker suggests two answers: first, 'doubt everything anyone in power tells you'; second, look for other opinions (1998: 91). Like Dalton (1959), in his classic study of middle managers, case study researchers should systematically attempt to assess the likely linkages between opinions, activities and interests.

- *I have so little data, just one case.* This is a more serious problem. As we shall see below, even in qualitative research it is important to consider what kind of generalizations can be made from a single case.

The rest of this chapter will be devoted to the issue of **generalizability** in case study research. First, however, we need to define both 'case study' and 'generalizability'.

What Is a Case Study?

9.2

This question has a relatively simple answer. As Keith Punch puts it:

> The basic idea is that one case (or perhaps a small number of cases) will be studied in detail, using whatever methods seem appropriate. While there may be a variety of specific purposes and research questions, the general objective is to develop as full an understanding of that case as possible. (1998: 150)

There are, of course, an endless variety of possible 'cases'. If, like Becker, we are interested in occupations, cases to study may range from dancehall musicians to student physicians. By contrast, if you are interested in childhood, a case may be a single child, a classroom or clinic, or a charity or other organization concerned with the welfare of children. So, as Stake suggests: 'A case may be simple or complex … [but] it is one among others. In any given study, we will concentrate on the one' (2000: 436).

All this is purely descriptive. Table 9.1 identifies three analytic features of case study research.

TABLE 9.1 Case study research

1 Each case has boundaries which must be identified at an early stage of the research (e.g. if you are studying a school, whether this includes classroom behaviour, staff meetings, parent–teacher meetings, etc.)
2 Each case will be a case of something in which the researcher is interested. So the unit of analysis must be defined at the outset in order to clarify the research strategy
3 Case studies seek to preserve the wholeness and integrity of the case. However, in order to achieve some focus, a limited research problem must be established that is geared to specific features of the case

Source: adapted from K. Punch, 1998: 153

Generalizing from Cases

9.3 Generalizability is a standard aim in quantitative research and is normally achieved by statistical sampling procedures. Such **sampling** has two functions. First, it allows you to feel confident about the representativeness of your sample: 'If the population characteristics are known, the degree of representativeness of a sample can be checked' (Arber, 1993: 70). Second, such representativeness allows you to make broader inferences: 'The purpose of sampling is usually to study a representative subsection of a precisely defined population in order to make inferences about the whole population' (1993: 38).

Such sampling procedures are, however, usually unavailable in qualitative research. In such studies, our data are often derived from one or more cases and it is unlikely that these cases will have been selected on a random basis. Very often a case will be chosen simply because it allows access. Moreover, even if you were able to construct a representative sample of cases, the sample size would be likely to be so large as to preclude the kind of intensive analysis usually preferred in qualitative research (Mason, 1996: 91).

This gives rise to a problem, familiar to users of quantitative methods: 'How do we know ... how representative case study findings are of all members of the population from which the case was selected?' (Bryman, 1988: 88).

Types of Case Studies

9.4 Robert Stake (2000: 437–8) has identified three different types of case study:

1 The *intrinsic case study* where 'this case is of interest ... in all its particularity and ordinariness'. In the intrinsic case study, according to Stake, no attempt is made to generalize beyond the single case or even to build theories.
2 The *instrumental case study* in which a case is examined mainly to provide insight into an issue or to revise a generalization. Although the case selected is studied in depth, the main focus is on something else.
3 The *collective case study* where a number of cases are studied in order to investigate some general phenomenon.

The idea of a purely *intrinsic case study* is resisted by many qualitative researchers. If all you aim to do is simply to 'describe a case', you may rightly get the response: 'So what?' Such scepticism arises from the following concerns:

- Description is a tricky activity which is inevitably theoretically laden (if you doubt this, you might look back at Table 7.1).
- To call something a 'case' implies that it is a case of 'something'; so we can only understand the distinctiveness of a case by making theoretical assumptions about what is typical for a certain population.

- Given how behaviour varies in different contexts, we need to understand how any one setting may be different from others (see Gobo, 2008: 97–8).

In this context, most supervisors of student qualitative research would expect your study of a case to be based upon some concept(s) which are developed as a result of your study. For examples of concept development through case study research, see Chapter 3.

Furthermore, empirical issues arise in case studies just as much as theoretical concerns. It is reasonable to ask what knowledge your case study has produced. If you are to answer this question, you must consider the degree of generalizability of your research. As Jennifer Mason puts it:

> I do not think qualitative researchers should be satisfied with producing explanations which are idiosyncratic or particular to the limited empirical parameters of their study ... Qualitative research should [therefore] produce explanations which are *generalizable* in some way, or which have a wider resonance. (1996: 6)

So description of a case for description's sake (the *intrinsic* case study) is a weak position. Quite rightly, the problem of 'representativeness' is a perennial worry of many qualitative or case study researchers. How do they attempt to address it? Can we generalize from cases to populations without following a purely statistical logic?

In the rest of this chapter, I will discuss four different but positive answers to this question of how we can obtain generalizability:

- combining qualitative research with quantitative measures of populations
- purposive sampling guided by time and resources
- theoretical sampling
- using an analytic model which assumes that generalizability is present in the existence of *any* case.

Combining Qualitative Research with Quantitative Measures of Populations

9.5 Quantitative measures may sometimes be used to infer from one case to a larger population. Hammersley (1992) suggests three methods through which we can attempt to generalize from the analysis of a single case:

- obtaining information about relevant aspects of the population of cases and comparing our case to them
- using survey research on a random sample of cases
- coordinating several ethnographic studies.

Hammersley argues that such comparisons with a larger sample may allow us to establish some sense of the representativeness of our single case.

However, two of Hammersley's methods are very ambitious for the student researcher. For instance, you are unlikely to have the funds for even a small piece of survey research, while the coordination of several ethnographic studies requires substantial resources of time and personnel as well as good contacts with other researchers. Such contacts allowed Miller and Silverman (1995) to apply the comparative approach in describing talk about troubles in two counselling settings: a British haemophilia centre counselling patients who are HIV-positive, and a family therapy centre in the US. In this study, we focused on similarities in three types of discursive practices in these settings: those concerned with trouble definitions, trouble remedies, and the social contexts of the clients' troubles (see also Gubrium, 1992).

Without such contacts and resources, the student researcher is left with Hammersley's first method: obtaining information about relevant aspects of the population of cases and comparing our case to them. This is more useful because, at its simplest, this method only involves reading about other cognate studies and comparing our case to them. For instance, in my study of HIV counselling (Silverman, 1997) I compared my counsellor–client interviews to Heritage and Sefi's (1992) data on interviews between health visitors and first-time mothers. Although this had little to do with establishing the representativeness of my sample, it gave a firmer basis to my generalizations about advice sequences in my data (1997: 124–8). The comparative method used here allows you to make larger claims about your analysis without leaving your library. As Peräkylä puts it:

> The comparative approach directly tackles the question of generalizability by demonstrating the similarities and differences across a number of settings. (2004: 296)

In this sense, your literature review (see Chapter 18) has as much to do with the issue of generalizability as with displaying your academic credentials.

Purposive Sampling

9.6 Before we can contemplate comparing our case to others, we need to have selected our case. Are there any grounds other than convenience or accessibility to guide us in this selection?

Purposive sampling allows us to choose a case because it illustrates some feature or process in which we are interested. However, this does not provide a simple approval to any case we happen to choose. Rather, purposive sampling demands that we think critically about the parameters of the population we are studying and choose our sample case carefully on this basis. As Denzin and Lincoln put it: 'Many qualitative researchers employ ... purposive, and not random, sampling methods. They seek out groups, settings and individuals where ... the processes being studied are most likely to occur' (1994: 202).

TABLE 9.2 A typology of children's museums

	Type of museum		
Programme type	Art	Science	History
Exhibitory	1	2	3
Participative	4	5	6

Source: adapted from Stake, 2000: 446–7

Stake (2000: 446–7) gives the example of a study of interactive displays in children's museums. He assumes that you only have resources to study four such museums. How should you proceed? He suggests setting up a *typology* which would establish a matrix of museum types as in Table 9.2. The typology yields six cases which could be increased further by, say, distinguishing between museums located in small and big cities – bringing up the cases to 12. Which cases should you select?

You will be constrained by two main factors. First, there may not be examples to fit every cell. Second, your resources will not allow you to research every existing unit. So you have to make a practical decision. For instance, if you can cover only two cases, do you choose two participatory museums in different locations or in different subjects? Or do you compare such a museum with a more conventional exhibit-based museum?

As a student researcher, your limited time and resources will usually determine how you settle these questions. However, the very fact that you have asked yourself these questions will satisfy most examiners.

┌─── **TIP** ┌───────────────────────────────────

When designing your research, resist the assumption that qualitative research merely describes a single case. Then adopt the simplest design that will allow you properly to address your research question(s).

Take the case of the mathematics teacher I met in Tanzania who was trying to design a qualitative study to discover what made maths lessons 'effective'. We came up with two factors that might be important here:

- the teaching style used (loosely 'traditional' or 'non-traditional')
- background features (school resources, staff turnover, parental support) which were likely to make maths lessons more or less 'effective'.

This suggested a simple 2 × 2 purposive sample as set out in Table 9.3. The simplicity of the research design set out in the table made for a study that showed the necessary critical thinking about the research problem and was achievable within the constraints of time and resources.

TABLE 9.3 A typology of mathematics lessons

		Teaching methods	
		Traditional	**Non-traditional**
Background	Favourable	1	2
	Unfavourable	3	4

However, in thinking through issues of sampling, we are following our quantitative colleagues. Before reading on, think what this student might gain from using a qualitative perspective on each of his 'cells'.

My answer to this question arises from the way in which the analytical models we use in qualitative research allow us to problematize matters that our quantitative colleagues may be compelled to take for granted or to settle prior to the commencement of research. In the context of this study, although our sample will be based upon prior assumptions, we can problematize:

- whether the categories 'traditional' and 'non-traditional' do justice to the variety of lessons we observe in the classroom

- what 'effective' education looks like in different contexts, so that we can go beyond scoring examination performance in each cell to considering how 'effectiveness' may be used as a rhetoric in settings as diverse as parent–teacher meetings, teacher promotion reviews and government documents.

In both cases, the beauty of qualitative research design is that it allows us to put 'scare marks' around apparently 'objective' concepts such as 'effectiveness'.

This shows that how you set up your typology and make your choice between cases should be grounded in the theoretical apparatus you are using. Sampling in qualitative research is neither statistical nor purely personal: it is, or should be, theoretically grounded.

 ■ **Attempt Exercise 9.1**

To improve your understanding of this point, you could now attempt Exercise 9.1.

Theoretical Sampling

9.7
Theoretical and purposive sampling are often treated as synonyms. Indeed, the only difference between the two procedures applies when the 'purpose' behind 'purposive' sampling is not theoretically defined. Bryman argues that qualitative research follows a theoretical, rather than a statistical, logic: 'The issue should be couched in terms of the generalizability of

cases to *theoretical* propositions rather than to *populations* or universes' (1988: 90, my emphasis).[1]

The nature of this link between sampling and theory is set out by Jennifer Mason:

> theoretical sampling means selecting groups or categories to study on the basis of their relevance to your research questions, your theoretical position ... and most importantly the explanation or account which you are developing. Theoretical sampling is concerned with constructing a sample ... which is meaningful theoretically, because it builds in certain characteristics or criteria which help to develop and test your theory and explanation. (1996: 93–4)

Theoretical sampling has three features which I discuss below:

- choosing cases in terms of your theory
- choosing 'deviant' cases
- changing the size of your sample during the research.

Choosing cases in terms of your theory

9.7.1 Mason writes about 'the wider universe of social explanations in relation to which you have constructed your research questions' (1996: 85). This theoretically defined universe 'will make some sampling choices more sensible and meaningful than others'. Mason describes choosing a kind of sample which can represent a wider population. Here we select a sample of particular 'processes, types, categories or examples which are relevant to or appear within the wider universe' (1996: 92). Mason suggests that examples of these would include single units such as 'an organization, a location, a document ... [or] a conversation'.

Mason gives the example of a **discourse analysis** of gender relation as discourses which construct subjects of gender relations. In this approach, as she puts it, 'You are ... unlikely to perceive the social world in terms of a large set of gender relations from which you can simply draw a representative sample of people by gender' (1996: 85).

So in qualitative research the relevant or 'sampleable' units are often seen as theoretically defined. This means that it is inappropriate to sample populations by such attributes as 'gender', 'ethnicity' or even age because how such attributes are routinely defined is itself the *topic* of your research.

As an example of theoretically defined sampling, Bryman uses Glaser and Strauss's discussion of 'awareness contexts' in relation to dying in hospital:

> The issue of whether the particular hospital studied is 'typical' is not the critical issue; what is important is whether the experiences of dying patients are typical of the broad class of phenomena ... to which the theory refers. Subsequent research would then focus on the validity of the proposition in other milieux (e.g. doctors' surgeries). (1988: 91)

We can understand better the theoretical logic behind choice of a sample in a further example of a study of policework. Say you are interested in the arrest and booking of suspects (see Miles and Huberman, 1984: 37–8). You are now confronted with a series of choices which relate to:

- the particular setting to be studied
- the elements or processes on which you will focus
- how you might generalize further.

Let us look at each of these in turn.

Settings

In independent, unfunded research, you are likely to choose any setting which, while demonstrating the phenomenon in which you are interested, is accessible and will provide appropriate data reasonably readily and quickly. In the police study, this might well lead you to study the police station rather than a squad car, the scene of the crime, the suspect's residence or hangout. In the police station, at the very least, you will keep warm and dry, you will be safe and you can expect several arrests and bookings on any visit. However, so far you are being guided by quite practical influences.

The research focus

In focusing your research, you necessarily are making a theoretically guided choice. By opting to focus on particular individuals, events or processes, you are electing particular theoretical frameworks. For instance, a focus on differential behaviour between police officers and suspects with different characteristics may draw on some version of the structural determinants of action. Conversely, a focus on how laws are interpreted in practice (cf. Sudnow, 1968b) may derive from a concern with the creative power of common-sense interpretive procedures.

Generalizing further

When wedded to other studies which share your theoretical orientation, your research on a single police station may provide enough data to develop all the generalizations you want about, say, how common-sense reasoning works. However, if you have a more 'structural' bent, it may now be necessary to widen your sample in two ways: first, to add more observations of arrests in this police station; and second, to compare it with other stations, perhaps in a range of areas.

In all these cases, the sample is not random but theoretical. It is 'designed to provide a close-up, detailed or meticulous view of particular units which may constitute ... cases which are relevant to or appear within the wider universe' (Mason, 1996: 92).

As Kathy Charmaz argues, this kind of 'theoretical sampling directs you where to go' (2006: 100) when you need to make further generalizations from the cases you have already selected.

Choosing 'deviant' cases

9.7.2 Mason notes that you must overcome any tendency to select a case which is likely to support your argument. Instead, it makes sense to seek out negative instances as defined by the theory with which you are working.

> **TIP**
>
> When designing your research, it is useful to contemplate the kind of experiences or situations that you initially think are most unlikely. One of Howard Becker's 'tricks of the trade' is: 'Just to insist that nothing that can be imagined is impossible, so we should look for the most unlikely things that we can think of and incorporate their existence, or the possibility of their existence, into our thinking' (1998: 85–6).

For instance, in a study of the forces that may make trade unions undemocratic, Lipset et al. (1962) deliberately chose to study a US printing union. Because this union had unusually strong democratic institutions, it constituted a vital deviant case compared to most American unions of the period. Lipset et al.'s union was also deviant in terms of a highly respected theory which postulated an irresistible tendency towards 'oligarchy' in all formal organizations.

So Lipset et al. chose a deviant case because it offered a crucial test of a theory. As our understanding of social processes improves, we are increasingly able to choose cases on such theoretical grounds.

Changing the size of your sample during the research

9.7.3 So far we have been discussing theoretical sampling as an issue at the *start* of a research study. However, we can also apply such sampling during the course of a piece of research. Indeed, one of the strengths of qualitative research design is that it often allows for far greater (theoretically informed) flexibility than do most quantitative research designs. As Mason puts it:

> Theoretical or purposive sampling is a set of procedures where the researcher manipulates their analysis, theory, and sampling activities *interactively* during the research process, to a much greater extent than in statistical sampling. (1996: 100)

Such flexibility may be appropriate in the following cases:

- As new factors emerge you may want to increase your sample in order to say more about them (for instance, a **gatekeeper** has given you an explanation that you doubt on principle).

- You may want to focus on a small part of your sample in the early stages, using the wider sample for later tests of emerging generalizations.

- Unexpected generalizations in the course of data analysis lead you to seek out new deviant cases.

Alasuutari has described this process using the analogy of an hourglass:

> A narrow case-analysis is broadened ... through the search for contrary and parallel cases, into an example of a broader entity. Thus the research process advances, in its final stages, towards a discussion of broader entities. We end up on the bottom of the hourglass. (1995: 156)

Alasuutari (1995: 155) illustrates this hourglass metaphor through his own study of the social consequences of Finnish urbanization in the 1970s. He chose local pubs as a site to observe these effects and eventually focused upon male 'regulars'. This led to a second study even more narrowly focused on a group where drinking was heavier and where many of the men were divorced. As he puts it: 'Ethnographic research of this kind is not so much generalization as extrapolation ... the results are related to broader entities' (1995: 155).

Generalizability Is Present in a Single Case

9.8 The fourth and final way of thinking about how we generalize in qualitative research is far more radical than our earlier alternatives. According to this approach, since the basic structures of social order are to be found anywhere, it does not matter where we begin our research. Look at *any* case and you will find the same order.

For this linguistically inspired approach, the possibility something exists is enough. As Peräkylä suggests:

> Social practices that are possible, i.e., *possibilities of language use*, are the central objects of all conversation analytical case studies on interaction in particular institutional settings. The possibility of various practices can be considered generalizable even if the practices are not actualized in similar ways across different settings. (2004: 297)

Peräkylä illustrates his argument by the example of his own study of AIDS counselling in a London teaching hospital (Peräkylä, 1995). This study focused on specific questioning practices used by counsellors and their clients. As he puts it:

> As possibilities, the practices that I analyzed are very likely to be generalizable. There is no reason to think that they could not be made possible by any competent member of (at least any Western) society. In this sense, this study produced generalizable results. The results were not generalizable as descriptions of what other counsellors or other professionals do with their clients; but they were generalizable as descriptions of what any counsellor or other professional, with his or her clients, *can* do, given that he or she has the same array of interactional competencies as the participants of the AIDS counselling sessions have. (2004: 297)

As the most cogent proponent of this view once put it: 'tap into whomsoever, wheresoever and we get much the same things' (Sacks, 1984b: 22).

Sacks had a strategy of working with any data that crossed his path. This clearly conflicts both with the standard approach of quantitative social scientists, who usually work with random samples from particular populations, and with the common defensiveness of their qualitative brethren about the representativess of the cases that they study.

Sacks's lack of defensiveness on this issue stems from his argument about the obvious pervasiveness of the social forms (or what he calls the 'machinery') with which he is concerned. For example, Sacks notes the ability of a child to learn a culture from very limited contacts and of the sociolinguist Whorf to build a Navajo grammar from talking to just one person (1992, Vol. 1: 485).

For Sacks, the pervasiveness of structures which these examples suggest carry the implication that it does not matter what data you select. As he argues:

> Now if one figures that that's the way things are ... then it really wouldn't matter very much what it is you look at – if you look at it carefully enough. And you may well find that you [have] got an enormous generalizability because things are so arranged that you *could* get them; given that for a **member** encountering a very limited environment, he has to be able to do that, and things are so arranged as to permit him to. (1992, Vol. 1: 485, bold added)

However, apprentice researchers have to be very cautious about simply parroting Sacks's 'solution' to the problem of the generalizability of research findings. This solution is really only appropriate to the most basic research on social order guided by theoretically sophisticated positions like Sacks's own **conversation analytic** (CA) approach (or, perhaps, French **structuralism**).

 ■ Attempt Exercise 9.2

If you are interested in this sort of research, you should now attempt Exercise 9.2.

Within CA, following Sacks: 'The baseline assumption is that the results are or should be generalizable to the whole domain of ordinary conversations, and to a certain extent even across linguistic and cultural boundaries' (Peräkylä, 1995: 214). However, Peräkylä notes that even this depends on the type of CA research:

> Even though the most primordial conversational practices and structures – such as **turn-taking** or **adjacency pairs** – are almost universal, there are others, such as openings of telephone calls (see Schegloff, 1986; Houtkoop-Steenstra, 1991; Lindström, 1994), which show considerable variation in different cultures. This variation can only be tackled through gradual accumulation of studies on ordinary conversation in different cultures and social milieux. (1995: 156–7)

Peräkylä's observation about the need for comparative work shows that even the most potentially radical approach, like CA, has to take seriously the issue of the empirical generalizability of its findings. Sometimes, an appeal to 'possibilities' will be sufficient. Often, however, other examples will be required.

■ Attempt Exercise 9.3

■ LINK ■

For an excellent discussion of generalization from case study research, see Giampietro Gobo's *Doing Ethnography* (2008) Chapters 5 and 14 and the associated website at:

http://www.sagepub.co.uk/gobo/resources.htm

Concluding Remarks

9.9

In this chapter, I have set out various strategies which you can use to defend your research against the charge that it 'merely' depends upon a single case. My overall message is that there is usually no need to be defensive about the claims of qualitative research. As Howard Becker argues:

> Sampling is a major problem for any kind of research. We can't study every case of whatever we're interested in, nor should we want to. Every scientific enterprise tries to find out something that will apply to *everything* of a certain kind by studying *a few examples*, the results of the study being, as we say 'generalizable' to all members of that class of stuff. We need the sample to persuade people that we know something about the whole class. (1998: 67)

Following Becker, sampling is not a simple matter even for quantitative researchers. Indeed, as we have seen, the relative flexibility of qualitative research can improve the generalizability of our findings by allowing us to include new cases after initial findings are established.

The crucial issue here seems to be thinking through one's theoretical priorities. Providing that you have done that and can demonstrate a research design driven by those priorities, nobody should have cause for complaint.

So the secret seems to be to substitute theoretical cogency for the statistical language of quantitative research. In this sense, as Alasuutari (1995) has suggested, perhaps 'generalizability' is the wrong word to describe what we attempt to achieve in qualitative research. As he puts it:

> Generalization is ... [a] word ... that should be reserved for surveys only. What can be analyzed instead is how the researcher demonstrates that the analysis relates to things beyond the material at hand ... *extrapolation* better captures the typical procedure in qualitative research. (1995: 156–7)

KEY POINTS

There are four positive answers to the question of how we can generalize from qualitative data:

- combining qualitative research with quantitative measures of populations

- purposive sampling guided by time and resources

- theoretical sampling

- using an analytic model which assumes that generalizability is present in the existence of *any* case.

Note

1 As Clive Seale (personal correspondence) has pointed out, theoretical sampling may have more to do with generating theories than with empirical generalization. I take up Seale's point at the end of this chapter in relation to Alasuutari's argument that the idea of empirical generalization 'should be reserved for surveys only' (1995: 156).

■ ■ Further Reading ■

Seale, Gobo, Gubrium and Silverman's edited book *Qualitative Research Practice* (Sage, 2004: 420–72) contains three very useful chapters on case studies by Flyvberg, Gobo and Emerson. The most thorough book on this topic is Clive Seale's *The Quality of Qualitative Research* (Sage, 1999). For chapter length treatments of this topic, see Kathy Charmaz's excellent *Constructing Grounded Theory: A Practical Guide through Qualitative Analysis* (2006: 96–122). Other useful discussions are: Jennifer Mason's *Qualitative Researching* (second edition, Sage, 2002); Pertti Alasuutari's *Researching Culture* (Sage, 1995: Ch. 12); and Howard

Becker's *Tricks of the Trade* (University of Chicago Press, 1998: Ch. 3). Robert Stake's chapter 'Case studies' is a good account of the conventional qualitative methods position on generalizability (in N. Denzin and Y. Lincoln (eds), *Handbook of Qualitative Research*, Sage, 2000) and Anssi Peräkylä's chapter 'Reliability and validity in research based upon transcripts' is an excellent, more specialist treatment (in David Silverman (ed.), *Qualitative Research*, second edition, Sage, 2004).

 ■ **Exercise 9.1**

Assume that you are studying a single case. On what basis do you think you might generalize from your findings? Distinguish your possible empirical contribution from any potential development of concepts.

 ■ **Exercise 9.2**

Imagine that you have the resources to study *four* cases of the phenomenon in which you are interested. Following my discussion of Stake (Table 9.2), draw up a typology to indicate the universe of cases potentially available. This typology should include between six and 12 possible cases.

Now explain why you propose to select your four cases in terms of the logic of purposive sampling.

 ■ **Exercise 9.3**

Using conversation analysis, Harvey Sacks has argued: 'tap into whomsoever, wheresoever and we get much the same things' (1984b: 22).

Consider how far your own theoretical model might allow you to use Sacks's argument to justify working with a very small dataset.

|10|

Ethical Research

Chapter Objectives

By the end of this chapter you will be able to:

- **Recognize the up-to-date standards required for ethical research.**

- **Understand why ethics matters.**

- **Interpret ethical guidelines in the context of actual qualitative research practice.**

- **Understand how research governance works.**

Introduction

10.1 Given the many demands faced by the apprentice researcher, obtaining ethical approval for your project may seem like a further unnecessary chore. However, because qualitative research inevitably involves contact with human subjects in the 'field', ethical problems are not usually far away. Consider the following examples of ethical dilemmas in qualitative research:

- In the course of gathering data for a study of male sexuality, a doctoral student guarantees confidentiality to the men he interviews. Taking him at his word, a number of them confide that they have been involved in the sexual abuse of children. To tell or not to tell? (adapted from Education Guardian, 22 August 2006)

- A sociology student gains access to an inner-city gang. The gang leader asks him to decide if and how two subordinates should be punished for a minor misappropriation of drug funds. What should he do? (Venkatesh, 2008)

Although these may be extreme examples, you will be lucky if you do not come across some ethical dilemmas in the course of your research. That is why modern universities make so much fuss about protecting the dignity and safety of the research participants and the general public.

You can read reviews of Venkatesh's (2008) book on a Chicago gang at:

http://www.amazon.co.uk/review/product/1594201501?sortBy=bySubmissionDateDescending

While such concerns are widely shared among social scientists today, we should remember that this has not always been the case. Most of us are aware that the Nazis used concentration camp victims as guinea pigs in their diabolical medical experiments, but relatively few are familiar with equally egregious but lesser publicized violations of human rights under the auspices of research here in democratic societies. In one of the most troubling examples of unscrupulous research, a group of 399 African-American men afflicted with syphilis unknowingly became participants in a medical experiment that lasted nearly 40 years until it was finally exposed in the early 1970s (Jones, 1981: 1–23). From the 1930s to the 1970s, the physicians assigned to these men deliberately did not treat them for their ailment, even after penicillin was developed and could have been used as a cure. Instead, the patients were secretly experimented on to examine the effects of untreated syphilis. By the time this US Public Health Service study was exposed and subsequently terminated, many of the patients whose condition had gone untreated for years had either died horribly or become severely ill.

Instances of unethical research are not limited to medical experiments. Among social scientists in the United States, a well-known example of unethical research is Laud Humphreys's *Tearoom Trade* (1970). Humphreys studied anonymous homosexual encounters in semi-public places. Specifically, he was interested in the background of men who had sex with other men in public restrooms. After positioning himself in a restroom in a city park, he gained the trust of the men who frequented it by acting as a lookout for them while they engaged in sexual activities. Humphreys secretly recorded their licence plate numbers, and with the help of the police discovered who they were and where they lived. Months later, he visited the men in their homes disguised as a survey researcher. He gathered additional information about these men and their families and subsequently published his research in a book that was widely praised before questions were raised about its ethics. One of the main findings of his work was that many of the men in his study were married and of middle class background – a discovery that was made possible through the covert invasion of the subjects' privacy.

Such flagrant abuses of research subjects in the name of science have led to the establishment of codes of research ethics. While these may vary across disciplines and national boundaries, there are a number of general principles that most researchers would agree with. Most prominent among these are:

- voluntary participation and the right to withdraw

- protection of research participants

- assessment of potential benefits and risks to participants

- obtaining informed consent

- not doing harm.

In many countries, including the UK, your supervisor is the person who decides whether your planned research meets appropriate ethical guidelines. Many if not most universities now have research ethics committees by which all research involving human subjects must be approved. Particularly when you are seeking to obtain access to an outside organization, you will often need to comply with the demands of such an ethics committee. This tends to be mandatory when you are studying healthcare organizations.

Ideally, when you successfully obtain ethical approval for your research, you accomplish two things. First, you have benefited from the advice of at least one academic trained to detect any potential flaws in your research design that could pose a threat to the participants. The advantage of this guidance cannot be overstated. A qualitative researcher's enthusiasm and desire to become intimately familiar with a topic could blind her to the adverse consequences of her research. Your supervisor or organization's research ethics committee could alert you to problems before any inadvertent harm is done.

Second, when you assure your research participants that your study has been approved by a university and/or medical research ethics committee, you earn their confidence that you are a trained researcher with the backing of a legitimate academic institution. This could help you establish rapport and address any reservations people might have about answering your questions or sharing their private lives with you.

The Standards of Ethical Research _____

10.2 Throughout this chapter, I will offer further advice about ethical issues illustrated by many student examples. However, now is a good time to confront the 'official line'. Table 10.1 sets out the instructions regarding ethical research provided by the British Economic and Social Research Council (ESRC). Do not despair if you find this too dense or demanding. Shortly, we will see how other graduate students have handled such matters.

■ LINK ■

For a useful discussion of ethical issues which includes tips from experienced researchers, go to:

www.the-sra.org.uk/documents/pdfs/ethics03.pdf

TABLE 10.1   What is ethical research?

1   *Research staff and subjects must be informed fully about the purpose, methods and intended possible uses of the research, what their participation in the research entails and what risks, if any, are involved.*

(a)   This principle underpins the meaning of informed consent. Informed consent entails giving as much information as possible about the research so that prospective participants can make an informed decision on their possible involvement. Typically, this information should be provided in written form and signed off by the research subjects. The primary objective is to conduct research openly and without deception. Deception (i.e. research without consent) should only be used as a last resort when no other approach is possible. Consent here is not simply resolved through the formal signing of a consent document at the start of research. Instead it is continually open to revision and questioning. Highly formalised or bureaucratic ways of securing consent should be avoided in favour of fostering relationships in which ongoing ethical regard for participants is to be sustained, even after the study itself has been completed.

(b)   This emphasis on the individual can seem inappropriate or meaningless in some cultural contexts, where the individual may take less precedence than broader notions of kin or community. This may be especially so when social scientists work in developing countries.

(c)   In cases where research involves vulnerable groups such as children, older persons or adults with learning difficulties, every effort should be made to secure their informed consent. However, in cases where this is seen as impossible or where the research subjects are considered not competent to give their assent to the research, the issue of honesty and consent may need to be managed via proxies, who should be either those with a duty of care or who can provide disinterested independent approval depending on the individual circumstances). In the case of research on children, one cannot expect parents alone to provide disinterested approval on their children's behalf. In such cases, every effort should be made to deal with consent through dialogue with both children and their parents (or legal equivalent). Again, there may be circumstances where this could jeopardise the research (again in some areas of deviance, such as research into teenage sexuality or teenage pregnancy). In such circumstances, researchers will need to regard the potential risk to the principal subjects of the research as a priority.

2   *The confidentiality of information supplied by research subjects and the anonymity of respondents must be respected*
    This requires that researchers take steps to ensure that research data and its sources remain confidential unless participants have consented to their disclosure, and in this latter case ensure that plans have been made for their storage and access to them.

3   *Research participants must participate in a voluntary way, free from any coercion*
    In all cases of research, researchers should inform subjects of their right to refuse to participate or withdraw from the investigation whenever and for whatever reason they wish. There should be no coercion of research subjects to participate in the research. Consent has to be freely given in order to be valid.
    This is linked to the issue of covert research and deliberate deception. Deception by definition precludes consent and should only be used in a research setting where open and

(Continued)

TABLE 10.1   *(Continued)*

transparent research is impossible, whether because of the risks it might create for the researcher or participant, or in work where consent can be secured without providing the participant with full information about the project to avoid jeopardising its performance.

4   *Harm to research participants must be avoided*

This principle requires that social science research should be conducted in such a way that it minimises harm or risk to social groups or individuals. Participants' interests or well-being should not be damaged as a result of their participation in the research. [It is important to take account of] the way in which research is communicated, especially where material is sensitive or results could be misconstrued and subsequently used by third parties against the interests of the research participants or researchers themselves.

5   *The independence and impartiality of researchers must be clear, and any conflicts of interest or partiality must be explicit*

The research should be conducted so as to ensure the professional integrity of its design, the generation and analysis of data, and the publication of results, while the direct and indirect contributions of colleagues, collaborators and others should also be acknowledged. In addition, this principle requires that investigators ensure that there is no undeclared conflict of interest (which may be personal, academic or commercial) in their proposed work and that the relation between the sources of funding and researchers' control over results is made clear, specifically in relation to the ownership, publication and subsequent use of research data.

Source: Research Ethics Framework, ESRC, July 2005, pp. 23–5

Why Ethics Matter for Your Research

10.3

I would not be surprised if many readers are overawed by Table 10.1. Indeed, it is very tempting to think that simply by paying lip-service to these principles, one may save a lot of time for the 'real' topics of your research.

In this section, I am not going to preach you a sermon about ethical practice. Instead, I want to use a student example to show you why thinking through ethical issues properly can help you do better research.

John Moore's study of families' reactions to suicide shows that if you don't think through the issue of informed consent, your research access may sometimes disappear.

⌐ STUDENT EXAMPLES ⌐

Reactions to Suicide

I had been contacting various helplines and discussing the issue of data collection. I wanted somewhere where mental health topics and suicide were being discussed … I contacted a number of self-help groups in the search for data. I received a great response from one in Norfolk, which was for relatives of people who had committed suicide. I had many conversations on the

---

phone with the group's founder, who had told me that they met regularly, were all good friends, and had even been recorded for part of a TV show before, and he would tell them about my research. He came back to me saying that they had agreed to me coming down and video-recording one of their sessions, and they were all keen to be part of the research. I discussed discursive psychological research in great detail with him, and he liked what I was proposing.

When I got there and had set up the camera, people started to arrive. It soon became clear that they were not expecting me, had given no consent to being recorded, and did not know each other or meet regularly (one person said she had attended one session four years ago and had been phoned out of the blue and asked to attend that night). It also became clear very quickly that they were all still very much in a great deal of emotional distress and pain. I turned the camera off and decided to just sit the meeting out. The group leader then announced to the group that he had no idea what I wanted or what my research was about. It then turned very unpleasant, with one member telling me that I was making her pain worse by being there, and I felt physically threatened by another member who appeared quite angry. I cannot express how terrible I felt.

Lessons learned: I should have spoken to participants and not just the group leader before showing up with a camera to the meeting, and if I ever approach a similar group again, I would get consent forms signed before attempting any data collection. I think attending some meetings to get a feel for them before collection starts would also be the way to go. [John Moore, Social Sciences, Loughborough]

John Moore also studied helplines available to people contemplating suicide and their families. His experience shows that one aspect of ethical practice is thinking through what your research can offer participants. By doing this, as he shows, you are more likely to obtain research access. So good ethical practice can produce better research.

What's in It for Us?

When I started discussing data collection with MindinfoLine, it was very useful to bring along some sound-files of the ethics exchanges from another helpline where calls had been recorded for research. This helped them to decide to use a recorded message as opposed to asking each caller for individual permission, as they felt that the ethics exchanges sounded too disrupting to the calls. Most importantly, it helped to bring along examples of how similar research had been used in feedback to helplines in the past, to clearly demonstrate that the research could be beneficial to them. I also made a point of encouraging them (if they were to decide to go ahead with call recording) to give me some questions to answer for them, which they did. This feedback has been a great way to continue my relationship with the helpline staff, and I have been back once to discuss the way callers who cry during calls are supported, and will be back again to discuss callers who are unclear as to what they want from the line. [John Moore]

10.4

One could spend hours trying to decode the ESRC's list of principles set out in Table 10.1. A better learning strategy might be to consider how other graduate students have addressed ethical issues in their research. In this section, I consider what their experience can tell us about:

- obtaining consent
- research in different cultures
- research with vulnerable groups
- confidentiality.

Obtaining consent _____

10.4.1

My PhD student, Sally Hunt, sought to obtain audio-recordings of a mental health team's weekly case conference. As well as completing the paperwork for an ethics committee, Sally Hunt also discussed her proposal with the chairman of the trust's mental health board, a practising consultant psychiatrist. He voiced no objection in principle and recommended that she contact the team's consultant and team leader to seek their individual permission, which she did. As she remarks:

> Being a participant-observer raises a number of ethical issues which extend beyond formal consent to the research. Before the research began, I decided that the best way to carry out participant observation, both morally and practically, was to be as open as possible with the team. My rationale for making this decision was that this would permit me to be free to ask questions as the fieldwork progressed without creating too much suspicion. (Sally Hunt)

Rachael Dunn's PhD at Murdoch University, Western Australia, focused on a clinic treating young people with eating disorders. Like Sally, she needed approval from a participating organization and needed to adjust her proposal accordingly.

STUDENT EXAMPLES

Working with Ethics Committees

In the course of the ethics approval process, a number of stipulations were made by the committee concerning data collection protocols. To minimize any effect the taping of the therapy sessions might have on patients, or the therapeutic process, the participating clinicians made an informed clinical decision as to which patients to approach for consent. This potentially produced bias in which sessions were ultimately recorded, as clinicians could exclude certain patients. To minimize this, the clinicians were instructed to record a representative sample of therapeutic interactions. Patients were advised on the patient information sheet and verbally before recording commenced that they were able to withdraw their consent before, during or after the therapy sessions. Patients were also informed that withdrawal or non-participation in the study would not affect the care they received. Patients were further advised that no identifying details would be made public in the study and that the audio-tapings of therapy sessions would not be played publicly. In addition, the hospital ethics committee required a final amendment to the application, which stipulated that all original recordings and sound file copies be destroyed subsequent to the analysis phase of the study. [Rachael Dunn, Psychology, Murdoch University]

TIP

Note that Rachael allowed participants to withdraw their consent at any time. This is known as 'process consent' and is a better way of safeguarding participants than a once-and-for-all 'informed consent'. Process consent may also imply your commitment to debrief participants afterwards. This is a common feature in focus group research where people may be allowed to talk about their contributions immediately after the event and given a contact number should they wish to talk to a researcher at a later date (see Barbour, 2007: 82).

The information sheets you give to potential participants should be carefully constructed. Your research needs to be fully described in a way that the people concerned can understand. As noted above, it is also sensible to stress that, if consent is given, it can be withdrawn at any time. As examples of good practice, you will find below the information sheet used by Rachael Dunn.

STUDENT EXAMPLES

Patient Information Sheet

Project Title: Therapeutic Interaction in Anorexia Nervosa Treatment

Thank you for taking the time to read this information.

My name is Rachael Dunn and I am a PhD student at Murdoch University. The purpose of my study is to look at how language is used in therapy sessions between clinicians and adolescents diagnosed with an eating disorder. Results from this study will have the opportunity to provide new information on the role of language in the therapeutic process with patients in the area of eating disorders. It is hoped that this will enhance our understanding of what is helpful for the adolescent with anorexia nervosa.

(Continued)

(Continued)

You can help in this study by consenting to have your therapy session recorded using a digital MP3 recording device. Participation in this study is voluntary. You may withdraw your consent at any time during or after the therapy session, at which time the recording will be destroyed. No names or other information that might identify you will be used in any publication or documentation arising from the research. If you decide to withdraw from the study or do not take part, this will not in any way affect the care you receive at [named] hospital.

Being in this study will not involve any extra time for you. It will only mean that the therapy session you are already having will be recorded. After transcription, the original recordings will be stored at the hospital in a locked filing cabinet on an MP3 recording device. The tapes will be kept through the data collection and transcription parts of the study (maximum 10 months) and then they will be destroyed. Written transcripts will be made from the recording and will contain no names or details that might identify you.

A report on this study will be given to the Eating Disorders Team at the hospital and will be available for you to read. If you are willing to participate in this study, could you please complete the attached consent form. If you have any questions about this study please feel free to contact me, Rachael Dunn, on [phone number] or my supervisor [name] from the Eating Disorders Team [phone number].

If you would like to speak to someone not involved in the study you can contact Murdoch University's Human Research Ethics Committee [phone number] or the Hospital's Executive Director, Medical Services [phone number].

Kind regards
Rachael Dunn
BA (Hons) (Psychology)

Rachael used a similar information sheet with the parents of the adolescent patients in her study. This is an excellent example of such information, which incorporates full description of the purposes of her research, details of what will actually happen if you participate, and provision for 'process consent' as well for extra information from respected others. My only minor reservation is that the description of her research in terms of 'the role of language in the therapeutic process' may be a little bit heavy on academic jargon. Can you think of a more down-to-earth way of phrasing Rachael's topic?

 ■ **Attempt Exercise 10.1** ■

| TIP |

When preparing information sheets it is sensible to avoid terms that are potentially sensitive. For instance, in a study of obesity management in general practice medicine, the term 'weight management' was used with potential participants. In subsequent interviews it was discovered that most respondents found the terms 'obese' and 'obesity' hurtful (Barbour, 2007: 75).

10.4.2

What is a 'different' culture? Does this mean a different society, or can 'different' cultures be much closer to home?

Of course, it is always wise for researchers to consider the way in which their assumptions and practices may be different from those they study. Even in the familiar medical settings studied by Sally and Rachael, they did not take for granted the way participants would understand what they were doing. In this section, however, I focus on the specific issues in studying people from another society.

Sometimes this can be a quite straightforward matter. Maddie Sandall studied the experience of international students. During her research, she interviewed 'partnership programme' students who have transferred to the UK for the final year of their degree.

STUDENT EXAMPLES

Studying International Students

I didn't require ethics committee approval, but did create an ethics statement which I sent to each interviewee which covered issues of anonymity and confidentiality. This was particularly important as I had been seen as a member of staff in one light and then a 'fellow student' in another. I wanted them to be clear that I was in my student role for the interviews.

Other ethical considerations included ensuring I had knowledge of their cultural differences and also being clear on the questions which could have different meanings in different cultures. I also reassured the students that the research will only read by the markers and will not in anyway be fed back to their partner college or to the university.

One particularly tricky issue was when one of the students turned the interview around and started to interview me – asking me what the Western view of Asians was – I felt like I was really put on the spot and asked to generalize on behalf of all Westerners! Although I do of course have an opinion, it's quite difficult to know the 'right thing to say'. An issue I am sure the interviewees had themselves … . [Maddie Sandall, Management, University of the West of England]

It is often difficult to import ethical principles from one culture and apply them without modifications to another. The experienced sociologist, Catherine Riessman, conducted research in villages in Kerala, South India, between 1993 and

1994. Her interest was in the meaning and management of infertility which, she remarks, was 'an invisible problem in the Indian context'. Here is a shortened account of how she describes her ethical dilemmas.

Researching Indian Villagers

My research proposal ... included procedures for obtaining informed consent from childless women. But ... the very language of Western research practice – 'obtaining' informed consent – indicates who will be in control.

The first hint of trouble happened shortly after I joined my host institution, the research unit of a small college in Kerala. [My] research assistant, Liza – a 26 year old Malayali graduate level social worker, educated in Kerala ... was surprised ... by my consent form: 'we don't do that here,' she told me gently ... I persisted, and asked her to translate into Malayalam the form I had prepared according to my University's guidelines ...

Because women in Kerala are educated and literate, many informants read along as we communicated the contents of the consent form. Most women signed it. A significant number, however, were reluctant to affix their names. They were suspicious, not about interviewing or taping, but about the form. Perhaps they thought it a government document.

Reflecting now on the refusal of some women, I hear their worry. The consent form *was* a government document – an import from the West, designed to meet my University's Institutional Review Board requirement ... Signing documents in the Indian context carries a history of well-deserved suspicion: government intrusion into property rights, inheritance, marriage customs, and reproductive health. Strangers seeking information and bearing forms are not easily trusted, especially in rural villages. (Riessman, 2005: ms 8–9)

It is not always just a case of suspicion. People in non-Western cultures may regard their consent to research as a purely instrumental matter. As Anne Ryen observes:

I have frequently met expectations that I will reciprocate in one way or another in African settings ... These have been of different kinds, from expecting me to cope with local poverty and offering grants, to gift exchanges and sexual offers. (2004: 238)

In some cultures, however, it may be difficult to say 'no' to a researcher's request for access. As Anne Ryen notes, on the basis of her research in East Africa:

For many poor Third World interviewees, local norms make it difficult to turn down a request from a visitor to be interviewed or they do not know the potential implications of participating in research. [This means that] the general ethical correctness of informed consent irrespective of the location of the field may be questionable with reference to the North–South dimension in Third World projects. (2004: 232)

Queenie Eng (S. Eng) did her PhD research on Chinese people with diabetes living in the UK. Like Anne Ryen, she found that 'informed consent' was quite different to that imagined in Western-based research protocols.

STUDENT EXAMPLES

Why Do Non-Western People Give Consent?

In the UK, the rules of engagement in research are modelled along the Western ethical framework. On the other hand, the research participants are Chinese migrants whose rules of engagement are moulded by the Eastern customs and traditions.

Within the group setting, the social role of the researcher is problematic because of her position as an academic amongst participants who were largely illiterate. The reverence for and importance of education in Chinese culture is documented in literary and historical texts. In accordance with the Western framework of conducting research, participants are asked for their consent, and this is indicated by their signature on a consent form. However, the signing of a form between individuals who have verbally consented to carrying out a promise is a foreign import. Within the Chinese tradition, agreements are sealed by the 'gentleman's honour', not a signature on a piece of paper.

So, what does one do in this case? Should the researcher get the participants to sign before or after the interview? Some researchers have said that given the participants had agreed to come to the meeting, their presence indicates consent. Whether the consent form is signed before or after the interview is insignificant. In this study, the signing of the consent form was negotiated with the participants as to whether they preferred to sign before or after the interview. Interestingly, the belief that putting one's signature is associated with dealing with officialdom is reflected in one of the queries raised by one participant who asked if this research was related to government activities. When reassured that it was for educational purposes, participants appeared content to contribute to the discussion.

The point is, when dealing with people who come from a non-Western culture, a seemingly simple act of the signing of a consent form has cultural repercussions. Researchers need to be aware of this and know what it means for the participants as it can impact on how much information they are willing to divulge.

The participants also misunderstood the benefits they were to get out of the research. One of the reasons for participation was because some of the participants thought that they would learn something about their illness from the researcher. Despite thorough explanation at the outset of the discussion from the researcher and her assistant about the nature of the focus group discussions, misunderstanding persisted. One reason for this apparent misunderstanding was that some of the gatekeepers told me that they did not mention the word 'research' to the participants because of the various ideas evoked from the word 'research'. Failure to mention the word 'research' and what it entailed led participants to feel 'cheated' into attending the focus group discussions. They were angry when SE did not accede to their demands for

(Continued)

(Continued)

information on diabetes in exchange for participation in the focus groups. Arguably, the 'mutiny' was justified.

As an inferior member of the group, I depended on one of the in-groupers to appease the group on my behalf. One of the in-groupers, participant MN, explained to the other group members about the nature of the meeting. As an in-grouper, MN was also a volunteer as a medical interpreter for some of the users of the Chinese community centre. In line with Confucian ethics, MN appealed to their duty of care towards younger members of the group. She reminded the group members that information contributed to the researcher was for the sake of the future generation. Hence, whatever information they gave to the researcher about their illness, this would eventually become useful in their future medical consultations. Given that MN supported SE's research, all the group members felt obliged to stay for the remainder of the session.

In the process of sharing their experience, both participant and researcher had to find a middle ground to satisfy the needs of both parties. [In this setting] deviation from the Western norm of conducting research is inevitable. These deviations include recruitment, obtaining consent, upholding confidentiality and anonymity, handling reciprocity and managing conflicts. [Queenie Eng, Medicine, Leeds]

Eng, Ryen and Riessman's research with non-Western people shows that obtaining consent can be far more complicated than Western ethical guidelines would suggest.

> **TIP**
>
> **As with every aspect of your research, success is not measured by passive rule following. Understand the rules but then ensure that you think through their relevance for the people and situations you wish to study. Success depends upon thoughtful, well-informed ethical practice. Sometimes this can mean deviating from rules.**

 ■ **Attempt Exercise 10.2** ▬▬▬▬▬▬▬▬▬▬

Research with vulnerable groups _____

10.4.3 Issues of consent become even more complicated when you want to study vulnerable people such as children or adults with disabilities. For instance, I welcomed the idea of colleagues researching the old people's home where I do voluntary work. However, the ethical issues involved in studying people with dementia are vast and apparently intractable, particularly if you want to use video data. Families, carers and care managers will all have to be consulted. But what happens when the camera accidentally includes a resident or carer for whom you have no permission to record? Moreover, how satisfactory is it to use family permission to record intimate details of somebody's daily life?

Anne Patterson carefully attended to these issues in her PhD research on young people with learning disabilities. Her account is as follows.

STUDENT EXAMPLES

Studying People with Disabilities

In my PhD research, which studies telephone calls between family members, one of whom has a learning disability, the 'dilemma' is associated with ethics in what I think is a fairly unique way. I obtained appropriate ethics committee approval (at university level) since some of the participants were in a recognized 'vulnerable' group, and I approached three families direct, asking them to record their telephone calls with the young adults in their families who were at residential school or college and were making calls home. I gained informed consent as far as possible from all individuals involved, but it is still a concern whether it is possible to obtain 'true' informed consent or whether the motives of the research are truly understood and the individual's rights to refuse to take part are fully appreciated. Some researchers question whether individuals truly understand the research and their position within it. With this in mind, an information sheet was designed which could be read by or read to all participants. This contained information about the purpose of the research and outlined the rights of participants taking part in the study and the rights of the researcher to share data with other academics, though it guaranteed anonymization of the data. This provided a good basis for most participants to be able to give informed consent. In the case of the young adults with learning disabilities the form was supplemented with extra explanation of the contents therein. It was possible then to be satisfied that the interests of these participants had been fairly served and that informed consent had been given as far as was practically possible. In order to build an even greater awareness of the purpose of the research it has been possible to show one of the young people some transcripts and allow them to listen to the recordings (much to everyone's amusement). This certainly provided a further, very practical opportunity to try to ensure that one of the young adults was aware of what was being done in the study and to understand their part in it, and so at the first available opportunity this is something that the researcher hopes to replicate with and for the other young adult. [Anne Patterson, Social Sciences, Loughborough]

Sometimes the complex ethical issues involved in studying potentially vulnerable groups may be redefined in terms of the research design itself. Pia Kontos applied to the research ethics board (REB) of a long-term care facility where she proposed to conduct ethnographic research on their Alzheimer's support unit. While the proposal was approved by the REB, in their letter of approval there were concerns expressed about her methodology. It was indicated that while they appreciated that there are significant differences between quantitative science and qualitative studies, they had an ethical responsibility to ensure that the residents of their facility were only subjected to research which was based on sound design. Of particular concern to the REB was that she intended to be the sole observer, which in their view carries an inherent potential for bias. In the interests of increasing her ability to obtain meaningful data, it was thus strongly recommended that she strengthen the validity of her study design by including triangulation of observations through the involvement of secondary observers. It was suggested that family members might be particularly appropriate in this role. Pia's response is shown below.

STUDENT EXAMPLES

Using Your Supervisor To Support You

In response to the REB's recommendation, my thesis supervisor wrote a letter indicating that their recommendation to involve 'secondary observers' was not methodologically appropriate. She explained that verification or trustworthiness is a central topic in the qualitative research literature and that verification in the case of my thesis research would be ensured by following standard qualitative methodology criteria including: (1) the articulation of an explicit theoretical framework which informs data collection and analysis; (2) prolonged engagement in the field; (3) the production of detailed fieldnotes ('thick description') after each engagement in the field; (4) iterative data collection and data analysis ('constant comparison method'); (5) attending to negative or disconfirming evidence; and (6) frequent debriefing with thesis committee members about the research process and development of preliminary coding categories.

This experience highlighted the importance of having qualitative researchers on REBs to ensure that qualitative studies are properly and fairly reviewed. [Pia Kontos, Department of Public Health Sciences, Toronto]

Confidentiality

10.4.4 Issues relating to confidentiality can usually be met straightforwardly. This is Sally Hunt's account of how she approached this topic when making audio-recordings of a mental health team's weekly case conference.

STUDENT EXAMPLES

Keeping Sensitive Information under Wraps

I undertook to use pseudonyms for the names of staff, clients and care areas throughout the research to preserve anonymity and to safeguard confidentiality. In the event, even references to months or seasons of the year in the transcripts were changed as the work got under way. Dates of legislation were retained as were dates of fieldwork and any reference to clients' ages, as such data were necessary to the analysis. As it is not usual for a PhD thesis to be published, this further helped to maintain anonymity. In addition, I undertook to write a report on the progress of the study for the ethical committee, should this be required at any stage of the work. [I did not seek] to interview clients or to access their case records. I guaranteed to keep all audiotapes at home under lock and key and to do all my own transcribing rather than eliciting secretarial assistance. I also promised to destroy the tapes at the end of the study. [Sally Hunt]

However, as we saw at the beginning of this chapter, confidentiality issues can be more complex. When I showed this chapter to my Sage editor, he remarked that, in his own PhD research, anonymity was not the choice of most of the people he interviewed.

STUDENT EXAMPLES

Do People Want To Be Anonymous?

One thing that I encountered doing oral history interviewing for my PhD was that many of my interviewees did not want to be anonymized. They regarded their interview as public testimony and stated that they were looking forward to seeing their names in print in my book. When I put it to the interviewees that I would have to change their names and hide their identity they became quite upset, and one of them said that she would not have let me interview her if her identity was to be concealed.

Which made me think: who are we trying to protect? Once it was anonymized, there was nothing to stop me from tampering with the testimony knowing that there could be no comeback from the respondent. I did not, of course, but anonymization would have made it easy to do so. So a critical question for me is always: who benefits? [Patrick Brindle]

What respondents want is not the only issue regarding anonymity. Should you keep quiet when people reveal criminal offences in the course of a 'confidential' research interview? And, if you are using video data, what can you properly reveal in seminar presentations and publications? Once again, there are no easy answers.

TIP

If you are faced with an apparently intractable ethical problem, consult your supervisor and read about how more experienced researchers handled such a problem. Here, as elsewhere, don't try to reinvent the wheel!

Complex Ethical Issues _____

10.5

Here the waters muddy still further. In this section I deal with a number of issues which are barely mentioned in ethical guidelines such as those provided by the ESRC, namely:

- consent to observational research
- whether there can be 'appropriate' deception
- paying participants
- the unintended consequences of good ethical practice.

Consent to observational research _____

10.5.1

Qualitative researchers sometimes encounter unique problems in obtaining ethical approval, particularly when their data depend upon observation. Indeed, a guidebook published by the US Department of Health and Human Services explicitly notes the difficulties confronting qualitative researchers where informed consent is concerned. Specifically, in a section titled 'Fieldwork' the guidebook states:

> Fieldwork, or ethnographic research, involves observation of and interaction with the persons or group being studied in the group's own environment, often for long periods of time. Since fieldwork is a research process that gains shape and substance as the study progresses, it is difficult, if not impossible, to specify detailed contents and objectives in a protocol.
>
> After gaining access to the fieldwork setting, the ongoing demands of scientifically and morally sound research involve gaining the approval and trust of the persons being studied. These processes, as well as the research itself, involve complex, continuing interactions between researcher and hosts that cannot be reduced to an informed consent form. Thus, while the idea of consent is not inapplicable in fieldwork, Institutional Review Boards [US ethical committees, referred to henceforth as IRBs] and researchers need to adapt prevailing notions of acceptable protocols and consent procedures to the realities of fieldwork. IRBs should keep in mind the possibility of granting a waiver of informed consent. (Penslar, 2007)

Evidently, even the US government agency in charge of defining and enforcing guidelines for dealing with human subjects is aware that qualitative researchers face unique challenges in gaining IRB approvals (it is worth noting that this guidebook was prepared by a lawyer, Robin Levin Penslar JD, the 'ORRR Program Officer', and a physician, Joan P. Porter DPA).

A case study illustrates how the student ethnographer may need to work out different forms of consent for different groups. Keith Abbott carried out doctoral (sociological) research into spiritual enlightenment at Loughborough University, and his subjects included internationally famous spiritual gurus as well as some lesser known individuals who teach about enlightenment.

Fieldwork On Spiritual Enlightenment

I have been using audio- and video-recordings, and photos I have taken. I have recorded people to whom the gurus speak during short courses or fairly public events. I've taken the view that different 'subjects' require different levels of consent (so gurus have massive long consent forms; people in the audience at public events being recorded anyway may not get a form at all).

When recording live events where there is an audience, I generally did not seek prior consent from all present, only the main speaker. I tried several times to catch up with people who had contributed to the event from the audience afterwards, to ask retrospective consent, but was never quick enough to intercept them and soon gave up on this as a strategy. However, such events were generally rather ostensibly recorded by the organizers anyway, sometimes unannounced and sometimes with something like the mention of a possible podcast or CD/DVD becoming available. I took it that on such occasions all those who spoke or remained had already implicitly consented to becoming part of a worldwide spectacle and so were ethically available to my own recordings. In such cases I tried to anonymize all but the main speaker or anyone who had explicitly consented.

For small events running over several days or encounters, particularly where I was using video-as well as audio-recordings, I had a very short single-page consent form, different from my more elaborate 'guru form', which in essence simply allowed course delegates the possibilities of altogether opting out of being recorded, being recorded anonymously (such as by their images being edited), or being recorded without anonymizing. There were occasions however where producing even the short form would have been hugely disruptive and instead I relied upon being open about my research intentions and simply asked people if they minded being audio-recorded, refraining if there seemed to be any hint of concern. [Keith Abbott, Social Sciences, Loughborough]

Although Queenie Eng's study of Chinese people living in the UK used focus groups rather than fieldwork data, she faced similar issues to Keith in deciding what counted as 'appropriate' consent.

Delayed Consent with Non-Western Respondents

For people who come from a non-Western culture, a seemingly simple act of signing of consent form has cultural repercussions. Researchers need to be aware of this and know what it means for the participants as it can impact on how much information they are willing to divulge. The participants' attendance of the focus group meeting was construed by the researcher as a sign of consent and hence agreement to take part in the study. Therefore, it can be argued that signing the consent form would only formalize the whole interaction and put the participant into another

(Continued)

(Continued)

mindset. For this reason, I delayed the signing of the consent form till towards the end of the session and did this in conjunction with the distribution of gift vouchers.

Thus, apparently simple protocols were difficult to adhere to. For example, the signing of consent forms which were advocated to be done before the beginning of each session was sometimes left to the last part of the interview, as the act of signing could affect the terms of engagement. Ironically, it was my moderator who reminded me that I should do what the Western protocol expects, i.e. obtain written consent before conducting the interview. As it turned out, the signature *per se* was not to be an issue but the verbal explanation of the consent form was. This was due to the low levels of literacy among these groups of Chinese participants. [Queenie Eng, Medicine, Leeds]

What Queenie calls 'the Western protocol' may be inappropriate to many fieldwork settings even when the participants are Western Europeans. Sally Hunt's account reveals that, faced with an ethical form based on medical research, the fieldworker needs to show considerable mental agility.

STUDENT EXAMPLES

Redefining 'Hazard'

I put forward my proposal to the ethical committee of the trust hospital to which the team was attached. I found the form I was required to complete somewhat problematic. It conformed to the standard type for purely *clinical* research involving human subjects rather than to any proposed sociological research. Predictably, it was very 'physically' oriented. One question asked for 'potential hazards' and the precautions I might take to meet them. The possible contravening of confidentiality was my written response to this enquiry. [Sally Hunt]

Sally's experience involving inappropriate ethical issues is very common in research involving fieldwork. If you are studying a public setting like a shopping mall, football stadium or concert, it may be impossible to obtain consent from the people you are observing. Moreover, as Giampietro Gobo (2008: 108) argues, such consent may not even be necessary because you do not interact with anyone and people know that their behaviour is open to public inspection.

Appropriate deception?

10.5.2 Informed consent suggests that you should be entirely open with participants about the purposes of your research and that any other course involves an unacceptable degree of deception. However, such openness gives rise to two problems:

1 Revealing your true interests may influence what people say or do.

2 People may not be able to make sense of the scientific terms you use to define your research problem.

These issues have been directly confronted in psychological experiments where a fully open statement of the research problem is thought to 'contaminate' the results. In these cases, a degree of deception is thought to be appropriate providing the wellbeing of participants and their privacy is respected. Indeed, one should never deceive people about what procedures they will undergo during your research, and always undertake to answer any questions they have both before and after the research has taken place (for further discussion of these issues, see Christians, 2005: 144–5).

Paying participants?

10.5.3 Sometimes it may be tempting to offer some reward to respondents who agree to be interviewed or to participate in a focus group (notice Queenie Eng's use of gift vouchers in the earlier example). This follows the practice of many psychological studies involving students and of drug companies in certain kinds of drug trials. However, both can raise ethical issues if the reward offered tempts people to participate against their initial judgement. One way of handling this problem is to avoid advertising the payment or to omit to provide details of the payment involved (Barbour, 2007: 80).

Unintended consequences of good ethical practice

10.5.4 Just as there can be no rules that cover every instance, following ethical rules can sometimes have quite unintended consequences. In Keith Abbott's research, a well-meant gesture (sharing data with participants) led to potential copyright problems.

STUDENT EXAMPLES

Consequences of Sharing Data

Legal and ethical rights and obligations relevant to researchers' own materials can also cause problems. I left some research subjects with some jpeg digital images I had taken from a personal development course I had researched as a memento and 'thank you'. All people in the data were

(Continued)

(Continued)

happy for others to share their images in this way. However, some of those photographs were used in a training manual prepared by the course organizers without asking for any further permission, thus becoming part of a text intended to elaborate and teach the practices being researched. I did not anticipate such usage, and the publication in what was in effect a commercial manual prompted me to check the university's position on what was potentially an infringement of its (and possibly my) copyright in the images and a usage which demanded some consideration to its ethicality. Thankfully, after a few emails the manual was altered to record my authorship and the university's permission for the usage, and everyone was content with this. By this time of course to impose conditions on usage would seem critical and negative towards the research subjects and jeopardize future cooperation. In retrospect all of this might have been much more destructive to the research relationship and did little to benefit my own project. Since in any case, ethically and under the Data Protection Act, subjects may expect to be given copies of recordings of themselves (or their works), it can be wise for researchers to give some early thought, before any such request is made and certainly before passing on research recordings, to limiting further reproduction of released materials (by for instance annotating prints or images, or only releasing low-quality or watermarked materials). If subjects are only happy if researchers share recordings fully with them, researchers may need to question whether or not such research is acceptable to them. [Keith Abbott]

Fortunately, following ethical guidelines can unintentionally sometimes enrich the analytic breadth of a research study. Sally Hunt's efforts to achieve informed consent with her homelessness workers meant that they were prepared to allow her to audio-record as well as observe their meetings.

Keith Abbott's pursuit of materials went in the opposite direction, moving him away from recording equipment towards observation. As he puts it:

> I've had some particular 'troubles' to do with getting permission for visual recordings, and objections leading me unintentionally into ethnographic research on one particular occasion, though this made future recordings easier as I thus became something of an insider. (Keith Abbott)

A further unintended consequence for the research process arises from the fact that 'ethical practice' as a matter of concern is now widespread among many occupational groups. On some occasions, this offers a fascinating topic for the fieldworker, as Sally Hunt recognized.

STUDENT EXAMPLES

Participants Doing Ethics

There were almost certainly times in this study when members responded to my presence in terms of what might be called 'ethical correctness'. I sensed that there were some occasions when members overtly displayed their moral adequacy as a consequence of being observed. My general *impression* was that members responded to me as a more senior member of staff, i.e. as an older, experienced professional now working in higher education. I felt that the team's display of moral adequacy in my presence was particularly marked especially where ethical dilemmas were prominent. [Sally Hunt]

Research Governance

10.6

Sally's observations of nursing staff doing 'ethical correctness' reveal that 'ethics' has become much more than a matter of individual researchers seeking to employ good practice. Instead, a vast system of interlocking organizations (governmental, semi-governmental, medical and legal) now confronts the contemporary Western researcher. The way in which these organizations survey and discipline researchers is described as 'research governance'. Linnie Price gives an example of what this can mean to an experienced qualitative researcher.

STUDENT EXAMPLES

Surveying the Researcher

As well as ethics, research governance is now a huge hassle. For our project, for which ethics approval was in place when I came in post, research governance delayed the start by four months, and we had to go cap in hand for more funding. For any contact with 'vulnerable' service users (some of ours had long-term mental illness), *every* person having contact needed an honorary contract with the local health authority *and* a Criminal Records Bureau check. In one of our sites, everyone had to have an occupational health medical with HIV test, including the principal researcher who is dean of a medical school.

The other pitfall is service user (SU) involvement. Few funding bodies will now support a project without SU involvement, which raises all sorts of other issues. Similarly, kapo-like data protection officers in health trusts can completely sabotage your ethics approved recruitment procedures. [Linnie Price]

While ethical and governance requirements can play a significant role in ensuring the safety of research participants, their survey-friendly protocol may in the long run discourage more innovative research projects, especially those aimed at investing social inequality (e.g. poverty, racism, sexism). Such studies may invariably involve some degree of risk, both for the subjects and for the organization where inequality is practised. As Nelson states:

> Of course, 'respect for persons' can hardly entail respect for every human action, but IRBs are ill equipped to negotiate the difference. Instead, they often give unquestioned allegiance to a concept that might be given more nuanced application to, say, Ku Klux Klan or Nazi Party members, who might merit humanity qualified with disapproval and

who might on occasion appropriately be challenged aggressively in an interview. A historian might well wish to investigate the self-understanding of a Ku Klux Klan member and might choose to present a neutral account of the organization, but academic freedom means that the decision to do so needs to be the historian's, not that of an IRB. One consequence of an unreflective commitment to 'respect for persons' is that IRBs have great difficulty accepting research destined to be critical of its 'human subjects'. (2003: 32)

As seen in the passage above, an increasing number of US social scientists, and academics in general, are concerned about IRBs' growing 'ethics creep' (Haggerty, 2004) into their research. Initially, the social scientists responded to IRB demands with incredulity and amusement. For example, in a magazine interview, Howard Becker joked that if he was required to undergo rigorous IRB reviews, he would circumvent the bureaucracy by redefining his research as 'conceptual art' (Shea, 2000). Four years later, in response to Haggerty's 'Ethics creep: governing social science research in the name of ethics', Howard Becker writes:

> What began years ago as a sort of safeguard against doctors injecting cancer cells into research patients without first asking them if that was OK has turned into a serious, ambitious bureaucracy with interests to protect, a mission to promote, and a self-righteous and self-protective ideology to explain why it is all necessary ... I never had occasion to try out the idea I suggested to the reporter from Lingua Franca, of describing my work as conceptual art or performance art ... But if I did I suspect the response would be to change the rules to include art projects. (2004: 415–16)

Becker goes on to point out that some of his research on medical students, for example, could not have been conducted with the same academic rigour under the new IRB rules. His final recommendation to social scientists is: 'Start fighting this thing full time and don't give up an inch we don't have to' (2004: 416). Increasingly, UK research ethics committees are taking on the function of IRBs (see Richardson, 2007; and see Flynn, 2000, on the cost of REC review).

Research ethics committees and North American IRBs may inadvertently block the aspirations of researchers who want to dig deeper, as it were. Moreover, in their capacity to monitor and approve research, IRBs can become a sort of 'university research police' that controls the production of knowledge. Given that IRBs are a relatively new institutional invention, it remains to be seen how they will evolve to fulfil their mission.

TIP

One way of cutting through the jargon used in research governance is simply to ask yourself: what might my research question mean to possible participants? What will they be confronted with if they agree to participate? As an exercise, think about the experience of being interviewed about your future if you have early-stage dementia, or what it may be like for a homeless person to be asked about their earlier family life (Flick, 2007: 71). Although Flick's idea will help your application, you do need to be aware of the time it can take to get ethical approval, and so you need to start seeking approvals in good time.

Conclusion: Managing Ethical Demands

10.7

The challenge for student researchers is to package the open-ended contingencies of qualitative research in a way that convinces your supervisor and any organization that you are studying that no risk is involved. Survey researchers have an easier job with this because the survey questions are designed in advance and clearly demarcate the boundaries of the project. In contrast, qualitative research moves in unpredicted directions; an informant's answers to a question may result in a line of inquiry that was not planned from the start. In the example below, Michelle Miller-Day offers advice for overcoming this sort of challenge.

STUDENT EXAMPLES

Planned Flexibility

The biggest problem for qualitative researchers, as I see it, is that in our data collection we have to be flexible and attuned to 'emergent data'. While qualitative researchers can dance to our particular rendition of flexible and emergent, lawyers and some quantitative researchers find this rendition lacking in rhythm (structure) and believe it is chaotic (not systematic). We need to provide structure and a systematic *outline* of what is planned and give possible outcomes of 'planned flexibility'. The phrase 'planned flexibility' is one way of handling ethical issues in qualitative research proposals. It may not be enough to inform your supervisor that you are doing qualitative research and therefore are not sure about the type of questions asked, where, and how. This applies even more to the organization you want to study. They just won't understand and agree with that line of reasoning. Instead to the best of your ability, give an outline of what shape or direction your research might take. In other words, give them something they can work with within the parameters of their institutional roles. [Michelle Miller-Day, USA]

Some research projects have to be considerably modified due to ethical constraints. For example, Michael Arter states about his PhD on a US police force:

> In the earliest planning for my research I had considered interviewing the spouses of the officers for the familial aspect of police stress. Based upon past decisions of the IRB at my institution, the plan to attempt to interview anyone other than police officers was abandoned. (Michael Arter)

Other researchers go through such a complicated ethical approval process that the experience itself becomes part of the dissertation. This was certainly the case with Sylvia Ansay who encountered particularly stringent demands in her research on US citizens under house arrest.

Which Organization Is Doing the 'Governance'?

I experienced a major hurdle that seemed to come out of nowhere. I had worked closely with the IRB administrator in writing my proposal. She assured me that we had covered all our bases and there appeared to be no problems. Approval should be automatic, she said, just a matter of waiting a couple weeks until the board met. The process became complicated when the IRB decided that, although I was not receiving funding from the National Institute of Health (NIH), I should have NIH approval for the project. The board didn't give me any reasons for the decision; however, I filed the proposal with NIH as they required. An administrator at NIH telephoned me, surprised at the request because I was not seeking funding from them. I had no answers for her. She ended the conversation by saying the requirement raised 'red flags' which they'd have to check out. That was the first of three or four phone calls between us. (I instigated two of these in response to letters from the administrator.) The first criticized the methodology, saying they had never heard of using life stories or narrative analysis as research. It wasn't 'good science,' she said. Later, I had to explain and defend every aspect of the research point by point. In the end, their argument against approval shifted to a concern with my personal safety. They requested a conference call with my professor, during which an NIH attorney urged him not to support the in-home interviews, to consider the liability. When he could not be persuaded, they approved the project with a disclaimer that approval would not have been given if I had been applying for NIH funding. My experience with NIH became a chapter of my dissertation and has been published in *Studies in Symbolic Interaction* (Vol. 25). [Sylvia Ansay, USA]

The IRB committee in this case seems to have been overly protective of Sylvia and her research participants. Though she eventually secured approval for her project, it is evident that her research would have been completely stymied without the support of her dissertation chair. This sort of overprotection is especially noticeable where 'sensitive topics' or 'deviant populations' are concerned. Consider, for example, Sara Crawley's description of the IRB mandates for her research with lesbians.

Governance Bodies Unhappy with Research On Minorities

I did have to take some pains to make the IRB comfortable with the group I was interviewing. Given that I wanted to interview 'lesbians!', the IRB was more worried about protecting confidentiality than most of my narrators. Although I was careful to respect narrators, I found most participants were very willing and expected that they might talk about lesbian experience in the lesbian groups they normally attended to talk about lesbian experience. Ironically, for me, getting IRB approval was more about making the IRB comfortable about issues that the naturally occurring community was already comfortable discussing. [Sara Crawley, USA]

In Sara's case the IRB approval seems to hinge around the board's comfort level with lesbians and talk of lesbianism rather than the community members' ease about discussing their lifestyles. In a related case, Eileen O'Brien, in her study of anti-racists, found that the research participants wanted to be identified by name in the research despite the IRB requirements for anonymity.

STUDENT EXAMPLES

Breaking Confidentiality?

I was dealing with an area of activists who are pretty silenced/ignored in history – white anti-racists – and some people felt that this neglect was very calculated because it prevents whites from having visible alternative models of whiteness to follow, thereby subverting any major transformations of the dominant group in society. So I asked my adviser about it, and he said as long as I had it documented that they gave me permission to use their real names, he didn't think it would be a problem. But this issue never actually went back to IRB. I think this illustrates how qualitative research needs to be adaptable, and that following 'standard protocol' will not always work best depending on the topic and context of the data you need to obtain. [Eileen O'Brien, USA]

I conclude with Eileen O'Brien's experience because it demonstrates once again that what she calls the 'standard protocol' may not always be entirely appropriate to a qualitative research study. Indeed, thoughtless rule following may blind you to unexpected ethical dilemmas. In this context, Table 10.2 gives a jargon-free list of questions to ask yourself when you pursue informed consent.

TABLE 10.2 Ethical questions for researchers

- What am I expecting participants to do?
- How will I explain my research questions to participants?
- What will happen to my data (e.g. who will see any transcripts or recordings?)
- Where will I store my data?
- How can I ensure confidentiality and anonymity?
- How can I try to make my study harm-free?
- What are the communication barriers between me and my participants (e.g. culture, age, gender, impairments?)
- Have I satisfied my accountability to my university, my supervisor, my participants, any gatekeepers and the wider research community?

Source: adapted from Churchill and Sanders, 2007: 48–52

┌─────┐ **KEY POINTS** ┌

While these may vary across disciplines and national boundaries, there are a number of general principles that most researchers would agree with. Most prominent among these are:

- voluntary participation

- protection of research participants

- assessment of potential benefits and risks to participants

- obtaining informed consent.

However, good ethical practice means that one should think through the appropriateness of each ethical principle to the precise context of one's research.

■ ■ Further Reading ■

Israel and Hay's (2006) *Research Ethics for Social Scientists* (Sage, 2006) is a valuable textbook on research ethics. Judith Green and Nicki Thorogood's *Qualitative Methods for Health Research* (Sage, 2004) provides an excellent account of ethical issues in health research. Anne Ryen's chapter 'Ethical Issues' (in C. Seale et al. (eds), *Qualitative Research Practice*, Sage, 2004) is a key source which includes fascinating material on her ethnographic research in East Africa. For more details of some fascinating case studies, see Les Back (2004) and Catherine Riessman (2004).

 ■ **Exercise 10.1**

Draw up an information sheet for participants in your research. Now consider whether you have succeeded in the following:

- providing a clear and truthful account of your research

- avoiding jargon

- avoiding potentially sensitive terms.

■ **Exercise 10.2**

Earlier in this chapter, I listed some features of good ethical practice:

- voluntary participation and the right to withdraw

- protection of research participants

- assessment of potential benefits and risks to participants

- obtaining informed consent

- not doing harm.

Assess your research proposal in terms of each of these rules. Now consider if there are any circumstances in which you might need to bend any of these rules.

11

Writing a Research Proposal

Chapter Objectives

By the end of this chapter you will be able to:

- Understand the key components of a qualitative research proposal.

- Recognize the importance of clarity, planning and persuasiveness in writing a proposal.

- Understand that writing of any kind must be recipient designed for a particular audience.

Introduction

11.1 Before you can set out on your research, you will usually need to submit a research proposal for approval. Although this is, in one sense, a bureaucratic hurdle, it is also an opportunity for you to make sure that you are perfectly clear about the direction which you want your research to take.

Writing a research proposal allows you to clarify in your own mind that you have fully grasped the issues we have been discussing in Part Two of this book. Moreover, it adds a useful discipline. Now it is not just a matter of convincing yourself but of convincing a potentially sceptical audience who will expect you to answer briefly and clearly a set of difficult questions. These questions are set out in Table 11.1.

The best way to answer these questions with brevity and clarity is to follow a standard format. Table 11.2 indicates a basic structure for a qualitative research proposal.

In preparing your proposal, it is worth bearing in mind the special difficulties qualitative researchers can face in achieving credibility. Particularly if you are within a university department where quantitative research is the mainstream, bear in mind that your proposal is likely to receive highly sceptical reviews.

TABLE 11.1 Questions answered by a research proposal

1 *What?* What is the purpose of my research? What am I trying to find out?
2 *How?* How will the proposed research answer these questions?
3 *Why?* Why is the research worth doing (and/or funding)? What will we learn and why is it worth knowing?

Source: adapted from K. Punch, 2006: 20

TABLE 11.2 A structure for a qualitative research proposal

1 Title
2 Abstract (further advice on titles and abstracts is found in Chapter 17)
3 Background or introduction, e.g. contemporary debates in social policy and social science
4 Statement of purpose or aims: the research question ('The intellectual problem(s) I may help solve through this research is (are) ... ')
5 Review of the relevant literature (showing the importance of the project in the context of the classic or definitive pieces of research in this area)
6 Methods (description of case(s) chosen, procedures for data collection and data analysis in terms of (a) their appropriateness to your theoretical orientation and (b) how they satisfy criteria of **validity** and **reliability**) (see Chapters 8 and 15)
7 Ethical issues (see Chapter 10)
8 Dissemination and policy relevance: explain how you will communicate your findings (see Chapters 26 and 27)
9 A timetable indicating the length of time to be devoted to each stage of the research
10 References: use a standard system like Harvard.[1]

Source: adapted from Morse, 1994: 228; Kelly, 1998: 115–21; Rudestam and Newton, 1992: 18

The sceptics may make the following assumptions:

- qualitative research is unstructured

- the results of qualitative research are unpredictable

- the outcome is uncertain (Morse, 1994: 227).

Moreover, most experienced qualitative researchers will expect their potential students to be aware of such concerns and to have thought about how to respond to them. At the very least, they will want to be reassured that:

- Your research is feasible and doable.

- Your research is worth doing.

- You can do it.

- When completed, it will produce a successful dissertation as an MA or a PhD (K. Punch, 2006: 11).

How, then, can one convince a potential university supervisor to support your research proposal? Following the format set out in Table 11.2 should help. But how should you frame your proposal in a way likely to maximize acceptance?

The following suggestions form the rest of this chapter:

- Aim for crystal clarity.

- Plan before you write.

- Be persuasive.

- Be practical.

- Make broader links.

Aim for Crystal Clarity

The proposal should use language and terminology that is understandable to an intelligent lay person as well as to a subject expert. (Cryer, 1996: 15)

11.2 Although it is tempting to seek to display your newly acquired technical jargon, bear in mind that your proposal is likely to be read, in the first instance, by a faculty member who is unlikely to be a specialist in your area of the discipline. So never be content with a proposal which can look like a stream of (perhaps undigested) theories or concepts. Always aim for clear language that describes your research in a way that non-specialists can comprehend.

As Morse suggests, this means that you should resist the temptation to lapse into pure jargon: 'Because some of the reviewers will be from other disciplines, the proposal writer should assume nothing and explain everything' (1994: 227).

By explaining everything, you will have demonstrated the ability to think (and write) clearly. Not only is this the way to write a research proposal, it is also the best indicator that your research itself will be organized in a clear and logical way:

A sloppily prepared proposal will, at best, send a message to the agency that if it funds the proposal, the research may also be sloppy. (1994: 226–7)

For instance, your objectives 'should be clear and it should be easy to decide whether they have been achieved or not' (Kelly, 1998: 117). The ways to achieve this are:

- Be concise (there is no reason why a proposal for a piece of student research should be more than 500 words).

- Use short, simple sentences.

- Use headings as in Table 11.2.

Plan Before You Write

> The writer must show that the design is the result of a series of decisions that she made because of knowledge gained from the ... literature. (Marshall and Rossman, 1989: 13)

11.3 Not only must the proposal demonstrate that it is based on an intelligent understanding of the existing literature, it must show that you have thought about the time you will need to conduct each stage of the research from obtaining access to writing up your data analysis. So, as Sara Arber notes, your research proposal will partly be judged by how you state you are going to use your time:

> You need to adopt a systematic and logical approach to research, the key to which is the planning and management of your time. (1993: 33)

Kelly (1998: 120–1, adapted here) offers an example from an interview study planned to last 32 weeks:

A research timetable

Week 2   Submit proposal to university ethical committee
Week 6   Draw up sample
Week 8   Begin interviews
Week 15   End interviews
Week 23   Complete data analysis
Week 26   First draft sent out for comments
Week 32   Submission of final report

We are not born with a natural ability to prepare research timetables! To help you plan such a timetable, seek the assistance of a trusted teacher in your department. Failing that, seek out an existing research student. With their help, make a list of all the options available in relation to your research problem, method and case(s) to be studied. Now you are in a better position to write a reasoned research proposal that explains the actual choices you have made.

Be Persuasive

> It is easy to get very wrapped up in the subject and think that, because we are convinced of the particular value of our research, others will be too. The way in which the proposal is presented can enable the reader to appreciate what you are planning to do. (Kelly, 1998: 121)

11.4

Kelly is reminding us that, in framing a research proposal, one must think first of the audience who is going to read it (and judge it). This means that it should set out to convince such readers that this is something worth supporting:

> The first principle of grantsmanship is to recognize that a good proposal is an argument ... for the researcher's project. The proposal must make a case to the granting agency that the research question is interesting [and] that the study is important ... Thus the proposal must be written persuasively. (Morse, 1994: 226)

Morse is suggesting that you try to 'sell' your proposal. This means that you must recognize that the craft of selling (your proposal, yourself) is not incongruent with working in a university. 'Ivory towers' were never so isolated as the term suggests!

However, this persuasiveness must be balanced with a realistic understanding about what you can achieve within a few years as a single researcher. Like any good salesperson, do not oversell your goods!

Be Practical

11.5

One way to persuade non-specialists, Morse suggests, is to show the specific ways that your research can address a social problem or solve an organizational trouble (e.g. staff turnover).

Such a concern with practical problems cannot be shrugged off even if you are proposing to do a purely academic piece of research with no expectation that it will be read outside the university. Academic funding bodies are increasingly demanding practical payoffs as well as analytic insights. For instance, Kelly quotes a policy statement by the body that funds social science PhDs in the UK:

> Any lingering public perception of social science as a source of irrelevant, introverted and incoherent output is set for radical alteration ... In future, research which makes a difference to the health and wealth of the population, rather than merely supports 'ivory tower' academic excellence, will be the ESRC's priority. (1998: 112, quoting the Economic and Social Research Council)

The issue of *audiences* for your research is discussed further in Chapter 27. However, if what you are proposing is 'basic research', i.e. a study deriving from debates and concepts internal to social science, then all is not lost. You can strengthen the persuasiveness of your case by showing non-specialists why they ought to take your ideas seriously. One way to do this is to try to make broader links between your (very narrow) research proposal and wider issues.

Make Broader Links

11.6 Realism need not mean that you must present your research as a narrow, anaemic exercise. Even if you cannot cover every aspect of the field yourself, you should demonstrate your understanding of the broader implications of your proposed research. One way to do that is to hint at a wider context: 'Place the problem in context to show, for instance, that "when we understand this, we will be able to work on that"' (Morse, 1994: 227).

Of course, you will be studying very few cases, or maybe only a single case. Be positive about the gains as well as the losses of this! Show how a relatively small database will enable you to conduct an in-depth analysis (see Chapters 9 and 13). And argue that your case can indicate far larger phenomena: 'The writer must show how, in examining a specific setting or group of individuals, she is studying a case of a larger phenomenon' (Marshall and Rossman, 1989: 12).

LINK

For a short, introductory discussion of qualitative research design, go to:

http://64.233.169.104/search?q=cache:1vgd7_cjOm0J:www.usd.edu/~mbaron/edad810/Chapter08.doc+qualitative+research+design&hl=en&ct=clnk&cd=12&gl=uk

---

■ Attempt Exercise 11.1

Concluding Remarks

11.7 If you eventually submit a research proposal with the kind of logical structure I have been suggesting, you may be plagued by a horrible thought. Will I actually have to follow, word for word, every idea I have suggested? If things turn out differently to the way I now expect, will my supervisor insist that I follow my self-prescribed route?

Fortunately, the answer to these kinds of questions is 'generally no'. Your research proposal should not be regarded as some kind of contract which, if approved, is legally enforceable. Every practitioner recognizes that all researchers may, at some stage, find it worthwhile to divert from an initial path. This is particularly true of qualitative research where analysis of field data often leads in unexpected but fruitful directions (see Chapter 13).

Of course, this does not mean that you may not be asked to justify any diversion. But any research proposal should not be set in stone for all time.

What, then, is the point of having to write an initial proposal? Let me suggest two answers to this reasonable question.

TABLE 11.3 Questions a research proposal must answer

1 Why should anyone be interested in my research?
2 Is the research design credible, achievable and carefully explained?
3 Is the researcher capable of doing the research

Source: adapted from Marshall and Rossman, 1989: 2

First, having had to work out a clear, persuasive research proposal is a wonderful discipline which will help you work out exactly what it is you want to do. As such, it can guide you in the initial stages of your research.

Second, such a proposal helps others. In particular, it allows your potential supervisors to see if you are the kind of student who is able to think critically and, just as important, to move outside her own inner world in order to work out what others may be looking for.

This means that ultimately a research proposal should be regarded not as a legal contract but as a way of responding to the potential questions experienced researchers may ask about your plans. These questions are summarized in Table 11.3.

KEY POINTS

When preparing a research proposal, try to find answers to three questions suggested by Keith Punch (2006: 20):

1 *What?* What is the purpose of my research? What am I trying to find out?

2 *How?* How will the proposed research answer these questions?

3 *Why?* Why is the research worth doing (and/or funding)? What will we learn and why is it worth knowing?

You can answer these questions better by following *five* principles:

- Aim for crystal clarity.

- Plan before you write.

- Be persuasive.

- Be practical.

- Make broader links.

■ ■ Further Reading ■

A research proposal is crafted according to the level of your research. MA researchers should turn to Moira Kelly's 'Writing a research proposal' (in C. Seale (ed.), *Researching Society and Culture*, Sage, 1998: 111–22). At PhD level, useful references are Pat Cryer's *The Research Student's Guide to Success* (third edition, Open University Press, 2006: Ch. 4) and Keith Punch's *Developing Effective Research Proposals* (second edition, Sage, 2006) (a much shorter version is contained in Punch's book *Introduction to Social Research*, Sage, 1998: 268–79. Beyond the PhD, you should consult Janice Morse's 'Designing funded qualitative research' (in N. Denzin and Y. Lincoln (eds), *Handbook of Qualitative Research*, Sage, 1994: 220–35).

Note

1 The Harvard system presents references in this order:

- in the main body of your text (not in footnotes): surname of author, followed by date and page reference
- in your references: author (with initials), date, title, place of publication, publisher and page references (for articles or chapters).

 ■ **Exercise 11.1**

Prepare a draft proposal about your research (no more than 1500 words) covering the following elements:

1 Title

2 Abstract

3 Background or introduction

4 Statement of purpose or aims

5 Review of the relevant literature

6 Methods (description of case(s) chosen, procedures for data collection and data analysis)

7 Ethical issues

8 Practical relevance

9 A timetable

10 A set of preliminary references.

Part Three
Collecting and Analysing Your Data

Contents

Part Three moves you on to issues in data collection and analysis. In Chapter 12, I outline what is involved in collecting interview and fieldwork data. Chapter 13 discusses how to develop your data analysis by working early with datasets. The next two chapters in this part of the book consider the use of computer-aided qualitative data analysis and validity and reliability. Chapter 16 shows you how to apply what you have learned in Part Three to evaluate qualitative research.

|12|

Collecting Your Data

```
┌─────────┤ Chapter Objectives ├─────────┐

By the end of this chapter, you will be able to:

• Recognize the key questions involved in collecting interview and observa-
  tional data.

• Know about how to answer each of these questions.

• Understand that such questions and answers are shaped by the theoretical
  model that you are using.
```

Most qualitative studies are based on asking respondents questions or making observations in the field. In this chapter, I will walk you through many of the practical problems involved in collecting and recording such data.

As I will show, collecting data is much more than a technical matter. Following Chapter 7, I will demonstrate that how you conceive and resolve practical research problems is always shaped by your model of how the social world works.

Collecting Interview Data

12.1

In some respects, doing an interview is the most natural thing in the world. After all, a fair proportion of what appears on the Internet, television, radio and newspapers consists of interviews. And these interviews seem not to have a predetermined pattern (as in survey research) but to be fairly free-flowing and open-ended (as in qualitative research). It is hardly surprising, then, that most student researchers identify qualitative research with the open-ended interview. For we all know what an interview looks like and have no difficulty in interviewing or being interviewed.

If you have had any experience of interview research, you will realize that things are not quite so straightforward as this might suggest. In this section, I will discuss:

- defining your research problem
- deciding how many interviews you need
- the interview protocol
- recording and transcribing interviews
- using multiple methods.

Defining your research problem

12.1.1 How do we describe a *qualitative* research design? Interview studies which are based on a relatively small number of cases and use open-ended questions are usually treated as examples of qualitative research. However, as we have already learned, the presence or absence of numbers and rigid structures is insufficient to distinguish between qualitative and quantitative research. Much more important is how you define your research problem using a particular **model** of reality.

Many interview studies seek to find out how a particular group of people perceive things. By assuming that interviews can give a direct access to 'experience' (providing the research design is reliable), such qualitative researchers depend upon a **positivist** model of research shared by quantitative interviewers, such as survey researchers. By contrast, where the emphasis veers more towards the elicitation of 'feelings', an **emotionalist** model is being applied.

Here are some actual student examples of positivist or emotionalist ways of framing a research problem using qualitative interviews:

- How residents in a community of elderly people feel about their life (Tippi, Information Studies/Sociology, Finland).
- Job satisfaction and occupational 'burnout' among female primary school teachers (Sanath, Community Medicine, Sri Lanka).
- The factors and contexts of gender discrimination and how they combine to affect opportunities and circumstances and choices, and how these are reflected in the realization of life and employment trajectories (Martina, Sociology/Human Geography, Czech Republic).
- How do different actors experience the implementation of labour standards in the construction industry in Chennai, India (Annika, Sociology/Human Geography, Norway)?
- Responses of patients who consult unqualified Western medical practitioners (Sachin, Community Medicine, Sri Lanka).

These kinds of research problems exemplify a style of qualitative interviews which aims to 'get inside the heads' of particular groups of people and to tell things from their 'point of view'. Yet, as we saw in Chapter 4, how far is it appropriate to think that people attach a single meaning to their experiences? May not multiple meanings of a situation (e.g. living in a community home) or of an activity (e.g. consulting an unqualified medical practitioner) be represented by what people say to the researcher, to each other, to carers and so on (Gubrium, 1997)?

This raises the important methodological issue of whether interview responses are to be treated as giving direct access to 'experience' and 'feelings' or as actively constructed 'narratives' involving activities which themselves demand analysis (Holstein and Gubrium, 1995). Both positions are entirely legitimate but the position you take will need to be justified and explained.

TIP

Always think through whether qualitative interviews are appropriate to your research problem. For instance, if you are collecting facts or perceptions, would a quantitative survey make more sense?

Now let us review examples of students who use qualitative interviews to address research problems based on a **constructionist** model:

- How family members construct stories about their grief and recovery processes after the death of their baby (Katarin, Psychiatry, Finland).

- How versions of postgraduate life are discursively constructed and sustained by postgraduates in interviews about doing their PhDs (Steven, Social Sciences, UK).

- How drug users and dealers present themselves in order to manage identity and keep self-respect during the interviews (Sveinung, Sociology, Norway).

In these three examples, notice the use of words like 'construct' and 'manage' in the definition of the research problem. This shows how constructionist researchers want to examine the active 'work' that interviewees do in producing their answers. This is very different from positivist projects which simply seek accurate reports of experiences or feelings which are taken to lie inside people's heads.

We have seen two strikingly different ways of conceptualizing your research problem which lead to contrasting ways of looking at interview data. It is worth adding that neither approach is without its own problems. Our positivist examples may de-emphasize the multiple meanings that people attach to what they do. A constructionist way of defining a research topic overcomes that problem but lays itself open to the criticism of losing sight of important substantive issues. For instance, critics might suggest that our three studies gain theoretical sophistication at the risk of downplaying 'real' problems like 'grief' or drug use. So constructionist researchers face a real challenge in translating their findings back to social problems.

━━━━━━━━━━━━━━━━━━━━ LINK ━━━━━━━━━━━━━━━━━━━━

Sage Publications has a very useful methodology site:

www.methodology.co.uk

This includes a blog on interview research with responses to a short piece that I wrote on this topic. Go to:

http://asksage.typepad.com/methods/

A final observation is in order. How you formulate the topic of a qualitative interview study is not just a matter of the research model you employ. You also have to ask questions that are answerable by your data. Sometimes this is merely a matter of narrowing down your topic (see Chapter 6). On other occasions, students may be tempted to use interviews to answer the wrong kind of questions.

A little while ago, I was advising some PhD students at a university in Tanzania. A politics student was interested in what seemed to be an important social issue: how water and sanitation policy had been influenced by the decentralization of Tanzanian local government since 2000. He proposed to find answers by interviewing key stakeholders.

Can you see what the problem is with this approach?

As we learn from our quantitative colleagues, it is difficult to find out what happened in the past by asking present-day respondents. This is not because they may lie but simply because we all view the past through the lens of the present. Hence this kind of *retrospective* study is likely to offer inaccurate information.

Now can you see possible solutions? I suggested that the student could meet this difficulty in one of two ways:

* reformulate his research problem as a study of contemporary stakeholder views

* stick with the original research problem and use different, contemporary data (for instance, contrasting newspaper reports today with those in 2000).

How many interviews do I need?

12.1.2 This question is very common among beginning research students. Remembering what they have been taught on quantitative methods courses, they are terrified that they may be torn to shreds for not having enough data.

One solution is to copy quantitative methods and study all cases or use random samples from a population. Many of the PhD students I taught in Sri Lanka had medical training and followed this quantitative route. Here are two examples:

- A study of unqualified medical practitioners which focused on one province district and included 10 (out of 14) practitioners who gave their consent and 350 of their patients.

- A study of 'burnout' among female primary school teachers using a sample of 15 teachers randomly selected from the participants of a much larger, quantitative, prevalence study.

These examples solve the problem of representativeness but raise other issues. Can detailed qualitative methods of analysis be fully used if you do 350 interviews? Apart from anything else, will you have time to transcribe properly your data? And may not data gathering be so time-consuming that you have little time for data analysis?

Or, in the second example, do you really need a fully random selection of cases in order to do credible qualitative research? A case might look highly illuminating; should we reject it just because it is the only one to which we have access?

Ultimately, the question 'How many cases do I need?' depends upon your research problem. As we saw in Chapter 9, many qualitative researchers use purposive sampling to choose a case because it illustrates some feature or process in which we are interested. This does not provide a simple approval for any case we happen to choose. Rather, purposive sampling demands that we think critically about the parameters of the population we are studying and choose our sample case carefully on this basis.

Here are some examples of students who used purposive sampling to find people to interview:

- A study of 16 students which contained samples of doctoral postgraduates and young lecturers who were registered as PhD candidates, in different departments (psychology and social science) in universities in two UK regions (Steven, Social Sciences, UK).

- Using observation of street drug scenes to recruit 60 young people composed of 40 adolescent street dwellers picked up in the area around an 'open drug scene' and 20 street cannabis dealers aged 15–30 selling at a more dispersed drug scene (Sveinung, Sociology, Norway).

- Studying gender inequalities through biographic interviews with a sample of women selected to include various stages of the life cycle and situations where they are at risk of being disadvantaged in the labour market (Martina, Sociology/Human Geography, Czech Republic).

- A study of care providers of children whose mothers work overseas. Some of the care providers were the fathers of children while the others were their grandparents, aunts and other relatives, and a sample of 20 care providers was selected to represent these different categories (Kamala, Community Medicine, Sri Lanka).

- A study of the links between homeland orientation/connections and the integration of immigrants in Norway from war-torn countries using a contact pool of people within immigrant communities to find informants and respondents (Sunil, Sociology, Norway).

- Studying the local understanding of 'cultural landscapes' (biophysical) and the processes behind different landscape changes using 16 informants found in the Norwegian agricultural registry, grouped according to work, sex and age in a balanced manner (Anders, Geography, Norway).

- A study of work/family balance among a segment of professionals in high-commitment occupations where confrontations between care and career might be expected to be accentuated. Based on a sample of 43 semi-structured, in-depth interviews collected in 2005–2007 with female (26) and male (17), white, heterosexual, lawyers (29) and consultants/managers (14) in the process of establishing different work/life adaptations. Informants were recruited formally through firms, and informally through different (non-related) social networks (Selma, Sociology, Norway).

These examples show you can select your interviewees purposively based on the groups which your research problem addresses. In addition, as in the final example ('work/family balance'), it can be helpful to use a 'snowball sample', using the social networks of one or two initial informants. In an MSc study of the experience of international students at a UK university, Maddie Sandall used email addresses to contact people. She then asked her respondents if they could persuade any of their friends to encourage them to come along for interview.

What questions should I ask?

12.1.3 Survey researchers use a predefined, fixed set of questions which are often derived from pre-tested measures used in other studies. This set of questions is usually known as a *research protocol*. When you have large samples and wish to use statistical tests of significance, fixing your questions can help to increase the reliability of your findings.

By contrast, qualitative interview studies tend to be conducted with quite small numbers and with rather informal patterns of questioning where the aim is to allow the interviewee to set the pace. Usually, the interviewer will have a prepared set of questions but these are used only as a guide, and departures from the guidelines are not seen as a problem (as would be the case in surveys) but are often encouraged.

The following example shows how qualitative interviews can be conducted with a minimal number of prepared questions. This is how one student describes the methods used in his study of doing a PhD:

> In-depth semi-structured interviews [were conducted] with a sample of 16. Participants were asked about their experiences of doing doctorates, whether they considered themselves to be academics, their views on academia more generally, and so forth. (Steven, UK)

By contrast, some qualitative researchers prefer to use a more structured set of questions. For instance, a Sri Lankan PhD student used the following detailed interview guide in his study of the coping mechanisms of women subject to domestic violence.

STUDENT EXAMPLES

Interview Guide

Introduce self
Permission to record
Purpose of study

Date/time
Setting
Respondent
Observations

- Tell me about your visit today, why did you come, who advised you to come?
  about services

- How did the problems start (tell me from the beginning)?
  create timeline

- Tell me about you and your family, where did you live before marriage?
  family background, community

- Was there physical (sexual) abuse/violence?
  specify

- Were the children involved?
  children abused, coping

- What did you do about the problem (why/why not)?
  coping strategies, cultural factors

- What is the reason for the problem (in your opinion/others/family)?
  perspective, opinions and influence

- What would you like to see happening?
  expectations, knowledge

- How can we help you?

Anything additional?

[Ravi, Community Medicine, Sri Lanka]

If you have ever tried to conduct a research interview, you will know that such guidelines, while helpful, only take you so far. As one student comments:

> Although the schedules include complete questions for the interviewees to answer, it was not the aim of the interviewing procedure to read these out verbatim. Throughout the interviews I adopted an in-depth semi-structured or 'conversational' interviewing style. The general aim was to encourage the respondents to speak personally and at length about their lives as doctoral students, while at the same time covering the issues which I was interested in as a researcher. There was a constant balance to be struck therefore between what was interesting to me and what was interesting to them, and as such the interviewer–interviewee relationship veered between impersonality and rapport. (Steven, Social Sciences, UK)

The kinds of problems to which Steven alludes are illustrated by the following questions raised by research students.

STUDENT EXAMPLES

Research Students' Questions on Interviewing

- In the interviews I need to ask many direct questions in order to get specific information about working conditions, how institutions function, etc. However, in order to get information on matters I have not thought of beforehand, it is important also to ask more open questions which encourage the informants to reflect more freely. I find it a bit challenging how to formulate such questions, and would appreciate any input in this regard. [Labour standards in developing countries, using the construction industry in the city of Chennai, South India, as a case. Annika, Sociology and Human Geography, Norway]

- How can I try to make the interviews more open-ended (though based on an interview guide)? [Transnationalism, integration and the Norwegian policy environment: remittance practices and integration among Pakistanis in Norway. Marta, Human Geography, Norway]

- I would appreciate a lot of input from you on issues important to discuss when interviewing elites. As my previous work deals with school research (observing and interviewing pupils and teachers), this PhD project is my first experience of 'researching upwards' – if not in terms of cultural capital, most certainly in terms of economic and social capital. How am I to frame an interview situation opening up for accounts of own – or observation of others' – exclusion or 'failure' in settings where the individualized ideology of meritocracy and the importance of 'successful' presentation of self (competent, resourceful, successful, high power, positive, result oriented, independent, self-sufficient, energetic, bursting with self-confidence, in control of the situation, etc.) are accentuated? With some of the informants I was hardly able to get beyond a definition of the interview situation more similar to a pitch or 'beauty contest' of the informant as a professional or his/her company than a research interview ... compared to informants in my previous work (teachers and students), these elite interviewees generally seemed much less comfortable – and/or acquainted – with conversation frames focusing on their own – or even others' – difficult experiences. [Selma, Sociology, Norway]

The highly intelligent questions posed by these three students ask how to make interviews more open-ended. However, as the last student recognizes, much depends upon the kind of people you are interviewing. When you interview 'up', you may find elite members unhappy about 'opening up' about themselves.

So there are no recipes for successful open-ended interviews. But there are ways of proceeding which give you more hope of success. In the rest of this section, I will discuss:

- avoiding posing your research question directly to the participants
- beginning with a focus group in order to get an initial understanding of how your target group sees things
- piloting your interview schedule.

Don't ask your research question directly

Thoughtless researchers sometimes present their main research question directly to the respondents themselves. This causes two problems. First, as is well known in quantitative surveys, if respondents are made aware of your interests, this can affect their responses. Second, it can lead to lazy research in which careful data analysis is simply replaced by reporting back what people have told you.

As Clive Seale (personal correspondence) has pointed out:

> This is a very common problem in all kinds of studies, but particularly ones where people mistakenly use a qualitative design to answer a question better suited to an experimental or quasi-experimental design. People decide, say, that they are going to see if TV violence encourages violent behaviour. Instead of doing a survey of what people watch on TV and a parallel survey of their tendency to violence, and then seeing whether there is a correlation (hoping that there are no spurious reasons for such a correlation of course), they just select a group of people and ask them (more or less), 'Do you think TV watching causes violence?'

Precede interviews with a focus group

Setting up a **focus group** prior to interviews can help to clarify the issues which you wish to raise. For instance, prior to interviews with carers of Sri Lankan children whose mothers worked overseas, the researcher identified the schools which the children attended. Subsequently:

> Teachers in these schools who teach the target children were invited to take part in focus group discussions. The difficulties and problems of the children at school were identified through these focus group discussions. (Kamala, Community Medicine, Sri Lanka)

Pilot your interview schedule

It is often sensible to try out different styles of questioning prior to your main study. This kind of *piloting* is a feature of most kinds of good research – both qualitative and quantitative.

In the following example, a Finnish PhD student of marketing talks about how she used a pilot study to learn from her early mistakes.

Going Wrong and Putting It Right

Most of the interviewees turned out to be good narrators. Some demanded more information – what the others had talked about, for example – and some interviewees hopped over many years of their working life without mentioning them, which led me to asking a few specific questions. In some interviews I participated a bit too enthusiastically, sometimes because the topic at hand was interesting, sometimes – especially at the beginning – because of the imagined need to reassure them about my knowledge of the themes discussed, or because I was too nervous to tolerate any silence. Before starting the interviews, I was confident about my ability to listen, but seeing the first transcripts and listening to the tapes was a shock. For example:

E: How have you ended up here?
I: I have only been here two years …
E: As an assistant?
I: … senior assistant …
E: So, you are senior …
I: … Now I'm an assistant again, and I don't know about the future (…) It is like this in the academia.
E: That's correct. How long ago, you've graduated from here, haven't you?
I: Yes, I graduated in 19XX and I'm finishing the doctoral thesis this year …
E: You are in a hurry, so to speak!
I: Well, I don't know, if you do research full-time, so you should come up with something as well. There's not much else to do …

I did not allow this interviewee to start his own narrative, but kept on interrupting him. However, as my confidence grew and my knowledge of the subject increased, I started to relax and let people talk at their own pace. I also learned to be careful with leading questions or the use of words with strong connotations – terms like 'career' or 'to drift'. Although many respondents told me that they had 'drifted' into academia, I should never have asked one interviewee: 'How did you drift into this profession?' However, I never repeated that mistake. [Emma, Sociology, Finland]

A British student concurs with Emma about the advantages of pilot interviews.

The Advantages of a Pilot Study

At the beginning of the first year of my PhD I carried out two pilot interviews with fellow PhD students, who were studying at the same university as myself. These initial pilot interviews served several different functions:

- They allowed me to practise interviewing. Although I had used the method of interviewing for my first degree, I did not have much experience of carrying out in-depth interview discussions. In this sense the first few interviews served as useful practices, as I gradually changed my interviewing style ...

- [They helped me] to find out whether I was going to get interesting and substantial data from my participants. Qualitative research can be a risky business in the sense that you literally do not know what you're going to get before going out into 'the field'. You are not sure whether your interests will be reflected in what your participants say. As it turned out the doctoral students I interviewed often spoke at length about the various issues, experiences and dilemmas they were negotiating in their lives. They generally seemed to appreciate the opportunity to speak openly about their dilemmas in the presence of a fellow student. Indeed, this was mentioned in the letter of introduction sent out to potential doctoral student participants.

- [They] ... were helpful in developing interview schedules for the interviews subsequently carried out with doctoral postgraduates at institutions other than my own. [Steven, social sciences, UK]

However, Steven adds that his constructionist approach limits the advantages of piloting. As he points out:

> This 'improvement' in my capability as an Interviewer did not necessarily equate with 'improved' data. When I carried out my first interview I was relatively inexperienced and tended to ask awkward questions of my participant. This generated some interesting data. However, as I became more experienced, my subsequent interviews tended to be somewhat less interesting. (Steven)

| TIP |

Steven's and Emma's successful piloting of their interviews shows there are ways to improve your interviewing skills. However, one caution is in order. Protocol design is less important if you are using a constructionist model and are, therefore, interested in how interviewers and interviewees co-construct a version of 'reality'. In this approach, questions and answers are made a topic as well as a resource (see Rapley, 2004).

■ Attempt Exercise 12.1

Recording and Transcribing interviews

12.1.4 It goes without saying that your interviews should always be recorded. With improved technologies and a growing recognition of the advantages of being able to play back interviews, the old days of pen and paper recording are long gone! Here is Steven's account of how he recorded and transcribed his interviews with PhD students.

STUDENT EXAMPLES

Recording and Transcribing Interviews

The audio of each interview was recorded using a minidisc recorder and lapel microphone. The main benefit of using digital as opposed to analogue recordings of interviews is that audio from a minidisc is of a much higher quality than that from an ordinary analogue cassette tape. Good sound quality is important for the present research as the interest is not only with what the participants say but also with how they say it. Also the process of transcription is speeded up using a Minidisc because of the instant and reliable access which digital recording equipment affords. The interviews could be listened to repeatedly without fear of wear and tear of the disc itself, and textual transcripts could be produced relatively quickly compared to transcribing from a cassette tape with moving parts.

Initial transcripts were made of all the interviews with doctoral students, at first recording only the words which were said by the interviewer and the respondents. These early verbatim transcripts were organized around topics and themes going across the interviews, such as doctoral postgraduate identity work, descriptions of the supervisory relationship, and stories of publishing from doctoral theses. When, after repeated reading, particular extracts were chosen for detailed discursive analysis, they were then retranscribed using a simplified and modified version of the notation developed by Jefferson (1984) for conversation analysis [see the Appendix of this book]. This system captured not only what doctoral students said about their identities and experiences, but also how they said it. The system includes notation to represent the paralinguistic features of spoken interaction, such as emphasis, repair, pauses, and so forth. The Jefferson system is appropriate for a discursive approach which treats talk as a thoroughly interactional phenomenon, bound up with the performance of social actions. [Steven]

The issue of transcription is important in at least two ways. First, transcribing takes a great deal of your time. The danger is that after having spent ages defining your research problem, finding your interviewees and piloting your interview protocol, you then lose yourself in transcription. The end product is that you have very little time to analyse your data when, as I stress throughout this book, this is the *crucial* part of writing a dissertation.

However, my second point is that transcription quality should not be neglected. Too many dissertations, not to mention publications, fail to show sufficient detail in their extracts from interview data, sometimes excluding the researcher's question which provoked a particular answer as well as the 'hm, hms' and other sound particles which can be crucial in guiding an interviewee in a particular direction (see Rapley, 2004).

I have three suggestions to deal with these problems:

- Be comforted by the fact that there is no 'best' method for transcribing interviews: so transcribe in a way that is appropriate to your research problem and theoretical model (for instance, constructionists will need more detailed methods of transcription than positivists or naturalists).

- Don't try to reinvent the wheel: use a standard set of transcription symbols (see the Appendix for a version that constructionists like Steven Stanley tend to use).

- Don't try to transcribe all your interviews at once: select a few to be transcribed in detail, analyse these, and then decide how many and which other interviews need detailed transcription.

Do I need multiple methods?

12.1.5 Whatever research method you use, it is tempting to seek out more data using other methods. Sometimes, this can be a good use of time. For instance, in her MSc study of the experience of international students, Maddie found that a broader comparison would overcome the limitations of her handful of interviews. As she puts it:

> Although the data I have gathered had been quite rich and interesting, I felt that more was needed, therefore this has been backed up by a largely quantitative survey of students in Malaysia. (Maddie)

However, you may recall my earlier advice to students contemplating the use of multiple methods: 'Keep it simple'! Sometimes, multiple methods seem to offer little more than a 'comfort blanket' to give you the feeling that, whatever the deficiencies of your research, you have, at least, covered your research topic from many angles.

There are at least three reasons to be wary of venturing beyond your interview data:

- Ironically, multiple datasets, assembled through different methods, can encourage laziness: as soon as you have a problem analysing one dataset, you switch to another (thereby resolving nothing).

- Using multiple methods can involve you in intractable problems about where the 'truth' lies. As I argue later in this book, this kind of **triangulation** is highly problematic.

- Is there a unitary phenomenon 'out there' which you need to study? Positivists and emotionalists tend to think there is, but constructionists prefer to talk about '*hyphenated* phenomena' (e.g. the family-as-narrated-to-an-interviewer, the family-as-displayed-on-a-photograph, the family-as-reported-in-a-newspaper-story, etc.).

However, we should not throw the baby out with the bathwater. Let me try to answer a student question on the use of multiple methods. In a study of remittance practices and integration among Pakistanis in Norway, a student asks:

> How can I combine data from interviews with data from other conversations and observations in a good way in a study which is mainly interview based? (Marta, Geography, Norway)

My answer is straightforward and in two parts. First, keep things simple by using non-interview data as a guide to conducting your interviews. For instance, in her study of the balance between work and family among female professionals, Selma preceded her interviews by participant observation of five female informants for one work day each.

Second, but only when you have completed the analysis of your interviews, collect further data which may help put your findings into a wider context. For instance, in a PhD study based on interviews with Sri Lankan women subject to domestic violence, the final phase of the research involved an evaluation of an existing hospital-based intervention programme for abused women in a provincial hospital using case profiles and interviews with care givers (Ravi).

I now move on to collecting observational data in ethnographic fieldwork. As you will see, many similar issues arise, for example sampling and recording.

Collecting Ethnographic Data

12.2
In this section, I will be discussing the issues that arise if you are working in the field gathering ethnographic data. Although such fieldwork can use interviews, it always involves observation and recording.

Student researchers face four difficult issues when doing fieldwork:

- access
- narrowing down your research problem
- deciding whether one case is enough
- recording observations.

I discuss below these questions. Each question will lead on to suggestions for possible 'solutions' and several case studies will be used for illustration.

Gaining access

12.2.1
Textbooks (e.g. Gobo, 2008: 118–33; Hornsby-Smith, 1993: 53; Walsh, 1998: 224–5) usually distinguish between two kinds of research setting:

- 'closed' or 'private' settings (organizations, deviant groups) where access is controlled by **gatekeepers**

- 'open' or 'public' settings (e.g. vulnerable minorities, public records or settings) where access is freely available but not always without difficulty, either practical (e.g. finding a role for the researcher in a public setting) or ethical (e.g. whether we should be intruding upon vulnerable minorities).

Depending on the contingencies of the setting (and the research problem chosen), two kinds of research access may be obtained:

- 'covert' access without subjects' knowledge

- 'overt' access based on informing subjects and getting their agreement, often through gatekeepers.

Covert access, particularly to 'closed' settings, raises difficult ethical issues, discussed in Chapter 10. However, we should not assume that 'covert' access always involves possible offence. For instance, on a course I used to teach, students were asked to observe people exchanging glances in an everyday setting (see Sacks, 1992, Vol. 1: 81–94). Providing the students are reasonably sensitive about this and refrain from staring at others, I do not envisage any problems arising.

However, in other cases, covert observation can lead to severe ethical problems as well as physical danger to the researcher. For instance, Fielding (1982) obtained permission to research a far right British political party but still felt it necessary to supplement official access with covert observation (see also Back, 2004).

Student researchers more commonly seek to obtain *overt* access to field settings. What does this involve?

In Chapter 3, we saw how my students Sally Hunt and Simon Allistone sought access for fieldwork. Sally was interested in how mental health professionals define patient diagnoses. As she recognized, observing mental health practice involves highly sensitive ethical issues and her early attempt to gain access to an inpatient setting was unsuccessful. Then what she describes as a 'chance happening' occurred:

> I met up with a former colleague in a local supermarket. After I recounted my difficulty in negotiating access to an inpatient area, he invited me to meet the community team with whom he worked ... Following two separate meetings with the team's psychiatric consultant and with the team leader (a community psychiatric nurse), I was eventually given permission to audio-record the team's weekly case meetings on the understanding that I destroy the tapes when the study concluded. (Sally Hunt, Sociology, Goldsmiths)

Simon's access for his MA research was even easier. He already had contacts at a primary school (children between 5–11) where his partner was a teacher. As he puts it:

At the time my partner was a relatively new primary school teacher, and her exposure to the realities of parents' evening led to her assertion that such meetings had not been directly addressed within her teacher-training course ... My ongoing unofficial pastoral role at my partner's school meant that I had already built up a rapport with the head teacher, so approaching him with a proposal to record some parents' evening meetings was straightforward enough. Once the process of the research was explained and agreed upon, he was happy for the recording to take place, with one stipulation: my access was restricted to the recording of only one teacher in the school, namely my partner. Not wanting to risk what rights to conduct the research I had already gained, I decided not to make any representations regarding the recording of any of the other Year 6 teachers. This did not unduly worry me at the time, since this restriction sat well with the time frame within which I could gather, transcribe and analyse the data for my MA dissertation. As it transpired, I only used a single meeting for the dissertation, leaving me (so I thought) with a surfeit of data. (Simon Allistone, Sociology, Goldsmiths)

Like Simon, Piera was interested in educational settings and found access very straightforward. She comments:

My doctoral dissertation is on classroom data in an Italian primary school ... My data were collected in one school where I worked as a teacher at the time. My working position helped in having access to data. (Piera Margutti, Sociology, York)

These experiences show that it is not uncommon for qualitative researchers to use their existing relationships and contacts for their research. For example, Sara writes about how she used her existing rapport with the lesbian community to collect data for her research on gender roles among lesbians:

I had chosen to study lesbians, an identity that I hold myself. I was already familiar with the local community and knew where to access narrators. I found focus groups particularly easy to organize because I was looking for 'naturally occurring' settings (in the sense that I did not arrange them, but participants would be there regardless of my research). So for focus groups I approached pre-existing groups and simply asked to be their topic for the evening. As a result, I not only intervened less as a researcher in creating the groups, but also needed to expend little energy organiz-ing places, time, participants, etc. (Sara, Sociology, USA)

Similarly, in his research on undercover police officers, Michael drew upon his existing contacts for fieldwork access:

I capitalized on my prior law enforcement experience to gain access to the depart-ments from which I collected data. Some of the agencies I contacted were person-ally known to me and others had individuals who worked there who knew me from my time in law enforcement. (Michael, Sociology, USA)

The lesson from these five accounts is that, if you are contemplating fieldwork, it simplifies access if you draw upon your existing circle of contacts. Trying to enter new fields is likely to involve time-consuming negotiations and may end in failure, particularly if you want to research an ethically sensitive area. In the example below (the ethical aspects of this study are discussed in Chapter 10), John tells what he himself describes as 'a horror story' in his attempt to study suicide helplines.

STUDENT EXAMPLES

Entering New Fields: a Horror Story

[My story is] positive in part, but essentially a horror story in places. I had been contacting various helplines and discussing the issue of data collection. I wanted somewhere where mental health topics and suicide were being discussed. Before long, I had negotiated access to CALM (Campaign Against Living Miserably) which was set up by the NHS to address the rise in depression and suicide in young men. As soon as they agreed, I stopped searching, but then three months went by where I found it difficult to get answers about when and how recording would start. Suddenly I was called to Glasgow to discuss things with the helpline staff, and I also delivered an expensive piece of recording equipment that day. We agreed that recording would start the following week.

As is typical of the 'eggs in one basket' story, the helpline shut down three days later and I was left to start from scratch. Of course I felt somewhat stupid having stopped after getting initial agreement from CALM, but there is always the dilemma of continuing access negotiations with other organizations which you then have to cut short once your data start coming in from another source. Also, the first three months after getting an initial 'yes' were wasted, and I could have collected more than enough calls had I kept the pressure up and got the recording started earlier.

When I realized that CALM had shut down, I contacted a number of self-help groups in the search for data. I received a great response from one in Norfolk, which was for relatives of people who had committed suicide. I had many conversations on the phone with the group's founder, who had told me that they met regularly, were all good friends, and had even been recorded for part of a TV show before, and he would tell them about my research. He came back to me saying that they had agreed to me coming down and video-recording one of their sessions, and they were all keen to be part of the research. I discussed discursive psychological research in great detail with him, and he liked what I was proposing.

When I got there and had set up the camera, people started to arrive. It soon became clear that they were not expecting me, had given no consent to being recorded, and did not know each other or meet regularly (one person said she had attended one session four years ago and had been phoned out of the blue and asked to attend that night). It also became clear very quickly that they were all still very much in a great deal of emotional distress and pain. I turned the camera off and decided to just sit the meeting out. The group leader then announced to the group that he had no idea what I wanted or what my research was about. It then turned very unpleasant, with one member telling me that I was making her pain worse by being there, and I felt physically threatened by another member who appeared quite angry. I cannot express how terrible I felt.

Lessons learned: I should have spoken to participants and not just the group leader before showing up with a camera to the meeting, and if I ever approach a similar group again, I would get consent forms signed before attempting any data collection. I think attending some meetings to get a feel for them before collection starts would also be the way to go. [John, Social Sciences, UK]

In his concluding paragraph, John offers some very useful suggestions to novice researchers. It is dangerous to assume that consent from one person is sufficient, and it helps for others to get to know you before you begin to gather your data. The impression you give may be very important in deciding whether you get overt access:

> Whether or not people have knowledge of social research, they are often more concerned with what kind of *person* the researcher is than with the research itself. They will try to gauge how far he or she can be trusted, what he or she might be able to offer as an acquaintance or a friend, and perhaps also how easily he or she could be manipulated or exploited. (Hammersley and Atkinson, 1983: 78)

Given these kinds of issues of trust, there are a number of ways that help fieldwork students to secure and maintain access:

- *Impression management* related to the 'fronts' that we present to others (see Goffman, 1959). It involves avoiding giving an impression that might pose an obstacle to access, while more positively conveying an impression appropriate to the situation (see Hammersley and Atkinson, 1983: 78–88). For instance, I have failed to gain access, despite initial expressions of interest, to two settings. In a paediatric clinic in the early 1980s, a very conservatively dressed physician, spotting my leather jacket, said I was being 'disrespectful of his patients' and threw me out! Fifteen years before that, as a novice researcher, I let slip over lunch that I was thinking of moving from the UK to North America when I had completed my PhD. This attitude was apparently viewed as improperly 'instrumental' by my host organization and the promised access was subsequently refused. The implication of the latter incident is that there is no 'time out' in field relations and that the most apparently informal occasions are times when you will often be judged.

- *Obtaining bottom-up access* can sometimes be forgotten at great cost. For instance, in the early 1970s, the access granted by the head of personnel at a large local government organization was put in danger by the fact that I had not explained my aims properly to his subordinates. This underlines the point that access should not be regarded as a once-and-for-all situation.

- *Being non-judgemental* is often a key to acceptance in many settings including informal subcultures and practitioners of a particular trade or profession. While the relativist tendencies of many social sciences may allow the researcher sincerely to profess non-judgementality on particular groups' values and practices, this is not always the case when you are studying certain forms of professional practice. Indeed for the researcher who thinks (s)he knows something about 'professional dominance' or even just basic communication skills, it is very easy to appear judgemental.

- *Offering feedback* because some research subjects will actually want your judgements – providing they are of an 'acceptable' kind. For instance, public or business organizations will expect some 'payoff' from giving you access.

12.2.2
Let us assume you obtain access to the field. Suddenly, vast amounts of possible data flow around your ears and eyes. Yet, as I argue in Chapter 6, narrowing down your topic and data is essential if you are to complete a successful dissertation. How are you to do this?

Sometimes, quite pragmatic considerations become relevant. Sally Hunt chose to record the meetings of a mental health team because:

> To undertake a case study of 'single homelessness' in the context of full-time employment makes heavy demands on the researcher in terms of personal resources and operational constraints. The field is so vast and the nature of subjects' lives so dispersed that I elected to observe professional caseworkers rather than service users. For practical reasons, then, I became a participant-observer at the mental health team's (MHT's) weekly case conferences ... These were 'scheduled events', so I would not waste time waiting to see whether or not relevant data would appear but rather would have them to hand. (Sally)

Having decided what she would observe, Sally decided to narrow down her research topic using a constructionist model which involved an **ethnomethodological** focus on **members**' knowledge and an ethnographic attention to **frames**. As she puts it, this focus provided her with a set of questions:

> My focus on members' activities generated initial questions about what they had to know to do their work. It also built on my original interest in diagnostic construction ... I attempted to find 'the sense' of what members were saying, and what was *made* of what they were saying. I then shifted my emphasis to the **discourse**-based question: 'How do participants *do* things?' My desire to pose such a question derived from my reading of other **ethnographic** work as I strove to define my research problem.

Like Sally, Simon narrowed down his research using the literature and models with which he was familiar. His focus was on what was 'routine' and apparently 'obvious' about parent-teacher meetings. He comments:

> the view that parents' evening meetings are events in which 'nothing much was accomplished' ... which, as Baker and Keogh point out, 'is an invitation, if not provocation, to ethnomethodological inquiry' (1995: 265) ... [So I attempted] what Psathas (1990: 45) has called 'unmotivated looking'. This is summed up by Sacks's assertion that 'when we start out with a piece of data, the question of what we are going to end up with, what kind of findings it will give, should not be a consideration' (1984b: 27). (Simon)

Piera decided early on that her classroom research would focus on what the ethnomethodological and CA literature calls 'instruction sequences' (see Mehan, 1979). Her task was to discover whether such sequences are the most representative way of describing classroom interaction. With such a clearly defined topic, Piera's worries shifted to how she should narrow down her data.

┌── **STUDENT EXAMPLES** ┌──

Narrowing Down When Data Are 'Extremely Available'

The first obstacle arose from the extreme availability of the data. Paradoxically, the less you have troubles in having access to data, the more you risk being paralysed, worrying about whether your own choice in selecting how much/what/where to record might influence the findings of the research and be detrimental to their reliability. The decisions I faced were just the very basic ones for an absolute beginner: (1) of everything that goes on in classrooms, what should be recorded; (2) which year group is the most representative, or should all year groups be recorded; (3) for how long the recording should last; (4) how many different classes; (5) how many teachers; (6) would the topic matter; and if so (7) would some lessons be excluded, and why, etc. I had no limits as to which and how many groups I was allowed to record. However, a selection was necessary and it was decided on the two third-year groups, each consisting of 25 children all of the same age (8–9). The choice was made on several grounds: first, I was not interested in a longitudinal perspective; second, presumably in the first two year groups the activities and interaction would have been about learning the school routines and discipline management, mostly; third, it is exactly during the third year of primary school that specific disciplines are introduced to the children for the first time. The main teaching goals are precisely to introduce pupils to each discipline's specialized language (history, geography, natural sciences, etc.) and to their very basic notions. This was very much in line with the primary interest of the project. Finally, I excluded the last two year groups for other reasons. Perhaps other institutional goals, besides imparting basic instruction and the associated interactional practices, may foreground in the fourth and fifth year in teacher/students interaction, especially owing to the fact that students started their training for the final examination. [Piera Margutti, Sociology, York]

Piera's experience shows that having a clear research topic by no means solves the problem of narrowing down so that you can do a piece of manageable student research. Once you have defined your topic, you must rigorously examine the relevance to your research of all the settings to which you have access. Following Piera's example, you need to choose the setting which will most obviously fit your topic and the previous research literature and findings.

Is one case enough?

12.2.3 There is something more we can learn from Piera's experience. Her account reveals that even a single case, like a school, contains infinite possibilities for comparison.

However, it is important to be balanced about the claims you make about your fieldwork when it uses material from a single setting. In his study of one teacher's meetings with parents, Simon acknowledges the limitations of his research but concludes with a theoretical justification.

STUDENT EXAMPLES

Single Cases and Generalizations

Focusing upon a single teacher has certain limitations in terms of generalizing the findings of this research to a wider population. It can be argued that the conversational techniques utilized by the teacher in this research are unique to her, and therefore not easily extrapolated to the parents' evening practice of other teachers. Equally, the fact that the teacher in the data was a class teacher rather than a set teacher could have been an important influential factor. Perhaps set teachers do things differently in such meetings by dint of the fact that they are dealing with the specificities of their curriculum area. Furthermore, the entire format of the meetings might have been different at another stage of the academic year, even if carried out by the same teacher studied in this research. In short, various permutations in the actual accomplishment of parents' evening could be hidden by the fact that the data sample consists of a single teacher on a single parents' evening.

How, then, should this research be seen in terms of both sampling variety and external validity? Indeed, given the tension between the specific difficulties associated with the gathering of the data and the ideal research design outlined above, can this study say anything useful about the phenomenon that has been studied?

I believe the answer lies in seeing this research not as an attempt to provide categorical 'truths' about all parents' evenings in general, but as an attempt to raise questions about such meetings by looking at a single case in detail. To some extent, raising questions in this way relies upon the perspective within CA that '*social practices that are possible*, that is, *possibilities of language use*, are the central objects of all conversation analytic case studies on interaction in institutional settings' (Peräkylä, 2004: 297, original emphasis). [Simon]

The language of 'possibilities' which Simon uses is more or less specific to CA. However, whatever model you use, you need not feel overly self-conscious when your fieldwork is based on a single case. Three simple ways of managing this concern are available:

- Be open about the limitations of your study.

- Show how your narrowing down even within a single setting has been rigorously conducted.

- Emphasize that qualitative researchers treat single cases as crucial in attempting to *refute* initial hypotheses. Flyvbjerg (2004) reminds us of Popper's suggestion that the observation of a single black swan would be sufficient to falsify the generalization that all swans are white. As a consequence: 'Falsification is one of the most rigorous tests to which a scientific proposition can be subjected: if just one observation does not fit with the proposition it is considered not valid generally and must therefore be either revised or rejected ... The case study is well suited for identifying "black swans" because of its in-depth approach: what appears to be "white" often turns out on closer examination to be "black" (2004: 424).

12.2.4

Recordings of **naturally occurring** interaction allow you to return to your data in their original form as often as you wish. The problem with fieldnotes is that you are stuck with the form in which you made them at the time and that your readers will only have access to how you recorded events.

There are two partial solutions to this problem: following strict conventions in writing fieldnotes, and adhering to a consistent theoretical orientation. The issue of fieldnote conventions will be discussed in Chapter 13. In this chapter, I discuss an observational research study which began from a well-defined theory.

In the early 1980s, I obtained access to a number of clinics treating cancer patients in a British National Health Service (NHS) hospital. Following Phil Strong's (1979) account of the 'ceremonial order of the clinic', I was interested in how doctors and patients presented themselves to each other. For instance, Strong had noted that NHS doctors would adhere to the rule 'politeness is all' and rarely criticize patients to their faces.

While at the hospital, I noticed that one of the doctors regularly seemed to 'go missing' after his morning clinics. My curiosity aroused, I made enquiries. I discovered that most afternoons he was conducting his 'private' practice at consulting rooms in a salubrious area of London's West End.

Nothing ventured, nothing gained, so I tried asking this doctor if I could 'sit in' on his private practice. To my great surprise, he consented on condition that I did not tape-record. I happily agreed, even though this meant that my data were reduced to (what I saw as) relatively unreliable fieldnotes.

Obviously, in making fieldnotes, one is not simply recording data but also analysing them. The categories you use will inevitably be theoretically saturated – whether or not you realize it! Given my interest in Strong's use of Goffman's (1974) concept of **framing**, I tried to note down the activities through which the participants managed their identities. For instance, I noted how long the doctor and patient spent on social 'small talk' and how subsequent appointments were arranged.

However, if the researcher is physically present, two different kinds of issues should never be neglected:

- what you can see (as well as hear)
- how you are behaving and how you are being treated.

What you can see

Both NHS clinics were held in functional rooms, with unadorned white walls, no carpets and simple furniture (a small desk, one substantial chair for the doctor, and a number of stacking chairs for patients, families and students). Like most NHS hospitals, heating pipes and radiators were very obtrusive.

To enter the consulting rooms of the private clinic is to enter a different world. The main room has the air of an elegant study, perhaps not unlike the kind of room in a private house where a wealthy patient might have been visited by an eighteenth-century doctor. The walls are tastefully painted and adorned with prints and paintings. The floor has a fine carpet. The furniture is reproduction antique and includes a large, leather-topped desk, several comfortable armchairs, a sofa, a low table covered with coffee table books and magazines, and a bookcase which holds ivory figures as well as medical texts. Plants are placed on several surfaces and the room is lit by an elegant central light and a table lamp. To add an executive touch, there are three phones on the desk, as well as a pen in a holder.

This room establishes an air of privacy as well as luxury. At the NHS clinics, patients are nearly always examined in curtained-off areas. Here, however, the examination couch is in a separate room which can only be entered through the consulting room. Although more functional than the latter, it is nonetheless carpeted and kept at a high temperature to keep patients warm. Even the doctor himself may knock before entering this examination room while the patient is dressing or undressing.

How you are being treated

The emphasis on privacy in British 'private' medicine creates a special problem for the researcher. While at the NHS clinics I sheltered happily behind a name-tag, at the private clinic my presence was always explained, if ambiguously ('Dr Silverman is sitting in with me today if that's alright?'). Although identified and accepted by the patient, I remained uncomfortable in my role in this setting. Its air of quiet seclusion made me feel like an intruder.

Like the doctor, I found myself dressing formally and would always stand up and shake hands with the patient. I could no longer merge into the background as at the NHS clinics. I regularly experienced a sense of intruding on some private ceremony.

My impression was that the private clinic encouraged a more 'personalized' service and allowed patients to orchestrate their care, control the agenda, and obtain some 'territorial' control of the setting. In my discussion of the data, like Strong, I cite extracts from consultations to support these points, while referring to deviant cases and to the continuum of forms found in the NHS clinics.

My interest in how observers are treated in medical settings is nicely demonstrated in Anssi Peräkylä's (1989) study of a hospital ward for terminally ill people. Peräkylä shows how staff use a 'psychological' frame to define themselves as objective surveyors of the emotional reactions of such patients. The psychological frame is a powerful means of resolving the identity disturbances found in other frames; when a patient resists practical or medical framing, staff can explain this in terms of his psychological state.

However, the psychological frame also turns out to be highly relevant to understand the staff's response to Peräkylä himself. By seeing him as a researcher principally interested in patients' feelings, the staff had a ready-made explanation of his presence to give to patients and also were able to guess which of their own activities might need explaining to him.

Like Peräkylä, by examining my own involvement in the 'framing' of the interaction, and using my eyes as well as my ears, I had kick-started my analysis. However, were there other ways in which I could systematically compare the two NHS clinics with the private clinic? In Chapter 13, I discuss some simple quantitative measures I used in order to respond to this problem.

As already noted, I relied on fieldnotes in this study because I was refused permission to record. Obviously, recording (audio or visual) is the preferred option since it gives you the opportunity to replay data uncontaminated by your assumptions at the time of the recording.

In her PhD on mental health casework, Sally Hunt gathered audio-recordings of team meetings which were supplemented by contemporary fieldnotes. As I recommended earlier in this chapter, she began by transcribing only a few meetings. This allowed her to begin early data analysis and to guide which (parts of) other recordings should be transcribed. Her research diary is a useful illustration of the nitty-gritty issues that arise when you first try to record and transcribe fieldwork settings.

STUDENT EXAMPLES

Decisions about Recording and Transcribing

The practicalities of audio-recording multiple voices in a less-than-soundproof environment exerted certain constraints. It was not possible to denote overlapping voices for example. Neither was it possible to decipher the simultaneous secondary interactions which frequently occurred alongside the main action. I tried to transcribe what I heard as faithfully as possible using standard spelling and punctuation so that members' accounts would not appear 'unnecessarily odd' to the reader. I did not attempt to represent accented talk, and lengths of pauses were not timed exactly.

The act of producing the transcripts was not a straightforward matter. In the main, they were constructed according to my own common-sense reasoning as I had no precedent for the process of transcribing. Because of this, transcripts do not always conform to accepted conventions. However, there is no perfect transcript and what I have adequately serve my analytic purposes … With hindsight, I might use more conventional transcription devices if I were to do the transcripts again. This would save the 'creative' work of devising my own. However, lacking the quality of recording more commonly associated with CA, it remains a matter of debate as to whether this could have been a practical option. From a methodological perspective, I did not need the fine detail required by those working with the CA method. [Sally]

A basic technical problem for all forms of recording is where you place your equipment. As Sally discovered, the location of microphones can lead to too much background noise. In collecting video-recordings of physiotherapy treatment sessions within the British health services, Ruth had to come up with original solutions to obtain the sound and images she needed.

STUDENT EXAMPLES

Coping with Recording 'Troubles'

I encountered a number of troubles, and worked out various solutions as a result. Sound was a challenge, since treatments go on in curtained-off areas of large rooms or gyms. After trying several mics, I found that I could best capture the local sound by fitting the therapist with a tiepin (sometimes called a Lavalier) microphone, attached to a transmitter. The transmitters come with small clips to attach to the clothing, rather like those worn by some TV presenters. The therapists, whose work involves a lot of moving around, found themselves constantly having to reattach these. I ended up sourcing a security belt from a travel shop, into which we slipped the transmitter; the wiring to the tiepin mic then ran up under the therapist's uniform and attached to their lapel. The receiver was also a challenge: small models are now available (particularly those designed especially for camcorders by Sennheiser), but mine was rather bulky, and I attached it to the camera's tripod using the rubberized band material (Thera-Band ®) that physiotherapists often use in treatment activities. When recording, I turned on the sound and the camera as soon as the therapist went to greet the patient and bring them to the treatment area, and tried to avoid turning off until the final goodbyes; this maximized the capture of the interaction.

I used various practices and equipment in order to minimize intrusiveness and yet capture as much as possible during treatment sessions where participants are more mobile than they are during doctors' consultations. Equipment-wise, I used a heavy tripod which could extend to almost 2 metres. The tripod was positioned behind the screens or curtains which surrounded the treatment area, with the camera thus poking over the top. I sat nearby, but behind the screens, listening to the action via a pair of headphones attached to the camera. If I could discern that some pretty large-scale movement was going on, e.g. if the patient moved from a lying to a standing position, I climbed onto a conveniently positioned stool and adjusted the camera angle as necessary. Other practices for reducing intrusiveness included the usual ones of having equipment set up for as much time as possible. In addition, I found that therapists often wanted to directly remind the patients about the camera just as they entered the treatment area. I began to pre-empt this, asking them not to do so, in order to reduce the direct attention paid there and then to the recording equipment. I decided that this was justified within the informed consent procedures used, since I had extensive discussions with patients about the proposed recordings beforehand, and I also checked patients' consent following completion of their recordings. [Ruth, Social Sciences, UK]

Ruth's story shows that, however well prepared you are, unforeseen contingencies will arise when you first try to make recordings. As Menisha implies, it may turn out that quite basic things go wrong.

STUDENT EXAMPLES

Getting the Basics Right

Just after starting my PhD I went to my first setting for data collection, a fire service control room, to film the staff at work. Here I hoped to capture some rich data of staff interacting with one another and technology, imagining a dramatic environment: it was a fire department control room, after all! Needless to say, things did not transpire as I had imagined. The environment itself was not the 'action packed', drama filled one that I had envisaged, but rather more subdued. So I was a little disappointed. Nevertheless, through my recordings I did obtain rich data that raise some interesting issues to begin an analysis.

I remembered to take all the right equipment – camcorder, microphone, tripod and power supply – and set it up correctly. Whilst I was pleased at the time that everything was running smoothly, I was horrified to discover afterwards that in the four hours that I had been 'recording', only one and half hours had recorded. My camera angle was also a bit dubious, as a few times, instead of capturing the correct angle, where participants were gathering around a desk to solve a problem, I was filming a desk and its empty chair – not the most stimulating subjects for analysis. From personal experience, what advice would I have to offer? As well as ensuring that you have camera angles set up carefully, and that microphones are positioned so you can hear the participants on playback, there are simpler things to remember. Ensure you know how to set up equipment, such as how the camera fits on the tripod, and understand the features of the camera you will use. Charge batteries, and before recording, ensure you have checked the recording time of the tape, so that it does not run out mid filming. Planning and preparation are essential. Finally, go into an environment with an open mind; things might not be as you expect, but this is not necessarily a bad thing. [Menisha, Management, UK]

Menisha's and Ruth's experiences show the complicated issues that arise when you are trying to produce images and sound relevant to your research problem. The clear implication is that you should pre-test the effectiveness of your recordings before you gather your main data. And, of course, even when you have obtained your recordings, you still have to sort out adequate methods of transcription (see Heath, 2004, on video transcription).

However, I would not want to conclude this chapter on a note of despair. As in Piera's research on a primary school classroom, technical issues in recording naturally occurring interaction can sometimes be readily resolved.

Simple Problems, Simple Solutions

Deciding where to place the cameras was clear from the beginning. In fact, it is rather typical of the Italian school system that each year group is assigned to a classroom that actually 'belongs' to the group for the whole school year. Here students do most of their learning activities, except for gymnastics and foreign language classes. In each classroom, one teacher and 25 students had fixed positions most of the time: one facing the others in parallel rows of seats. In order to capture both sides, it was necessary to place two cameras facing each other. The cameras I used at the time (2000) worked with cassettes lasting 45 minutes, with the disadvantage of having to enter the classroom frequently in order to replace the cassette in each camera – a great disturbance for the ongoing activity. The problem was resolved by connecting the cameras with video-recorders operating with VHS cassettes. In this way, four-hour recording without interruption was granted. The cassettes were replaced at the routine and natural interruptions of the school days, while the children were having their lunch in another room and at the end of the schoolday. It was possible to gather data without the participants seeing me. Furthermore, everything that happened in the classroom was recorded. I believe that now digital cameras have their own hard disk, long sessions of talk can be recorded without difficulties. [Picra, Sociology, York]

TIP

Make use of the technologies you already possess. Maddie's interviews with international students for her MSc were recorded using a digital recorder. She adds that these recordings were then 'converted to MP3 and downloaded to my iPod to allow easy transcription from the comfort of my sofa!'

■ Attempt Exercise 12.2

Concluding Remarks _____

12.3 In this chapter, we have reviewed many of the practical problems that can arise in collecting, recording and transcribing qualitative data. In most cases, I have shown that there are straightforward solutions to these problems.

However, as I have emphasized throughout, doing qualitative research is not quite like following a cookbook. To produce a worthwhile study depends upon first sorting out what features of the social world attract your interest. And this, in turn, depends upon working with a consistent model of social reality.

| | KEY POINTS | |

KEY POINTS

1 Collecting data is never just a technical matter. Data collection must be organized in terms of answering a specific research question which itself is shaped by a particular analytical model of the social world.

2 If you are gathering interview data, you need to think through the following issues:

- How many interviews are sufficient?
- Do I need some kind of interview schedule?
- Do I need to pilot my interviews?
- How do I propose to transcribe my data?
- Should I use other sources of data?

3 If you are collecting field data, you need to consider:

- how you are going to obtain access (and the implications of such access)
- how your initial observations may help you to narrow down your research problem
- how you should record your observations
- whether one 'case' is enough.

■ ■ Further Reading ■

Steinar Kvale's *Doing Interviews* (Sage, 2007: 33–66) is a great source of practical advice on conducting interviews. If you are considering using interviews to access narratives, I recommend Jaber Gubrium and James Holstein's *Analyzing Narrative Reality* (Sage, 2009) and Catherine Riessman's *Narrative Methods for the Human Sciences* (Sage, 2008). Barbara Czarniawska's *Shadowing and Other Techniques for Doing Fieldwork in Modern Societies* (Liber, 2007) is a goldmine of insightful advice on collecting fieldwork data.

 ■ Exercise 12.1

The following research on burnout among Sri Lankan female primary school teachers includes a detailed interview guide.

- What advantages and disadvantages do you see in this guide in the context of a qualitative research study?

- If you plan to do interview research, what sort of guide (if any) will you use? Why?

Interviewer guide

1 Socio-demographic factors of the teacher:

- Age
- Ethnicity
- Religion
- Marital status

- Husband's occupation
- Number of children
- Family income
- Place of residence: district, urban or rural
- Distance of school
- Method of travel to school

2 Capacity and experience of the teachers:

- Highest educational qualification
- Total experience in teaching
- Number of years in current school
- Grade of the class

3 Satisfaction:

- Are you satisfied with your job?
- If yes, what more than anything do you feel leads to this job satisfaction?
- If no, what more than anything do you feel prevents you from being satisfied with your job?

4 Satisfaction regarding factors in the classroom:

- Number of children
- Space, ventilation, temperature
- Teaching materials

5 Satisfaction regarding student interaction:

- Students' achievements
- Students' behaviour

6 Satisfaction regarding cooperation from colleagues and superiors:

- Colleagues
- Superiors

Source: Sunil, Sri Lanka

 ■ **Exercise 12.2**

If you are planning to do some fieldwork observations, write a short research plan covering the following issues:

- How will I obtain access to the field (and why are access negotiations important ethically and as a source of data)?

- How can I use my fieldwork to narrow down my research topic?

- Am I going to use one or more settings? Will one 'case' be enough?

- How do I plan to record my observations?

|13|

Developing Data Analysis

| | Chapter Objectives | |

By the end of this chapter, you will be able to:

- **Kick-start your data analysis.**

- **Work systematically with interviews, observational data, audio-recordings or visual images.**

- **Recognize the useful role that theoretical models play in shaping your research.**

Introduction

13.1 After their first year of PhD research, people have varying degrees of certainty about the future. As Coffey and Atkinson (1996) put it, the end of year 1 sees two kinds of researcher. The uncertain one feels she is drowning in data and asks: 'I've collected all these data, now what should I do?' The other, more confident, researcher states: 'I've collected all my data, now I'm going to analyse them and write them up.'

The temptation might be to find merit in both positions. After all, self-questioning and self-confidence both seem to be worthy qualities in a researcher. In fact, *neither* position is satisfactory and both reflect a more or less wasted first year of research:

> Both positions imply a woeful lack of appreciation of what is and can be meant by analysis ... [Such analysis] is a *pervasive* activity throughout the life of a research project. Analysis is not simply one of the later stages of research, to be followed by an equally separate phase of 'writing up results'. (1996: 10–11, my emphasis)

Research designs which devote the first year solely to a literature review and/or data gathering may look excellent on paper. Indeed, they may be just the thing in quantitative studies more concerned with implementing pre-designed 'measures' rather than employing a theoretical imagination. But in most qualitative research, unless you are *analysing* data more or less from day 1 you will always have to play 'catch-up'.

All very well, you might respond, but where on earth am I going to get my data from on day 1? Whether I'm doing an MA or a PhD, surely most of my early work will involve getting access to some research site or set of respondents and then, if successful, gathering my data. How is it going to be possible to start data analysis so quickly?

In the rest of this chapter, I show you how to kick-start your data analysis very early on. I then discuss ways to begin data analysis on many different kinds of qualitative data: interviews, fieldnotes, transcripts of conversation and visual data.

Kick-Starting Data Analysis

13.2 As already noted, you might well ask: where am I going to get my data on day 1? For both MA and PhD students, there are five very practical, complementary solutions to this puzzle:

- Analyse data already in the public sphere.
- Beg or borrow other people's data.
- Seek advice from your supervisor.
- Analyse your own data as you gather them.
- Ask key questions about your data.

I briefly discuss each strategy below.

Analyse data already in the public sphere

13.2.1 Some types of naturally occurring materials are already waiting for you. For instance, when undergraduate students doing a dissertation at my London college used to approach me with their concerns about gathering and analysing data in, say, a three-month time slot, I usually gave the following advice – still relevant today. Hop on a train to Colindale in North London. Turn right out of the station and you will come to a big building marked British Museum Newspaper Library. Now select a few newspapers which covered a particular story (e.g. Princess Diana's death, the O.J. Simpson trial or the financial crash of 2008).

Of course, you still lack a research problem and a method of analysis, and you will need to think long and hard about both. But you have your data, so go to it!

Needless to say, the public sphere contains much more than newspapers. There are all the other kinds of written texts from novels to the contents of different websites on the Internet. There are the products of the broadcast media, radio and TV programmes, from phone-ins to soap operas and news broadcasts. Then there are those rare qualitative studies which reproduce large portions of data, making them available for your own reanalysis, perhaps following up different questions from those originally asked.

Even if you intend, in due course, to gather your own data, these materials are immediately available. As such, they provide a marvellous opportunity to refine your methods and to get a feel of the joys (and torments) of 'hands-on' data analysis.

Beg or borrow other people's data

13.2.2 Perhaps your research interests cannot be accommodated by data in the public sphere. If so, it is always worth making enquiries in your department about relevant data that other people may be willing to share with you.

Your supervisor is an obvious person to turn to. Having agreed to supervise you, and thereby acknowledged a common research interest, it is probable that your supervisor will have already gathered data that may be relevant to your project. Don't be shy to ask if you might have access to them. This was exactly the strategy that my student Vicki Taylor followed. I was delighted to pass on my counselling audiotapes to her so she could explore a research problem which was different to mine.

Of course, there may be ethical or other reasons why such access is not always possible. But most supervisors will be delighted, perhaps even flattered, if you are interested in their own data. After all, your research may lead to new ideas which will help them in their own work.

If your supervisor cannot deliver the goods, explore your various peer groups. Fellow research students in your department, perhaps two or three years into their research, may, like your supervisor, welcome passing on some of their own data. Or perhaps you can turn to members of study groups in your area, or even to visiting speakers talking on a relevant topic.

Above all, you must remember that, in most disciplines, no 'brownie points' are usually given for having your own data. It is the quality of your data *analysis* that will matter, not whether you can show how clever you were to access your data. Perhaps only in anthropology may the display of how, in pursuit of your 'tribe', you have travelled thousands of miles, learnt a foreign language and endured endless hardships count for something – but not much, I suspect.

Even if you feel happier to have your own data, remember that this does not exclude the first two strategies. In the early stages, analysis of other people's data or public data may still give you the impetus you need for research 'lift-off' when you are ready to analyse your own materials.

Seek advice from your supervisor _____

13.2.3 As an undergraduate, your main face-to-face contact with a faculty member may have been when you submitted a term-paper or, occasionally, when you got some feedback after such a submission. However, this model of a student–staff relationship is totally inappropriate when you are doing your own research.

Supervisors are there to offer support when you most need it (see Chapter 22). If you feel that you are 'drowning in data', that is a prime time to ask for help.

One way they can help you gain focus is to suggest a small and hence achievable task. Two examples of such tasks from Howard Becker and Harry Wolcott are given below:

- Offering a snap characterization of what seems to be happening in your data and asking you to respond to it. It really doesn't matter how wide of the mark this idea is if it can get you to start working with your data (Becker, 1998).

- Asking you to take 'some manageable *unit of one* as a focus' (Wolcott, 1990: 69, discussed at greater length in Chapter 5). In this way, instead of confronting your data as one large, threatening mass, you can narrow down and achieve a focus on one topic, one activity or one day (or one minute).

These kinds of task should help you overcome the kind of mental blocks we all too readily erect for ourselves when first confronting data. If we are set a small task, we are more likely to succeed and to gain confidence. Moreover, through such small tasks, we can start to see subtleties in our data which may be hidden if we ask big questions at the outset. As Becker (1998) reminds us, don't over-theorize early on in data analysis. Instead, begin from a situation or a datum and then build theories out of this limited material.

Analyse your own data as you gather them _____

13.2.4 Data analysis should not only happen after all your data have been safely gathered. If you only have one interview or recording or set of fieldnotes, go to it! Where appropriate, start transcribing. In all cases, start reviewing your data in the light of your research questions.

Now is the time to test out methods, findings and concepts. Here are some good questions to ask yourself:

- Do I feel comfortable with my preferred method of data analysis (e.g. grounded theory, narrative, conversation or discourse analysis)?

- Is my data analysis method suggesting interesting questions?

- Is it giving me a strong grip on my data that looks like it might generate interesting generalizations?

- Do previous research findings seem to apply to my data? If not, why not? If so, how can I use my data to develop these findings?

- How do particular concepts from my preferred model of social research apply to my data? Which concepts work best and hence look likely to be most productive?

None of these questions can be properly answered from the armchair or drawing board. No matter how elegant your original research proposal, its application to your first batch of data is always salutary. In most qualitative research, sticking with your original research design can be a sign of inadequate data analysis rather than demonstrating a welcome consistency.

None of this will you know until you begin analysing your data. Of course, this will mean committing yourself to writing up your analysis at a very early stage. As Wolcott argues: 'You cannot begin writing early enough' (1990: 20). Even a 200-word shot at data analysis will give your supervisor something to go on. And even if your understandable initial hesitancy means that you are not 'off and running', at least you will have started.

 ■ **Attempt Exercise 13.2**

Ask key questions about your data

13.2.5 Of course, what is a 'key' question will depend upon your research topic and your preferred model of qualitative research. Although this means that there are few if any 'free-floating' key questions, the following list has worked with my own students and is worth posing about your own research:

- What are the main units in my data and how do they relate to one another? Remember that no meaning resides in a single unit and so everything depends on how your units fit together. This is an issue of *articulation*.

- Which categories are actually used by the people you are studying? Remember that, unlike quantitative researchers, we do not want to begin with our own categories at the outset. This is an issue of *definition*.

- What are the contexts and consequences of your subjects' use of categories? Remember that it is rarely right to ask 'why' questions before you have identified the local phenomena involved. This is an issue of *hows* and *whats*.

- How do my difficulties in the field over, say, access and how I am defined by my research subjects, provide me with further research topics? Remember that the beauty of qualitative research is that it offers the potential for us to topicalize such difficulties rather than just treat them as methodological constraints. This is an issue of the creative use of *troubles*.

However, a checklist of 'suggestions' can appear somewhat anaemic and without substance. Let me illustrate these general points with an account of how data analysis developed in one qualitative study. The beauty of qualitative research is that it gives you access to the nitty-gritty reality of everyday life viewed through a new analytic lens. Through the example that follows, you will learn how to take advantage of that access in order to focus and then refocus your data analysis.

A Case Study

13.3 In the early 1980s (see Silverman, 1987: Chs 1–6) I was directing a group of researchers studying a paediatric cardiology (child heart) unit. Many of our data derived from tape-recordings of an outpatient clinic that was held every Wednesday.

It was not a coincidence that we decided to focus on this clinic rather than upon, say, interaction on the wards. Pragmatically, we knew that the clinic, as a scheduled and focused event, lasting between two and four hours and tied to particular outcomes, would be likely to give us a body of good quality data. By contrast, on the ward, tape-recording would be much more intrusive and produce tapes of poorer quality because of multiple conversations and background noise. Even if these technical problems could be overcome, the (apparently) unfocused character of ward life meant that it would be far harder to see order than in the outpatient clinic. For instance, unlike the latter, there would be no obvious repetitive structures like scheduled meetings by appointment, physical examinations and announcements of diagnosis and prognosis.

Of course, this does not mean that a researcher should never study apparently unfocused encounters – from the hospital ward to the street corner. But it does mean that, if you do, you must be prepared for long vigils and apparently unpromising data before researchable ideas start to gel.

At our hospital clinic, we became interested in how decisions (or 'disposals') were organized and announced. It seemed likely that the doctor's way of announcing decisions was systematically related not only to clinical factors (like the child's heart condition) but to social factors (such as what parents would be told at various stages of treatment). For instance, at a first outpatients' consultation, doctors would not normally announce to parents the discovery of a major heart abnormality and the necessity for life-threatening surgery. Instead, they would suggest the need for more tests and only hint that major surgery might be needed. They would also collaborate with parents who produced examples of their child's apparent 'wellness'. This step-by-step method of information giving was avoided in only two cases. If a child was diagnosed as 'healthy' by the cardiologist, the doctor would give all the information in one go and would engage in what we called a 'search and destroy' operation, based on eliciting any remaining worries of the parent(s) and proving that they were mistaken.

In the case of a group of children with the additional handicap of Down's syndrome, as well as suspected cardiac disease, the doctor would present all the clinical information at one sitting, avoiding a step-by-step method. Moreover, atypically, the doctor would allow parents to make the choice about further treatment, while encouraging them to dwell on non-clinical matters like their child's 'enjoyment of life' or friendly personality.

We then narrowed our focus to examine how doctors talked to parents about the decision to have a small diagnostic test on their children. In most cases, the doctor would say something like:

> **What we propose to do, if you agree, is a small test.**

No parent disagreed with an offer which appeared to be purely formal – like the formal right (never exercised) of the Queen not to sign legislation passed by the British Parliament. For children with Down's syndrome, however, the parents' right to choose was far from formal. The doctor would say things to them like the following:

> **I think what we would do now depends a little bit on parents' feelings.**
>
> **Now it depends a little bit on what you think.**
>
> **It depends very much on your own personal views as to whether we should proceed.**

Moreover, these consultations were longer and apparently more democratic than elsewhere. A view of the patient in a family context was encouraged and parents were given every opportunity to voice their concerns and to participate in decision making.

In this subsample, unlike the larger sample, when given a real choice, parents refused the test – with only one exception. Yet this served to reinforce rather than to challenge the medical policy in the unit concerned. This policy was to discourage surgery, all things being equal, on such children. So the democratic form coexisted with (and was indeed sustained by) the maintenance of an autocratic policy.

The research thus discovered the mechanics whereby a particular medical policy was enacted. The availability of tape-recordings of large numbers of consultations, together with a research method that sought to develop hypotheses inductively, meant that we were able to develop our data analysis by discovering a phenomenon for which we had not originally been looking.

The lessons to be drawn from this study are summarized in Table 13.1.

TABLE 13.1   Four ways to develop data analysis

- Focus on data which are of high quality and are easiest to collect (tape-recordings of clinics)
- Look at one process within these data (how medical 'disposals' are organized)
- Narrow down to one part of that process (announcing a small diagnostic test)
- Compare different subsamples of the population (children with Down's syndrome and the rest)

So much for general issues. We will now see how you can kick-start data analysis in the context of using four different kinds of data:

- interviews
- fieldnotes
- audiotapes of naturally occurring talk
- visual images.

Interviews

13.4 In Chapters 4 and 12, I examined the various ways that researchers can read sense into answers that respondents give to open-ended interviews. The most popular approach is to treat respondents' answers as describing some external reality (e.g. facts, events) or internal experience (e.g. feelings, meanings). Following this approach, it is appropriate to build into the research design various devices to ensure the accuracy of your interpretation. So you can check the accuracy of what your respondents tell you by other observations (see Chapter 15 on the method of **triangulation**). And you can treat such measures as inter-coder agreement (see Chapter 15) and computer-assisted qualitative data programs (see Chapter 14) as a means of securing a fit between your interpretations and some external reality. Containing elements of positivism (facts) and emotionalism (feelings), we can call this a realist approach to interview data.

As Clive Seale has pointed out (personal correspondence), 'realism' is here used in the sense of the literary genre whose aim is to describe the 'gritty' reality of people's lives. In this approach, typical of tabloid journalism, 'confessional' stories are gathered and presented to the reader as new 'facts' about personalities. This form of realism has had much influence on qualitative research (see Atkinson and Silverman, 1997).

An alternative approach treats interview data as accessing various stories or **narratives** through which people describe their world (see Riessman, 2008; Gubrium and Holstein, 2009). This approach claims that, by abandoning the attempt to treat respondents' accounts as potentially 'true' pictures of 'reality', we open up for analysis the culturally rich methods through which interviewers and interviewees, in concert, generate plausible accounts of the world. Although this second approach may use similar measures to achieve 'quality control' (e.g. group data sessions to ensure agreement about the researchers' reading of a transcript), these measures are used in pursuit of a different, 'narrated' reality in which the 'situated', or locally produced, nature of accounts is to the fore.

■ LINK ■

You can read many of Cathy Riessman's papers using narrative analysis by going to:

http://www2.bc.edu/~riessman/papers.html

I am aware that many readers of this volume will favour the former approach. At the same time, I do not want to neglect the latter, **constructionist** approach – particularly as it is closer to my own theoretical orientation. Fortunately, there are examples available which show how you can kick-start a piece of interview research using both these approaches.

In a course on interview research I gave with Anne Ryen in 2007 at Oslo University, students were asked to submit a short report describing their research topic and then to ask us some questions. One such report, set out below, raised some intriguing issues.

STUDENT EXAMPLES

Citizenship and Feminism

My PhD asks how feminism, ethnic identity and religion are brought together in the policies of women's movements and in the daily lives of women. I have started to conduct interviews with women who are active in women's organizations. I do two interviews with each: one primarily about the organization's work (women's issues, relations with other organizations and political work), and one more 'personal' about the person's everyday life including questions about citizenship (identity, belonging, participation in different areas of society and so on).

The issues overlap, but when the person is representing the organization my impression is that some of them are afraid that they will say something 'wrong' on behalf of the organization and they want to say what's considered to be 'politically correct'. My question is related to ways to handle the interview material when the people I'm interviewing are speaking with 'several voices'. [Cecilie Thun, Women's Studies and Gender, Oslo University]

Cecilie's question emerges from a well-designed project which is right on the cusp between positivist and constructionist approaches to interview data. Viewed from a positivist (factual) perspective, people 'speaking with several voices' is a problem in need of a technical solution. For instance, you might ask the 'same' question in several different ways or compare what respondents say with what they do.

By contrast, constructionists argue that 'identity' is never a fixed entity lying somewhere inside people's heads. We present different aspects of ourselves in different contexts. So, rather than eliminate multiple voices, we need to examine what voices people use, how they use them and with what consequences. In other words, constructionists assume that interview participants actively create meaning. This lies behind Holstein and Gubrium's idea of 'the active interview':

Construed as active, the subject behind the respondent not only holds facts and details of experience, but, in the very process of offering them up for response, constructively adds to, takes away from, and transforms the facts and details. The respondent can hardly 'spoil' what he or she is, in effect, subjectively creating. (1995: 117)

In a project on the quality of care and quality of life of nursing home residents, Gubrium (1993) noted how residents adopted varying 'standpoints':

In speaking of the quality of care, for example, nursing home residents, as interview respondents, not only offer substantive thoughts and feelings pertinent to the topic under consideration, but simultaneously and continuously monitor who they are in relation to the person questioning them. For example, prefacing her remarks about the quality of life in her facility with the statement 'speaking as a woman', a nursing home resident informs the interviewer that she is to be heard as a woman, not as someone else – not a mere resident, cancer patient, or abandoned mother. (Holstein and Gubrium, 1995: 122)

Viewed in this light, the constructionist answer to Cecilie's question is threefold:

- Treat the 'several voices' you have identified as a finding rather than a problem.

- Delineate the range of voices that your respondents use ('what' questions).

- Examine how these voices are articulated in relation to each other and the interactional contexts in which this happens ('how' questions).

In what Holstein and Gubrium call 'the active interview': 'Data can be analyzed to show the dynamic interrelatedness of the *whats* and the *hows*' (1995: 127, emphasis in original).

TIP

Holstein and Gubrium (1995: 33–4) cite telltale phrases which respondents use to signal shifts in roles, e.g. 'speaking as a mother now'; 'thinking like a woman'; 'wearing my professional hat'; 'if I were in his shoes'; and 'now that you ask'. When analysing your interview data, look for prefaces of this kind and try to identify the range of subject positions your respondents invoke.

Note that this approach is a useful antidote to the assumption that people have a single identity waiting to be discovered by the interviewer. By contrast, it reveals that we are active narrators who weave skilful, appropriately located, stories.

Two further Norwegian student projects follow this focus on the 'whats' and 'hows' of interview accounts. We first came across Sveinung Sandberg's research on the street drug scene in Chapter 12. Here is how he describes the 'self-presentations' of users and dealers.

STUDENT EXAMPLES

Street Drug Narratives

The topics of my research are street drug scenes, illegal drug dealing and drug consumption, violence, ethnicity, and hip-hop culture. The data are observation (partly participatory) over a two-year period and interviews with 60 young people. Of these, 40 were adolescent street dwellers picked up in the area around an 'open drug scene' (Plata/Skippergata). The rest were street cannabis dealers aged 15–30 selling at a more dispersed drug scene (Akerselva), all ethnic minorities.

It is often emphasized that qualitative interviews are social situations where data are constructed as a result of the interaction between the interviewer and the interviewed. In this paper I wish to discuss how qualitative interviews can be analysed as social situations, struggles for power, and self-presentation. The paper presents six strategic self-presentations my research participants use in order to manage identity and keep self-respect during the interviews: (a) 'I'm a nice guy'; (b) 'It was my own choice'; (c) Excuses/sad tales/neutralization; (d) Emphasizing similarity between interviewer and research participant; (e) Posing as gangsters; (f) Exaggerating in order to get attention. [Sveinung Sandberg, Sociology, Oslo]

In a related project, Mette has examined the narratives produced about drug dealing within the prison system.

STUDENT EXAMPLES

Drug Narratives and the Penal System

The project 'A qualitative study of the heroin market' is based on 24 qualitative interviews with imprisoned offenders, two interviews with dealers on the outside, and six interviews with policemen who have followed the development of the heroin market over time. As a starting point these interviews were only meant to illuminate the organizational aspects of the heroin trade, but in meeting with the offenders and hearing their narratives, issues of self-presentation and power also became apparent and need addressing. Some central questions: how do the heroin smugglers and dealers present themselves and their illegal activities? What explanation do they give for their illegal actions? What types of representations of normality, deviance, health and sickness are found in their narratives? [Mette, Sociology, Norway]

Topics like 'self-presentation' and multiple 'voices' are a very nice way to kick-start constructionist interview research. But a problem remains. Issues like drug use, the penal system and citizenship are important substantive and political topics. If we treat our respondents' accounts only as 'self presentations' or 'narratives', aren't we losing sight of such broader issues?

Fortunately, both Mette and Sveinung are very much aware of these issues. Mette asks:

> Do the offenders create their narratives in meeting with different institutionalized practices? How does the practice of criminal law shape the narratives of the offenders? And how freely do the offenders create their narratives, and in what way should perspectives of power be integrated in the analyses of the heroin smugglers' and dealers' narratives?

And Sveinung observes:

> An important argument in the discussion will be that analysing self-presentations is more important than methodological reservations; it is crucial in order to understand the social world of the research participants.

Put in other terms, although Sveinung and Mette begin with 'what' and 'how' questions, they want to go beyond such questions in order to ask 'why?' Or, as Sveinung tellingly puts it: 'What can lies tell us about life?'

By moving from 'what' and 'how' to 'why' questions, constructionist interviewers seek to understand the varied contexts out of which we 'draw from experience' to convey accounts of who and what we are. A telling example is provided in an anecdote about one of Jay Gubrium's doctoral students (Gubrium and Holstein, 2002: 21–2). The student interviewed pharmacists who had engaged in substance abuse. His aim was to understand how those who 'should know better' accounted for what had happened to them. As it turned out, what these pharmacists said closely fitted the familiar recovery rubrics of self-help groups. Indeed, many had attended groups like Alcoholics Anonymous (AA) and Narcotics Anonymous (NA). So in what sense were these accounts the pharmacists' 'own' stories? As Gubrium pointed out, don't these stories 'belong' not only to individuals but to particular organizational discourses which are merely 'voiced' here?

Fieldnotes

13.5

We now move on to ethnographic studies based on observation and fieldnotes. In Chapter 12, we considered the nitty-gritty questions involved in gathering field data. Now we need to see how we can kick-start the analysis of such data. The following areas will be discussed:

* why detail is important
* expanding fieldnotes in order to develop your sense of what is going on
* thinking about what you are seeing as well as hearing

TABLE 13.2 Functions of detailed fieldnotes

- To identify and follow processes in witnessed events
- To understand how members themselves characterize and describe particular activities, events and groups
- To convey members' explanations for when, why or how particular things happen and, thereby, to elicit members' theories of the causes of particular happenings
- To identify the practical concerns, conditions and constraints that people confront and deal with in their everyday lives and actions

Source: adapted from Emerson et al., 1995

- examining how interactions and events are articulated or put together

- progressive focusing

- the relevance of simple counting techniques

- the limits of coding observational data.

Why detail is important

13.5.1

> Field researchers seek to get close to others in order to understand their way of life. To preserve and convey that closeness, they must describe situations and events of interest in detail. (Emerson, et al., 1995: 14)

By preserving the details of interaction, you are in a better position to analyse the issues set out in Table 13.2.

Like any set of animating questions, the kinds of issues set out in Table 13.2 reflect a particular **model** of the social world. As in my study of heart clinics, Emerson et al. assume a **constructionist** or **ethnomethodological** model in which the meaning of events is not transparent but is actively constructed by the participants (**members**).

Two methodological imperatives flow from this model. The first is a concern with what participants take to be *routine* or obvious. The second is a recognition that what is routine is best established through watching and listening to what people do rather than asking them directly. So, unlike much ethnographic fieldwork, the interview is not regarded as a major research tool. Instead:

> the distinctive procedure is to observe and record naturally occurring talk and interaction ... [while] it may be useful or essential to interview members about the use and meaning of specific local terms and phrases ... the researcher's deeper concern lies in the actual, situated use of those terms in ordinary interaction. (1995: 140)

TABLE 13.3   Six initial questions for fieldnote analysis

1 What are people doing? What are they trying to accomplish?
2 How exactly do they do this? What specific means and/or strategies do they use?
3 How do members talk about, characterize and understand what is going on?
4 What assumptions are they making?
5 What do I see going on here? What did I learn from these notes?
6 Why did I include them?

Source: Emerson et al., 1995: 146

Such a concern with what participants take to be ordinary and unexceptional gives a clear focus to making and analysing fieldnotes. Data analysis can then develop through asking the sort of questions set out in Table 13.3.

▬▬▬▬▬▬▬▬▬▬▬▬▬ LINK ▬▬▬▬▬▬▬▬▬▬▬▬▬

For details of Robert Emerson's books on field research, go to:

http://www.sscnet.ucla.edu/soc/faculty/emerson/#Books

Expanded fieldnotes

13.5.2

Fieldwork is so fascinating and coding usually so energy-absorbing, that you can get preoccupied and overwhelmed with the flood of particulars – the poignant quote, the appealing personality of a key informant. You forget to *think*, to make deeper and more general sense of what is happening, to begin to explain it in a conceptually coherent way. (Miles and Huberman, 1984: 69)

In order to make 'deeper and more general sense of what is happening', Spradley (1979) suggests that observers keep four separate sets of notes:

1 short notes made at the time

2 expanded notes made as soon as possible after each field session

3 a fieldwork journal to record problems and ideas that arise during each stage of fieldwork

4 a provisional running record of analysis and interpretation (discussed by Kirk and Miller, 1986: 53).

Spradley's suggestions help to systematize fieldnotes and thus improve their **reliability** (see Chapter 15). Like Spradley, Miles and Huberman (1984) offer systematic ways of expanding what gets recorded in fieldnotes. They suggest

TABLE 13.4   Questions for contact summary sheets

- What people, events or situations were involved?
- What were the main themes or issues in the contact?
- Which research questions did the contact bear most centrally on?
- What new hypotheses, speculations or guesses about the field situations were suggested by the contact?
- Where should the fieldworker place most energy during the next contact, and what sorts of information should be sought?

Source: Miles and Huberman, 1984: 50

writing 'contact summary sheets' or extended memos after each observation (1984: 50–1, 69–71).

An example of how to use a contact summary sheet to encourage analytic thinking is set out in Table 13.4.

Miles and Huberman suggest five reasons why such contact sheets are valuable:

1   to guide planning for the next contact

2   to suggest new or revised codes

3   to coordinate several fieldworkers' work

4   to serve as a reminder of the contact at a later stage

5   to serve as the basis for data analysis (adapted from Miles and Huberman, 1984: 51).

How we record data is important because it is directly linked to the quality of data analysis. In this sense, fieldnotes and contact sheets are, of course, only means to an end: developing the analysis.

Using your eyes

13.5.3 In a study of the social organization of a restaurant, W.F. Whyte (1949) reaped rich rewards by using his eyes to observe the spatial organization of activities. More recently, in a study of interaction in hospital wards, Anssi Peräkylä (personal correspondence) notes how spatial arrangements differentiate groups of people. There are the wards and patient rooms, which staff may enter anytime they need to. Then there are patient lounges and the like, which are a kind of public space. Both areas are quite different from areas like the nurses' room and doctors' offices where patients enter only by invitation. Finally, if there is a staff coffee room, you never see a patient there.

As Peräkylä points out, one way to produce different categories of human beings in a hospital is the allocation of space according to categories. At the same time, this allocation is reproduced in the activities of the participants. For instance, the perceptive observer might note the demeanour of patients as they approach the nurses' room. Even if the door is open, they may stand outside and just put their heads round the door. In doing so, they mark out that they are encroaching on foreign territory.

Unfortunately, we have all become a little reluctant to use our eyes as well as our ears when doing observational work. However, there are exceptions. Stimson has noted how 'photographs and diagrams are virtually absent from sociological journals, and rare in sociological books' (1986: 641). He then discusses a room set out for hearings of a disciplinary organization responsible for British doctors. The Professional Conduct Committee of the General Medical Council sits in a high-ceilinged, oak-panelled room reached by an imposing staircase. There are stained-glass windows, picturing 16 crests and a woman in a classical Greek pose. As Stimson comments:

> This is a room in which serious matters are discussed: the room has a presence that is forced on our consciousness ... speech is formal, carefully spoken and a matter for the public record. Visitors in the gallery speak only, if at all, in hushed whispers, for their speech is not part of the proceedings. (1986: 643–4)

In such a room, as Stimson suggests, even without anything needing to be said, we know that what goes on must be taken seriously. Stimson aptly contrasts this room with a McDonald's hamburger restaurant:

> Consider the decorations and materials – plastic, paper, vinyl and polystyrene, and the bright primary colours. [Everything] signifies transience. This temporary character is further articulated in the casual dress of customers, the institutionally casualised dress of staff and the seating that is constructed to make lengthy stays uncomfortable. (1986: 649–50)

Stimson and Peräkylä show that ethnographers who fail to use their eyes as well as their ears are neglecting a crucial source of data. This lesson is most readily learnt if you imagine a sighted person being forced to make sense of the world while blindfolded!

The articulation of different elements

> The move from coding to interpretation is a crucial one ... Interpretation involves the transcendence of 'factual' data and cautious analysis of what is to be made of them. (Coffey and Atkinson, 1996: 46)

13.5.4

As Miles and Huberman (1984) point out, qualitative data come in the form of words rather than in numbers. The issue, then, is how we move from these words to data analysis. They suggest that data analysis consists of 'three concurrent flows of activity: data reduction, data display and conclusion drawing/verification' (1984: 21):

- *Data reduction* 'refers to the process of selecting, focusing, simplifying, abstracting, and transforming ... "raw" data'. Data reduction involves making decisions about which data chunks will provide your initial focus.

- *Data display* is 'an organized assembly of information that permits conclusion drawing and action taking'. It involves assembling your data into displays such as matrices, graphs, networks and charts which clarify the main direction (and missing links) of your analysis.

- *Conclusion drawing* means 'beginning to decide what things mean, noting regularities, patterns, explanations, possible configurations, causal flows and propositions'.

- *Verification* means testing our provisional conclusions for 'their plausibility, their sturdiness, their "confirmability" – that is, their validity' (1984: 21, 22).

Miles and Huberman demonstrate that in **field** studies, unlike much quantitative research, we are not satisfied with a simple coding of data. As I argued in Chapter 4, this means that qualitative researchers have to show how the (theoretically defined) elements that they have identified are articulated or mutually laminated. The distinctive contribution qualitative research can make is by utilizing its theoretical resources in the deep analysis of usually small bodies of publicly shareable data.

This means that coding your data according to some theoretical scheme should only be the first stage of your data analysis. You will then need to go on to examine how these elements are linked together. At this second stage, lateral thinking can help. For instance, you can attempt to give your chosen concept or issue a new twist, perhaps by pursuing a counter-intuitive idea or by noting an additional feature little addressed in the literature.

In any event, as I show below, one way of achieving better data analysis is by a steadily more narrow focus.

Progressive focusing in fieldwork

13.5.5 We only come to look at things in certain ways because we have adopted, either tacitly or explicitly, certain ways of seeing. This means that, in observational research, data collection, hypothesis construction and theory building are not three separate things but are interwoven with one another.
This process is well described by using an analogy with a funnel:

Ethnographic research has a characteristic 'funnel' structure, being progressively focused over its course. Progressive focusing has two analytically distinct components. First, over time the research problem is developed or transformed, and eventually its scope is clarified and delimited and its internal structure explored. In this sense, it is frequently only over the course of the research that one discovers what the research is really 'about', and it is not uncommon for it to turn out to be about something quite remote from the initially foreshadowed problems. (Hammersley and Atkinson, 1983: 175)

Atkinson (1992) gives an example of such a redefinition of a research problem. Many years after completing his PhD, Atkinson returned to his original fieldnotes on medical education. He shows how the original data can be reread in a quite different way. Atkinson's earlier method had been to fragment his fieldnotes into relatively small segments, each with its own category. For instance, a surgeon's description of post-operative complications to a surgical team was originally categorized under such headings as 'unpredictability', 'uncertainty', 'patient career' and 'trajectory'. When Atkinson returns to it, it becomes an overall narrative which sets up an enigma ('unexpected complications') which is resolved in the form of a 'moral tale' ('beware, unexpected things can always happen'). Viewed in this way, the surgeon's story becomes a text with many resemblances to a fairytale!

Two studies of British medical clinics that I carried out in the 1980s also nicely illustrate Hammersley and Atkinson's funnel. As I showed above, my observation of a paediatric cardiology unit moved unpredictably in the direction of an analysis of disposal decisions with a small group of children with Down's syndrome. Similarly, my research on cancer clinics, discussed in Chapter 8, unexpectedly led into a comparison of fee-for-service and state-provided medicine (Silverman, 1981; 1987).

These two cases had three features in common:

1   The switch of focus – through the 'funnel' – as a more defined topic arose.

2   The use of the comparative method as an invaluable tool of theory building and testing.

3   The generation of topics with a scope outside the substantive area of the research. Thus the 'ceremonial orders' found in the cancer clinics are not confined to medicine, while the 'democratic' decision making found with the children with Down's syndrome had unexpected effects of power with a significance far beyond medical encounters.

As I have noted elsewhere (Silverman, 2001), working this way parallels Glaser and Strauss's (1967) famous account of **grounded theory**. A simplified model of this involves three stages:

• an initial attempt to develop categories which illuminate the data

• an attempt to 'saturate' these categories with many appropriate cases in order to demonstrate their relevance

• the development of these categories into more general analytic frameworks with relevance outside the setting.

Glaser and Strauss use their research on death and dying as an example. They show how they developed the category of 'awareness contexts' to refer to the kinds of situations in which people were informed of their likely fate. The category was then saturated and finally related to non-medical settings where people learn about how others define them (e.g. schools).

'Grounded theory' has been criticized for its failure to acknowledge implicit theories which guide work at an early stage. It also is more clear about the generation of theories than about their testing. Used unintelligently, it can also degenerate into a fairly empty building of categories or into a mere smokescreen used to legitimize purely empiricist research (see my critique of four qualitative studies in Chapter 16; and see Bryman, 1988: 83–7). At best, 'grounded theory' offers an approximation of the creative activity of theory building found in good observational work, compared to the dire abstracted empiricism present in the most wooden statistical studies.

LINK

www.groundedtheory.com

> **| TIP |**
>
> **For a really good, student-friendly account of how grounded theory can be used in constructionist research, see Kathy Charmaz's book *Constructing Grounded Theory* (Sage, 2006).**

However, quantification should not be seen as the enemy of good field research. In the section below, I discuss one example of how simple tabulations were used to test an emergent hypothesis in the study of cancer clinics.

Using tabulations in testing fieldwork hypotheses _____

13.5.6
In the cancer study, I used a coding form which enabled me to collate a number of crude measures of doctor and patient interactions (Silverman, 1984). The aim was to demonstrate that the qualitative analysis was reasonably representative of the data as a whole. Occasionally, the figures revealed that the reality was not in line with my overall impressions. Consequently, the analysis was tightened and the characterizations of clinic behaviour were specified more carefully.

The crude quantitative data I had recorded did not allow any real test of the major thrust of this argument. Nonetheless, they did offer a summary measure of the characteristics of the total sample which allowed closer specification of features of private and NHS clinics. In order to illustrate this, let me briefly show you the kind of quantitative data I gathered on topics like consultation length, patient participation and the scope of the consultation.

My overall impression was that private consultations lasted considerably longer than those held in the NHS clinics. When examined, the data indeed did show that the former were almost twice as long as the latter (20 minutes as against 11 minutes) and that the difference was statistically highly significant. However, I recalled that for special reasons, one of the NHS clinics had abnormally short consultations. I felt a fairer comparison of consultations in the two sectors should exclude this clinic and should only compare consultations taken by a single doctor in both sectors. This subsample of cases revealed that the difference in length between NHS and private consultations was now reduced to an average of under 3 minutes. This was still statistically significant, although the significance was reduced. Finally, however, if I compared only *new* patients seen by the same doctor, NHS patients got 4 minutes more on average: 34 minutes as against 30 minutes in the private clinic. This last finding was not suspected and had interesting implications for the overall assessment of the individual's costs and benefits from 'going private'. It is possible, for instance, that the tighter scheduling of appointments at the private clinic may limit the amount of time that can be given to new patients.

As a further aid to comparative analysis, I measured patient participation in the form of questions and unelicited statements. Once again, a highly significant difference was found: on this measure, private patients participated much more in the consultation. However, once more taking only patients seen by the same doctor, the difference between the clinics became very small and was *not* significant. Finally, no significant difference was found in the degree to which non-medical matters (e.g. patient's work or home circumstances) were discussed in the clinics.

These quantitative data were a useful check on over-enthusiastic claims about the degree of difference between the NHS and private clinics. However, as I argued in Chapter 8, my major concern was with the 'ceremonial order' of the three clinics. I had amassed a considerable number of exchanges in which doctors and patients appeared to behave in the private clinic in a manner deviant from what we know about NHS hospital consultations. The question was: would the quantitative data offer any support to my observations?

The answer was, to some extent, positive. Two quantitative measures were helpful in relation to the ceremonial order. One dealt with the extent to which the doctor fixed treatment or attendance at the patient's convenience. The second measured whether patients or doctor engaged in polite small-talk with one another about their personal or professional lives. (I called this 'social elicitation'.) As Table 13.5 shows, both these measures revealed significant differences, in the expected direction, according to the mode of payment.

Now, of course, such data could not offer proof of my claims about the different interactional forms. However, coupled with the qualitative data, they provided strong evidence of the direction of difference, as well as giving me a simple measure of the sample as a whole which contexted the few extracts of talk I was able to use. I do not deny that counting can be as arbitrary as qualitative interpretation of a few fragments of data. However, providing researchers resist the temptation to try to count everything, and base their analysis on sound concepts

TABLE 13.5   Private and NHS clinics: ceremonial orders

	Private clinic (*n* = 42)	NHS clinics (*n* = 104)
	(% in all such clinics)	
Treatment or attendance fixed at patients' convenience	15 (36%)	10 (10%)
Social elicitation	25 (60%)	31 (30%)

Source: adapted from Silverman, 2001: 243

linked to actors' own methods of ordering the world, then each type of data can inform the analysis of the other.

In Chapter 15, I return to the role of counting as an aid to **validity** in qualitative research. In the case of observational studies, such counting will often be based on the prior coding of fieldnotes. I now, therefore, turn to the issues that arise in such coding.

Limits in coding fieldnotes

13.5.7
The tabulations used in the cancer study derived from:

> that well-established style of work whereby the data are inspected for categories and instances. It is an approach that disaggregates the text (notes or transcripts) into a series of fragments, which are then regrouped under a series of thematic headings. (Atkinson, 1992: 455)

Such coding by thematic headings has been supported by computer-aided qualitative data analysis systems as discussed in Chapter 14. In larger projects, the reliability of coding is also buttressed by training coders of data in procedures which aim to ensure a uniform approach.

However, there remain two problems with coding fieldnotes. The first, and more obvious, problem is that every way of seeing is also a way of not seeing. As Atkinson points out, one of the disadvantages of coding schemes is that, because they are based upon a given set of categories, they furnish 'a powerful conceptual grid' (1992: 459) from which it is difficult to escape. While this 'grid' is very helpful in organizing the data analysis, it also deflects attention away from uncategorized activities. Therefore, as Clive Seale (personal correspondence) has noted:

> a good coding scheme would reflect a search for 'uncategorized activities' so that they could be accounted for, in a manner similar to searching for deviant cases.

The second, less obvious, problem is that, as I pointed out in Chapter 4, 'coding' is not the preserve of research scientists. All of us 'code' what we hear and see in the world around us. This is what Garfinkel (1967) and Sacks (1992) mean when they say that societal **members**, like social scientists, make the world observable and reportable.

Put at its simplest, this suggests that researchers must be very careful how they use categories. For instance, Sacks quotes from two linguists who appear to have no problem in characterizing particular (invented) utterances as 'simple', 'complex', 'casual' or 'ceremonial'. For Sacks, such rapid characterizations of data assume 'that we can know that [such categories are accurate] without an analysis of what it is [members] are doing' (1992, Vol. 1: 429).

How should we respond to Sacks's radical critique of ethnography? The first point is not to panic! Sacks offers a challenge to conventional observational work of which everybody should be aware. In particular, Sacks's lecture "Doing 'being ordinary'" (1992, Vol. 2: 215–21) is essential reading for every fieldworker.

However, awareness does not mean that everybody has to follow Sacks's radical path. So one response is to state something like 'thanks but no thanks'. For instance, **grounded theory** is an equally respectable (and much more popular) way of theorizing (about) fieldwork.

To this effective but essentially defensive manoeuvre, we can add two more ambitious responses. First, we can seek to integrate Sacks's questions about 'how' the social world is constituted with more conventional ethnographic questions about the 'whats' and 'whys' of social life (Gubrium and Holstein, 1997). Or, second, as I describe below, we can make this everyday 'coding' (or 'interpretive practice') the object of inquiry by asking 'how' questions about talk-in-interaction.

=== LINK ===

For a series of highly relevant case studies illustrating what is involved in analysing field-work data, visit:

www.sagepub.co.uk/gobo and go to Chapters 9 and 10.

Transcripts

13.6 The two main social science traditions which inform the analysis of transcripts of tapes are **conversation analysis** (CA) and **discourse analysis** (DA). For an introduction to CA, see ten Have (1998; 2007); for DA, see Potter and Wetherell (1987) and Potter (2004).

In this book we are, of course, more concerned with the practicalities of doing qualitative research. In the rest of this chapter I will, therefore, deal with two practical issues:

- the advantages of working with tapes and transcripts

- the elements of how to do analysis of such tapes.

Why work with tapes?

[The] kind of phenomena I deal with are always transcriptions of actual occurrences in their actual sequence. (Sacks, 1984b: 25)

13.6.1 The earlier ethnographers had generally relied on recording their observations through fieldnotes. Why did Sacks prefer to use an audio-recorder?

Sacks's answer is that we cannot rely on our recollections of conversations. Certainly, depending on our memory, we can usually summarize what different people said. But it is simply impossible to remember (or even to note at the time) such matters as pauses, overlaps, inbreaths and the like.

Now whether you think these kinds of things are important will depend upon what you can show with or without them. Indeed, you may not even be convinced that conversation itself is a particularly interesting topic. But, at least by studying tapes of conversations, you are able to focus on the 'actual details' of one aspect of social life. As Sacks put it:

> My research is about conversation only in this incidental way, that we can get the actual happenings on tape and transcribe them more or less, and therefore have something to begin with. If you can't deal with the actual detail of actual events then you can't have a science of social life. (1992, Vol. 2: 26)

Tapes and transcripts also offer more than just 'something to begin with'. In the first place, they are a public record, available to the scientific community, in a way that fieldnotes are not. Second, they can be replayed, transcriptions can be improved, and analyses can take off on a different tack unlimited by the original transcript. As Sacks told his students:

> I started to play around with tape recorded conversations, for the single virtue that I could replay them; that I could type them out somewhat, and study them extendedly, who knew how long it might take ... It wasn't from any large interest in language, or from some theoretical formulation of what should be studied, but simply by virtue of that; I could get my hands on it, and I could study it again and again. And also, consequentially, others could look at what I had studied, and make of it what they could, if they wanted to disagree with me. (1992, Vol. 1: 622)

A third advantage of detailed transcripts is that, if you want to, you can inspect sequences of utterances without being limited to the extracts chosen by the first researcher. For it is within these sequences, rather than in single turns of talk, that we make sense of conversation. As Sacks points out:

> having available for any given utterance other utterances around it, is extremely important for determining what was said. If you have available only the snatch of talk that you're now transcribing, you're in tough shape for determining what it is. (1992, Vol. 1: 729)

It should not be assumed that the preparation of transcripts is simply a technical detail prior to the main business of the analysis. The convenience of transcripts for presentational purposes is no more than an added bonus.

As Atkinson and Heritage (1984) point out, the production and use of transcripts are essentially 'research activities'. They involve close, repeated listenings to recordings which often reveal previously unnoted recurring features of the organization of talk.

Such listenings can most fruitfully be done in group data sessions. As described by Paul ten Have (1998), work in such groups usually begins by listening to an extract from a tape with a draft transcript and agreeing upon improvements to the transcript. Then:

> the participants are invited to proffer some observations on the data, to select an episode which they find 'interesting' for whatever reason, and formulate their under-standing or puzzlement, regarding that episode. Then anyone can come in to react to these remarks, offering alternatives, raising doubts, or whatever. (1998: 124)

However, as ten Have makes clear, such group data sessions should be rather more than an anarchic free for all:

> participants are, on the one hand, *free* to bring in anything they like, but, on the other hand, *required* to ground their observations in the data at hand, although they may also support them with reference to their own data-based findings or those published in the literature. (1998: 24)

======== LINK ========

For resources on CA go to:

http://www.paultenhave.nl/resource.htm

For resources on DA go to:

http://www.lboro.ac.uk/research/mmethods/resources/links/da.html

---

Analysing tapes

13.6.2 There is a strongly inductive bent to the kind of research that ten Have and Sacks describe. As we have seen, this means that any research claims need to be identified in precise analyses of detailed transcripts. It is therefore necessary to avoid premature theory construction and the 'idealization' of research materials which use only general, non-detailed characterizations.

Heritage sums up these assumptions as follows:

> Specifically, analysis is strongly 'data-driven' – developed from phenomena which are in various ways evidenced in the data of interaction. Correspondingly, there is a strong bias against *a priori* speculation about the orientations and motives of

TABLE 13.6 How to do CA

1 Always try to identify sequences of related talk
2 Try to examine how speakers take on certain roles or identities through their talk (e.g. questioner–answerer or client–professional)
3 Look for particular outcomes in the talk (e.g. a request for clarification, a repair, laughter) and work backwards to trace the trajectory through which a particular outcome was produced

Source: Silverman, 2006: 222

TABLE 13.7 Common errors in CA

1 Explaining a turn at talk by reference to the speaker's intentions
2 Explaining a turn at talk by reference to a speaker's role or status (e.g. as a doctor or as a man or woman)
3 Trying to make sense of a single line of transcript or utterance in isolation from the surrounding talk

Source: Silverman, 2006: 222

> speakers and in favour of detailed examination of conversationalists' actual actions. Thus the empirical conduct of speakers is treated as the central resource out of which analysis may develop. (1984: 243)

In practice, Heritage adds, this means that it must be demonstrated that the regularities described can be shown to be produced by the participants and attended to by them as grounds for their own inferences and actions. Further, **deviant cases**, in which such regularities are absent, must be identified and analysed.

However, the way in which CA obtains its results is rather different from how we might intuitively try to analyse talk. It may be helpful, therefore, if I conclude this section by offering a crude set of prescriptions about how to do CA. Table 13.6 summarizes how to do CA, and Table 13.7 sets out things to avoid when doing CA.

If we follow these rules, the analysis of conversations does not require exceptional skills. As Schegloff puts it, in his introduction to Sacks's collected lectures, all we need to do is to:

> begin with some observations, then find the problem for which these observations could serve as ... the solution. (Schegloff in Sacks, 1992, Vol. 1: xlviii)

This means that doing the kind of systematic data analysis that CA demands is not an impossibly difficult activity. As Harvey Sacks once pointed out, in doing CA we are only reminding ourselves about things we already know. As Sacks remarks:

> I take it that lots of the results I offer, people can see for themselves. And they needn't be afraid to. And they needn't figure that the results are wrong because they can see them ... [It is] as if we found a new plant. It may have been a plant in your

garden, but now you see it's different than something else. And you can look at it to see how it's different, and whether it's different in the way that somebody has said. (1992, Vol. 1: 488)

━━━━━━━━━━━━━━━━━ ■ LINK ■ ━━━━━━━━━━━━━━━━━

www.conversation-analysis.net

Visual Data

13.7 Visual data comprise a very broad category which can encompass anything from videos to photographs to naturally occurring observational data like those discussed in Section 13.5.3, and to such aspects of our environment like street signs and advertisements (see Emmison and Smith, 2000).

> **TIP**
>
> The analysis of visual data can be very complicated and, in some hands, can be so over-theorized that one feels that the theoretical tail is leading the empirical dog! Gillian Rose (2007) provides a useful guide to data analysis of visual images which, while not short of theory, provides practical advice on the analysis itself.

To simplify matters for the beginning researcher, I will examine four ways in which visual data can be gathered and analysed:

- allowing people to produce their own images using content analysis
- studying pet photographs and videoing how people interact with their pets using grounded theory
- using family photographs in interviews and analysing the narratives produced
- workplace studies using conversation analysis to see how sequences of interaction get put together.

Content analysis

13.7.1 Sharples et al. (2003) had the interesting idea of studying the kinds of photographs made by children. One hundred and eighty children of three different ages (7, 11 and 15) were given single-use cameras and asked to use them in any way they pleased over a weekend. Over 4300 photographs were generated by this means.

Data analysis took off through using a form of content analysis which produced a kind of 'radar screen … a two-dimensional scatterplot showing the principal axes of variability' (2003: 311). These data were set up in this way in order to answer some early, key research questions, namely:

- What is the content of each photograph?

- Are the people or objects shown posed?

- Who are the people shown?

- How does each of these features vary by the age of the photographer?

The analysis showed significant variation by the age of the child. For instance, 7-year-old children were more likely to take photographs of toys and other possessions. They also took more photographs of their home and family. By contrast, the 11-year-olds concentrated on outdoor and/or animal photographs (usually their pets), while the 15-year-olds mainly took photographs of their friends, usually of the same sex and often in 'informal and striking poses' (2003: 316–17).

This study shows that an apparently simple count of such apparently basic features can raise a number of interesting issues (for a discussion of the nature and limits of content analysis, see Marvasti, 2004). In this case, the researchers sought to pursue these issues by qualitative interviews with their child photographers.

In terms of Section 13.2.5, this study took off by beginning with descriptive questions of 'what?' and 'how?' This generated 'why' questions which they later sought to answer through interviews with subjects. The interviews also allowed the comparison of the categories that the researchers used with those used by the children themselves.

Grounded theory

13.7.2 Kryzysztof Konecki (2005) used photographs to study various aspects of direct contacts between domestic animals and people. He was interested in the ways in which owners represented their relations with the animals by means of gestures and 'choreographic' arrangement of the bodies and objects. The research aimed at finding the cultural framework which would be useful in categorizing oneself through photographic representation.

Konecki used grounded theory to generate a set of workable categories and a set of hypotheses to be tested. This is how he describes this coding in the context of a further study reported shortly:

> Open coding in the methodology of grounded theory means ascribing labels to his data. The labels should usually have a conceptual character, shifting the researcher from direct description … Some of the labels become categories, which later become saturated with qualities, that is conceptual elements, which have their empirical references (that is references to actual events, situations, interactions, gestures, etc.). (Konecki, 2008)

Konecki's analysis of the photographs showed that hugging and touching animals is mainly depicted with children and women. By contrast: 'Men usually keep the animals on the leash or firmly in their hands in order to, practically, create an opportunity to take the photograph, which consequently, from the social perspective, represents men in a dominating social position' (2005: 163–4).

In the later paper, Konecki (2008) assembled video-recordings of human–animal interactions. Sixty video clips were recorded by means of a portable camera. The clips were transcribed and then analysed by means of grounded theory. The recordings were gathered in order to show typical everyday situations of interaction between humans and animals in their households. The context of the recording was also described thoroughly and the basic ethnographic information was provided, such as *who*, *where*, *when* and *why* regarding the particular animal or owner.

Among the activities that Konecki identified were: talking with animals, ascribing intentionality to them, playing, greeting, feeding and touching. He found that touching is a vital part of displaying close contact with family pets. He distinguished four kinds of touching shown in his videos:

- touching characterized by positive affection (showing feelings or support)

- entertaining touching (showing playful anger or attachment)

- controlling touching (showing compliance)

- ritual touching (showing greetings or farewells).

LINK

For an online journal debate on visual methods, which includes Konecki's paper, go to

http://www.qualitative-research.net/index.php/fqs/issue/view/11

Narratives

13.7.3 An interview is a researcher-provoked way of gathering data. As such, interviewers must be aware of the extent to which they are imposing their own categories on respondents. One way of limiting such imposition is to find a stimulus or topic which is relevant to the people being studied. Photographs can be such a stimulus. For instance, Jenkings et al. (2008) asked 16 military personnel each to choose 10 photos that best represented their experience of military life. Each person was then interviewed and their accounts of the photos were used to analyse how military identity is represented.

For most of us, family photographs are even more important than photographs of our working life. Moreover, talking about these photos to others is quite a common activity. Gillian Rose (2007) discusses interviews she conducted with women about their family photos. This is how she describes how she began analysis:

> I transcribed the interviews and then worked with them, working outwards from what I was told about the things that were done with photos, and gradually finding recurring themes and taken-for-granted assumptions which I felt were the meanings of the photos in this phase of their existence. (2007: 230–1)

However, these photos did not constitute the only visual data that were relevant. It also mattered what her women did with their photos, e.g. which photos were selected or emphasized and then displayed to her in particular ways. So Rose kept fieldnotes about what the women in her study were doing as they talked or remained silent and noted what she did in response.

Working with both interviews and fieldnotes, she discovered 'the way in which these photos helped to produce a relation of "togetherness"' (2007: 231). This involved:

- choosing photos showing family members together

- pointing out how photo frames or albums were presents from family members

- arranging photos in groups to show family links (e.g. children and other relatives)

- discussing which photos had been given to or received from other family members.

Conversation analysis using video data

13.7.4 We first came across conversation analysis (CA) in Chapter 2 when I discussed the research of several of my students. It is a method which involves recording naturally occurring situations, transcribing them in great detail using standardized conventions (see the Appendix) and analysing sequences of interaction in order to see how the participants produce various outcomes.

Until 1980, most CA was carried out using audio-recordings and this meant that the outcomes identified derived from the participants' conversation (e.g. an invitation preface or an acceptance of a piece of advice). More recently, however, the emergence of digital camcorders, in combination with the editing and playback possibilities of desktop computers, mean that video is likely to become as straightforward for social scientists to use in their research as photographs. The cutting-edge research now being done involves looking at workplace settings in order to document the tacit procedures and forms of common-sense reasoning involved in the performance of tasks (see Heath and Luff, 2000).

Ruth Parry collected video-recordings of physiotherapy treatment sessions within British NHS settings during her PhD using Transana software to support her analysis of video data.

━━━━━ LINK ━━━━━

www.transana.org

TIP

The Transana database should not be set up until you have carefully thought through and set up a consistent labelling and indexing system: the program creates links to your stored videos [and] you don't want to be reorganizing your filing system once you have started making links. Transana allows for the kind of ethnographic note taking or 'logging' that is useful in the first watch-through of data. It also facilitates transcribing, whether verbatim or the full Jeffersonian style. It allows collection of and keywording of multiple clips and extracts. [Ruth Parry, Social Sciences, Loughborough]

In the following account of her work, Ruth adds that video data analysis is helped by purposive sampling and group data sessions.

STUDENT EXAMPLES

Analysing Videos

Given the vast amounts of data contained in videos, the key thing for me has been learning how to purposefully sample from within the data so as to allow detailed analysis of a smaller amount, upon the basis of a sound selection strategy. This also works back to design issues: once access has been managed, it is easy to collect a good deal of video data pretty quickly, and though it is sometimes heartbreaking to realize how many of one's data one has not examined in detail, having this big 'bank' allows for appropriate selection and 'natural experiments'.

One other note on data analysis. Like everyone, I bring a certain perspective to my analysis. One element of this perspective is my past as a clinical physiotherapist. I find that joint data analysis sessions are a very useful way of helping balance this perspective with others. I have found that non-clinicians attending these sessions tend to 'take the perspective of', or at least primarily focus their attention upon, patients, whereas sometimes my attention tends to be skewed towards therapists and their practices. I think it is important to note that the non-clinicians don't have a neutral position themselves. [Ruth Parry]

Concluding Remarks

13.8
We have seen how data analysis can be developed during and after data collection. However, as I have implied throughout, good data analysis is never just a matter of using the right methods or techniques but always is based on theorizing about data using a consistent model of social reality. This commitment to theorizing about data makes the

best qualitative research far superior to the stilted empiricism of the worst kind of quantitative research.

Most readers will not bring to their research any very well-defined set of theoretical ideas. If you are in this position, your problem will be how you can use data to think in theoretical terms. The list below is intended merely as a set of suggestions. Although it cannot be exhaustive, it should serve as an initial guide to theorizing about data. It can also be read in conjunction with my discussion of the three kinds of research sensitivity in Chapter 6.

In carrying out your research, it is suggested that you think about the following six issues:

1 *'What' and 'how' questions.* Avoid the temptation to rush to explanations of your data. Don't begin with 'why' questions. Instead ask yourself 'what' verbal and behavioural and contextual resources are being used here, and look for the detail of 'how' they are being used (and with what consequences).

2 *Chronology.* Look at the timing of people's behaviour or their use of time in their accounts. Alternatively, gather data over time in order to look at processes of change. If appropriate, try searching out historical evidence which may at least suggest how your research problem came into being.

3 *Context.* How are your data contextualized in particular organizational settings, social processes or sets of experiences? For instance, as the Norwegian students' work shows, answering an interviewer's question may be different from engaging in the activity which is the topic of the interview. Therefore, think about how there may be many versions of your phenomenon.

4 *Comparison.* Always try to compare your data with other relevant data. Even if you cannot find a comparative case, try to find ways of dividing your data into different sets and compare each. Remember that the comparative method is the basic scientific method.

5 *Implications.* When you are reporting your research, think about how what you have discovered may relate to broader issues than your original research topic. In this way, a very narrow topic (e.g. self-presentation by drug dealers) may be related to much broader social processes (e.g. how crime is defined and treated).

6 *Lateral thinking.* Don't erect strong boundaries between concepts but explore the relations between apparently diverse models, theories and methodologies. Celebrate anomaly!

However, theorization without methodological rigour is a dangerous brew. In Chapter 14, we consider how computer software can aid qualitative research. Then, in Chapter 15, the issues of validity and reliability are discussed.

■ Attempt Exercise 13.3 ■

```
┌─────────┐ KEY POINTS ┌─────
            │            │

Develop data analysis by:

• working with data which are easy to collect and are reliable

• focusing on one process within those data

• narrowing down to one part of that process

• comparing different subsamples of the population concerned.
```

■ ■ Further Reading ■

Chapter 3 of my recent book *A Very Short, Fairly Interesting, Reasonably Cheap Book about Qualitative Research* (Sage, 2007) examines how you can develop data analysis by examining sequences of data. For a useful treatment of coding observational data, see Robert Emerson et al.'s *Writing Ethnographic Fieldnotes* (University of Chicago Press, 1995). Hammersley and Atkinson's *Ethnography: Principles and Practice* (third edition, Tavistock, 2007, Chs 8, 9) offers a classic discussion of how to analyse ethnographic data. A development of some of these ideas can be found in Martyn Hammersley's recent book *Questioning Qualitative Inquiry* (Sage, 2008). The best treatment of grounded theory is Kathy Charmaz's *Constructing Grounded Theory* (Sage, 2006). Sacks's work on conversation analysis is discussed in my book *Harvey Sacks: Social Science and Conversation Analysis* (Polity, 1998). The case studies of the cancer and heart clinics discussed here are found in my book *Communication and Medical Practice* (Sage, 1987, Chs 6, 7).

■ Exercise 13.1 ■

This gives you the opportunity to think about relevant datasets to which you may have early access.

1 Review relevant data already in the public sphere, for instance on the media (from newspapers to television and radio to the Internet). Select a dataset and begin to analyse it.

2 Ask your supervisor and/or fellow students about any relevant data that they might have which you could borrow either as a preliminary exercise or possibly to develop long-term collaboration. Do a brief analysis of some of the data.

■ **Exercise 13.2**

This gives you an opportunity to analyse your own data as soon as you obtain them.

1   Which questions does your preferred method of data analysis suggest? What interesting generalizations can you start to pull out of your data?

2   Do previous research findings seem to apply to your data? If not, why not? If so, how can you use your data to develop these findings?

3   How do particular concepts from your preferred model of social research apply to your data? Which concepts work best and hence look likely to be most productive?

 ■ **Exercise 13.3**

This exercise is based on the various ways to develop data analysis discussed in this chapter. With reference to your own data:

1   Focus on one process within those data. Now narrow down your focus to one *part* of that process. Survey your data in terms of this narrow focus. What can you now find?

2   Compare different subsamples of your data in terms of a single category or process. What does this show?

3   Decide what features of your data may properly be counted and tabulate instances of a particular category. What does this tabulation indicate? Identify 'deviant' cases and explain what you will do with them.

4   Attempt to develop your categories into more general analytic frameworks with relevance outside the setting you are studying.

|14|

Using Computers To Analyse Qualitative Data

Clive Seale

Chapter Objectives

By the end of this chapter, you will be able to:

- Understand the strengths and limitations of computer software for qualitative data analysis.

- Recognize the key features of some of the main CAQDAS software products.

- Find the details of CAQDAS software programs on the Internet and evaluate their usefulness for your research project.

Introduction

14.1 The use of computers for basic **content analysis** of text became popular in the humanities from the 1960s onwards. Scholars of literature, for example, found that they could use the large mainframe computers of the time for counting the number of times particular words occurred in a text. A computer might have been used to count the frequency of Shakespeare's use of a particular word or phrase and to compare this with some other dramatist; or to compare usage between Shakespeare's late plays and his early ones, or his comedies and his tragedies, or his plays and his poetry, and so on. The co-occurrence of particular words, or the incidence of particular phrases characteristic of particular writing genres, could be reported objectively, meaning that literary analysis could be based on apparently more rigorously reported evidence. Computers could do these things because of their capacity for rapidly processing large volumes of text (Miall, 1990).

Social researchers also exploited the advantages of computers for data analysis, but this was largely confined to statistical work until the early 1980s, when qualitative researchers began to catch up. There are several reasons for the delay. Before the widespread availability of personal computers, use of mainframes was expensive and slow, requiring a degree of certainty about the analysis required so that it could be pre-specified accurately. Statistical procedures could be programmed into computers because they were well described. They were planned on one day, and often run on data during the night, the results being examined the following morning. By contrast, qualitative analysis was (and still is) far less formulaic, often requiring an approach to computing that gives quick feedback on the results of emergent questions, involving an interactive cycle of thinking and innovation only really made possible with the personal computer.

Additionally qualitative research, as a social movement like many others, emerged as an initially radical response to a dominant orthodoxy: that of quantitative research work. This involved a heartfelt rejection of the technological appearance of statistical work, which smacked of dehumanization, over-control and obsession with technical puzzles. The computer symbolized these things, and many qualitative researchers remained distanced from this technology because of feelings that it might impose an alien logic on their analytic procedures. This, though, for some time impeded a more balanced assessment of the advantages and disadvantages of the computer-assisted analysis of qualitative data (CAQDAS), which is, of course, not suitable for all of the things that qualitative researchers wish to do with data, but does offer significant benefits.

In this chapter I propose to show you how CAQDAS can be helpful in doing the kind of qualitative data analysis discussed in the previous two chapters – while also pointing out its limitations. I will describe features which have been widely used by qualitative researchers since specialized software was introduced from the early 1980s onwards. I will also discuss some new developments, involving conjoint qualitative and quantitative analysis based on keyword searches which uses software that draws on the discipline of corpus linguistics (Baker, 2006).

While particular software will be mentioned, I do not aim to review all products of this sort, or seek to describe the finer details of how particular types work. Such information would probably become out of date quickly, since software developers continue to release new versions with extra features. The websites given in the text will enable you to access free demonstration versions of the latest software. As in statistical analysis, you will learn best when you have a specific project in mind, and have time to explore how various available techniques might benefit what you want to do.

What CAQDAS Software Can Do for You

14.2 It will become clear, as you read on, that there are many different kinds of CAQDAS software, each offering particular features. Lewins and Silver (2007) provide an excellent guide to the main software products. Described here are the basic core features of most of the mainstream CAQDAS packages. Some features offered by more specialized products will be touched on later. In this 'mainstream' category I include, for example:

NVivo	www.qsrinternational.com
MAXQDA	www.maxqda.com
ATLAS.ti	www.atlasti.com

To use this type of software, a 'project' is normally created, representing the particular research project that you are working on. In this project are, first, the raw materials associated with the project. These may be, for example, transcripts of interviews or other types of text such as documents or downloaded files. Sometimes CAQDAS software also supports the use of pictures and sound files.

Mainstream CAQDAS software allows the user to see these materials in the same way that a word processor allows a user to see a document. The software will also support the user in searching through documents for particular features, for example a particular word or phrase. Sometimes each instance of a word or phrase can be inspected in its context. Additionally, and this is perhaps the most commonly used core feature, such software allows the user to code segments of data (for example, some text) according to some conceptual scheme. Coded segments can then be searched for and retrieved. Together, this is known as the 'code-and-retrieve' element of such software. Searches can usually be done according to rules that involve Boolean logic (e.g. 'show me all instances where people talking about topic A are *also* talking about topic B' or 'show me all instances where people who talk about topic A are *not also* talking about topic B'). Retrieved material can normally be outputted in a way that can be easily copied and pasted into a word processor.

Such software will normally allow bits of information to be attached to particular files, or parts of files, contained in a project so that this information can be used in searches. For example, a researcher may have interviewed 20 men and 20 women of different ages. CAQDAS software will allow information about the gender and age of each interviewee to be attached to each interview transcript, and searches can then be done on subsets of the data (e.g. 'show me everything males over the age of 60 had to say about a topic, and then show me what females over 60 had to say about it'). This allows comparative analysis.

Very frequently such software will support the researcher in writing analytic notes or 'memos' that allow emergent ideas to be recorded in appropriate places. Additionally, most support the export and import of quantitative information about the project, so that work can be integrated with statistical or spreadsheet software. Some allow users to draw diagrams that give a visual display of relationships between coding categories, thus supporting the development of theoretical models grounded in data analysis.

Advantages of CAQDAS

14.3
The advantages of CAQDAS fall into three main categories:

1 Speed at handling large volumes of data, freeing the researcher to explore numerous analytic questions and increasing the capacity to analyse samples that are representative because they can be large

2 Improvement of rigour, including the production of counts of phenomena and searching for deviant cases

3 Facilitation of team research, including the development of consistent coding schemes.

Speed

14.3.1 This advantage is most obvious to the researcher faced with a large amount of qualitative data, wanting to sort them into categories or coded segments which may then be filed and retrieved easily. For someone in this position, the speed at which software can carry out sorting procedures on large volumes of electronically entered data is remarkable. This saves time and effort which might otherwise be expended on boring clerical work, perhaps involving mounds of photocopied paper, colour coded, sorted into piles on the floor, cut up, pasted and so on. In turn, this gives the data analyst more time to think about the meaning of data, enabling rapid feedback on the results of particular analytic ideas so that new ones can be formulated. Qualitative data analysis then becomes more devoted to creative and intellectual tasks, and less immersed in routine.

In the initial stages of analysis, the rapidity with which CAQDAS can identify patterns in large volumes of text can be useful. Fisher (1997) gives an example using a feature similar to those used in the Shakespeare example earlier. This was from a project involving 244 interviews with children, parents and social workers about local authority child care procedures. The data had been analysed previously using manual methods. Fisher's analysis was done in order to assess the contribution which different CAQDAS software products could make. He used CAQDAS software to search for the word 'discipline' in the interviews and found that different family members appeared to have different meanings for the word, a feature that had been missed in the original manual analysis. This led to some creative thinking about what could have led to this and what it might mean for child care issues. In turn, this thinking led to the development of ideas for **coding** segments of text. Fisher likens this sort of pattern searching to an aerial view of a landscape. Patterns can sometimes be seen from the air which, to the person on the ground, are merely random features.

A further example is a project at the University of Ulm, Germany, by Mergenthaler (1996) in which some 2 million words of transcription from 300 hours of transcribed psychotherapy sessions were searched for the incidence of particular words. It was found that a high incidence of certain words used in sessions, selected because they related to the researcher-generated concepts of 'emotion' and 'abstraction', were associated with particular sessions evaluated by participants as 'good'. Of course, the issue of why there is this connection requires more meaningful analysis of the interactions, perhaps using a coding approach or conversational analysis; but, as an initial finding generated by the simple word counting facilities of CAQDAS software, it helped focus the minds of the researchers on particular lines of enquiry rather than others.

This capacity to generate a quantitative 'aerial view' of large volumes of text, so that subsequent qualitative analysis can be more focused, is developed in more detail later in this chapter.

Rigour

14.3.2 An additional advantage of CAQDAS is that it can help researchers demonstrate that their conclusions are based on rigorous analysis. The demonstration of rigour can involve counting the number of times things occur, as well as demonstrating that you have searched for negative instances by examining the whole corpus of data rather than selecting only anecdotes supporting your interpretation. This is made relatively easy by CAQDAS.

Mention of counting is a reminder that the days of a great divide between qualitative and quantitative research work have now largely passed. The argument that each of these methodologies is inextricably linked to separate philosophical or theoretical positions (for example, Smith and Heshusius, 1986) is less and less convincing to most practising social researchers. The alternative position (for example, Bryman, 1988; Hammersley, 1992) is that for many purposes the two forms of analysis can be helpfully combined (see also Chapter 15).

CAQDAS helps you to make this combination. First, as already mentioned, events can be counted. These may be individual words or phrases, or coded segments of text. I can give an example of this from my own work, where I had used CAQDAS software to code interviews with 163 people who had known elderly people living alone in private households in the year before their deaths (Seale, 1996). I wanted to show what the speakers had said about the elderly people's attitudes to receiving help from others, and I wrote in the final report:

> It was very common for the people living on their own to be described either as not seeking help for problems that they had (65 instances covering 48 people), or as refusing help when offered (144 instances in 83 people). Accounts of this often stressed that this reflected on the character of the person involved, although other associations were also made. In particular, 33 speakers gave 44 instances where they stressed the independence which this indicated:
>
>> '[She] never really talked about her problems, was very independent ...';
>> '[She] was just one of those independent people who would struggle on. She wouldn't ask on her own';
>> 'She used to shout at me because I was doing things for her. She didn't like to be helped. She was very independent.'
>
> Being 'self sufficient', 'would not be beaten', and being said to 'hate to give in' were associated with resisting help. (1996: 34)

As you can imagine, the 163 interviews generated a large amount of text. Because I had read through each interview, marking segments of text with code called *Help* to indicate when speakers had discussed the topic of the elderly person's attitude to help, which I had then entered on the computer, I was able to generate a listing of all these coded segments. Reading through this, I was able to code these into subcategories, distinguishing segments describing elderly people not seeking help in spite of problems, instances where a refusal of help was described, and within this, those segments that involved explicit reflections on the character of the person. A code called *Indep* marked segments where independence was mentioned. For all these things, the CAQDAS software which I was using allowed me to generate counts, some of which can be seen in the text above. I could then select illustrative quotations that gave good, typical examples of the things I was talking about.

If I had wanted to take this analysis further, I could have asked the computer to show me quotations about women separately from men, or to compare what neighbours as opposed to adult children said about the elderly person's attitude to help. Such an analysis might have been done as part of a more general investigation of the effect of gender on the experience of living alone towards the end of life, or as a part of an investigation into kinship obligations in contemporary society. The computer would have generated lists of quotations separately, which might then have been subjected to more detailed scrutiny (for example, how women discuss 'independence' compared with men) but would also have enabled these to be counted. Such counts help the reader to see how widespread phenomena are, guarding against excessive emphasis on rare things that happen to suit the researcher's preferred arguments. These types of systematic comparison between subgroups are greatly facilitated by the rapid retrieval of coded segments enabled by CAQDAS.

Team research

14.3.3 Durkin (1997) notes the impact of using CAQDAS software in the context of an international, collaborative research project where researchers needed to agree on the meaning of codes and so had to assess inter-rater **reliability**. Some qualitative researchers who claim a separate philosophical position from the majority have suggested that a concern with inter-rater reliability smacks of naive realism (see the review in Armstrong et al., 1997, for more details on this debate), preferring the view that all researchers will see a different reality in a given text. Most, however, feel that for collaborative work to proceed it is necessary to create some sort of shared agreement about the meaning of particular segments of data. Durkin found that CAQDAS helped the team check whether they were interpreting segments in the same way. This was particularly useful as coding moved from the more descriptive and mundane codes to those that reflected broader theoretical concerns. Researchers could pass coded interviews between them, and compare the results of blind second coding rapidly, using the counting facilities made available by the computer. Lee and Fielding (1995), who interviewed many researchers about their use of CAQDAS, note that in collaborative projects one of the major impacts has been the encouragement that this gives to agree shared meanings for codes, a matter that is easier to ignore without the discipline imposed by the use of computers.

Limitations and Disadvantages

14.4 Three issues are often raised in objection to the use of CAQDAS software and I consider each in turn in this section. They are as follows:

1 Does specialist CAQDAS software do anything that cannot be done by a good word processor?

2 Do computers impose a narrowly exclusive approach to the analysis of qualitative data?

3 While clearly of use in analysing large volumes of data, CAQDAS software is of little help in examining small data extracts, of the sort often studied by conversation analysts and some discourse analysts.

Using word processors for CAQDAS

14.4.1 Reid (1992) originally made the first point, going on to describe ways in which word processors could help the qualitative data analyst. Hahn (2008) develops this idea further, showing how Microsoft Office word processing, database and spreadsheet software can be used to carry out many of the tasks of qualitative research.

Most CAQDAS software expects text to have been entered electronically using a word processor, although inclusion of pictures and sound files is also often supported. The task of transcription from an audio-recording remains a major, time-consuming element of many qualitative research projects. Use of speech recognition software can help. Such software has to be 'trained' to recognize a particular voice in a quiet environment, but once this is done the person doing the transcription can play back an audio file into headphones and then dictate the words heard into the computer. Transcription speeds are then considerably faster than keying in text.

Alternatively, qualitative researchers may analyse text that is already in electronic form, such as that which is archived in various locations on the Internet. Nexi® (www.lexissnexis.com), for example, allows the media researcher to download news articles relevant to a topic from the world's newspapers going back over several years. Qualitative analysis of Internet forums, website content and blogs can all be done without original data entry, although these may require the conversion of files from one format into another that is readable by CAQDAS software (for example, from html to txt format). And qualitative data archives offer resources to the researcher looking for material to analyse, without the need to enter text (see, for example, www.esds.ac.uk/qualidata). Optical character recognition enables the text of printed documents to be scanned into a word processor for importing into CAQDAS software.

Thus, software other than CAQDAS can be used to prepare material for analysis. Reading and coding material is clearly time-consuming and CAQDAS does not remove this requirement, although keyword analysis (see later) can help in some respects with this. But what about the view that a word processor contains features that make CAQDAS software redundant?

For example, it is possible to use a word processor to search for strings of text. This feature can be exploited if the researcher enters code words near particular topics, which can subsequently be retrieved using the string search facility. Microsoft Word enables the use of 'macros' (a sequence of keystrokes contained in a command file) which will search for paragraphs in which a particular code word (say 'discipline') is embedded, saving each paragraph which it finds to a separate 'results' file. One can then repeat a similar macro on this results file to search and save only those paragraphs containing a second code word (say 'children'), in which case one will have retrieved data where the two codes ('discipline' and 'children') overlap. The file management capacities of most word processors mean that this can be done for separate files if need be, so that perhaps one could compare files for male with female interviewees. Microsoft Word also contains a feature known as a 'spike' which enables a text to be visually inspected and segments of text extracted, to be temporarily stored in a clipboard, then added to by the contents of the next 'spiking' operation. All of the spiked material thus collected can then be copied to a separate document.

Clearly, then, word processors can do some of the things done by specialized software. However, to an experienced user of CAQDAS, these procedures appear unnecessarily time-consuming. In CAQDAS software the complex macro-style instructions are already programmed and are available with just a few simple clicks or keystrokes. Additionally, they offer facilities not available on word processors, such as the export of counts to statistical software, or the visualization of conceptual maps.

We can conclude, then, that only some of the features of CAQDAS software can be carried out by other types of commonly available software, and this, somewhat laboriously. The researcher planning to use CAQDAS, though, will find that other products, including word processors, are useful if used in conjunction with CAQDAS, particularly in preparing text for analysis.

A narrow approach to analysis

14.4.2 The second issue, concerning the possible imposition of a narrowly exclusive approach to analysis, has been raised most intelligently by

Coffey and Atkinson (1996). I say 'most intelligently' because I think concerns about the computer imposing a particular analytic logic, alien to the spirit of qualitative research, can be fuelled by the slight paranoia about technology still felt by some qualitative researchers. In contrast, Coffey and Atkinson begin with a description of a variety of analytic strategies used by researchers working within different qualitative genres. As well as the conventional and popular code-and-retrieve method, typical of researchers working within the grounded theory approach, they also describe analysis of the formal structures of **narratives** (see also Riessman, 1993; 2008) and what they call 'domain analysis', which involves close examination of actors' use of language, seen through their choice of particular words, phrases and metaphors. Domain analysis involves a fine-grained attention to the way in which language constructs meaning, along the lines of a **semiotic** or discourse analytic approach (see, for example, Potter and Wetherell, 1994). This contrasts with the code-and-retrieve approach of grounded theory which relies on common-sense interpretations of the meaning of particular segments of text. Coffey and Atkinson's comment therefore reflects a balanced analysis of the extent to which CAQDAS software supports particular forms of analysis, though they do not discuss conversation analysis in any depth.

By now, you should be convinced that CAQDAS supports the code-and-retrieve operations of grounded theorizing adequately. Indeed, several early CAQDAS programs were designed with this methodology in mind. For discourse analysts, concerned to discover how particular speakers use particular words and phrases, the capacity for rapid retrieval of word strings in large bodies of data will be attractive in a preliminary identification of areas of text likely to repay closer analysis. For such researchers it is useful, too, to make comparisons of different settings or speakers, to identify systematic differences in the language chosen. However, for the discourse analyst or semiotician CAQDAS would be pointless for detailed analysis of short data extracts and would not substitute for in-depth consideration of the meaning of particular, telling instances. Barthes (1973) would not have found CAQDAS particularly useful for *Mythologies*.

Coffey and Atkinson (1996) make the point that most CAQDAS software does not support analysis of the formal structure of narratives, but note that one of them, ETHNO (www.indiana.edu/~socpsy/ESA/), is devoted to this. This program helps analyse sequential events by producing a visual display of how some events are necessary for other events to occur, offering the capacity to code (for example) the agent, action, setting, product and beneficiary of each event.

Heise (1988) shows this by using the software to analyse the formal structure of the Little Red Riding Hood story. The analyst identifies events in **narratives** and enters them into the computer. For example, there may be a point in most stories where the hero's task is outlined, another point where the first difficulty is overcome, another where good defeats evil, and so on. The computer generates diagrams of such events and allows the user to explore and test logical relationships between events across different narratives, as well as to compare different narrative structures. The formal structure of fairy stories, biographical accounts, observed rituals and so on can all be analysed and compared in this way.

Thus CAQDAS software does not have to impose a particular style of analysis; it is more usually a question of knowing what analytic procedures are wanted and either finding the particular package that enables these, or bending an existing package to one's purpose.

Small data extracts

14.4.3 The point I have been discussing merges with the third limitation of CAQDAS listed at the head of this section: the issue of small data extracts. This is not controversial. It has long been conventional advice to users of statistical software that there is no point in spending time entering data from a 10-question interview schedule, done with 10 people, in order to find out how many people answered 'yes' or 'no' to each question. You can work this out by hand more quickly. This advice also applies to CAQDAS. For the conversation analyst interested in reading and rereading a particular 10-second extract of talk, or the discourse analyst paying close attention to a single paragraph of text, there is no point in using CAQDAS.

Having said this, it is increasingly recognized that these more advanced modes of qualitative analysis have established a body of basic findings that can be extended by the comparative analysis of different data extracts. This can involve quite large bodies of data. For example, Silverman (1997) presents a conversation analytic study of a large number of HIV counselling sessions, drawn from several different clinics. He finds that counselling sessions in this highly focused setting vary, for the most part, between a directive 'information delivery' (ID) format that has the virtue of being brief, but is not designed to elicit or address the particular concerns of clients, and an 'interview' (IV) format which takes longer, is more recognizable as being 'counselling' in the conventional sense implying elicitation of clients' concerns, and has the virtue of resulting in 'recipient designed' advice. The IV format is effective, in that it is accompanied by overt acknowledgement of the relevance of advice by clients, whereas the ID format sometimes shows clients resisting advice. These findings are based on an unusually large body of data, by comparison with most other CA studies. Clearly, it would be possible to build on these findings by examining data from a variety of other counselling settings, searching and marking transcribed extracts for the formal characteristics of ID or IV formats, perhaps as a part of some broader enterprise searching for the co-occurrence of particular formats and particular outcomes. For a study like this, CAQDAS would have some relevance in storing, retrieving and counting coded segments.

Like narrative analysis, though, the more popular CAQDAS software (see later) is unable to support many of the things conversation analysts wish to do. This is particularly evident when it comes to transcription of talk from sound recordings. Here, it is useful to have software that can both replay sound files and time events within talk, such as the length of pauses. A software product called Code-A-Text (www.code-a-text.co.uk) allows the computer storage and replay of sound recordings, and the user can work concurrently with transcript and sound or video. One can also add codes to audio segments without transcription. The transcription system of Code-A-Text has a number of features useful for CA, including the automatic recording of the length of silences and the insertion of this into the transcript, as well as supporting the use of CA transcription symbols (see the Appendix to this book). The software can export counts of words or other letter strings, and counts of code words, to spreadsheets for numerical analysis.

Different CAQDAS software offers different things, and if you think you want to do something that your software can't do, search for one that can and you will often find it. I hope the examples of ETHNO and Code-A-Text in this section, neither of which are mainstream CAQDAS products, will show you that that this can result in some welcome finds.

I'll now give you a brief description of three 'mainstream' software products, before discussing some more advanced analytic strategies supported by CAQDAS.

 ■ **Attempt Exercise 14.1** ▬▬▬▬▬▬▬

Theory Building with CAQDAS

14.5
Most researchers who use CAQDAS confine their use to coding and retrieval of text segments, using the computer as an electronic filing cabinet (Lee and Fielding, 1995). Theory building is generally done in the mind, or with the aid of paper, if at all. Although in one sense all research studies, indeed all observations, are 'theory driven', not all research studies need to be explicitly 'theorized'. Much qualitative research is, in common-sense parlance, 'descriptive' and does not require the explicit elaboration of conceptual thought generally referred to as theory. However, CAQDAS does support theorizing and examples of this are available in the literature. Additionally, I use the term 'theory building' to incorporate both the generation of theory and its testing. It is in fact hard to discuss one without the other, and an important perception of later researchers responding to the original outline of **grounded theory** (Glaser and Strauss, 1967) has been that the testing of emerging ideas is important in contributing new theoretical ideas. Indeed, the constant comparative method for generating theory (see Chapter 15) can be understood as involving continual tests of ideas against data. The concept of 'abduction' (see Blaikie, 1993) is a helpful half-way house between the poles of induction and deduction, indicating this understanding of data analysis.

The capacity to map out ideas in diagrams or conceptual networks, supported by most mainstream CAQDAS software such as NVivo or ATLAS.ti, has already been mentioned. Links between concepts can be visually represented in a variety of forms, so that one type of link can mean 'X causes Y', another 'X is associated with Y', or 'X loves Y', 'X depends on Y', 'X is a property of Y' and so on. Since the network is linked to coded segments of data, instances of X and instances of Y, or instances of X where Y also occurs, or instances of Y where X is not present (and so on) can be generated by the application of Boolean search statements.

Let us imagine, for a moment, that CAQDAS had been available when Glaser and Strauss (1964) generated their grounded theory of social loss, an example of the use of the constant comparative method. These researchers recorded, amongst other things, instances of nurses talking about the care of patients who had died. Let us imagine that they searched through all of these stories, perhaps coded as *Nursetalk*, and discovered that, of what they found through manual methods in the 1960s, some were instances of 'social loss stories'. These were comments made that indicated the extent to which nurses felt a particular death constituted a serious loss or not. A code (let us imagine that it is called *Socialoss*) might have been attached to these stories, enabling their later retrieval and further analysis.

Glaser and Strauss report that the category 'social loss story' contained some variable examples, whose properties Glaser and Strauss were able to explore by comparing different incidents where nurses spoke about the deaths of patients. Thus a nurse might regretfully say of a 20-year-old man, 'He was to be a doctor', or of a 30-year-old mother, 'Who will look after the children?', or of an 80-year-old widow, 'Oh well, she had a good life.' This might have been established by close examination of these stories, retrieved by computer. Such an examination could have involved searches for word strings like 'age' or 'years'. Glaser and Strauss concluded that the age of a patient was a key factor in determining the properties of social loss stories, as well as the educational and occupational class of the person who died. Additionally, they found that nurses' 'composure' (itself a category with variable properties) was often disrupted at moments of high social loss. Thus relationships between two categories were mapped out. Eventually Glaser and Strauss were to incorporate this into a general theory of relationships between professionals and their clients, suggesting that clients of high social value were more likely to receive rapid attention from professionals.

The conceptual network that might then have helped this developing theory to emerge would have looked like that shown in Figure 14.1 (created with the NVivo modeller). The arrows indicate the features of patients considered in social loss stories, which can have two different outcomes, depending on the content of the story. At each stage, retrievals of data would have supported or refuted the emerging theory. Note too that further refinement is then possible. Glaser and Strauss (1964) suggest, for example, that the properties of social loss stories interact. If an elderly person of high education and social class status died, this would be less likely to result in loss of composure than a situation involving a younger person of high education and social class. Such relationships might be indicated by further arrows indicating the conditions influencing particular outcomes. Other types of diagram are possible for representing these ideas.

This example can also help in understanding the theory-testing capabilities of CAQDAS. Before going into this, though, it is important to distinguish between two broad types of code. It is possible to code material *factually* rather than *heuristically*.

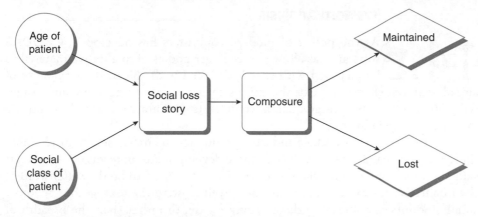

FIGURE 14.1   Social loss and composure

Thus, for example, a segment of text might be described as being about 'composure' or about 'religion' or about 'alienation'. These are examples of heuristic codes, often reflecting the researcher's theoretical concepts, useful for retrieving segments of data so that examples of such talk can be thought about more deeply, subcategorized and so on. However, one might also want to code that composure, in a particular segment, has been retained or lost, that a person is a Catholic or a Protestant, or that someone is alienated or not. These are examples of factual codes. It is necessary to code 'factually' in this way in order to pursue the rigorous hypothesis testing supported by CAQDAS.

Hesse-Biber and Dupuis (1995) give an example of hypothesis testing from a study of the causes of anorexia. Using factual coding with CAQDAS, these researchers could test the proposition that weight loss related to certain antecedent conditions. A logical relationship between factual coding categories was written along the following lines: '*If* mother was critical of daughter's body image *and* mother–daughter relationship was strained *and* daughter experiences weight loss *then* count as an example of mother's negative influence on daughter's self-image.' Once particular interviews were identified as containing the codes involved, the text could be retrieved for further examination in order to see whether support for this causal interpretation could be justified for each case.

Clearly, the example from Glaser and Strauss could have been treated in a similar fashion. Selecting all examples of the loss of composure, the researchers could have examined to see whether these were accompanied by co-occurrences of codes for high education and class and low age, or particular combinations of these. This strategy would have searched out and retrieved negative instances, thus supporting an approach to data analysis that in Chapter 15 we describe as analytic induction. Kelle (1995) contains a number of examples of these uses of CAQDAS, as well as references to software that has been developed to support particular approaches to theory testing.

Keyword Analysis _____

14.6

As the power of modern computers has developed, CAQDAS software has allowed ever larger bodies of qualitative material to be analysed with speed. Coupled with the ready availability of already-entered electronic text, this means that it is easy to generate and potentially analyse extremely large qualitative datasets. Qualitative research is thus no longer a cottage industry!

Like the move from cottage industry production to mass factory production, there are potential dangers involved in these developments, in terms of loss of craft skill and close contact with the fine details of text. It used to be the watchword of the qualitative researcher that he or she stayed close to the text, getting to know small amounts of material in detail, going for depth rather than the breadth of the quantitative researcher. Keyword analysis, adapting software developed in the discipline of linguistics, is a computer-assisted analytic method that maintains the capacity to focus on small amounts of material in considerable depth, but also exploits the availability of large qualitative datasets.

WordSmith Tools (www.lexically.net/wordsmith) is the leading software here, although AntConc (www.antlab.sci.waseda.ac.jp/antconc_index.html), a free programe, also enables many of the procedures used in keyword analysis. This type of software works on different principles from the mainstream CAQDAS packages reviewed earlier in that it does not support a 'code-and-retrieve' approach but instead builds on the core capacity of the software to produce wordlists. A wordlist is a list of all the words that occur in a given group of texts, sorted by frequency of occurrence or by alphabetical order. Comparative keyword analysis identifies the words that occur more frequently in one collection of text when compared with another collection. Thus in Seale et al. (2006) we established that men with prostate cancer used the following words significantly more frequently than women with breast cancer:

wife, he, men, man, chap, male, his, chaps, guy

On the other hand, women with breast cancer used the following words more frequently than men with prostate cancer:

I, she, husband, her, you, women, my, people, mum, sister, everybody, me, children, mother, friends, woman, lady, dad, she'd, daughter, she's, yourself, myself, sisters, I'd, auntie, ladies, who've, someone, somebody, your

In each case, these represent all of the words referring to people in the top 300 most statistically significant keywords. They support an argument saying that women's experience of illness incorporates consideration of a wider range of people than men's. The important point to note is that this analysis, after the files were imported into the software, took about five minutes to carry out, although it was done on 97 interviews comprising about 730,000 transcribed words.

In itself this is not a qualitative analysis, but it is a quick snapshot or 'aerial view' of a large volume of text that precedes a more detailed look at particular features. WordSmith Tools software, for example, showed that men who posted messages on a breast cancer forum, where they were in a minority amongst women who otherwise dominated the postings, were rather different from men elsewhere in that they used words relating to their feelings a lot, and to other family members, particularly children. Descending from the 'aerial view' provided by keyword analysis and reading the stories of these men showed that they were mostly men experiencing or anticipating loss of a partner, so that they found themselves inhabiting a new role in the family, looking after children and attending to emotional needs in a manner which many of them claimed was quite inconsistent with masculine norms. Thus 'macho' appeared as a keyword, indicating their tendency to reflect on masculinity.

Keyword analysis is a specialized aspect of CAQDAS which has considerable potential. It is described more fully in Baker (2006) from the point of view of a discourse analyst, and by Seale and Charteris-Black (2009) from the viewpoint of a CAQDAS networking project at Surrey University, United Kingdom.

============================ LINK ============================

For the CAQDAS networking project at Surrey University, United Kingdom, visit:

http://caqdas.soc.surrey.ac.uk

Concluding Remarks

14.7
In this chapter I have introduced you to some of the basic features of CAQDAS, emphasizing the utility of many such products for the electronic storage, filing and retrieval of large bodies of textual data.

The time-saving element of this has been stressed, as well as the advantages that are gained in addressing issues of validity and reliability by the simple counting enabled by such software. The limitations of CAQDAS have also been discussed, including the issue of whether computer software is likely to impose a narrowly exclusive approach to qualitative data analysis.

As a result I hope that you will feel able to use CAQDAS for your own ends, rather than have it dictate an analytic strategy to you. There are many such software products available and, if you find that a particular one does not support what you want to do, the odds are that another product will contain something more useful if you look hard enough. More elaborate uses of CAQDAS, for theory building and testing, were also described, as well as keyword analysis which exploits the ready availability of very large volumes of electronic text usable for social research purposes.

~ ■ Attempt Exercise 14.2 ■■■■■■■■■■■■

KEY POINTS

- Specialized computer software (CAQDAS) can speed up the routine tasks of sorting and searching through large quantities of qualitative data. This frees up time for analytic thought.

- Such software also tends to promote certain aspects of rigour. It does not tie the researcher to a particular form of qualitative analysis.

- CAQDAS does not do the thinking for you. It may not be needed where small segments of data are being considered.

- Code, search and retrieve are basic and much used features of most CAQDAS software. However, you should not neglect other features designed to facilitate theory building and other innovative approaches such as keyword analysis.

■ ■ Further Reading ■

Lewins and Silver's *Using Software in Qualitative Research* (Sage, 2007) is an excellent guide to CAQDAS. Kelle's *Computer Aided Qualitative Data Analysis* (Sage, 1995) is a good collection of articles showing a variety of uses of CAQDAS, and this author has written thoughtfully on coding for computerized analysis elsewhere (Kelle, 2004). Fielding and Lee's *Using Computers in Qualitative Research* (Sage, 1991) is an edited collection of similar pieces. The websites listed in the text contain plentiful advice and training and self-help tutorials on the subject, as well as links to books and articles.

~ ■ Exercise 14.1 ■■■■■■■■■■■■

If you have an Internet connection, visit the websites listed in this chapter. Download a demonstration version of one of the mainstream software products described (i.e. NVivo, MAXQDA or ATLAS.ti). You could also try out WordSmith Tools or, for free, get a copy of AntConc. When you have spent some time getting to know the software and what it can do, jot down answers to the following questions:

1   How could I use this software to save time on my research project?

2   How could I use this software to improve the rigour of my study?

3   How could I use this software to develop the theoretical aspects of my study?

4   What are the limitations and disadvantages of using this software for my study? Would another product overcome these, or should I opt for a 'manual' approach ?

Select a published qualitative research project that you already know quite well, which was done without the use of CAQDAS. It could, for example, be an early 'classic' study of Chicago School ethnography, or a well-known study relevant to your research topic. Examine the way in which the researcher appears to have collected and analysed the data and answer the following questions:

1   How might CAQDAS software have been used to aid data collection in this study?

2   How might CAQDAS software have been used to develop a coding scheme in this study?

3   How might the use of CAQDAS have improved the quality and rigour of data reporting in this study?

4   What other questions might have been asked of the data in the study, and could CAQDAS software have helped in answering these?

15

Quality in Qualitative Research

| Chapter Objectives |

By the end of this chapter, you will be able to:

- **Understand the concepts of validity and reliability.**

- **Incorporate into your research design a number of methods for improving validity and reliability.**

- **Design and generate research sensitive to quality issues.**

Introduction

15.1 This chapter is the first of two chapters which deal with quality considerations. In this chapter, I will attempt a diagnosis of the problem and suggest some practical solutions for you to use in your own research. In Chapter 16, I suggest how you can apply quality rules to evaluate research publications.

Quality has been a continuing theme of this book. Deciding to do qualitative research is not a soft option. Such research demands theoretical sophistication and methodological rigour.

Just because we do not use complicated statistical tests or do much counting, does not mean that we can wallow in comforting hot baths of 'empathic' or 'authentic' discussions with respondents. After all, if this is the limit of our ambitions, can we do better than a talk show presenter?

Why does 'quality' matter, and what does 'quality' mean? To get a feel of the issues involved, let us begin with how students frame these matters.

Maddie Sandall's research for her MSc was based on interviews with foreign students who had transferred to the UK for the final year of their degree. Having gathered her data, she worried about her sample as follows.

Do I Need More Data?

The request for interviewees generated a relatively small response rate, possibly due to the characteristics of the students required for the sample, or it could have been due to the numerous coursework assignments due in during that term. Although the data I have gathered had been quite rich and interesting, I felt that more was needed, therefore this has been backed up by a largely quantitative survey of students in Malaysia. [Maddie Sandall, MSc Management, UWE]

In a focus group study of Chinese people with diabetes living in the UK, Queenie Eng had similar concerns. Like Maddie, she worried about the representativeness of her respondents. Unlike Maddie, she did not gather more data but spent time explaining the rationale behind the composition of her focus group.

Representativeness Again

It is extremely important that findings obtained with convenience samples are critically evaluated against the following questions:

Q1: What types of people were systematically excluded from the sample, and why? The following individuals were excluded from the study:

- Students, asylum seekers and refugees were excluded because of their limited length of stay and the lack of fixed abode in the UK.
- Non-Chinese-language speakers were excluded because the study is focused on Chinese people and the researcher cannot communicate fluently in other non-Chinese languages.
- Those with cognitive impairment were excluded because of potential inability to articulate thoughts and feelings effectively.

Q2: What types of people were over-represented in the sample? Given the nature of diabetes, where males are more predisposed than women, proportionately more men were involved in Phase 2 of the study. [S. Eng, Medicine, Leeds]

As I noted in Chapter 9, given the small numbers of people or situations with which qualitative research is concerned, many students worry about the representativeness of their case studies. Yet there are two straightforward solutions to this worry:

- an emphasis on the value of even a single case since, like a black swan, it can test a general rule (Flyvbjerg, 2004: 421)
- as Queenie Eng shows, the choice of a purposive sample based on logical grounds.

The logic of purposive sampling is well illustrated by the following extract. Rachael Dunn carried out a study of individual therapy sessions between therapists and patients with eating disorders. Twenty-four therapy sessions of between 30 and 60 minutes were audiotaped via digital recorders operated by the participating therapists. Below you can see how she explains the nature of her sample.

STUDENT EXAMPLES

The Logic of Purposive Sampling

The reason for the number of sessions taped was predominantly informed by pragmatic considerations. Given my project's overall timeline, data collection was scheduled to occur over a six-month period. However, after I experienced some initial technical obstacles, this eventually exceeded 12 months. The total quantity of taped sessions was 34; however, 10 of the early sessions were unusable due to inaudible and corrupted sound files. This was mainly due to the external microphone not being switched on, or the incorrect activation of the record function of the taping device. These problems were resolved by employing more user-friendly recording equipment and providing additional operational training for participating clinicians.

There were no criteria regarding patients' number of previous therapy sessions, or number of hospital admissions that excluded participation; nor were there requirements in the study regarding the sequence of session recordings in terms of taping a certain trajectory, or order of sessions with the same patients. This decision was again based on pragmatic grounds, in order to expedite the data collection period. Therefore, the clinicians were instructed to record a range of sessions with different patients, at varying stages of treatment. [Rachael Dunn, Psychology, Murdoch University]

Representativeness is not the only quality issue that troubles students. Many have doubts about the extent to which respondents' answers really relate to what they do outside the interview (see Hammersley, 2008: 89–100). In the 2008 US presidential election, pollsters were asked whether people might be concealing their racist feelings about Barack Obama. Similarly, in an interview study of perceptions of race in New Zealand, Farida Tilbury was concerned about whether she could take at face value her respondents' expressions of non-racist sentiments.

Truth or Rhetoric?

Speakers about race relations use a number of rhetorical devices to convince and to manage the impression they make when giving accounts of their views. One device is to claim a personal relationship with members of the group one goes on to criticize, producing the oft-heard justification, 'Some of my best friends are Maori …, but …'. The purpose of this research was to determine the influence such friendships *actually* have on identity and attitudes. When a friendship is reported by a respondent, is it possible to tell whether a respondent is using their 'friendship' as a rhetorical device, or whether they are reporting a genuine friendship? When is a friend a friend, and not a rhetorical device? Basically, if respondents were reporting close friendships which did not exist, how can the data be taken as valid? A person may have reported two good friendships across ethnic boundaries, but if they reported these purely for impression management reasons, the relationship between attitudes reported and friendships is going to be misleading. This is a special case of the more general question – how are accounts related to 'reality'? [Farida Tilbury, Sociology, Murdoch University]

Farida nicely illustrates a dilemma about validity common to interview researchers. There are two ways of responding to this dilemma:

- insisting on a more detailed analysis of the data in order to sort 'fact' from 'fiction' (the positivist solution)
- changing the focus away from the 'facts' of racism towards the rhetoric of racism (the constructionist solution).

Although Farida's use of **discourse analysis** leads towards the second response, she also makes use of a more positivist solution, as the extract below illustrates.

Sorting 'Fact' from 'Fiction'

[Because] there was inevitably a degree of impression management influencing the choice of friendships reported by the participants … it was necessary to analyse the entire interviews much more closely to try to glean whether these friendships had a strong influence on respondents' views, taking note of how frequently they were used as warrants for particular views, and how often other influences were mentioned, the manner in which they were referred to,

(Continued)

(Continued)

the nature of the story told, the tone of surrounding comments, and noting the ways they were used as examples to support certain attitudes. It became easier to tell whether friendships reported were simply credentials or justifications, or were genuine close friendships, from the ways that they were talked about. [Farida Tilbury]

Irrespective of the theoretical model that lies behind your research problem, the kind of in-depth analysis that Farida uses here is an essential way to achieve valid findings. Later I will refer to this approach as 'comprehensive data treatment'.

Once again mobilizing a positivist model, in the following extract Farida worries about the **reliability** of her chosen 'research instrument' – the open-ended interview.

STUDENT EXAMPLES

The Reliability of Open-Ended Questions

Perhaps their extreme open-endedness left respondents a little unsure how to respond, or with less time to consider their response [to my questions]. For example, if the interviewer merely says 'affirmative action', respondents may not have time to consider their response, not know where to start, or not understand the concept. On the other hand, if the issue were framed in terms of a longer question, such as, 'Some people have argued that special quotas for Maori or other disadvantaged groups are a good idea in order to give them access to jobs or educational opportunities that they might not otherwise have access to. Do you have any views on affirmative action programmes such as this?', respondents would have a clear explanation of the topic and time to collect their thoughts and consider their answer. I still feel that the longer format tends to lead respondents to answer in particular ways, and so prefer the format used, but it is interesting to consider the effect of this approach on the forms of respondents' expressions. [Farida Tilbury]

A logical way of testing whether different question formats produce different answers, as Farida suspects, is to pre-test questions before the main research starts. A more constructionist solution is to examine long sequences of talk to examine how interviewer and interviewee co-assemble particular versions of 'reality' (see Rapley, 2004).

Whatever your theoretical model, it is good practice to address how your relationship with the people in your study might affect your findings. In ethnographic studies, using participant observation, the researcher–researched relation has been a continuing interest. Ben Heaven's ethnography of the conduct of a randomized controlled trial (RCT) is a case in point.

Collecting Data among Friends

Using ethnographic techniques and aspects of Strauss's theory of action, I explored the work of my colleagues as they went about their daily tasks as a trial team, in addition to interviewing enrolled practice nurses and participating patients. Unsurprisingly, over the five-year period of the research, the social and working relationships I formed with the 'triallists' influenced the process of data collection and analysis. In particular the trial team and I worked in the same building, and therefore had contact across a range of working and social contexts that extended beyond the immediate study. In order to produce what I could regard as a 'successful' and personally satisfying ethnography, I needed to find a solution to a key problem; how to produce a critical account of the process of this RCT whilst not undermining, alienating or downplaying the work of my colleagues. This issue was complicated by the sometimes unenthusiastic accounts of the RCT offered by the practice nurses and participating patients, and indeed by my own occasionally sceptical views of the trial.

A key difficulty I experienced in my interpretation of the data was a sense of loyalty to the trial team. I was exposed to the daily frustrations of these researchers, and sometimes participated in their struggle to make the trial work. It was difficult at times therefore to question their actions or perspectives.

My mind raced with the uses to which I could apply certain quotes: in paper titles, conclusions to conference presentations and formal reports. However, I was also mindful that I was amongst colleagues and friends, and that such statements were typically made out of frustration. The dilemma was: should they be reported, and if so how?

To address the dilemma of utilizing inflammatory statements in the thesis, I employed a single, relatively risky strategy. The risk in this sense stemmed from an increased opportunity for censorship. When an inflammatory action or statement was recorded I discussed my interpretation of the event with the actor in question. In the case of the dietician's comments I presented her with a section of written analysis in which I had quoted her verbalization. This was followed with a detailed 'debriefing' in which I expressed my interpretation of her actions in the broader context of the collaborative research project. My intention in these situations was to gain supplemental consent and achieve a level of transparency with my colleagues. However, my motivations were in part also driven by self-interest. I found that by situating perspectives in their broader contexts and by explicitly acknowledging the trajectories preceding them, none of the trial team vetoed my use of potentially inflammatory material. Given this attention to context – the broader narrative – even inflammatory comments appeared to have some reason. In addition, the debriefing approach relieved me of some of the discomfort inherent in recording and reporting the professional behaviour of colleagues.
[Ben Heaven, Health Studies, Newcastle]

Ben's thoughtful account of his research raises several ethical problems about what you owe to the people you study (discussed in Chapter 10). However, it also addresses two important quality issues:

- going 'native', i.e. being so personally involved with the people you are studying that it is difficult to be objective

- anecdotal use of data extracts (like spectacular quotes from participants) out of context.

Ben offers two solutions to the problem of **anecdotalism**. First, he takes his interpretations back to the people concerned. This method, known as 'respondent validation', is discussed later in this chapter. Second, instead of choosing a few spectacular data extracts, he elects to situate 'perspectives in their broader contexts … explicitly acknowledging the trajectories preceding them'. Like Farida's work, this is another excellent example of 'comprehensive data treatment'.

 ■ **Attempt Exercise 15.1** ▬▬▬▬▬▬

All of the student examples used here employ what Clive Seale has called 'methodological awareness':

> Methodological awareness involves a commitment to showing as much as possible to the audience of research studies … the procedures and evidence that have led to particular conclusions, always open to the possibility that conclusions may need to be revised in the light of new evidence. (1999: x)

It follows that unless you can show your audience the procedures you used to ensure that your methods were reliable and your conclusions valid, there is little point in aiming to conclude a research dissertation. Having good intentions, or the correct political attitude, is unfortunately never the point. Short of reliable methods and valid conclusions, research descends into a bedlam where the only battles that are won are by those who shout the loudest.

In Chapter 9, I was able to be reassuring about the scientific status of case studies based upon small amounts of data. However, I am less tempted to assure qualitative researchers that they need not be concerned about the reliability of their methods or the quality of their interpretations. The reader has only to refer to Chapter 16 to see that my concerns about these matters extend to some published research.

But first it is important to be clear about the relevant terms: validity and reliability. For simplicity, I will work with the two straightforward definitions set out in Table 15.1.

Using examples of actual research studies, I review below the pitfalls and opportunities that the demands of validity and reliability create for the novice researcher. Let me begin with validity.

TABLE 15.1   Validity and reliability

Validity

By validity, I mean truth: interpreted as the extent to which an account accurately represents the social phenomena to which it refers. (Hammersley, 1990: 57)

Reliability

Reliability refers to the degree of consistency with which instances are assigned to the same category by different observers or by the same observer on different occasions. (Hammersley, 1992: 67)

Validity

15.2 'Validity' is another word for truth. Sometimes one doubts the validity of an explanation because the researcher has clearly made no attempt to deal with contrary cases or to locate an example in a broader context (as Ben and Farida do). Or sometimes, the demands of journal editors for shorter and shorter articles and the word limits attached to university courses mean that the researcher is reluctantly led only to use 'telling' examples.

Of course, such challenges to validity are not confined to qualitative research. The same sort of problems can happen in the natural sciences. The demands of journal editors and university courses are little different in most fields. Nor is the temptation to exclude contrary cases unique to qualitative research. Moreover, the large research teams that sometimes collaborate in the natural sciences can unexpectedly threaten the credibility of findings. For instance, laboratory assistants have been shown to select 'perfect' slides for their professor's important lecture, while putting on one side 'slides' about which awkward questions might be asked (see Lynch, 1984).

It also should not be assumed that quantitative researchers have a simple solution to the question of validity. As Fielding and Fielding point out, some interpretation takes place even when using apparently 'hard' quantitative measures:

> ultimately all methods of data collection are analysed 'qualitatively', in so far as the act of analysis is an interpretation, and therefore of necessity a selective rendering. Whether the data collected are quantifiable or qualitative, the issue of the *warrant* for their inferences must be confronted. (1986: 12, my emphasis)

So, as you prepare your qualitative study, you should not be overly defensive. Quantitative researchers have no 'golden key' to validity.

Nonetheless, qualitative researchers, with their in-depth access to single cases, have to overcome a special temptation. How are they to convince themselves (and their audience) that their 'findings' are genuinely based on critical investigation of all their data and do not depend on a few well-chosen 'examples'? This is sometimes known as the problem of 'anecdotalism' (Silverman, 2001: 222–3), which we met in the previous section.

As Mehan (1979) notes, the very strength of ethnographic field studies – its ability to give rich descriptions of social settings – can also be its weakness. Mehan identifies three such weaknesses:

1   Conventional field studies tend to have an anecdotal quality. Research reports include a few *exemplary* instances of the behavior that the researcher has culled from field notes.
2   Researchers seldom provide the criteria or grounds for including certain instances and not others. As a result, it is difficult to determine the typicality or *representativeness* of instances and findings generated from them.
3   Research reports presented in tabular form do not preserve the materials upon which the analysis was conducted. As the researcher abstracts data from raw materials to produce summarized findings, the original form of the materials is *lost*. Therefore, it is impossible to entertain alternative interpretations of the same materials. (1979: 15, my emphasis)

Some years later, this problem was succinctly expressed by Bryman:

There is a tendency towards an anecdotal approach to the use of data in relation to conclusions or explanations in qualitative research. Brief conversations, snippets from unstructured interviews ... are used to provide evidence of a particular contention. There are grounds for disquiet in that the representativeness or generality of these fragments is rarely addressed. (1988: 77)

Let me use one more student example to show how a proper degree of 'methodological awareness' can help you overcome anecdotalism and improve the validity of your findings. Alan Quirk's dissertation examined how mental health professionals made decisions about the 'careers' of mental patients (from being compulsorily admitted or 'sectioned', to their hospital stay and discharge). Below you will find his discussion of how he improved the validity of his findings using three interrelated studies. In this long example, look out for Alan's discussion of:

• following the trajectory of patients' careers (longitudinal design, i.e. over time)

• examining negative instances rather than rushing to early conclusions

• triangulating different methods to address a particular topic

• using simple tabulations of the frequency of certain phenomena

• employing member validation to check his findings.

Striving for Validity

Combining the findings from my three studies means I am able to comment not only on how people are admitted onto an acute psychiatric ward – both under mental health legislation and voluntarily (two of the audiotaped outpatient consultations resulted in an informal admission) – but also what happens to them when they get there. Further, in the Prescribing Decisions Project I observed some people's first outpatient appointment after their discharge from hospital. This offers some insight into people's experiences after a stay in hospital, as do the follow-up interviews undertaken with discharged patients for the MHA study. In short, the observations presented in this thesis span events leading up to, during, and after hospital admission. To my knowledge this is the first combined observational study to encompass all of these aspects of psychiatric practice. [Alan goes on to explain how he has attempted to improve the validity of his findings:]

- All three studies have been undertaken in a *spirit of grounded theorizing*, with attempts made to search and account for negative instances.

- Various methods of *triangulation* have been used. In the two ethnographic studies various types of evidence were collected before concluding that a thing is true, and in the Prescribing Decisions Project, the CA research complemented our interview study. It did so because while the analysis of consultation transcripts revealed activities that psychiatrists failed to mentioned in research interviews (e.g. what patients do to construct safe conversational environments in which to discuss non-compliance), the interviews helped one-off psychiatric consultations to be understood in the context of the unfolding doctor–patient relationship in which they take place.

- *Simple counts* of well-defined phenomena have been included in the findings chapters where appropriate. This is aimed at increasing the credibility of claims and guarding against accusations of anecdotalism that can be levelled at certain qualitative studies.

- *Member validation* techniques were used. [Alan Quirk, Human Sciences, Brunel University]

Alan's use of multiple methods and settings was ambitious and well beyond the range of most PhD (let alone MA) research. Nevertheless, his high degree of 'methodological awareness' and resistance to 'anecdotalism' is something to which we can all aspire.

Now let us look more closely at some of the strategies that Alan uses.

Triangulation refers to the attempt to get a 'true' fix on a situation by combining different ways of looking at it (method triangulation) or different findings (data triangulation). In Chapter 3, I showed some of the difficulties that novice researchers can get into by attempting such triangulation. In Chapter 8, I discussed in more detail the analytical limitations of this approach.

Broadly, using a constructionist model is simply not compatible with the assumption that 'true' fixes on 'reality' can be obtained separately from particular ways of looking at it. Of course, this does not mean that you should not use different datasets or deploy different methods. The problem only arises when you use such multiplicity as a way of settling validity questions.

Respondent validation suggests that we should go back to the subjects with our tentative results and refine them in the light of our subjects' reactions (Reason and Rowan, 1981). Like triangulation, however, I fear it is a flawed method.

Of course, the subjects we study can, if we ask them, give us an account of the context of their actions. The problem only arises if we attribute a privileged status to that account (see Bloor, 1983; Bryman, 1988: 78–9). As Fielding and Fielding put it:

> there is no reason to assume that members have privileged status as commentators on their actions ... such feedback cannot be taken as direct validation or refutation of the observer's inferences. Rather such processes of so-called 'validation' should be treated as yet another source of data and insight. (1986: 43)

Of course, this leaves on one side the ethics, politics and practicalities of the researcher's relation with subjects in the field (see Chapters 10 and 12). Nonetheless, these latter issues should not be *confused* with the validation of research findings.

If triangulation and respondent validation are fallible paths to validity, what more satisfactory methods remain? I discuss below five interrelated ways of thinking critically about qualitative data analysis in order to aim at more valid findings. These are:

- the refutability principle
- the constant comparative method
- comprehensive data treatment
- deviant case analysis
- using appropriate tabulations.

The refutability principle

15.2.1 One solution to the problem of anecdotalism is simply for qualitative researchers to seek to refute their initial assumptions about their data in order to achieve objectivity. As Kirk and Miller argue:

> The assumptions underlying the search for objectivity are simple. There is a world of empirical reality out there. The way we perceive and understand that world is largely up to us, but the world does not tolerate all understandings of it equally. (1986: 11)

Even if we do not employ Kirk and Miller's positivist language, we need to recognize that 'the world does not tolerate all understandings of it equally'. This means that we must overcome the temptation to jump to easy conclusions just because there is some evidence that seems to lead in an interesting direction. Instead, we must subject this evidence to every possible test.

The critical method implied here is close to what Popper (1959) calls 'critical rationalism'. This demands that we must seek to refute assumed relations between phenomena. Then, only if we cannot refute the existence of a certain relationship are we in a position to speak about 'objective' knowledge. Even then, however, our knowledge is always provisional, subject to a subsequent study which may come up with disconfirming evidence. Popper puts it this way:

> What characterises the empirical method is its manner of exposing to falsification, in every conceivable way, the system to be tested. Its aim is not to save the lives of untenable systems but, on the contrary, to select the one which is by comparison the fittest, by exposing them all to the fiercest struggle for survival. (1959: 42)

Of course, qualitative researchers are not alone in taking Popper's critical method seriously. One way in which *quantitative* researchers attempt to satisfy Popper's demand for attempts at 'falsification' is by carefully excluding spurious correlations.

To do this, the survey researcher may seek to introduce new variables to produce a form of 'multivariate analysis' which can offer significant, non-spurious correlations (see Mehan, 1979: 21). Through such an attempt to avoid spurious correlations, quantitative social scientists can provide a practical demonstration of their orientation to the spirit of critical inquiry that Popper advocates.

How can qualitative researchers satisfy Popper's criterion? The remaining four methods suggest an interrelated way of thinking critically during data analysis.

The constant comparative method

15.2.2 The comparative method means that the qualitative researcher should always attempt to find another case through which to test out a provisional hypothesis. In an early study of the changing perspectives of medical students during their training, Becker and Geer (1960) found that they could test their emerging hypothesis about the influence of career stages upon perceptions by comparing different groups at one time and also comparing one cohort of students with another over the course of training. For instance, it could only be claimed with confidence that beginning medical students tended to be idealists if several cohorts of first-year students all shared this perspective.

Similarly, when I was studying what happened to children with Down's syndrome in a heart hospital, I tested out my findings with tape-recordings of consultations from the same clinic involving children without the congenital abnormality (Silverman, 1981). And, of course, my attempt to analyse the ceremonial order of private medical practice (Silverman, 1984) was highly dependent on comparative data on public clinics.

However, beginning researchers are unlikely to have the resources to study different cases. Yet this does not mean that comparison is impossible. The constant comparative method involves simply inspecting and comparing all the data fragments that arise in a single case (Glaser and Strauss, 1967; Charmaz, 2006: 178–80).

While such a method may seem attractive, beginning researchers may worry about two practical difficulties involved in implementing it. First, they may lack the resources to assemble all their data in an analysable form. For instance, transcribing a whole dataset may be impossibly time-consuming – as well as diverting you from data analysis! Second, how are you to compare data when you may have not yet generated a provisional hypothesis or even an initial set of categories?

Fortunately, these objections can be readily overcome. In practice, it usually makes sense to begin analysis on a relatively small part of your data. Then, having generated a set of categories, you can test out emerging hypotheses by steadily expanding your data corpus. This point has been clearly made by Anssi Peräkylä using the example of studies based on tape-recorded data:

> There is a limit to how much data a single researcher or a research team can transcribe and analyse. But on the other hand, a large database has definite advantages ... a large portion of the data can be kept as a resource that is used only when the analysis has progressed so far that the phenomena under study have been specified. At that later stage, short sections from the data in reserve can be transcribed, and thereby, the full variation of the phenomenon can be observed. (2004: 288)

I employed this constant comparative method, moving from small to larger datasets, in my study of AIDS counselling (Silverman: 1997). For example, having isolated an instance of how a client resisted a counsellor's advice, I trawled through my data to obtain a larger sample of cases where advice resistance was present.

However, the constant comparative method, because it involves a repeated to and fro between different parts of your data, implies something much bigger. All parts of your data must, at some point, be inspected and analysed. This is part of what is meant by 'comprehensive data treatment'.

Comprehensive data treatment

15.2.3 Paul ten Have notes the complaint that in CA, like other kinds of research:

> findings ... are based on a subjectively selected, and probably biased, 'sample' of cases that happen to fit the analytic argument. (1998: 135)

This complaint, which amounts to a charge of anecdotalism, can be addressed by what ten Have, following Mehan (1979), calls 'comprehensive data treatment'. This comprehensiveness arises because, in qualitative research, 'all cases of data ... [are] incorporated in the analysis' (1979: 21).

Such comprehensiveness goes beyond what is normally demanded in many quantitative methods. For instance, in survey research one is usually satisfied by achieving significant, non-spurious, correlations. So, if nearly all your data support your hypothesis, your job is largely done.

By contrast, in qualitative research, working with smaller datasets open to repeated inspection, one should not be satisfied until one's generalization is able to apply to every single gobbet of relevant data you have collected.

The outcome is a generalization which can be every bit as valid as a statistical correlation. As Mehan puts it: 'The result is an integrated, precise model that comprehensively describes a specific phenomena [*sic*], instead of a simple correlational statement about antecedent and consequent conditions' (1979: 21).

Deviant case analysis

15.2.4 What is important in depicting anomalies precisely? If you cannot do it, that shows you do not know your way around the concepts. (Wittgenstein, 1980: 72e)

Comprehensive data treatment implies actively seeking out and addressing anomalies or deviant cases. Again Mehan makes the point:

> The method begins with a small batch of data. A provisional analytic scheme is generated. The scheme is then compared to other data, and modifications made in the scheme as necessary. The provisional analytic scheme is constantly confronted by 'negative' or 'discrepant' cases until the researcher has derived a small set of recursive rules that incorporate all the data in the analysis. (1979: 21; see also Becker, 1998: 211–12)

Mehan notes that this is very different from the sense of 'deviant case analysis' in quantitative, survey research. Here you turn to deviant cases in two circumstances:

- when the existing variables will not produce sufficiently high statistical correlations
- when good correlations are found but you suspect these might be 'spurious'.

By contrast, the qualitative researcher should not be satisfied by explanations which appear to explain nearly all the variance in their data. Instead, as I have already argued, in qualitative research, every piece of data has to be used until it can be accounted for.

Let me show you two examples which use deviant case analysis with the aim of a comprehensive data treatment. The first is drawn from an interview study of reports by relatives about family members who had died alone (Seale, 1996; discussed in Seale, 1999: 79–80).

Most relatives reported that a relative dying alone was an unwelcome event and that they would have wanted to be present at the death if they had been able. Seale argued that such accounts worked to display a relative's moral adequacy.

However, in a small minority of cases, people said they had not wanted to be present at such a death. Rather than treat these examples as statistically insignificant, Seale examined them in greater detail to see if his overall argument needed to be modified.

In all these deviant cases, it turned out that respondents offered legitimations for their position. For instance, in one case, a son said that his father's dementia meant that he would have been 'oblivious' if his son had been present. In another case, a husband referred to his own potential distress at being present at the death of his wife. He also added that it 'didn't make any difference as she was in a coma' (1999: 79).

Seale concluded that, in his five deviant cases, respondents did not depart from displays of moral adequacy but:

> successfully demonstrated their moral adequacy by alternative means. In doing this, they showed an orientation towards the event [i.e. not being present at the death of a loved one] as deviant from normal behaviour, requiring explanation, so strengthening the general case that accompaniment of dying people is perceived as a generally desirable social norm. (1999: 80)

My second example of deviant case analysis is drawn from my ethnographic research on paediatric clinics (Silverman, 1987). In this research, I compared the heart clinic discussed in Chapter 13 with a clinic treating children born with hare lip and/or cleft palate. The latter is another congenital defect but, unlike cardiac anomalies, is self-evident and treatable by routine, low-risk, cosmetic surgery usually carried out when the patient is in their teens. In both clinics, I observed and tape-recorded what was said. Transcription was for ethnographic purposes and this meant that its level of detail did not follow all the conventions used in CA.

The rationale for delaying cosmetic surgery in the cleft-palate clinic is that, since appearance is a matter of personal judgement, it is best left until somebody is of an age when they can decide for themselves rather than be influenced by the surgeon or their parents. In practice, this reasonable assumption meant that the doctor (D) would ask the young person concerned a question in this general format:

Extract 15.1 [Silverman, 1987: 165]

D: What do you think about your looks Barry? (3.0)
B: I don't know
D: You heh heh doesn't worry you a lot.

Barry's answer was common at the clinic. Short of a later self-correction or a persuasive parental intervention (both difficult to engineer), it meant that many such patients did not get cosmetic surgery.

Drawing upon evidence of this kind, I argued that questioning such young people about their looks set up the consultation as a psychological interrogation likely to lead to non-intervention. This was strengthened by the fact that, later in the consultation, it became clear that Barry, after all, did want cosmetic surgery. Barry's case and that of others showed that these adolescent patients had far less difficulty when they were simply asked whether they wanted an operation.

However, a visit to a clinic in Brisbane, Australia, provided me with the deviant case shown in Extract 15.2:

Extract 15.2 [Silverman, 1987: 182]

D: Do you worry at all about your appearance?
S: Oh I really notice it but I um if it could be improved, I'd
     Like to get it done. I really worry about it.

In one leap, Simon seems to have overcome the communication difficulties that a question about your appearance usually generates. He freely admits that he 'notices' and 'worries' about his looks and, consequently, would 'like to get it done'. What are we to make of this apparently deviant case?

The first thing to report is that, at 18 years of age, Simon is considerably older than Barry and the other children seen in my English clinic. So reticence to discuss one's appearance may be age related and different medical strategies may be applied to different age groups.

However, there was something more interesting about Simon's case. This was how his reports about his worries were treated by doctors in his clinic. Extract 15.3 is a continuation of 15.2:

Extract 15.3 [Silverman, 1987: 183]

S: I really worry about it.
D: *Really*?
D: Not really but *really*?
S: But *really* yes.

What is going on in Extract 15.3? Why is Simon's apparently straightforward response subject to further questioning? To answer these questions, I noted comments made by a doctor before Simon had entered the room. These are shown in Extract 15.4:

Extract 15.4 [Silverman, 1987: 180]

D: He's er (0.5) it's a matter of deciding whether he should have an operation. And, er, what we are concerned about is his degree of maturity which it will be very interesting for you [D turns towards me] to make a judgment on when he comes in.

We see from Extract 15.4 that, even before Simon enters the room, his 'degree of maturity' will be an issue. We are advised that Simon's answers should not stand alone as expression of his wishes but should be judged as mature or immature and, perhaps, discarded or reinterpreted. After Simon leaves, this doctor worries some more about what Simon's answers 'really' mean:

Extract 15.5 [Silverman, 1987: 186]

D: It's very difficult to assess isn't it? Because he's pretty sophisticated in some of his comments and it's er (1.0) it's just the, you know, continuously sunny nature that's troubling me a little bit about the problem as to whether it should be done.

Eventually, this doctor concludes that Simon's relaxed manner is merely 'a cover-up' for his self-consciousness about his appearance. Although this is rather an odd conclusion, since Simon has freely admitted that he is concerned about his appearance, it generates general consent and all the doctors present agree that Simon is 'motivated' and should have his operation.

This deviant case considerably added to my understanding of the mechanics of decision making in the cleft-palate clinic. The English data had suggested that asking young people about their appearance tended to set them problems which could lead away from the cosmetic surgery they might want. The Australian data showed that, even where a patient confidently reported his concern about his appearance, this created a further complication. In this case, the doctors worried about how someone so concerned could present themselves in such a confident (or 'sunny') manner.

A Catch-22 situation was now revealed. The doctors' practical reasoning unintentionally resulted in the following impasse:

1 To get surgery, you needed to complain about your appearance.

2 Those who were most troubled about their appearance would often be the least able to complain, so they would not get surgery.

3 Patients who did complain would be viewed as self-confident. Hence their underlying troubles were open to doubt and they too might not get surgery.

The impasse derived from the coupling of the doctors' understandable desire to elicit their patients' own views with psychological versions of the meaning of what their patients actually said.

These two studies show how the identification and further analysis of deviant cases can strengthen the validity of research. As implied here, it is important to underline the fact that such identification needs to stem from a theoretical approach to the data. Seale's work derived from a way of treating interview responses as moral **narratives**. My own research was based upon an ethnographic interest in the 'ceremonial order' of the clinic (Strong, 1979).

So pieces of data are never intrinsically 'deviant' but rather become so in relation to the approach used. This theoretically defined approach to analysis should also properly apply to the compilation and inspection of data in tabulated form.

Using appropriate tabulations _____

15.2.5 A very nice example of how simple tabulations can improve the quality of data analysis is provided by Koppel et al. (2003). Their earlier ethnographic research had revealed that hospital computer-based ordering systems were often associated with errors when doctors prescribed patients' medications. A quantitative survey now showed that over 75 per cent of doctors had used the computer system incorrectly.

It turned out that the computer display tended to convey a false sense of accuracy to many doctors. For example, by focusing solely on the electronic medication chart, doctors would tend to miss crucial paper stickers attached to the hardcopy casenotes. Various features of the computer software also seemed to be associated with these errors. For instance, the display on the screen would show amounts of a medication appropriate for warehousing needs and purchasing decisions. Yet this level might be clinically inappropriate. In addition, it was possible for a doctor to add a new medication without cancelling an existing prescription for something very similar.

Koppel et al.'s survey increased the validity and generalizability of their qualitative study. Using both sets of data, they were able to argue more convincingly about how the computer software could be improved.

However, it is usually mistaken to count simply for the sake of counting. Without a theoretical rationale behind the tabulated categories, counting only gives a spurious validity to research.

For instance, in the observation of classroom behaviour, Mehan suggests that many kinds of quantification have only limited value:

> the quantitative approach to classroom observation is useful for certain purposes, namely, for providing the frequency of teacher talk by comparison with student talk ... However, this approach minimizes the contribution of students, neglects the inter-relationship of verbal to non-verbal behavior, obscures the contingent nature of interaction, and ignores the (often multiple) functions of language. (1979: 14)

I do not attempt here to defend quantitative or positivistic research *per se*. I am not concerned with research designs which centre on quantitative methods and/or are indifferent to how participants construct order. Instead, I want to try to demonstrate some uses of quantification in research which is qualitative and interpretive in design.

To some extent, the tabulations I developed in my study of cancer clinics (see Table 13.5) fell foul of Mehan's criticisms. Although my comparison of clinics derived from Strong's (1979) discussion of 'ceremonial orders', the tabulation was based upon dubious, commonsensical categories. For instance, it is very problematic to count participants' questions when your only data are fieldnotes. Without being able to reinspect a tape-recording, my category of 'question' has an unknown relation to the participants' orientations.

An alternative is to count members' own categories as used in naturally occurring places. For instance, in my analysis of cardiac consultations with children with

Down's syndrome (see Chapter 13), I constructed a table, based on a comparison of Down's and non-Down's consultations, showing the different forms of the doctor's questions to parents and the parents' answers. This tabulation showed a strong tendency with children with Down's syndrome for both the doctor and parents to avoid using the word 'well' about the child, and this absence of reference to 'wellness' proved to be crucial to understanding the subsequent shape of the clinic consultation. So there is no reason why qualitative researchers should not, where appropriate, use quantitative measures.

| TIP

Simple counting techniques, theoretically derived and ideally based on members' own categories, can offer a means to survey the whole corpus of data ordinarily lost in intensive, qualitative research. Instead of taking the researcher's word for it, the reader has a chance to gain a sense of the flavour of the data as a whole. In turn, researchers are able to test and to revise their generalizations, removing nagging doubts about the accuracy of their impressions about the data.

As Kirk and Miller remark: 'By our pragmatic view, qualitative research does imply a commitment to field activities. It does not imply a commitment to innumeracy' (1986: 10).

 ■ **Attempt Exercise 15.1**

Reliability

15.3 Counting based on members' own categories in the context of comprehensive data treatment is possible because, in principle, the quality of data should be high in qualitative research. By contrast, although quantitative researchers try to claim reliability by using pre-tested measures and scales, they can end up with highly unreliable tabulations. This is not because survey research questions are ambiguously worded but rather because asking and answering any question can never be separated by mutual interpretations which are inherently local and non-standardizable (see Antaki and Rapley, 1996).

By contrast with tabulated figures from survey research interviews, tapes and transcripts are open to further inspection by both researchers and readers. However, this opportunity is not always present in qualitative research. There are many observational studies where the reader has to depend on the researcher's depiction of what was going on. Indeed, perhaps the extended immersion in the 'field', typical of much qualitative research, leads to a certain preciousness about the validity and reliability of the researcher's own interpretation of 'their' tribe or set of interview respondents.

As Bryman notes about such studies:

> field notes or extended transcripts are rarely available; these would be very helpful in order to allow the reader to formulate his or her own hunches about the perspective of the people who have been studied. (1988: 77)

By implication, Bryman is calling for what Seale (1999) calls **low-inference descriptors**. Although, as Seale notes, no act of observation can be free from the underlying assumptions that guide it (see Chapter 2 of this book), detailed data presentations which make minimal inferences are always preferable to researchers' presentation of their own (high-inference) summaries of their data.

Low-inference descriptors involve 'recording observations in terms that are as concrete as possible, including verbatim accounts of what people say … rather than researchers' reconstructions of the general sense of what a person said' (Seale, 1999: 148). I would add that low-inference description also means providing the reader with long data extracts which include, for instance, the question preceding a respondent's comments as well as the interviewer's 'continuers' (e.g. 'mm hmm') which encourage a respondent to enlarge a comment (see Rapley, 2004).

Earlier in this book, I have discussed two ways of strengthening the reliability of **field** data: fieldnote conventions (see Chapter 12) and inter-coder agreement. In the remaining part of this chapter, I will concretize this discussion of reliability by looking at an example of how reliability was addressed in the context of one piece of student research. I will then examine practical issues of reliability in a study which worked with tapes and transcripts of **naturally occurring** interaction.

Anne Patterson's dissertation was concerned with the meaning of disability to family members. As this extract shows, rather than ask family members to talk about the 'disability experience', she studied whether and how 'disability' entered into ordinary situations (like talking on the telephone).

STUDENT EXAMPLES

Reliability and Research on Family Life

Much disability research relies on anecdotal accounts of life experiences of being in a family which contains someone with a learning disability, and a whole body of research continues to be derived from such experts by experience. In this study the researcher does not set out, as an outsider, to collect reflexive accounts of life experiences, but rather examines how family moments (chatting on the phone) are lived 'here and now' with the researcher as an intrinsic part. It provides for a non-filtered, viewable-by-all set of data from which to draw insights and conclusions.

(Continued)

(Continued)

In a conversation analytic approach researchers work with audio- or video-recordings, which means that the recordings and the transcripts they give rise to represent a source of data that is detailed, accurate and available for public scrutiny. Of course the quality of recording and of transcription can be variable, but as technology improves so can quality of recordings and transcription can benefit from input from other analysts in data sessions. Such was the approach taken in this current study; data were collected via digital recorders and transcripts were the subject of discussion and review with and by fellow analysts. Thus reliability in this study is built through factors that are intrinsic in CA methodology and through meticulous attention to issues of recording and transcription. [Anne Patterson, Social Sciences, Loughborough]

Anne's account offers an instructive way to manage reliability issues by thinking through the extent to which different types of data allow you to address your research problem and then recording and transcribing your data using an analytically informed method.

When people's activities are tape-recorded and transcribed, the reliability of the interpretation of transcripts may be gravely weakened by a failure to transcribe apparently trivial, but often crucial, pauses and overlaps. For instance, a recent study of medical consultations was concerned to establish whether cancer patients had understood that their condition was fatal. In this study (Clavarino et al.,1995), we attempted to examine the basis upon which interpretive judgements were made about the content of a series of audiotaped doctor–patient interviews between three oncologists and their newly referred cancer patients. It was during this interview that the patients were supposedly informed that their cancer was incurable.

Two independent transcriptions were performed. In the first, an attempt was made to transcribe the talk 'verbatim', i.e. without grammatical or other 'tidying up'. Using the first transcription, three independent coders, who had been trained to be consistent, coded the same material. Inter-coder reliability was then estimated. Inconsistencies amongst the coders may have reflected some ambiguity in the data, some overlap between coding categories, or simple coding errors.

The second transcription was informed by the analytic ideas and transcription symbols of CA. This provided additional information on how the parties organized their talk and, we believe, represents a more objective, more comprehensive and therefore more reliable recording of the data because of the level of detail given by this method.

By drawing upon the transcription symbols and concepts of conversation analysis, we sought to reveal subtle features in the talk, showing how both doctor and patients produced and received hearable ambiguities in the patient's prognosis. This involved a shift of focus from coders' readings to how participants demonstrably monitor each other's talk. Once we pay attention to such detail, judgements can be made that are more convincingly valid. Inevitably, this leads to a resolution of the problem of inter-coder reliability.

For instance, when researchers first listened to tapes of relevant hospital consultations, they sometimes felt that there was no evidence that the patients had picked up their doctors often guarded statements about their prognosis. However, when the tapes were retranscribed, it was demonstrated that patients used very soft utterances (like 'yes' or more usually 'mm') to mark that they were taking up this information. Equally, doctors would monitor patients' silences and rephrase their prognosis statements.

■ LINK ■

For useful case studies relevant to the credibility of qualitative research, visit:

www.sagepub.co.uk/gobo

and go to Chapter 14.

 ■ **Attempt Exercise 15.2** ■

Concluding Remarks

15.4
Some social researchers argue that a concern for the reliability and validity of observations arises only within the quantitative research tradition. Because what they call the 'positivist' position sees no difference between the natural and social worlds, reliable and valid measures of social life are only needed by such 'positivists'. Conversely, it is argued, once we treat social reality as always in flux, then it makes no sense to worry about whether our research instruments measure accurately (e.g. Marshall and Rossman, 1989).

Such a position would rule out any systematic research since it implies that we cannot assume any stable properties in the social world. However, if we concede the possible existence of such properties, why shouldn't other work replicate these properties?

As Kirk and Miller argue about reliability:

> Qualitative researchers can no longer afford to beg the issue of reliability. While the forte of field research will always lie in its capability to sort out the validity of propositions, its results will (reasonably) go ignored minus attention to reliability. For reliability to be calculated, it is incumbent on the scientific investigator to document his or her procedure. (1986: 72)

Of course, exactly the same point may be made about the claims to validity, or truth status, of qualitative research studies. So, to underline the point with which this chapter began, unless you can show your audience the procedures you used to ensure that your methods were reliable and your conclusions valid, there is little point in aiming to conclude a research dissertation.

KEY POINTS

Validity is another word for truth. We cannot say that the claims of a research study are valid when:

- Only a few exemplary instances are reported

- The criteria or grounds for including certain instances and not others are not provided

- The original form of the materials is unavailable.

Five ways of thinking critically about qualitative data analysis in order to aim at more valid findings were discussed:

- the refutability principle

- the constant comparative method

- comprehensive data treatment

- deviant case analysis

- using appropriate tabulations.

Reliability refers to the degree of consistency with which instances are assigned to the same category by different observers or by the same observer on different occasions. For reliability to be calculated, it is incumbent on the scientific investigator to document his or her procedure and to demonstrate that categories have been used consistently.

■ ■ Further Reading ■

Clive Seale's book *The Quality of Qualitative Research* (Sage, 1999) offers an excellent overall treatment of the issues discussed in this chapter. A shorter but more specialized treatment is to be found in Peräkylä (2004). Kathy Charmaz's *Constructing Grounded Theory* (Sage, 2006) is a thoughtful discussion of how credibility can be achieved in a constructivist version of grounded theory. Martyn Hammersley's recent book *Questioning Qualitative Inquiry* (Sage, 2008) has several chapters dealing with credibility issues. For a detailed discussion of deviant case analysis or 'analytic induction' see Becker (1998: 197–212).

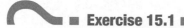 ■ **Exercise 15.1**

This is an exercise designed to help you think about the validity of your data analysis. It is best attempted when you have already written at least one substantial paper on your findings.

1 Choose any paper you have written on your data.

2 Explain on what grounds you chose those particular data extracts to report.

3 To what extent can you claim that these data were 'typical' or 'representative'?

4 To what extent have you investigated and reported 'deviant' cases?

 ■ **Exercise 15.2**

This exercise is meant to accustom you to the advantages and limitations of simple tabulations.

1 Select one dataset from your data corpus (e.g. a particular collection of interviews, observations or transcripts).

2 Count whatever seems to be countable in these data *according to your theoretical orientation*.

3 Assess what these quantitative data tell you about social life in this setting, e.g. what associations you can establish.

4 Identify deviant cases (i.e. items that do not support the associations that you have established). How might you further analyse these deviant cases, using either quantitative or qualitative techniques? What light might that throw on the associations which you have identified?

 ■ **Exercise 15.3**

The following is a quotation from Barry Glassner and Julia Loughlin about how they handled the issue of reliability in a study of adolescent drug users:

> In more positivistic research designs, coder reliability is assessed in terms of agreement among coders. In qualitative research one is unconcerned with standardizing interpretation of data. Rather, our goal in developing this complex cataloguing and retrieval system has been *to retain good access to the words of the subjects*, without relying upon the memory of interviewers or data analysts. (1987: 27, my emphasis)

Now write a short piece (say 1000 words) explaining how your own data analysis provides the reader with good access to your original dataset. Check out this piece with your supervisor and other students. If they think it works, you may be able to use it as part of your final methodology chapter.

16

Evaluating Qualitative Research

| Chapter Objectives |

By the end of this chapter, you will be able to:

- **Understand the key questions to ask about published qualitative research studies.**

- **Apply agreed criteria to evaluate the quality of research carried out by yourself or by other people.**

Introduction _____

16.1
In Chapter 15, we examined various strategies which can help to improve the quality of your research design and data analysis. Knowledge of such strategies also gives you a powerful set of tools through which to evaluate other people's research. Such evaluation skills are crucial in writing effective literature reviews (see Chapter 18). They will also stand you in good stead in preparing papers for publication (see Chapter 26) and in hallmarking your dissertation as the work of a truly professional researcher (see Chapter 5).

In this chapter, I will review evaluation criteria for qualitative research. As ever, I will use multiple case studies to illustrate what these criteria mean in practice.

I start from the assumption that all social science should base itself on a form of inquiry that is self-critical. This means that, if we wish to establish criteria for evaluating qualitative research, we will need to understand the similar issues faced by any systematic attempt at description and explanation, whether quantitative or qualitative.

Two Guides for Evaluating Research _____

16.2
Researchers are not the only people concerned about the quality of published research. Governments and smaller public and private organizations are currently inundated by research

TABLE 16.1 Criteria for assessing qualitative research

Appraisal Quality indicators	Question
Appropriate research design?	Convincing argument for different features of research design?
Reliable data?	Recording methods? Fieldnote or transcription conventions?
Clear theoretical assumptions?	Discussion of models employed?
Adequate documentation of research process?	Discussion of strengths and weaknesses of data and methods?
	Documentation of changes made to the research design?
How credible are the findings?	Are the findings supported by data? Clarity of links between data, interpretations and conclusions?
Can the findings be generalized?	Evidence for wider inference?

Source: adapted from Spencer et al., 2003: 9–15

reports that seem to have a bearing on policy. How can they assess the quality of such reports?

A very detailed list of evaluative criteria has recently been devised by a team of researchers commissioned by the British Cabinet Office (Spencer et al., 2003). An adapted version of these criteria is set out in Table 16.1.

LINK

To read Spencer et al.'s report in full, go to:

http://www.gsr.gov.uk/downloads/evaluating_policy/qqe_rep.pdf

---

Another useful set of evaluation criteria is provided in Table 16.2. Like Table 16.1, it can be employed when you are evaluating research publications. It also, of course, suggests a number of tricky questions that you should address in your own work!

 ■ **Attempt Exercise 16.1** ━━━━━━━━━

Four Quality Criteria

16.3
While Tables 16.1 and 16.2 set out a very rigorous set of criteria, they focus on purely methodological issues. By now you will be aware that, in this book, I have been arguing for a more broadly based set of criteria for evaluating qualitative research which weds methodological,

---

TABLE 16.2   Criteria for the evaluation of research

- Are the methods of research appropriate to the nature of the question being asked?
- Is the connection to an existing body of knowledge or theory clear?
- Are there clear accounts of the criteria used for the selection of cases for study, and of the data collection and analysis?
- Does the sensitivity of the methods match the needs of the research question? Were the data collection and record keeping systematic?
- Is reference made to accepted procedures for analysis?
- How systematic is the analysis?
- Is there adequate discussion of how themes, concepts and categories were derived from the data?
- Is there adequate discussion of the evidence for and against the researcher's arguments?
- Is a clear distinction made between the data and their interpretation?

Source: adapted from criteria agreed and adopted by the British Sociological Association Medical Sociology Group, September 1996

TABLE 16.3   Four criteria for assessing research quality

- How far can we demonstrate that our research has mobilized the conceptual apparatus of our social science disciplines and, thereby, helped to build useful social theories?
- How far can our data, methods and findings satisfy the criteria of reliability and validity or, put more crudely, counter the cynic who comments 'Sez you'?
- To what extent do our preferred research methods reflect careful weighing of the alternatives or simple responses to time and resource constraints – or even an unthinking adoption of the current fashions?
- How can valid, reliable and conceptually defined qualitative studies of healthcare processes contribute to practice and policy by revealing something new to practitioners, clients and/or policy makers?

theoretical and practical issues. To simplify matters, I limit the discussion to the four aspects of quality set out in Table 16.3.

Using classic case studies, I will now illustrate each of the four quality criteria set out in Table 16.3. My case studies are taken from sociology and anthropology. For a fascinating attempt to apply these criteria to media studies, see Barker (2003).

Building useful theories

16.3.1 My case study here is Mary Douglas's (1975) work on a Central African tribe, the Lele. Douglas notes that people in most cultures find certain things anomalous. For us, it may be a celebrity who refuses to 'reveal all', rejecting invitations to talk shows and eschewing public performances. For the Lele, it was an animal that seemed to be anomalous.

An anteater, called a pangolin by Western zoology, was seen by the Lele to combine apparently opposite characteristics. The Lele were puzzled by how this pangolin seemed to have some human features: for instance, it tended to have only one offspring at a time. Moreover, while most animals were either land or water creatures, it was both.

Douglas noted how most cultures tend to reject anomalous entities. Since anomaly seems to cast doubt on how we classify the world, it would appear to be dangerous to take it too seriously. However, the Lele are an exception. They celebrate their anomalous pangolin and this suggests that there may be no *universal* propensity to frown upon anomaly.

Douglas moves from this observation to an examination of the forms of social organization which may encourage different responses to perceived anomalies. In particular, she argues convincingly that successful exchange across borders with other groups may be associated with favourable responses to entities which match such border crossing. Since successful relations with other groups may not be all that common, it is hardly surprising that, in many cultures, anomaly is not tolerated.

Building on an ethnography of an obscure tribe, Douglas has developed an important theory about the relation between cultural categories and social organization. In doing so, she reveals how a simple qualitative case study can build social theory.

Using a self-critical approach

16.3.2 Mel Dalton (1959) carried out an early case study of an American factory. He was particularly interested in eliciting the perspectives of middle managers.

He reports that he was very pleased that, in the early stages of his research, he was approached by several managers prepared to tell him their stories. However, he then started to reflect on what these early informants shared in common and compared it to the background information he could gather on other managers.

It turned out that the keen informants tended to be managers whose position and prospects within the firm were the most marginal. In brief, they were keen to talk to Dalton because nobody else wanted to hear their stories!

Dalton used this insight to study the resources which gave different managers leverage at the firm. He began to see that power worked through a clique structure in which groups of managers with similar access to resources used collective tactics to oppose (or bring about) particular changes which favoured their own clique.

Dalton's study reveals the benefits of a self-critical approach. Rather than treat the accounts of willing informants as 'inside dope' on what was really going on at the firm, Dalton reflected on their motivation and, as a consequence, obtained a much broader understanding of the links between control over resources and managers' behaviour. In doing so, like Mary Douglas, he made a theoretical contribution (in Dalton's case, a theory about how cliques work within management).

A similar self-critical spirit is also present in good student research. In the following case study of psychiatric consultations, notice how Alan Quirk seeks to demonstrate why the reader should take his findings seriously.

┌──────┐ STUDENT EXAMPLES ┌─

Achieving Credibility

Trust in the findings presented in this thesis will hopefully have been enhanced in a number of ways. First, all three studies have been undertaken in a *spirit of grounded theorizing*, with attempts made to search and account for negative instances. Second, various methods of *triangulation* have been used. In the two ethnographic studies, various types of evidence were collected before concluding that a thing is true; and in the Prescribing Decisions Project, the CA research complemented our interview study. It did so because while the analysis of consultation transcripts revealed activities that psychiatrists failed to mention in research interviews, the interviews helped one-off psychiatric consultations to be understood in the context of the unfolding doctor–patient relationship in which they take place. Third, *simple counts* of well-defined phenomena have been included in the findings chapters where appropriate. This is aimed at increasing the credibility of claims and guarding against accusations of anecdotalism that can be levelled at certain qualitative studies. And fourth, *member validation* techniques were used. [Alan Quirk, Human Sciences, Brunel]

Notice how Alan uses four strategies to increase the credibility of his findings. While questions can legitimately be raised about the utility of some of these strategies (e.g. triangulation and member validation), the reader is left in no doubt that this is a self-critical piece of research.

Thinking about appropriate research methods _____

16.3.3 Like Douglas, Michael Moerman is an anthropologist interested in how a people categorized its world. Moerman (1974) studied the Lue tribe of northern Thailand.

First Moerman learnt the local language and then he started to interview Lue people. Like many Western ethnographers, Moerman was interested in how his people saw themselves and how they distinguished themselves from other peoples. As a result of his interviews, Moerman assembled a set of traits which seemed to describe the Lue.

At this stage, like Dalton and Alan Quirk, he thought critically about the status of his data. Put in its simplest terms, what does it mean when you answer the questions of a visiting ethnographer? Imagine someone coming to your town and asking you to identify your 'group'. You could certainly do it, but it would be an unusual activity of self-reflection. Surely most of the time we manage to live our lives without unduly worrying about our identities? As Moerman put it:

> To the extent that answering an ethnographer's question is an unusual situation for natives, one cannot reason from a native's answer to his *normal* categories or ascriptions. (1974: 66, my emphasis)

Moerman now started to see that perhaps he had been asking the wrong kind of questions. He had been using interviews to answer the question: 'Who are the Lue?' But a more interesting question was when, if at all, the people being studied actually invoke ethnic identities.

So Moerman changed his research question to: 'When are the Lue?' This meant abandoning interviews and using observation and audio-recording of the people in question engaged in 'ordinary' events like going to market. In such naturally occurring contexts, one could observe when (and with what consequences) people living in these Thai villages actually invoked ethnic identification labels.

By thinking critically about the relation between his research methods and research problems, Moerman rightly moved away from a conventional ethnographic research design.

Making a practical contribution

16.3.4 Unlike the three earlier studies, Lucy Suchman (1987) gathered data through a VCR. However, like Moerman, her method was entirely appropriate to her research problem.

Suchman was interested in the highly practical issue of how people use photocopying machines. Her video-recordings revealed that most people's behaviour bore little relation to the user's manual provided by the manufacturer. This was seen most clearly in the troubles that many users had in effectively responding when an order to the machine had produced an unexpected response and the user wanted to abort or repair an activity in which the machine had engaged. People's behaviour could exhibit a variety of actions which from the user's perspective turned out to be ineffective. However, from a design point of view, the machine was acting quite properly.

Suchman's study has clear practical implications. It suggests the constructive role of users' troubles in system design. As she notes, based on this kind of research, expert systems may seek not to eliminate users' errors but; 'to make them accessible to the user, and therefore instructive' (1987: 184).

Having cited a number of classic studies, I now want to present a more critical evaluation of some more recent research. As before, however, my evaluation will be based on the four criteria set out in Table 16.3.

Applying Quality Criteria

16.4 For convenience, I have simply selected the four articles reporting research studies in the last two 1996 issues of the US journal *Qualitative Health Research* (QHR). The Editor of QHR, Janice Morse, has a nursing background and many of its contributors are in university nursing departments. This nursing focus distinguishes QHR from other journals like *Sociology of Health and Illness* and *Social Science & Medicine*, although its explicit concern with practice has a parallel with *Social Sciences in Health*.

The contents of these papers can, therefore, only offer a taste of the kind of work that counts as qualitative health research, let alone qualitative research in general. Furthermore, such a 'taste' does not allow inspection of the deviant cases that I recommend below as a feature of good research practice. However, these papers allow me to develop a coherent focus with implications which extend well beyond health research.

Women's process of recovery from depression

16.4.1 Schreiber (1996) describes an interview study with a snowball sample of 21 women who identified themselves as having recovered from depression. She sets out to establish an account of the depression experience which, she claims, is 'grounded in the real world of the participant' (1996: 471). This 'real world', we are told, contains six 'phases' of '(re)defining the self', each with between three and five 'properties' or 'dimensions'.

Schreiber's discussion of her methodology shows some concern for the quality of her research. Like many researchers with an academic appointment in nursing, she holds up Glaser and Strauss's (1967) account of grounded theory as a *sine qua non* of good qualitative research. Indeed, three of the four papers I am considering here mentioned grounded theory at some point – usually as a central reference.

Following the logic of grounded theory, Schreiber searched her data for subjects' categories and only stopped when her analysis became 'saturated' because no new information about the emerging theory was forthcoming (1996: 472). These findings were then fed back to the participants and revised accordingly.

However, in my view, a number of problems remain with what we are told about this research, and I set these out in the following.

This was a retrospective study. This problem is recognized by the researcher, who comments that the first phase ('My Self Before') 'is only seen upon reflection' (1996: 474). Such recognition might have led her to abandon her claim to access the depression experience.[1] But instead Schreiber is satisfied with the rather glib assertion that 'there is merit in hearing the women's understandings of the people they were at the time' (1996: 474). What merit, we might ask? Moreover, despite the fragile status of her data, she has no hesitation in setting out to search for external causes of these accounts (1996: 489).

Schreiber presents extracts from her data. But, in place of analysis, we are simply presented with a common-sense précis of what each respondent said followed by an apparently arbitrary label. This gives the paper an anecdotal feel and makes this reviewer wonder why one needs social science skills to write this kind of report.

Of course, it is not difficult to find instances that fit a given set of categories. Despite this the paper does not report deviant cases, although such reporting and subsequent analysis are a central feature of grounded theory.

I am uncertain from where Schreiber is claiming her categories (phases and dimensions) derive. It is unclear whether these are the women's categories ('the recovery process was described by the women in this study as ...' (1996: 473)) or the researcher's. If the latter, the author gives no hint of the relevant social science theories from which her categories might derive (e.g. a theory of self-definition). If the former, then one wonders at the lack of analytic nerve which treats research as simply reporting what respondents tell you (see my comments in Chapter 4 on 'going beyond a list'; and see Gilbert and Mulkay, 1983).

Urban healers

16.4.2 Engebretson (1996) reports a participant observation and interview study of three groups of healers who 'heal' through the laying on of hands. She locates her findings in terms of three 'dimensions' (setting, interaction and cognitive process) and finds, unsurprisingly, that such healing differed from biomedicine on each of these dimensions.

Although she mentions no explicit theory and, unlike Schreiber, has no explicit quality controls, Engebretson does strengthen the reliability of her account by detailed ethnographic description. Through it, we learn about the setting, how healing was organized and how the sessions were opened and closed. All of this description has at least the potential to suggest practical relevance. However, three problems remain with the observational data presented:

- No data extracts are given (presumably what occurred was not taped, and for some reason the researcher's fieldnotes are not made available). This means that the reader has no basis to contest the researcher's account.

- No mention is made of the system used for recording fieldnotes and its impact on the reliability of her data (see Chapter 15).

- Like Schreiber's study, the account of the data is presented just as a simple description. Without a discussion of the analytic basis for the researcher's account, her report once more can only have a journalistic status.[2]

Again, like Schreiber, Engebretson groups her interview respondents' accounts into a number of categories (in this case, physical sensations, emotional experiences and visual images). But there is nothing to suggest that these are anything but *ad hoc* labels without a clear analytical basis (see the discussion in Chapter 14 of using categories in CAQDAS). Again the chosen extracts simply illustrate her argument and no deviant cases are provided or explored.

Quality care in the hospital

16.4.3 Irurita (1996) describes semi-structured interviews with a sample of 10 patients (one to two weeks after discharge) and 10 nurses from the same hospital wards. Respondents were asked about what they saw as the nature and causes of 'quality care'.

According to the author, patients saw themselves as 'vulnerable' and described what they and the nurses did to preserve patient 'integrity'. Nurses described the time and resource constraints which limited them in providing such care.

Like Schreiber, Irurita locates her research within the approach of grounded theory, particularly through her attempt at the constant comparative method. Like many interview researchers, she reports the use of a qualitative software program (in her case Ethnograph). Moreover, she argues that an important quality control was the separation of the studies of nurses and patients and because theory was built as 'an ongoing process' (1996: 346).

Nonetheless, in my view, three serious quality problems remain:

- Is 'quality care' a normative or a participants' category? Irurita's account of her research findings is unclear about this but her abstract implies that she accepts a normative category without question.[3]

- The interview protocol is not provided and, unlike Schreiber, no extracts from the interviews are given. Hence the reader is in no position to know how 'quality care' was investigated, or how the researchers analysed data.

- No analytic basis behind the researcher's selection of categories is given: for example, 'preserving integrity' is presented as a simple description of what respondents said and not, for instance, in relation to Goffman's (1961) account of identity in total institutions. Hence the findings appear, once more, to be journalistic.

Perinatal cocaine crack users

16.4.4 Pursley-Crotteau and Stern (1996) report a longitudinal interview study with nine female crack users during and after their pregnancies. The longitudinal research design allows a solution to the problem of retrospective accounts not found in Schreiber's study.

Moreover, these researchers make a real attempt to establish an analytic framework (based upon 'four dimensions of temperance') with which to make sense of how such women struggle with addiction (see Figure 16.1). Thus, unlike the other three studies, this paper does not simply offer lists of (common-sense) categories

		Having desire	
		+	−
Having structure	+	Holdin' on to the lifeline	Messin' up
	−	Goin' it alone	Dancin' with the devil

FIGURE 16.1   Four dimensions of temperance (adapted from Pursley-Crotteau and Stern, 1996: 360)

TABLE 16.4 Some defects in selected qualitative studies

They tend to be atheoretical:

- Categories are usually participants' own or are *ad hoc* and commonsensical, i.e. journalistic
- Normative concepts are sometimes accepted unproblematically

They use unreliable data:

- Only tidied-up data extracts are given (no interviewers' questions, no indication of how far a particular answer had to be extracted from a respondent, e.g. after a pause or a monosyllabic initial response)
- Data extracts are sometimes replaced by researchers' 'summaries'

The analysis can be of doubtful validity:

- No deviant cases
- Some accounts are retrospective

but combines them into an analytic scheme which holds out the possibility of generating formal theories of the kind that Glaser and Strauss (1967) recommend and which may well have practical relevance.

Unfortunately, Pursley-Crotteau and Stern (1996) do not, in my view, avoid some of the defects of the other studies. In particular:

- Data extracts are treated as having a self-evident meaning and no deviant cases are discussed (see Chapter 15).

- The question(s) which provoked the interviewee's responses are not given.

- An atheoretical reading of grounded theory is offered (for an intelligent, constructionist account of grounded theory, see Charmaz, 2006). For instance, the researchers suggest that grounded theory 'is used to discover the problem from the point of view of the actors' (Pursley-Crotteau and Stern, 1996: 352). But if this is all that research does, how is it different from 'human interest' journalism or indeed Oprah Winfrey?

Achieving quality

16.4.5 Obviously, from my own perspective, I have found many defects, as well as some good points, in these examples of qualitative research. Table 16.4 summarizes my criticisms.

You may now be asking yourself: is my criticism of these studies too harsh? After all, these were published papers. Have I raised the bar too high for student researchers?

Let me reassure you that it is perfectly possible to combine credibility and theoretical sensitivity within a student dissertation. Anne Patterson's research, like the studies we have been discussing, was in the health area. However, in the case study that follows (partly introduced in Chapter 15), notice how she combines theoretical awareness with an attempt to convince the reader of the credibility of her data and findings.

STUDENT EXAMPLES

From 'Life Experience' to Reliable Data

Much disability research relies on anecdotal accounts of life experiences of being in a family which contains someone with a learning disability, and a whole body of research continues to be derived from such experts by experience. In this study the researcher does not set out, as an outsider, to collect reflexive accounts of life experiences, but rather examines how family moments (chatting on the phone) are lived 'here and now' with the researcher as an intrinsic part. It provides for a non-filtered, viewable-by-all set of data from which to draw insights and conclusions.

It was also possible to be sure that the researcher-participant could not influence any phenomena-to-be-found through some very practical means. Most of the calls in the dataset in question were recorded well before preliminary analysis even began and thus well before any phenomenon was mooted. The subset of calls used in the first round of observation did not include those which involved the researcher-participant, so the noticeings which form the basis of this study were present initially in calls, which did not include the researcher-participant. There were also three other participants involved in the calls, each of which engaged in the interactional 'actions' that have become the main subject of the study. Thus the researcher was able to ensure that the phenomenon observed could not also have been one that was produced by her own involvement. A further way of ensuring this was by regular data sessions with other analysts who independently made similar observations. [Anne Patterson, Social Sciences, Loughborough]

Consider how Anne systematically demonstrates the steps that she has taken to ensure that her data are reliable and her analysis is valid.

TIP

The model of research you use is your own choice and the only credibility issue is whether you use it consistently. So Anne's work is not better than the studies reviewed earlier because, unlike them, she uses a constructionist model. When your research is evaluated, the issue is: how reliable are your data and how valid are your interpretations?

Four Quality Issues Revisited

16.5 Having given these examples of the failings (and successes) of several qualitative research studies, the rest of this chapter will contain some positive proposals about each of the four 'quality' issues identified in Table 16.3.

Analytic depth

16.5.1 *How far can we demonstrate that our research has mobilized the conceptual apparatus of our social science disciplines and, thereby, helped to build useful social theories?*

A continuing theme of my critiques above was that these researchers tended to describe their data in terms of sets of categories which either reproduced participants' categories or put a common-sense gloss upon them. Although it is arguable that this is a proper first-stage procedure within grounded theory, Glaser and Strauss (1967) and Charmaz (2006) make clear that such description cannot itself build theories. To do so, we need to move beyond *ad hoc* labels and redefine our data within a well-articulated analytic scheme.

As we saw above, one of the strengths of Pursley-Crotteau and Stern's (1996) account of pregnant crack users is precisely that it attempts to establish an analytic framework (based upon 'four dimensions of temperance') with which to make sense of how such women struggle with addiction. In this way, categories are combined into an analytic scheme in order to generate what Glaser and Strauss (1967) would call a 'formal' theory.

As I argue in Chapter 7, a theory is best understood as a set of concepts used to define and/or explain some phenomenon. A criterion for adopting a theory is its usefulness.

Some classical studies illustrate this sense of theory in sociology and anthropology:

- Using an interactionist theory concerned with 'labelling', awareness of dying is related to a set of 'awareness contexts' (Glaser and Strauss, 1968).

- Using a structuralist theory of the nature of binary oppositions, an African tribe's favourable response to an anteater is used to build a theory about the relation between perceived 'anomalies' and the experience of crossing boundaries (Douglas, 1975).

- Using a discourse analytic theory of the active use of language, scientists' accounts of their work are shown to function in local contexts (Gilbert and Mulkay, 1983).

- Using an ethnomethodological theory of accounting practices, the 'cause' of 'suicide' is to be found in the common-sense judgements of coroners (Atkinson, 1978).

Without the active employment of these and other theories, we are bound to lapse into *ad hoc* use of common-sense interpretations and may, like Irurita's (1996) appeal to the label 'quality care', even smuggle normative concepts into our data analysis. However, like many other people researching issues that affect our daily lives, health researchers may have two particular difficulties in thinking theoretically. First, their preference for the study of 'people' rather than, say, variables may lead to the pursuit of a kind of 'empathy' which does not permit sufficient distance. Second, if you research an area like health, which generates so many pressing social problems, it may sometimes be difficult to look beyond what your common-sense knowledge tells you about the 'meaning' of social situations.

How, then, can we aid our sluggish imaginations to think theoretically about data? In Chapter 6, I discussed how social science theory building can benefit from four types of sensitivity: historical, political and contextual.

I shall return to the question of whether such theoretically guided research can have a greater practical relevance as well as building a better social science. For the moment, I will turn to my second 'quality' issue.

Why should we believe qualitative research? _____

16.5.2 *How far can our data, methods and findings satisfy the criteria of reliability and validity or, put more crudely, counter the cynic who comments 'Sez you'?*

If we argue for the pre-eminence of analytic issues in research, the implication might follow that the sole requirement for any research study is analytic integrity. This would mean that the validity of a piece of qualitative research could be settled simply by asserting its pristine, theoretical roots.

Along these lines, it is sometimes suggested that the assessment of the quality of qualitative data should transcend the conventional methodological approaches. The quality of qualitative research, it is argued:

> cannot be determined by following prescribed formulas. Rather its quality lies in the power of its language to display a picture of the world in which we discover something about ourselves and our common humanity. (Buchanan, 1992: 133)

If Buchanan is saying that the main question in field research, is the quality of the analysis rather than the recruitment of the sample or, say, the format of the interview, then I would agree (see Mitchell, 1983). However, Buchanan's opposition to 'prescribed formulas' can amount to something which might be called 'methodological anarchy' (see Clavarino et al., 1995).

How far do you want to go with such anarchism? First, does it make sense to argue that all knowledge and feelings are of equal weight and value? Even in everyday life, we readily sort 'fact' from 'fancy'. Why, therefore, should science be any different? Second, methodological anarchy offers a clearly negative message to research funding agencies, namely: don't fund qualitative research because even its proponents have given up claims to reliability and validity. Moreover, in such an environment, can we wonder that qualitative research's potential audiences (e.g. the medical professions, corporations, trade unions) take its 'findings' less than seriously?

In Chapters 9 and 15, I examined in detail methods for improving the validity, reliability and generalizability of qualitative research. I now turn to my third 'quality' issue.

Only interviews? _____

16.5.3 *To what extent do our preferred research methods reflect careful weighing of the alternatives or simple responses to time and resource constraint – or even an unthinking adoption of the current fashions?*

TABLE 16.5 Type of research method (*Qualitative Health Research*)

	Articles (*n* = 91)	
	Number	% of total
Qualitative interviews	65	71
Other methods	26	29

Source: qualitative data articles in Qualitative Health Research, 1991–6

In 1996, while writing a paper for a methodology conference, I did a crude survey of recent published research-based articles which used qualitative methods. In my own subspeciality, the sociology of health, the preference for the open-ended interview was overwhelming. Table 16.5 is based on articles in *Qualitative Health Research*.

The results in the table are consistent with the four non-randomly selected health research articles discussed above, all of which used interviews as their sole (or main) method. The skewing towards qualitative interviews in *Qualitative Health Research* probably reflects the fact, already noted, that many of the authors are in nursing where the open-ended interview is regarded as both an appropriate research technique and a preferred model of communicating with the patient.

Of course, we should not make too much of findings based on such a tiny and perhaps unrepresentative dataset. Nonetheless, Table 16.5 may not be strikingly out of line with the preference for interview-based qualitative research found in the articles published in the more mainstream journals.

To test out this hypothesis, I turned to the journal of the British Sociological Association called *Sociology*. My findings are set out in Table 16.6.

The table shows a preference for the use of the interview method in recent qualitative papers published in *Sociology*. Although the proportion is only 55:45, given that the category 'other methods' lumps together every other non-interview based qualitative method, the interview-method clearly predominates as the single most preferred method.

Other social sciences may vary in the extent of use made of the interview-method. Anthropologists, for instance, may pay relatively more attention to observational methods (but see my discussion of Moerman's study above). However, I suspect that the choice of the open-ended interview as the gold standard of qualitative research is pretty widely spread. For example, information systems

TABLE 16.6 Type of research method (*Sociology*)

	Articles (*n* = 49)	
	Number	% of total
Qualitative interviews	27	55
Other methods	22	45

Source: qualitative data articles in Sociology, 1991–6

(IS) is a discipline which studies the human consequences of information technology. In preparing a recent talk to an IS conference, I surveyed the methodologies chosen in research articles published in a number of recent IS journals. Of the six qualitative research articles, five were derived from interviews.

Qualitative researchers' almost Pavlovian tendency to identify research design with interviews has blinkered them to the possible gains of other kinds of data. For it is thoroughly mistaken to assume that the sole topic for qualitative research is 'people'. Seale (personal correspondence) has noted how he seeks to contest this common supposition:

> I find that, in order to counteract the tendency towards wanting to do interviews, it helps to repeatedly make the point that many textbooks assume that when one is going to do a research study one always wants to sample 'people' (rather than, say, documents). This helps [students] realise that all kinds of phenomena can be studied for social research purposes (e.g. building design, music lyrics, websites, small ads etc.) and it is then obvious that interviews aren't the only thing to do.

Even when the choice of interviews is thought through (for instance, interviews undoubtedly give you far more rapid results than observation which, when done properly, can take months or years), many research reports offer journalistic 'commentaries' or merely reproduce what respondents say rather than provide detailed data analysis.

Such a situation suggests that we need to look twice at the unthinking identification of the open-ended interview as the gold standard of qualitative research (see my discussion of naturally occurring data in Chapter 8). Note that this is not to reject each and every interview study. I merely suggest that the choice of any research instrument needs to be defended and that the pursuit of people's 'experience' by no means constitutes an adequate defence for the use of the open-ended interview (for further discussion of interviews, see Silverman, 2007: 37–60).

━━━━━━━━━━━━━━━━━━━━━ LINK ━━━━━━━━━━━━━━━━━━━━━

For a useful blog on the value of interviews which includes contributions from Jonathan Potter and myself, go to:

http://asksage.typepad.com/methods/

I now turn to my final 'quality' point.

Research and practitioners

16.5.4 *How can valid, reliable and conceptually defined qualitative studies of healthcare processes contribute to practice and policy by revealing something new to practitioners, clients and/or policy makers?*

Research instruments, like interviews, focus groups and questionnaires, which ask respondents to provide facts, attitudes or experiences, have an important part to play in areas like health which affect us all. In particular, they can give policy makers a reasonable sense of how, at one moment in time, their clients are responding to a particular service (see Chapter 27). Moreover, unlike observational or conversation analytic studies, interview studies can be completed relatively quickly and, in this sense, can give rapid 'answers'.

Unfortunately, as I have already suggested, some qualitative interview studies may lack the analytic imagination to provide anything more than anecdotal 'insights'. When there are also legitimate doubts about the rigour of the data analysis, then, I suggest, policy makers and practitioners should doubt the quality of the 'answers' such research provides.

One response might be to return to purely quantitative research, given the serious attention it usually pays to issues of reliability and validity. Indeed, if the only alternative was *impressionistic* qualitative research, I would certainly always back quantitative studies such as well-designed questionnaires or randomized controlled trials.

However, this is not the only alternative. As already suggested, both the 'in-depth' accounts apparently provided by the 'open-ended' interview and the seemingly unequivocal measures of information retention, attitude and behaviour that we obtain via laboratory or questionnaire methods have a tenuous basis in what people may be saying and doing in everyday health contexts.

Take the case of general practice consultations. In an interview study of patients involved in 50 British GP consultations, Webb and Stimson (1976) noted how doctors were routinely portrayed as acting insensitively or with poor judgement. By contrast, patients presented themselves as having acted rationally and sensibly.

As Webb and Stimson (1976) imply, we only get into difficulties if we treat patients' responses as standing in a one-to-one account with what happened in the actual consultation. This is not to suggest that these patients were lying. Rather, Webb and Stimson suggest, by telling 'atrocity stories', the patients were able to give vent to thoughts which had gone unvoiced at the time of the consultation, to redress a real or perceived inequality between doctor and patient and to highlight the teller's own rationality. Equally, atrocity stories have a dramatic form which captures the hearer's attention – a point of which qualitative researchers become aware when asked to give brief accounts of their findings.

Webb and Stimson reject the assumption that lay accounts can do the work of sociological explanations. They do not want to take the actor's point of view as an explanation because this would be to equate common sense with sociology – a recipe for the lazy field researcher. Only when such a researcher moves beyond the gaze of the tourist, bemused with a sense of bizarre cultural practices ('Goodness, you do things differently here'), do the interesting analytic questions begin.

To underline my earlier point, this is not to suggest that interview studies of patient satisfaction have *no* place in health research. Rather it implies that such studies must be supplemented by data on what actually happens in the consultation itself. Fortunately, from the pioneering work of Byrne and Long (1976) through to Heath's (2004) precise analysis of videos of the consultation, this is what we now possess. Because of this work, practitioners and clients can be informed of interactional skills they did not know they possessed and of communication dilemmas of which they may have been unaware. Moreover, policy makers can make decisions on far fuller evidence than provided by simple records of respondents' 'opinions' or 'attitudes' (see Silverman, 1987: Ch. 8; Silverman, 2007: 100–10).

A further bonus of studying communication *in situ* is that both findings and raw data can be valuable resources in training practitioners. Although the researcher cannot tell practitioners how they should behave, understanding the intended and unintended consequences of actions can provide the basis for a fruitful dialogue.

Concluding Remarks

16.6 The ability to evaluate published research is a key skill which will help you to locate gaps in the field which can inspire your own research and to write your literature review (see Chapter 18). In this chapter, I have critically assessed four published qualitative research articles using four criteria of 'quality'.

I am aware that many readers will feel that I have raised the bar too high for student researchers. So let me make clear the limits of my argument.

I am *not* suggesting that you should be so consumed by 'quality' issues that you become paralysed or lose the excitement of your encounters with the 'field'. As Geraldine Leydon comments in her PhD:

> To be sure, in choosing one route, other just as feasible and reasonable routes were ruled out. So in choosing a way, certain critiques become all the more apparent. As well as criticisms from external sources, those engaged in the business of qualitative enquiry have become ever more self-conscious and reflective about their own shortcomings. This general tendency towards a more self-critical line on the representation of data, and claims that can be made of those data, can become unhelpful when taken to their extreme. There is, as Gubrium and Holstein (1997) argue, a danger of empirical analysis being threatened or overwhelmed by 'procedural self-consciousness'. A more pragmatic line of being aware of and attempting to confine the limitations is a more realistic approach. Striving for perfection can only promise 'methodological paralysis'. [Geraldine Leydon, Sociology, Goldsmiths]

Like Geraldine, I acknowledge the danger that constant self-criticism can lead to 'methodological paralysis'. So don't take self-criticism too far. But also don't become so involved with your subject that you lose your critical senses.

KEY POINTS

Good quality research satisfies the following criteria:

- It thinks theoretically through and with data.
- It develops empirically sound, reliable and valid findings.
- It uses methods which are demonstrably appropriate to the research problem.
- Where possible, it contributes to practice and policy.

State-of-the-art accounts of qualitative research which fit the criteria discussed in this chapter are to be found in David Silverman's (ed.) *Qualitative Research: Theory, Method and Practice* (Sage, 2004). Martin Barker's paper 'Assessing the "quality" in qualitative research: the case of text–audience relations' (*European Journal of Communication* 2003, 18 (3): 315–35) applies the criteria set out in Table 16.3 to research in cultural studies. Good treatments of theoretically inspired but rigorous qualitative research are: Pertti Alasuutari's *Researching Culture: Qualitative Method and Cultural Studies* (Sage, 1995); Jennifer Mason's *Qualitative Researching* (Sage, 1996); Amanda Coffey and Paul Atkinson's *Making Sense of Qualitative Data* (Sage, 1996); and Kathy Charmaz's *Constructing Grounded Theory* (Sage, 2006).

 ■ **Exercise 16.1** ■

Select a qualitative research study in your own area. Now go through the following steps:

1 Review the study in terms of the quality criteria set out in Table 16.3 (if you prefer, you may use the criteria in Table 16.1 or Table 16.2).

2 If the study fails to satisfy all these criteria, consider how it could have been improved to satisfy them.

3 Consider to what extent these criteria are appropriate to your area. Are there additional or different criteria which you would choose?

Notes

1 Abandoning the claim that interview accounts directly represent 'experience' need not be disastrous to interview research, as I show elsewhere (Silverman, 2001: 110–14). As Gubrium and Holstein (1997) point out, we can say analytically and practically interesting things about interviews analysed as locally structured narrative forms.

2 This is not to criticize journalism which, at its best, can be highly illuminating. It is simply intended to distinguish between journalism and social science.

3 Note that how 'quality care' gets defined is not treated as problematic in the following sentence: 'The delivery of quality care, although acknowledged as being vital to health care systems, is a complex, poorly understood phenomenon' (Irurita, 1996: 331).

Part Four
Writing Up

Contents

Pertti Alasuutari describes writing a thesis as rather like learning to ride a bicycle through gradually adjusting your balance: 'Writing is first and foremost analyzing, revising and polishing the text. The idea that one can produce ready-made text right away is just about as senseless as the cyclist who has never had to restore his or her balance' (1995: 178).

Alasuutari reminds us that 'writing up' should never be something left to the end of your research. Instead, writing should be a continuous process, with you learning as you go from your supervisor, your peers and from your own mistakes.

In the following five chapters, we will examine how this writing up can be accomplished efficiently if rarely painlessly. Its five chapters address the following topics: how to begin your research report; how to write effective literature review and methodology chapters; how to structure your data chapters; and what to put in your concluding chapter.

17

The First Few Pages

Chapter Objectives

By the end of this chapter, you will be able to:

- Recognize why the first few pages of your thesis are very important.

- Construct a title, an abstract, a list of contents and an introduction which are appropriate, informative and attention grabbing.

Introduction

17.1

Nearly all dissertations begin with four elements:

- a title

- an abstract

- a list of contents

- an introduction.

If you follow my advice and devote most attention to your data analysis chapters, then you may tend to treat these beginnings as routine matters, speedily disposed of. However, the impression you create at the start of your dissertation is very important and the writing of the first few pages should never be regarded as 'busy work', i.e. as a triviality.

In this short chapter, I offer some practical advice about each of these beginning sections of your dissertation.

The Title

17.2
In the early stages, you will probably be asked to give a short title to your research for administrative purposes. You will almost certainly change this title before long, so do not attach too much importance to it. However, as Harry Wolcott (1990: 70–1) suggests, it is a good idea to be thinking about an effective final title and to keep notes about your ideas.

Titles should catch the reader's attention while properly informing them about the main focus of your research. My own preference is for a two-part title, a snappy main title, often using a present participle to indicate activity; and then a more descriptive subtitle. For illustration, two of my books were entitled:

> *Reading Castaneda: A Prologue to the Social Sciences*
> *Interpreting Qualitative Data: Methods for Analysing Talk, Text and Interaction.*

Among my papers, you will find the following titles:

> 'Describing sexual activities in HIV counselling: the co-operative management of the moral order'
> 'Unfixing the subject: viewing "Bad Timing"'
> 'Policing the lying patient: surveillance and self-regulation in consultations with adolescent diabetics'

Of course, using a present participle in the main title is merely my preference, intended to stress the *active* nature of my research as well as the fact that I study people's *activities*. Nor do I always follow my own rule. For instance, my 1997 book on AIDS counselling was entitled *Discourses of Counselling: HIV Counselling as Social Interaction.*

But titles do matter and need careful thought, as any marketing person will tell you. So give this matter thought and discuss it with your supervisor.

 ■ **Attempt Exercise 17.1** ▬▬▬▬▬▬▬

The Abstract

17.3
This should succinctly cover the following:

- your research problem

- why that problem is important and worth studying

- your data and methods

- your main findings
- their implications in the light of other research.

There is usually a word limit for abstracts (100 words is common). So, as Punch points out: 'abstract writing is the skill of saying as much as possible in as few words as possible' (1998: 276). Within the word limitations, try to make your abstract as lively and informative as possible.

Read the abstracts of other dissertations in your area; try out drafts on other students and see if they find your abstract clear and pithy. Know what your audience is likely to be most interested in and 'emphasize your problem and content, not your fieldwork techniques' (Wolcott, 1990: 81). Harry Wolcott nicely sums up what makes a good abstract:

> An abstract can offer a valuable opportunity to inform a wide audience, to capture potential readers, and to expand your own interactive professional network. Whether others will pursue their reading may depend largely on their assessment of your abstract, including Its style. (1990: 81)

The List of Contents

17.4

You may think this is a very trivial matter. Not so! A scrappy or uninformative table of contents (or, worse still, none at all) will create a terrible impression.

In order to be user-friendly, recipient design this table to achieve two ends:

1 to demonstrate that you are a logical thinker, able to write a dissertation with a transparently clear organization

2 to allow your readers to see this at once, to find their way easily between different parts of the dissertation and to pinpoint matters in which they have most interest.

One useful device which helps to achieve these two things is to use a double numbering system. So, for instance, the chapter containing the review of the literature may be listed as:

CHAPTER 3: REVIEW OF THE LITERATURE
3.1 The background studies
3.2 The core readings
3.3 The study closest to my own

Of course, this is only an illustration. More detailed discussion of what a literature review should contain is provided in the next chapter of this volume.

The Introduction

17.5 Anne Murcott (1997: 1) says that the point of an introduction is to answer the question: what is this thesis about? She suggests that you answer this question in four ways by explaining:

1 why you have chosen this topic rather than any other, e.g. either because it has been neglected or because it is much discussed but not properly or fully

2 why this topic interests you

3 the kind of research approach or academic discipline you will utilize

4 your research questions or problems.

Like this chapter, there is no reason why your introduction should be any longer than two or three pages, particularly if your methodology chapter covers the natural history of your research (see Chapter 19). The role of the introduction, like your abstract, is to orientate your readers. This is best done clearly and succinctly.

 ■ **Attempt Exercise 17.2** ▬▬▬▬▬▬▬▬▬

Concluding Remarks

17.6 The impression you create at the start of your dissertation is very important. Your title should catch the reader's attention while properly informing them about the main focus of your research. An abstract should describe your research problem; why that problem is important and worth studying; your data and methods; your main findings; and the implications of your findings in the light of other research.

Your list of contents should allow your readers to find their way easily between different parts of the dissertation and to pinpoint matters in which they have most interest. Your introduction should explain why you have chosen this topic rather than any other; why this topic interests you; the kind of research approach or academic discipline you will utilize; and your research questions or problems.

KEY POINTS

- The first few pages of your thesis are very important.

- Your title, abstract, list of contents and introduction should be appropriate, informative and attention grabbing.

Harry Wolcott's *Writing Up Qualitative Research* (second edition, Sage, 2001: Chs 2, 3) has an excellent discussion of how to present student dissertations. A further useful source is Pat Cryer's *The Research Student's Guide to Success* (third edition, Open University Press, 2006).

 ■ **Exercise 17.1**

This is an exercise to encourage you to find a good title and abstract for your dissertation.

1   Make a list of three or four possible titles for your dissertation. Try to make the main title intriguing and the subtitle descriptive.

2   Now reverse the order, putting the subtitle first. Which works best? Why?

3   Try out your titles on students working in similar areas or using similar methods or data. Which do they think works best? Why?

4   Now try out two different abstracts in the same way.

 ■ **Exercise 17.2**

Show the introduction to your dissertation to a range of fellow students. Encourage them to tell you whether they feel tempted to read more. If not, why not? If so, why?

Now use their response to revise your introduction.

18

The Literature Review Chapter

Chapter Objectives

By the end of this chapter, you will be able to:

- Keep usable records of your reading.

- Understand what a literature review should contain.

- Know the principles underlying a good literature review.

- Think about when is the most appropriate time to write a literature chapter.

- Consider the alternatives to having such a chapter.

In this chapter, I will make some practical suggestions about what a literature review should contain. Somewhat controversially, I will also question whether you really need a separate chapter dealing with the literature and what might replace it.

A good discussion of the literature in your area presupposes sensible recording of what you read. So I will ask first: what is the best way to record your reading?

Recording Your Reading

18.1 By the time you begin a research degree, it is likely that you will have learned the habit of keeping your reading notes in a word-processed file, organized in terms of (emerging) topics. I stress 'reading notes' because it is important from the start that you do *not* simply collate books or photocopies of articles for 'later' reading but read as you go. Equally, your notes should not just consist of chunks of written or scanned extracts from the original sources but should represent your ideas on the *relevance*

TABLE 18.1 Reading and note taking

1 Never pick up and put down an article without doing something with it
2 Highlight key points, write notes in the margins, and write summaries elsewhere
3 Transfer notes and summaries to where you will use them in your dissertation
4 Ensure that each note will stand alone without you needing to go back to the original

Source: adapted from Phelps, Fisher and Ellis, 2007: 175–6

of what you are reading for your (emerging) research problem. Table 18.1 offers suggestions for sensible note taking.

Table 18.1 makes it clear that you should always read *critically*. Don't just copy chunks of material. Strauss and Corbin (1990: 50–3, adapted here) suggest that the existing literature can be used for five purposes in qualitative research:

1 *To stimulate theoretical sensitivity,* 'providing concepts and relationships that [can be] checked out against (your) actual data'.

2 *To provide secondary sources of data* to be used for initial trial runs of your own concepts and topics.

3 *To stimulate questions during data gathering and data analysis.*

4 *To direct theoretical sampling* to 'give you ideas about where you might go to uncover phenomena important to the development of your theory'.

5 *To be used as supplementary validation* to explain why your findings support or differ from the existing literature.

Following Strauss and Corbin, you should always approach any publication or website with a set of questions, for instance:

• What are the relevant findings?

• What are the relevant methodologies?

• What are the relevant theories?

• What are the relevant hypotheses?

• What are the relevant samples?

• What is the relevance to how I now see my research problem?

• What possible new directions for my research are implied?

Exercise 18.1 gives you an opportunity to test out your skills in using the existing literature to help you in your own research. It emphasizes that we should never read such literature without having formulated some prior set of questions.

> **TIP**
>
> It goes without saying that you should use a consistent system for referencing authors and other details of the material you are reading. The Harvard method of referencing is usually the system chosen. This involves entering an author's surname, followed by date of publication and any page reference in your main text as follows:
>
> **Abrams (1984: 2); Agar (1986: 84)**
>
> By using this method, you can save footnotes for substantial asides rather than for (boring) references. Detailed references are then appended in a bibliography in a form such as the following:
>
> **Abrams, P. (1984) 'Evaluating soft findings: some problems of measuring informal care',** *Research Policy and Planning*, **2 (2), 1–8.**
> **Agar, M. (1986)** *Speaking of Ethnography*. **Qualitative Research Methods Series, Volume 2. London: Sage.**

When you come to write your literature review chapter, ideally towards the *end* of your research, you will have all the relevant material on file. But, just as important, you will also have a record of your changing thoughts about the literature and its relevance to your emerging research topic.

Writing Your Literature Review _____

18.2 There are four common misconceptions about the literature review chapter:

- It is done just to display that 'you know the area'.

- It is easier to do than your data analysis chapters.

- It is boring to read (and to write).

- It is best 'got out of the way' at the start of your research.

Later in this chapter, all these assertions will be questioned. By contrast I will argue that a literature review:

- should combine knowledge with critical thought

- involves hard work but can be exciting to read

- should mainly be written *after* you have completed your data analysis.

I will begin, however, by trying to answer some practical questions about writing a literature review. Namely, what should it contain? Where will you find what you need to read? How should you read?

18.3 Practical Questions
What should a literature review contain?

18.3.1 In part, a literature review should be used to display your scholarly skills and credentials. In this sense, you should use it:

> To demonstrate skills in library searching; to show command of the subject area and understanding of the problem; to justify the research topic, design and methodology. (Hart, 1998: 13)

Such justification also means, as I remarked in Chapter 6, that any literature review connected with a piece of research has as much to do with the issue of **generalizability** as with displaying your academic credentials. This involves addressing the questions set out in Table 18.2.

TABLE 18.2 Contents of a literature review

- What do we already know about the topic?
- What do you have to say critically about what is already known?
- Has anyone else ever done anything exactly the same?
- Has anyone else done anything that is related?
- Where does your work fit in with what has gone before?
- Why is your research worth doing in the light of what has already been done?

Source: adapted from Murcott, 1997

Once you start to see your literature review as dialogic rather than a mere replication of other people's writing, you are going in the right direction. Conceived as an answer to a set of questions, your reading can immediately become more directed and your writing more engaging and relevant.

Preparing a literature search

18.3.2 As Hart (2001: 24) points out, it helps to do some preliminary thinking about what you are doing before you begin the search itself. Below are some issues to think about (drawn from Hart, 2001: 24):

- What discipline(s) relate to my main topic?

- How can I focus my topic to make my search more precise?

- What are the main indexes and abstracts relevant to my topic?

- What means of recording will be most efficient for many tasks such as cross-referencing? (Hart points out that index cards are useful.)

Where will I find the literature?

18.3.3 Once you are prepared, it is time to review the many potential sources of information about what literature you need to read and where to find it:

- your supervisor

- the subject librarian in your university library

- bibliographies in the literature you read

- online searches on the World Wide Web

- the Social Sciences Citation Index

- newsgroups on the Internet

- your fellow students (past and present).

TIP

Excellent discussions of using the web for literature searches are provided by Phelps et al. (2007: 129–65) and O Dochartaigh (2007).

LINK

For a template for recording literature searches, go to:

http:/www.sagepub.co.uk/phelps

In literature searches, there is no need to worry about admitting your lack of knowledge. Indeed, the American sociologist Gary Marx recommends taking 'short cuts': 'learn how to use computer searches, encyclopaedias, review articles. Ask experts for help' (1997: 106).

Once you start looking, you will speedily find that you have a problem not with too little literature but with too much! Getting away from the books and towards your data is a leap that most of us need to make as early as possible. As Marx cautions: 'Don't become a bibliophile unless it suits you' (1997: 106). Or, more pointedly, 'know when enough is enough' (Phelps et al., 2007: 176).

There's so much: how will I find the time?

18.3.4 Before you panic, you need to remember that you would not have reached this stage of your academic career without learning the tricks of the reading trade. These tricks go beyond the skills of speed reading (although these help); your aim is usually to 'fillet' a publication in terms of your own agenda (not the author's!). Again, Marx makes the point well:

> Sample! Learn how to read by skimming, attending to the first and last sentence, paragraph or chapter. Read conclusions first, then decide if you want the rest. Most social science books probably shouldn't be books; they have only a few main (or at least original) ideas. (1997: 106)

If these are some answers to the usual 'nuts and bolts' questions, we still need to tackle the underlying principles behind a literature review. As my earlier discussion of 'misconceptions' suggested, these principles are not always obvious or clear-cut.

Principles

18.4 This is how the best recent book on the topic defines a literature review:

> The selection of available documents (both published and unpublished) on the topic, which contain information, ideas, data and evidence written from a particular standpoint to fulfil certain aims or express certain views on the nature of the topic and how it is to be investigated, and the effective evaluation of these documents in relation to the research being proposed. (Hart, 1998: 13)

Chris Hart's term 'effective evaluation' means, I believe, attending to the following principles.

Show respect for the literature

18.4.1 Your single-minded pursuit of your (ideally) narrow research topic should not lead you to show disrespect for earlier research or to disconnect your work from the wider debate in which it figures. Your dissertation will be assessed in terms of its scholarship, and being 'scholarly' means showing 'respect' as well as striking out on your own. In Marx's words:

> Even producers of literature must know the literature, and a major criterion for evaluating work is whether or not it is put in a context of prior scholarship. We are not only creators of new knowledge, but protectors and transmitters of old knowledge. Our inheritance is the astounding richness of the work of prior scholars. Beyond that, one has a strategic interest in the peer reciprocity inherent in the citing system. (1997: 106)

Be focused and critical

18.4.2 Respect can only get you so far. Scholarship also means advancing knowledge – although the level of the advance required will vary according to the degree at which you are aiming. Such advance involves a strict focus and a critical perspective on what you read:

> After some initial grovelling, know what you are looking for. Approach the literature with questions and remember that your goal is to advance it, not simply to marvel at its wonders. Seek an appropriate balance between appreciation and advancement of the literature. (Marx, 1997: 106)

Avoid mere description

18.4.3 Any academic has horror stories of literature reviews which were tediously and irrelevantly descriptive. Rudestam and Newton characterize well such failing reviews:

> [They consist of] a laundry list of previous studies, with sentences or paragraphs beginning with the words, 'Smith found …', 'Jones concluded …', 'Anderson stated …', and so on. (1992: 46)

In this vein, Gary Marx recommends avoiding writing 'a literature summary without an incisive critique that will help your peers to view the world differently' (1997: 106). Instead, you need to focus on those studies that are relevant for defining *your* research problem. By the end of the literature review:

> the reader should be able to conclude that, 'Yes, of course, this is the exact study that needs to be done at this time to move knowledge in this field a little further along.' (Rudestam and Newton, 1992: 47)

This entails giving different amounts of attention to what you read according to how central it is to your topic. Background literature can just be described in a sentence. By contrast, the most relevant studies 'need to be critiqued rather than reported' (1992: 49). Such critique can focus on failings of theory or method (see Chapter 16).

Write up after your other chapters

18.4.4 The common version of a student research trajectory suggests that a major early aim is to complete a literature review. This version is supported in the 'Time Checklist' provided by the British Research Councils (1996) for PhD students. This includes the following recommendation: 'First year … student to complete a literature survey. Elsewhere the same publication gives less dogmatic advice:

In some subjects a *literature survey* forms an important starting portion of the work, and this should be carried out in the early stages. Before the end of the first year, the student should have a good idea of relevant work carried out by others, but it will be necessary to keep up with new literature throughout the period, so that the thesis takes account of the latest developments in its subject area.

This more considered advice hints at the problems of completing your literature review at an early stage. These problems may include:

- Completing the literature survey in year one and writing it up can mean a lot of wasted effort. Until you have done your data analysis, you do not know what stuff will be relevant.

- You may be tempted to regard the literature review as a relatively easy task. Since it tests skills you have already learned in your undergraduate career, it may become potential 'busy work'. If so, it will only delay getting down to the data analysis on which you should be judged.

- As I asked in Chapter 6, can you ever get out of the library in order to write your thesis? One book will surely have a list of further 'crucial' references and so on, *ad infinitum*. Anybody who thinks a library PhD is a 'quick fix' would be well advised to ponder whether they have the willpower to stop reading.

These considerations mean that the bulk of your reading is usually best done in and around your data collection and analysis. In the end, this will save you the time involved in drafting your literature review chapter before you can know which literature will be most relevant to your treatment of your topic. It will also force you out of the library. As Marx comments: 'searching the literature must not become an end in itself or a convenient way to avoid the blank page' (1997: 106).

So: read as you do the analyses. By all means write notes on your reading, but don't attempt to write your literature review chapter early on in your research.

■ Attempt Exercise 18.2

LINK

For some short tips on literature reviews go to:

http://www.qmu.ac.uk/psych/RTrek/study_notes/web/sn9.htm

However, as researchers, we should be critical and innovative. In this regard, how far is the literature review chapter simply an unthought relic of an out-of-date version of scholarship. Do you need such a chapter?

18.5

The major unorthodox figure here is the American ethnographer Harry Wolcott. Wolcott (1990) argues that student researchers often mistakenly assume a need to defend qualitative research in general as well as the particular approach or method you are using. But, as he suggests, after a century of qualitative research (and several decades of more specific qualitative approaches):

> There is no longer a call for each researcher to discover and defend [qualitative methods] anew, nor a need to provide an exhaustive review of the literature about such standard procedures as participant observation or interviewing. Instead of having to describe and defend qualitative approaches, as we once felt obligated to do, it is often difficult to say anything new or startling about them. Neophyte researchers who only recently have experienced these approaches first-hand need to recognize that their audiences probably do not share a comparable sense of excitement about hearing them described once again. (1990: 26)

Wolcott also points to some positive gains of avoiding the statutory review chapter. As he puts it:

> I expect my students to know the relevant literature, but I do not want them to lump (dump?) it all into a chapter that remains unconnected to the rest of the study. I want them to draw upon the literature selectively and appropriately as needed in the telling of their story. (1990: 17)

This means that you can bring in appropriate literature as you need it, not in a separate chapter but in the course of your data analysis:

> Ordinarily this calls for introducing related research toward the end of a study rather than at the beginning, except for the necessary 'nesting' of the problem in the introduction. (1990: 17)

In the following example, you can see how one of my students followed Wolcott's suggestions. Instead of a separate literature review chapter, Geraldine 'nested' relevant literature in her data chapters and in an early chapter setting out the 'natural history' of her research.

STUDENT EXAMPLES

Telling my Research Story

A step-by-step appraisal of the broad literature read during the course of study carried a risk of providing an unnecessarily protracted read. In place of the conventional literature review chapter,

---

I opted to tell the *story* of the research and in so doing describe some of the literature that left an impression on me – *good* and *bad* – and which encouraged me to ask the questions that I eventually came to ask. To impose a structured description of *my literature* retrospectively would have failed to capture adequately a more 'honest' and oftentimes-chaotic journey toward achieving a coherent topic and analytic approach, and in being able to nest the problem in an apposite literature.

As well as situating the research in a broader context, I attempt to situate myself as an audience of the literature and explain how my reading of '*it*' led to the work reported on the following pages. In so doing, the constraints or limitations imposed by alternative analytic approaches are raised. The resulting critique is intended not to attack the utility of work already undertaken in the broad research domain of cancer, information and communication, but to demonstrate my rationale for choosing one way over another.

In providing a natural history chapter in place of a literature review, the insights and influences of other literatures are still drawn on at relevant points. Moreover, in line with a qualitative approach to data analysis, reference to the literature occurs throughout the data chapters to augment and illuminate the points conveyed. In short, the thesis engages with relevant literatures throughout, and not in a single chapter. [Geraldine Leydon, Sociology, Goldsmiths]

Geraldine's approach, which follows Wolcott's radical suggestions, is, no doubt, too radical for most students (and their supervisors!). Nevertheless, even if you decide to write the conventional literature review chapter, what Wolcott has to say is a salutary reminder that, in writing a research dissertation, you should cite other literature only in order to connect your narrow research topic to the directly relevant concerns of the broader research community. Making wider links should properly be left to your final chapter (see Chapter 21).

 ■ **Attempt Exercise 18.3** ▬▬▬▬▬▬▬

Concluding Remarks

18.6
In this chapter, I have argued that a literature review should combine knowledge with critical thought. It should involve hard work but be exciting to read and should mainly be written *after* you have completed your data analysis.

KEY POINTS

A literature review should contain answers to the following questions:

- What do we already know about the topic?
- What do you have to say critically about what is already known?

(Continued)

(Continued)

- Has anyone else ever done anything exactly the same?

- Has anyone else done anything that is related?

- Where does your work fit in with what has gone before?

- Why is your research worth doing in the light of what has already been done?

■ ■ Further Reading ■

The essential book on this topic is Chris Hart's *Doing a Literature Review: Releasing the Social Science Imagination* (Sage, 1998). This covers in detail all the issues discussed in this brief chapter as well as addressing the different requirements of literature reviews for BA, MA and PhD dissertations. Hart's later book *Doing a Literature Search* (Sage, 2001) is a helpful guide to planning and executing a literature search. For shorter, lively discussions see Harry Wolcott's *Writing Up Qualitative Research* (third edition, Sage, 2009) and Gary Marx's paper 'Of methods and manners for aspiring sociologists: 37 moral imperatives' (*The American Sociologist*, Spring 1997: 102–25). On keeping a record of your reading, see Phelps, Fisher and Ellis's *Organizing and Managing Your Research: A Practical Guide for Postgraduates* (Sage, 2007: 128–49); Strauss and Corbin's *Basics of Qualitative Research* (third edition, Sage, 2008, Ch. 4); Kathy Charmaz's *Constructing Grounded Theory* (Sage, 2006: 163–8); and Pat Cryer's *The Research Student's Guide to Success* (third edition, Open University Press, 2006).

 ■ Exercise 18.1

Select what you regard as the two or three most relevant pieces of literature. Now:

1 Make notes on each, attempting to use each one to answer the questions found in Table 18.2.

   Insert Table 18.2 here.

2 Incorporate these notes in a short literature review chapter which only refers to these two or three works.

3 Discuss this review with your supervisor.

 ■ Exercise 18.2

When you complete each data analysis chapter, look back over the literature you have discussed. Now ask yourself these questions:

1 Is there sufficient discussion of each reference to render further discussion (in a literature review chapter) redundant?

2 If not, practise writing about these references in a way that adds to how you have described them in your data analysis chapters. You may use Table 18.2 as a guide.

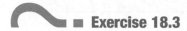 ■ **Exercise 18.3** ▬▬▬▬▬▬▬▬▬▬▬▬▬▬▬▬▬▬

Below is an extract of around 300 words from my book *Discourses of Counselling: HIV Counselling as Social Interaction*.

1 Read the passage and make notes from it (no more than 200 words) appropriate to a thesis on the nature of professional–client communication.

2 Now repeat the process on the assumption that your thesis topic is 'effective AIDS counselling'.

3 What relevance, if any, does this extract have to your own research? Note that such relevance can be methodological and theoretical as well as substantive. This means that a reading can be useful even if your substantive topic is very different.

Three major points have emerged from this discussion of a small number of post-test counselling interviews. First, following Peräkylä (1995), 'cautiousness' is seen, once more, to be a major feature of HIV counselling. This is true of the activities of both counsellors and clients. Thus these counsellors seek to align their clients to the disclosure of their test-result, while clients, to whom the character of counselling is presumably 'opaque', often demur at taking any action which might demand an immediate telling of their test-result (or indeed, many other activities, like directly demanding clarification of the validity of HIV-tests) even when, as here, given the right to decide the agenda of their counselling interview. However, these agenda-offers, unlike the alignment strategies discussed by Maynard (1991) and Bergmann (1992), are being used in an environment where the upcoming diagnosis is likely to be heard as 'good'.

Second, we have seen how, when clients respond to agenda-offers by introducing other topics than the test-result (e.g. volunteering statements about themselves or asking, usually indirectly, about the validity of the HIV-test), they seem to 'kick in' standard counselling responses (e.g. information and requests for specification). While such responses are consonant with normative standards of good counselling practice, they are, once again, produced in an environment in which their positioning (prior to the telling of the test-result) may be problematic.

Finally, we have demonstrated that, for at least one client, this delay in telling is problematic … this client analysed the delay in the delivery of his test-result as implying that C was about to deliver a 'positive' result – by referring to 'support groups' for HIV-positive people.

This apparent lack of fit between a delayed delivery of the test-result and its content (i.e. as HIV-negative) leads directly into some fairly clear practical implications. (Silverman, 1997: 106)

|19|

The Methodology Chapter

Chapter Objectives

By the end of this chapter, you will be able to:

- **Recognize what is involved in writing a methodology chapter which transparently documents the research process.**

- **Understand the key questions which this chapter must answer.**

- **Consider the nature and advantages of writing this chapter in a 'natural history' format.**

Introduction _____

19.1

We can distinguish three different kinds of student dissertation: theoretical, methodological and empirical. Each of these demands different discussion of 'methods'.

1 *Theoretical.* Here you claim to develop some theoretical insights by means of a critical review of a body of literature. In the theoretical dissertation, your methodology chapter will need to discuss your rationale for selecting your corpus of literature and any illustrative examples. It will also need to show how you have attempted to produce a systematic analysis, e.g. by considering the arguments for positions that you reject.

2 *Methodological.* Here you are mainly concerned to develop a method (e.g. focus groups or textual analysis) or to compare and contrast the use of several different methods. Here the whole thesis may be devoted to methodological matters, and so a separate chapter called 'methodology' may be redundant or simply devoted to explaining why you have chosen certain methods to compare and/or which data you choose to use for this exercise.

3 *Empirical.* In this, the most common form of research report or dissertation, you will analyse some body of data. Here you will be expected to show that you understand the strengths and weaknesses of your research strategy, design and methods.

TABLE 19.1   The methods chapter in a quantitative thesis

1   Subjects studied
2   Research instruments used
3   Procedures used in applying these instruments to these subjects
4   Statistical analysis

Source: adapted from Rudestam and Newton, 1992: 61

This chapter focuses on empirically based research reports. It argues for openness and clarity about what actually happened during your research. It argues that a bland account in the passive voice is an entirely inappropriate format for your methodology chapter.

Qualitative researchers are often interested in the **narratives** or stories that people tell one another (and researchers). Indeed, our data analysis chapters tell (structured) stories about our data. It is only natural, then, that our readers should expect to be told how we gathered our data, what data we ended up with, and how we analysed them.

This is why all research reports seem to have a methodology chapter, or at least a section devoted to 'data and methods'. Within that rubric, however, as I show later in this chapter, there are many different (non-bland) formats we can use to give an account of our data and methods. First, however, we need to clear the ground about the issues you need to cover in your methods chapter.

What Should the Methodology Chapter Contain?

19.2
In a quantitative study, there is a simple answer to this question. You will have a chapter usually entitled 'Data and Methods'. As Table 19.1 shows, this chapter will typically contain four elements.

The straightforward character of a quantitative methods chapter unfortunately does not spill over into qualitative research reports. At first sight, this simply is a matter of different language. So, in reporting qualitative studies, typically we do not talk about 'statistical analysis' or 'research instruments'.

These linguistic differences also reflect broader practical and theoretical differences between quantitative and qualitative research. More particularly, in writing up qualitative research, we need to recognize:

- the (contested) theoretical underpinnings of methodologies

- the (often) contingent nature of the data chosen

- the (likely) non-random character of cases studied

- the reasons why the research took the path it did (both analytic and chance factors).

Each of these four features raises issues which should not be concealed or generate guilt. Your research training courses and your reading should have made you aware of the theories on which your methods rest. So the rule here, in writing your methods chapter, is simply: *spell out your theoretical assumptions*.

Here is an example of how this can be done via an extract from Steven Stanley's PhD which used discourse analysis on interviews with other research students.

STUDENT EXAMPLES

The Theoretical Assumptions of Methodologies

Within qualitative, discursive and critical approaches to psychology it is generally acknowledged that methodological issues cannot be separated from theoretical assumptions. When one employs a particular method one is always drawing upon and consolidating ideas about how the world works, what people are like, and so on. In contrast to this, the methods sections of traditional psychological reports are often presented as purely descriptive accounts of 'what happened'. They often involve little theoretical discussion of methodological issues, implying that the practice of psychology can be separated from theory, interpretation and argument. From a discursive perspective, the methods one employs are inherently bound up with theory. The choice of how to investigate a given topic is intimately connected with epistemological and ontological issues relating to the very nature of that topic as a 'topic'. As such, the present chapter constitutes both a presentation of 'what happened' in this study, as well as a discussion of the particular issues surrounding method in discursive psychology and in studies of doctoral education. Each section will include descriptive details of how the study was developed and conducted, as well as a discussion of the associated theoretical issues. The aim is not to provide an exhaustive and complete account of the various methodological issues relating to the topics under discussion, but rather to highlight some of the central issues involved in adopting a discursive approach to the study of doctoral education, and to show how the presentation and practice of 'method' is inherently bound up with theoretical assumptions. It is hoped that these discussions will contribute both to studies of higher education and to debates on method within discursive and related constructionist approaches to psychology. [Steven Stanley, Social Sciences, Loughborough]

Notice how Steven is seeking an alternative to presenting a methodology chapter as a purely descriptive account of 'what happened'. However, 'theory' alone does not totally shape the course of your research. Everybody realizes that contingent events related to personal interest, access or even simply being in the right (wrong) place at the right (wrong) time, often determine which data you are able to work upon. So, when you write your methods chapter, be straightforward: *spell out the (sometimes contingent) factors that made you choose to work with your particular data*.

Finally, everybody knows that qualitative researchers can work fruitfully with very small bodies of data that have not been randomly assembled. If this is the case, *explain how you can still generalize from your analysis*. For example, in Chapter 9, I discussed four different but positive answers to this question of how we can obtain generalizability:

TABLE 19.2 How to document your research transparently

- Give an honest account of the conduct of the research
- Provide full descriptions of what was actually done in regard to choosing your case(s) to study, choosing your method(s), collecting and analysing data
- Explain and justify each of your decisions
- Discuss the strengths and weaknesses of what you did
- Be open about what helped you and held you back

Source: adapted from Spencer et al., 2003: 76

- combining qualitative research with quantitative measures of populations

- purposive sampling guided by time and resources

- theoretical sampling

- using an analytic model which assumes that generalizability is present in the existence of *any* case.

So, when writing your methodology chapter, avoid over-defensiveness. Many great researchers will have used similar methods with few qualms. So draw from their strength.

On the other hand, self-confidence should not mean lack of appropriate self-criticism. Your literature review chapter will already have considered other studies in terms of 'the strengths and limitations of different research designs and techniques of data collection, handling and analysis' (Murcott, 1997: 2). Treat your methodology chapter in the same way – as a set of cautious answers to questions that another researcher might have asked you about your work (e.g. 'Why did you use these methods?', 'How did you come to these conclusions?').

TIP

Your methodology chapter should aim to *document* the rationale behind your research design and data analysis.

Spencer et al. (2003) argue that this documentation process requires transparency about your methods. In other words, you should anticipate and answer reasonable questions about your research. Table 19.2 sets out the issues involved here.

Another way of putting these kinds of matters has been suggested by Anne Murcott. Table 19.3 shows how we can use our methods chapter to answer a set of questions.

To answer the questions in the table will usually mean describing the following:

- the data you have studied

- how you obtained those data (e.g. issues of access and consent)

TABLE 19.3 Questions for a qualitative methods chapter

1	How did you go about your research?
2	What overall strategy did you adopt, and why?
3	What design and techniques did you use?
4	Why these and not others?

Source: Murcott, 1997

- what claims you are making about the data (e.g. as representative of some population or as a single case study)

- the methods you have used to gather the data

- why you have chosen these methods

- how you have analysed your data

- the advantages and limitations of using your method of data analysis.

━━━━━━━━━━━━━━━ ■ LINK ■ ━━━━━━━━━━━━━━━

For a short introduction to the issues involved in writing this chapter, go to:

http://web.uvic.ca/spp/documents/methodology.pdf

A Natural History Chapter?

19.3
To answer Murcott's four questions in Table 19.3, in the context of my elaborations above, may now look to be a pretty tall order, particularly if you feel you have to devote a long section to each of these issues.

However, the methodology chapter of a qualitative study can be a much more lively, interesting affair than this suggests. In this context, there are three issues to bear in mind. First, a highly formal chapter can be dull to read as well as to write. Many is the time I have ploughed through a desperately boring methodology chapter, usually written in the passive voice. I often get the feeling that the chapter is there for purely formal purposes. In the words of a British song about the war, 'because we're here, because we're here, because we're here'! In such cases, I can hardly wait to get on to the (more lively) heart of the study.

Second, 'methodology' has a more flexible meaning in qualitative research than in its quantitative sister. In Chapter 7, I defined 'methodology' as 'a general approach to studying research topics'. As such, your readers will be more interested in a methodological discussion in which you explain the actual course of your decision making rather than a series of blunt assertions in the passive voice (e.g. 'the method chosen was ...').

Third, a research study submitted for a university degree, even up to the PhD level, is principally evaluated in terms of how far you can demonstrate that you have the makings of a competent researcher. Hence your examiners will be interested to know something about the history of your research, including your response to the various difficulties and dead ends that we all experience.

As Alasuutari argues, false leads and dead-ends are just as worth reporting as the method eventually chosen:

> It is precisely for this reason that taking 'fieldnotes' about the development of one's thinking is needed ... The text can be like a detective story, where one presents these 'false leads' until they are revealed to be dead-ends. (1995: 192)

Alasuutari's version of the history of research as a 'detective story' is incompatible with a formal methodology chapter in the passive voice. Instead of a formal, impersonal chapter, one offers the reader 'fieldnotes about the developments of one's thinking'. One way to do this is to rename the 'methodology' chapter 'The Natural History of My Research'.

In Chapter 3, we saw how some of my research students used their field diaries to write lively natural histories. These informed the reader, among other things about:

- the personal context of their research topic

- the reasons for their research design

- how they developed their research through trial and error

- the methodological lessons they learned.

Examples of how these topics can be treated in your 'natural history' chapter are set out in Table 19.4.

TABLE 19.4 Topics for a natural history chapter

The personal context
By the end of my period of undergraduate study, I was greatly vexed by issues surrounding the tendency within the various schools of sociology towards using 'social structure' too loosely as a way of accounting for data. [Simon]

The micro-analysis of social interaction seemed to me to be a valuable way of understanding some of the health issues and problems I had encountered in my experience working in clinical health settings as a psychiatric nurse and as a research nurse. Many of these problems appeared to hinge on the interactive practices and skills of the various parties involved. [Moira]

As with Silverman 's (1987) experience of gaining access to the field of paediatric cardiology, my entry to the field of mental health casework was a chance happening. I met up with a former colleague in a local supermarket. After I recounted my difficulty in negotiating access to an inpatient area, he invited me to meet the community team with whom he worked. [Sally]

Reasons for research design
I chose to collect data in the way that I did because it was appropriate to the study of situated action. Audiotapes provide detailed recorded talk which fieldnotes alone cannot provide, while preparing transcripts is itself a research activity. [Sally]

(Continued)

TABLE 19.4   (Continued)

Many qualitative research studies set out clear aims and objectives at the start of a project. These may often refer to collecting and analysing data on a particular topic, such as describing the views of patients about a particular type of illness experience. The aims of ethnomethodological studies such as this one tend to be quite general, centring on the examination of some data. Decisions therefore need to be made about objectives for particular pieces of analysis at each stage. [Moira]

Developing through trial and error
I had initially intended to undertake separate analyses of instances of criticisms of self and of the dead spouse. However, I decided a more constructive tack would be to conduct a closer analysis of members' practices in producing the accounts. This would involve taking a step back in order to take a closer look. [Moira]

To undertake a case study of 'single homelessness' in the context of full-time employment makes heavy demands on the researcher in terms of personal resources and operational constraints. The field is so vast and the nature of subject' lives so dispersed that I elected to observe professional caseworkers rather than service users. For practical reasons then, I became a participant-observer at weekly case conferences. [Sally]

Methodological lessons I have learned
I was attempting to describe something that I knew was going on but could not see at the start. The need to refrain from introducing my own categorizations before producing the description of members' practices that I was aiming for has not been easy. However, I believe that the fine grained analysis of the practices adopted by interview participants has enabled me to contribute new insights to the sociology of health and illness. [Moira]

With hindsight, I might use more conventional transcription devices if I were to do the transcripts again. This would save the 'creative' work of devising my own. [Sally]

How, then, should this research be seen in terms of both sampling variety and external validity? I believe the answer lies in seeing this research not as an attempt to provide categorical 'truths' about all parents' evenings in general, but as an attempt to raise questions about such meetings by looking at a single case in detail. This study can therefore be seen as being *exploratory* rather than *definitive*, examining the achievement of routine by a single individual in a specific setting in such a way that further analytical possibilities are opened up. [Simon]

As the student comments in Table 19.4 show, the more informal 'natural history' style of methodology chapter that I recommend should not be taken to mean that 'anything goes'. On the contrary, by asking readers to engage with your thinking *in process*, they are in a far better position to assess the degree to which you were self-critical. Moreover, an autobiographical style is only appropriate to the extent that it allows you to address properly the kind of crucial methodological questions set out in Tables 19.2 and 19.3. Clearly, your readers will not want to hear needlessly and endlessly about how your personal life impinged upon the process of obtaining your degree!

Concluding Remarks

19.4 Some universities (like some academic journals) still have a pretty fixed idea of what a methodology chapter (or section) should contain. Therefore, it is probably worth discussing with your teachers whether a 'natural history' format is appropriate to describe the methodology that you have chosen. But even if you do not write your chapter in this way, you will still gain by keeping dated fieldnotes about the trajectory of your project.

However, if you do write a 'natural history' chapter, it is much more likely that you will avoid boring your readers (and yourself). It is also more likely that you will overcome the common problem of failing to explicate to the reader what is now 'obvious' to you. As Alasuutari puts it. 'Researchers always become more or less blind to their texts and thoughts, so that they do not notice that they have failed in spelling out certain premises or starting points without which an outsider has a hard time understanding the text' (1995: 192). A 'natural history' chapter, based on contemporary fieldnotes, will be more likely to make your readers 'insiders' and to avoid you being an 'outsider' in relation to your own text.

KEY POINTS

All research reports have a methodology chapter, or at least a section devoted to 'data and methods'. In it, you will be expected to show that you understand the strengths and weaknesses of your research strategy, design and methods. In this chapter you should explain:

- your theoretical assumptions
- the factors that made you choose to work with your particular data
- how you can generalize from your analysis.

However, a highly formal methodology chapter can be dull to read as well as to write. Instead, it is often right to offer the reader fieldnotes about the developments of one's thinking called 'The Natural History of My Research'.

▬▬ ■ ■ **Further Reading** ■ ▬▬▬▬▬▬▬▬▬▬▬▬

The most helpful comments on writing a methodology chapter are to be found in Pertti Alasuutari's *Researching Culture: Qualitative Method and Cultural Studies* (Sage, 1995: Chs 13 and 14).

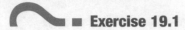 ■ **Exercise 19.1**

Assemble the various memos you have written during your research. Now write 500 words on each of the following topics related to your research:

1 the main things that have helped you finish and the main things that have held you back

2 what you have learned about your research topic

3 how you have improved your knowledge of (a) methodology and (b) theory

4 what lessons your research has for other students at your level.

Note: if you have not finished your research yet, do Exercise 2.1 instead.

|20|

Writing Your Data Chapters

Chapter Objectives

By the end of this chapter, you will be able to:

- **Plan the overall structure of your thesis.**

- **Recognize and choose between different stories you can tell about your research.**

- **Work out how to present data effectively.**

- **Appreciate the importance of writing in a clear and persuasive manner.**

Introduction

20.1 As we have already seen, many supervisors and funding bodies suggest that doing a research study falls into three equal phases. These phases are commonly defined as:

- reviewing the literature

- gathering your data

- analysing your data.

Faced with this convention, it may be necessary to restate the obvious. Assuming that you are writing an empirically based study, your data analysis chapters are (or should be) the key basis on which your dissertation will be judged. Unlike coursework essays, where knowledge of the literature and an ability to analyse it critically will stand you in good stead, dissertations that involve research are worth nothing without good data analysis.

TIP

There are usually no brownie points awarded for successfully gathering your data. Whether or not such data gathering involves discomfort, danger or the need to learn another language is, ultimately, neither here nor there. In the final assessment, everything comes down to what you *do* with your data. Hence your data chapters are the *crucial* part of your dissertation.

This situation implies two clear messages. First, as I have stressed throughout this book, you cannot begin too early in your data analysis. Second, when you write up data, you need to develop the skills to present your analysis clearly and cogently to your readers.

This is why, as Jay Gubrium (personal correspondence) has commented, students need advice on the actual writing up of their data analysis. They need to understand 'what to say first, next, where to place things, how to introduce extracts and what to say in relation to them, how to draw conclusions'. In this chapter, I offer advice addressed to the issues that Gubrium raises.

It will be useful at once to make a distinction between how you write up your analysis of particular sets of data and how you craft your overall argument. Alasuutari (1995) calls the former area the 'microstructure' of a thesis and the latter its 'macrostructure'. This is how he explains the difference between the two levels:

> The difference between the two could be compared to different dimensions of the architecture of a house. At the macrolevel one thinks how the rooms and different activities are placed in relation to each other, whereas at the microlevel one considers the furnishing and interior decoration of different rooms. (1995: 179)

This is a helpful distinction because, as Alasuutari suggests, different issues arise in relation to the organization of individual chapters (the microstructure) and the overall organization of your thesis (the macrostructure). In the rest of this chapter, I will consider each structure separately and then go on to explain how to make a final check that everything is in place before you tighten up the structure (Wolcott, 1990: 47).

The Macrostructure

20.2

> The macrostructure is how the investigation proceeds from one chapter to another so that it forms a logical and sound whole. (Alasuutari, 1995: 179)

How do you ensure that your data analysis chapters form 'a logical and sound whole'? I discuss below two answers to this question:

- Plan your table of contents at an early stage and continually revise it.

- In the final write-up, decide the form of the 'story' you want to tell about your research.

Early planning of table of contents

20.2.1 Plan what you may put into your data chapters as early as you can and then keep revising your list. As Harry Wolcott suggests, projecting a table of contents provides for:

an orderly progression, a clear identification of major points and subordinate ones, and an overview ... to assess whether the structure I have designed accommodates the data to be presented and provides an appropriate sequence for the presentation. (1990: 18)

By such early planning of the structure of your thesis you can help to clarify your research design and identify upcoming problems:

Insurmountable problems in finding a sound macrostructure may be a sign of weaknesses in the research design: problems which have to be sorted out first. (Alasuutari, 1995: 179)

Alasuutari gives the example of a set of chapters which veer unpredictably between different themes – a good indication of an unclear research design. This means that, if you have difficulty in working out your table of contents, then you are exhibiting symptoms of a confused research design.

To show you how tables of contents can be projected, I set out below examples from two of my research students: Sally Hunt and Kay Fensom. In each case, these research students started to project a table of contents at an early stage.

Sally gathered audio-recordings of case conferences of a community health team seeking to house mentally ill, homeless people. Her work, which was discussed in Chapter 3, is ethnographic in focus. The following is her draft table of contents, prepared while she was still writing her data chapters:

Sally's draft table of contents

'Producing single homelessness: descriptive practice in community mental casework'

1 Introduction: aims of the study

2 Natural history of the research

3 Literature used in the analysis

4–6 The ethnographic context

7 Constructing the case

8 Constructing the client

9 Gender as an interpretive framework

10 Constructing the mental health team

11 Conclusion: limitations and implications

In the final version of her thesis, Sally reorganized most of it into two parts: an introduction (which included Chapters 1–3) and the data analysis (Chapters 7–10). Sally recognized that her projected chapters on the ethnographic context were peripheral to her main argument. So her draft Chapters 4–6 were vastly shortened and incorporated in her introduction.

Kay analysed crime stories in local newspapers in London and Northern Ireland. To do this, she used Harvey Sacks's **membership categorization device (MCD)** analysis. The following are her early ideas about the organization of her thesis:

Kay's draft table of contents

'Locating newsworthiness in newspaper headlines: reading inference and 'motive'

1 Natural history: stages, directions and influences

2 Theoretical framework

3 The media, 'newsworthiness' and the activity of reading

4–7 Data chapters (each on a separate crime headline)

8 Dealing with critiques of MCD analysis

9 Conclusions: what has the analysis achieved?

By the time Kay submitted her PhD, she had one extra data chapter. She now felt that two of her draft chapters were based on literature reviews which were not distinctively original. So Chapters 3 and 8 disappeared from the final version of her thesis, although parts of each were used elsewhere. Kay's title also changed to: 'Crime, locality and morality: membership categorization and "newsworthiness" in local newspapers'. This improved title nicely reflected (what had turned out to be) Kay's key concepts and database.

Sally's and Kay's redrafting carries three important implications about how you should think about the structure of your thesis:

- Work out the main message and findings your data chapters should contain.

- Ensure that the structure of your thesis underlines that message.

- Strip out or minimize draft chapters that are peripheral to your argument.

Deleting or shortening chapters over which you have toiled requires a degree of ruthlessness on your part. Seek the guidance of your supervisor about whether such chapters might find a better home in, say, a conference paper or journal article (see Chapter 26).

More than a year before Sally and Kay finished their dissertation, they were already planning a draft table of contents. Planning is important because your research dissertation will probably be the longest piece of writing you have ever done. BA or MA research essays are commonly 10,000 words and PhDs are usually between 70,000 and 100,000 words. However, it is important not to focus upon your own difficulties in writing at this length, for I guarantee that in nearly every case you will find you have too *little* space.

Instead, think of how the reader needs a guide to follow a long story. Provide that guide at the start and repeat it, as appropriate, in every chapter (see Alasuutari, 1995: 180). This will mean giving regular 'signposts' to help the reader understand what you are going to do (or have done) and how these components relate to your overall theme. It also means planning the form of the 'story' you wish to tell.

Planning your story

20.2.2 There are at least three models to choose from in working out the macrostructure of your thesis:

- the hypothesis story
- the analytic story
- the mystery story.

Each is discussed briefly below.[1]

The hypothesis story

This is how many journals require you to organize your paper. It follows a standard three-part way of writing up research reports derived from quantitative studies:

1 State your **hypotheses**.
2 Test them.
3 Discuss the implications.

As Alasuutari (1995: 181) points out, there are two reasons why you are unlikely to want to use this model for writing up your qualitative dissertation. First, you may well be proceeding inductively, developing and testing hypotheses in the course of your data analysis. If so, then clearly you cannot state a prior hypothesis. Second, however, there are reasons to be suspicious of the hypothesis story because, even in quantitative studies, it often represents not the 'actual' logic of the research but a reconstructed logic fitted to how your cross-tabulations of variables actually worked out (see Alasuutari, 1995: 181–3).

The analytic story

The hypothesis story usually demands a passive voice format (for example, 'it was hypothesized that...' or 'the findings were ...') which can be difficult to write and still more painful to read! Telling an analytic story is a more conversational way of writing. It involves deciding 'the main analytic story line that you wish to tell' (Strauss and Corbin, 1990: 200). As Strauss and Corbin put it:

> think intently about the *analytic logic* that informs the story. Every research monograph, indeed every research paper, will have such a logic ... In a sense the entire thesis or monograph will represent a spelling out of this analytic story. (1990: 230)

To write this story, you need to ask yourself questions like:

- What are the key concepts that I have used in this study?
- How do my 'findings' shed light on these concepts and, through them, on the substantive topics I studied?
- What, therefore, has become of my original research problem and the literature regarding it?

Rather than hope that the reader will eventually find out these matters, telling an analytic story lays everything out on a plate at the outset.

There is much to be said for this model, for it helps the reader who can settle back knowing what (s)he will find in the rest of your thesis. Some readers, however, may actually want to be surprised. Such surprises can be planned rather than the mere outcome of sloppy design. This is where the mystery story comes in.

The mystery story

Alasuutari refers to an approach to writing that 'proceeds by pointing out mysteries and by gradually developing questions and answers'. In this approach, one:

> starts directly from **empirical** examples, develops the questions by discussing them, and gradually leads the reader to interpretations of the material and to more general implications of the results. (1995: 183)

Beginning one's data analysis in the form of a mystery story has at least two advantages. First, it may well capture your readers' attention as, like the readers of detective stories, they want to stay with you in order to find 'whodunnit'. Second, it more accurately mirrors the inductive form of much qualitative research where findings (and even topics) are only gradually revealed.

Set against this, you must remember that writing a mystery story requires many craft skills. Should you fail, you will certainly lose your readers' interest. So, in practice, many writers of good qualitative dissertations follow Strauss and Corbin's idea of telling an analytic story to lead the readers through the data analysis chapters.

In a sense, whichever story form you choose can be safely left to personal choice. More important is whether you are telling *some* coherent story. For, despite their differences, all three models share one important feature in common: they give the study focus and point. This means that the structure of your thesis should only rarely flow from the chronological order in which you happened to find out things. As Pat Cryer puts it: 'the final version of the thesis should be written, with hindsight, knowing where one has been' (1996: 178).

| TIP |

If you remember just one lesson from this chapter, it is this: avoid telling your story in the order which you found things out or wrote them up.

Discussing the order in which you discovered things is a story which is only appropriate for a natural history chapter (see Chapter 19). If the overall structure of your thesis just reflects the order in which you discovered things, then your examiners are unlikely to praise you for your verisimilitude. They are much more likely to criticize you for being too lazy to work out a coherent structure for your argument.

As Alasuutari puts it, returning to the motif of a 'mystery story':

> A good investigation is indeed like a murder mystery in that it does not contain much irrelevant text: themes or details that have nothing to do with the solution revealed in the end ... One could talk about the *economy principle* of a study: everything included must be related and tied in with the argumentation developed and presented in the investigation. (1995: 186, my emphasis)

■ Attempt Exercise 20.1

The Microstructure

20.3

With a clear macrostructure, you are well set up to write well-organized and well-argued data chapters. Whether it is a matter of setting out an overall argument (the macrostructure) or developing an analysis of a particular topic (the microstructure), you should always write in a way that helps the reader. As Gubrium (personal communication) notes, this is not always something that comes easily to inexperienced researchers:

> many students don't take their readers into account; they don't know how to 'teach' their readers what they should be reading into the empirical material present. Many just throw stuff into the text and expect the reader to get the point.

Thinking about your reader(s) turns out to be an excellent way of answering perennial problems that arise when you first write up a qualitative study. For instance, you may ask yourself: how much depth is needed in my data analysis? How much is enough? Strauss and Corbin suggest a good way of answering such questions:

> The answer is first that you must know what your main analytic message will be. Then you must give enough conceptual detail to convey this to readers. The actual form of your central chapters should be consonant with the analytic message and its components. (1990: 232–3)

So the answer to these questions is found in how you have depicted the main message of your thesis (the macrostructure). The point here is: know your message and stick to it!

Normally, each data analysis chapter will have three sections:

* an introduction in which you explain what you are going to do in advance

* the main section in which you work through your data in terms of what you have already said

* a conclusion in which you summarize what you have shown and connect to the next chapter.

I set out below some suggestions for writing each of these sections with an audience in mind.

Introduction

20.3.1 Never spring anything on your readers. Even if you have decided to tell a mystery story (see above), your audience should always know what the mystery is about and what kind of 'clues' they should be looking for. As Howard Becker has cautioned:

> Many social scientists ... think they are actually doing a good thing by beginning evasively. They reveal items of evidence one at a time, like clues in a detective story, expecting readers to keep everything straight until they produce the dramatic concluding paragraph ... I often suggest to these would-be Conan Doyles that they simply put their last triumphant paragraph first, telling readers where the argument is going and what all this material will finally demonstrate. (1986: 51–2)

So at the outset, preface each data analysis chapter with an explanation of how its topic relates to your thesis as a whole and how the chapter will be organized. As a broad rule, no subheading should ever appear in a chapter without it having received a prior explanation of its nature and logical place in your argument.

Along these lines, Pat Cryer suggests four components of a good introduction to a chapter. These are set out in Table 20.1.

TABLE 20.1 Components of a data chapter introduction

1 Scene-setting for the chapter, i.e. explaining the general area(s) that the chapter considers
2 Locating the gap in knowledge which the chapter addresses
3 Explaining how the chapter fills that gap
4 Providing a brief overview of what is in the chapter

Source: adapted from Cryer, 1996: 182

Main section

20.3.2 Now that your readers know the areas that this chapter will discuss, it is important that you initially pull apart these areas and discuss each one separately. The golden rule for writing data analysis is:

- Make one point at a time.

So, if you find yourself veering off in another direction, cut out the offending material and put it in another section. Sometimes this will mean returning to the same data but from a different perspective. Sometimes it will mean getting rid of some data altogether.

Your readers will find their life much easier if they are not distracted by too many different arguments. And it is also much more likely that you will be able to recognize holes in your argument if it is stripped to the bone.

If you are making just one point at a time, it is, of course, crucial that your readers should immediately grasp what that point is. Therefore, a second rule is:

- 'Top and tail' each data extract.

This means writing a sentence or two before every extract to context it in your argument. This way your readers will know what to look for while they read it.

Follow that up with a more detailed analysis of the extract in terms of the single point you are using it to make. If the extract is inconclusive, then admit to it. So, a third rule is:

- Always show that you understand the limitations of both your data and your analysis of them.

For your readers to be able to follow your analysis, they will need to be able to locate the extract(s) to which you are referring and where to find the relevant part of that extract. So a fourth rule is:

- Always number your extracts.

One effective way to do this is to give each extract two identifying numbers: the first will be the chapter number in which it appears, and the second the order in which it is placed in the chapter. So the first data extract in Chapter 3 of your thesis should be numbered Extract 3.1.

Line numbers should also be used for any extracts over two lines in length. In this way, for instance, you can refer to Extract 3.1, lines 5–7, without having to reprint the passage.

A fifth rule is:

- Convince the reader.

Not only must your readers be able to see why you interpreted your data in the way you did, they must be convinced by your interpretation. As Anne Murcott suggests: 'the basis for saying that the data say "x" rather than "y" has to be made apparent' (1997: 2). Murcott suggests that the way to display that your analysis has this kind of critical component is to 'discuss candidate interpretations and make the case for judging, and so discarding, alternatives as inferior or inadequate' (1997: 2).[2]

Conclusion

20.3.3 When you reach the end of a tight piece of data analysis, you may feel that nothing further needs to be done. Not so! You owe it to your readers to tie the whole chapter together again. Not only will this remind them of what you (and they) have learnt in the preceding pages, but it will also

TABLE 20.2 Components of a data chapter conclusion

1 Explain what the chapter has done
2 Describe the new questions the chapter has identified
3 Explain where these questions will be addressed (e.g. in the next chapter or in the overall conclusions)

Source: adapted from Cryer, 1996: 183

prepare them for the chapter(s) to follow. Table 20.2 sets out what the conclusion of a data chapter might contain.

It is worth remembering that it is unlikely that you will achieve a well-argued, reader-friendly thesis at one go. I conclude this chapter, therefore, with some suggestions about moving to a final draft or what Harry Wolcott calls 'tightening up' (1990: 47).

Tightening Up

20.4

> Make sure all parts are properly in place before tightening (directions for assembling a new wheelbarrow, reported by Wolcott, 1990: 47).

Wolcott's analogy of assembling a wheelbarrow reminds us that no subtle change of detail will work if the macrostructure of your thesis is not properly in place. As he puts it:

> Before you start tightening, take a look at how the whole thing is coming together. Do you have everything you need? (And do you need everything you have? Remember, you're only supposed to be tightening up that wheelbarrow, not filling it!) (1990: 48)

You are likely to be too close to your work to tell easily whether everything is properly in place. As Pat Cryer suggests, the author of a thesis 'will know it inside and out and back to front. So the link between its components may be clear to you, while not being as clear to those who have met your work only recently' (1996: 186).

There are two ways of giving yourself the critical distance necessary to see whether all the parts of your thesis are in place. First, if time allows, put it to one side for a while. Wolcott notes:

> I do a better job of strengthening the interpretation, spotting discrepancies and repetitions, locating irregularities in sequence or logic, and discovering overworked words, phrases, and patterns after periods of benign neglect. (1990: 52)

Locating what Wolcott calls 'irregularities' can mean deleting particular points to which you may have become attached but which detract from your overall argument (Seale, personal correspondence).

A second strategy to obtain distance is to give a talk on your research during the writing-up stage or to find 'someone new to your work who will listen to you explaining it or will read the draft thesis and tell you where they have trouble following' (Cryer, 1996: 186).

Once the macrostructure is in place, it is time to tighten up the microstructure. Among the things to look at here are:

- unclear or infelicitous language

- over-large claims about your data or analysis

- needless repetition

- insufficient detail (see Wolcott, 1990: 49–50).

When you have done all of these things, you must recognize that the tightening-up period is nearly over. Certainly, you can ask yourself: 'Have I really got the last details in? Got them right?' (Strauss and Corbin, 1990: 235).

To check this out, you can ask your supervisor and/or fellow students to have one final read and then respond to their comments. But remember: the revision process is potentially endless! The real cop-out is not submitting a less than perfect thesis but being stuck in a process of endless revisions:

> Part of an increasing maturity as a research-writer is to understand that no manuscript is ever finished. (1990: 235)

Just as parents eventually realize that their children have become adults and will leave home, now is the time to make the break with your manuscript. Like 'empty nest' parents, you should be ready to strike out in new directions. But first you must 'let go'.

■■■■■■■■■■■■■■■■ LINK ■■■■■■■■■■■■■■■■

For further advice on this topic, go to:

http://www.nova.edu/ssss/QR/QR2-3/presenting.html

For a weblog on writing up, visit:

http://forums.qsrinternational.com/index.php?showtopic=451

 ■ **Attempt Exercise 20.2** ■■■■■■■■■■■■■■■■■■■

Concluding Remarks _____

20.5 Your data analysis chapters are (or should be) the key basis on which your dissertation will be judged. However, different issues arise in relation to the organization of individual chapters (the microstructure) and the overall organization of your thesis (the macrostructure).

Good overall organization is based upon planning your table of contents at an early stage and continually revising it. You also need to decide the form of the 'story' you want to tell about your research and structure your data chapters accordingly. Each data chapter should have a microstructure based on three sections: an introduction in which you explain what you are going to do in advance; the main section in which you work through your data in terms of what you have already said; and, finally, a conclusion in which you summarize what you have shown and connect to the next chapter.

| **KEY POINTS**

In planning the overall (macro) structure of your thesis:

- Work out what main message and findings you want your data chapters to contain.
- Ensure that the structure of your thesis underlines that message.
- Strip out or minimize draft chapters that are peripheral to your argument.

When writing data chapters, it is wise to consider the following instructions:

- Make one point at a time.
- Context each data extract in your argument.
- Show that you understand the limitations of your analysis.
- Always number your data extracts.
- Realize that the reader will need to be convinced and that what is obvious to you will not always be so clear to others.

NOTES

1   As we shall see, the ideas of the hypothesis story and the mystery story derive from Alasuutari (1995).
2   See Chapter 15 for a discussion of these issues in terms of 'validity' and 'reliability' and Chapter 13 for an explanation of how diagrams and charts may illustrate your rigorous thinking. On this latter point, see also Mason (1996: 131–3) and Strauss and Corbin (1990: 131–7).

■ ■ Further Reading ■

Harry Wolcott's *Writing Up Qualitative Research* (third edition, Sage, 2009) is a marvellous account of how to write up data. Useful shorter treatments are: Pat Cryer's *The Research Student's Guide to Success* (third edition, Open University Press, 2006: Ch. 23); Pertti Alasuutari's *Researching Culture: Qualitative Method and Cultural Studies* (Sage, 1995: Ch. 14); and Anselm Strauss and Juliet Corbin's *Basics of Qualitative Research* (third edition, Sage, 2008: Ch. 13).

■ **Exercise 20.1**

Try organizing your data analysis into two chapters. Don't do this arbitrarily but find a logical approach. Now try reordering this material into five shorter chapters with a different logic. Consider which format works best and why.

 ■ **Exercise 20.2**

Select a coherent piece of your data analysis which might become a chapter. Give the chapter a title that fits what you are trying to do there. Using Tables 20.1 and 20.2, now:

1 Write an introduction for this chapter.

2 Write a conclusion.

3 Add in your data analysis and show the whole chapter to a colleague. Ask her (him) whether your introduction and conclusion helped her to see what you were getting at. If so, why? If not, why not?

4 Now revise the text and repeat the process.

|21|

Your Final Chapter

Chapter Objectives

By the end of this chapter, you will be able to:

- **Understand why a final chapter is necessary in a research report.**

- **See what this chapter should contain.**

- **Think about the theoretical implications of your research.**

- **Work out which audiences you are addressing and how you can shape your chapter accordingly.**

- **Recognize that writing a final chapter can be fun.**

Introduction

21.1 In the previous chapter, I concluded with the recommendation to 'let go'. However, since all research reports (including dissertations) seem to end with a set of 'conclusions', you cannot finally let go until your concluding chapter is written.

Having cycled painfully to the top of the hill, the great temptation at this point is to relax and freewheel down to the finish. In practice, such relaxation of effort is reflected in the all too common 'summaries' found in the final chapter of dissertations.

Although summaries are often quite useful devices at the end of data analysis chapters, I suggest that you should never write a summary as your concluding chapter. If your readers need a summary at this point, then your 'macrostructure' (Alasuutari's concept discussed in Chapter 20) is not in place. If it is in place, then what you have said should already be crystal clear. So resist the temptations of a final downhill freewheel.

But does this mean that you may not even need a final chapter? Cannot your thesis stop after you have finished your data analysis?

Think of a musical example. Classical symphonies typically end with a fast movement marked 'allegro' or 'presto'. Rather than a mere recapitulation of earlier themes, they take them up and develop them still more. As such, they seem designed to provide listeners with some of the most stimulating material in the composition. So your final chapter is, indeed, necessary. But it should function to stimulate your readers by demonstrating how your research has stimulated you.

This chapter begins by showing you the interesting and liberating functions of a concluding chapter. It then provides some practical suggestions about what this chapter should contain and reviews the balance between confessing to your errors and proclaiming your achievements. I go on to show how your concluding chapter should reconnect your data analysis to the basic analytic questions that have inspired you and should think through what your research can offer to a range of different audiences. Finally, I demonstrate why writing your final chapter can be fun.

■ Attempt Exercise 21.1

The Final Chapter as Mutual Stimulation

21.2 Your final chapter should be stimulating for you to write. If this is the case, it is likely to stimulate your readers. Part of that stimulation arises in linking the particularities of your own research back to the more general issues that arise within (your part) of your discipline. As the authors of the standard British text on PhDs comment:

> You are not doing some research for its own sake; you are doing it in order to demonstrate that you are a fully professional researcher, with a good grasp of what is happening in your field and capable of evaluating the impact of new contributions to it – your own as well as others. (Phillips and Pugh, 1994: 60)

Your contribution is what you must set out to demonstrate in your final chapter: 'It is here that you underline the significance [to your discipline] of your analysis, point out the limitations in your material, suggest what new work is appropriate, and so on' (1994: 59).

Phillips and Pugh's remarks suggest part of the answer to the practical question: what exactly should your final chapter contain?

What Exactly Should Your Final Chapter Contain?

> In the most general terms it [your final chapter] is a discussion as to why and in what way ... the theory that you started with [is] now different as a result of your research work. Thus your successors (who include, of course, yourself) now face a different situation when determining what their research work should be since they now have to take account of your work. (Phillips and Pugh, 1994: 59–60)

21.3

A helpful way of looking at this is in terms of Anne Murcott's question: 'What does the candidate want the reader to make of all this?' (1997: 3). As Table 21.1 shows, the final chapter offers you the opportunity to give your own twist to the wider implications of your research. Such implications must, of course, reflect your own critical sense of what is good and not so good in your own research. Always remember: unless you define your own sense of the limitations (and implications) of your work, your readers will do it for you!

TABLE 21.1 Suggested contents for your final chapter

- The relation between the work done, the original research questions, previous work discussed in the literature review chapter, and any new work appearing since the study began
- Some answer to the classic examiner's question, 'If you were doing this study all over again, is there anything you would do differently? Why so?'; that is, the lessons to be learned from the conduct of the study
- Any implications for policy and practice
- Further research that might follow from your findings, methods or concepts

Source: adapted from Murcott, 1997: 3

The example that follows shows how Rachael Dunn's dissertation (on therapeutic interaction in anorexia nervosa (AN) treatment) dealt with two of the issues in Table 21.1: the limitations of her research and recommendations for further research.

STUDENT EXAMPLES

Extract from a Final Chapter

Thesis limitations. This thesis has looked at *some* of the functions of the interactional practices identified in the analysis. Without question, any number of theses could have potentially been written about each analytic insight produced, and infinite alternative analytic directions could have been pursued in the data. Overall, the focus of the analysis could only be very narrow, and in the end I endeavoured to take a direction that had potential for clinical relevance ... It is important to note that I did not take preconceived ideas regarding therapeutic principles, and in a sense, code for them in the data ... Rather, I looked at how the practices and local organization of the interactions yielded analytic insights, that could *then* be viewed in terms of such principles. Furthermore, my own interpretations, analytic categories and institutional identities were not *imposed* onto the data corpus; instead, the analysis relied on the speakers' own orientations to elements and structures of the interactions.

A *further limitation* of this thesis is that it is potentially problematic to define the concept of therapeutic engagement generally, let alone as represented by a certain set of practices in therapeutic interactions … To address this, I endeavoured to show in the analysis reasonable links between certain recurrent practices in the interactions and specific theoretical principles of the therapists …

This thesis also did not directly address the issue of high dropout rates, reported in AN populations. While it can speculate on the link between certain interactional practices being representative of therapeutic engagement, it cannot make a direct association between engagement in therapy and reduced dropout rates (as discussed in the following section).

Future research. Though it is not a basis for this study, it could be proposed that increased engagement in therapy may be correlated with improved rates on external outcome measures, such as number of hospital admissions, as well as internal measures of AN symptomatology … Future studies could associate the presence or absence of certain interactional practices with specific treatment outcomes such as therapeutic withdrawal rates [and] could also study certain interactional circumstances in which therapeutic approaches in AN treatment such as individual or family-based therapies are more effective, as called for in the literature. [Rachael Dunn, Psychology, Murdoch University, my emphasis]

Notice how Rachael combines reflections on the limitations of her research with a discussion of how she addressed them. This shows that you can go too far in focusing solely on the limitations of your work. Research reports should not just be confessions! In the next section, I discuss the balance between owning up to where you feel you went wrong and blowing your own trumpet about your achievements.

Confessions and Trumpets

21.4 As Harry Wolcott notes, in assessing your thesis, your examiners will recognize that chance happenings as well as your research design have limited (as well as improved) your research. Be upfront about these matters. So, in your final chapter, write:

a broad disclaimer in which [you] make quite clear [your] recognition of all the limitations of the study (e.g. that it occurred in a particular place, at a particular time, and under particular circumstances; that certain factors render the study atypical; that limited generalization is warranted; etc.). (1990: 30)

However, what Wolcott calls 'this litany of limitations' should be coupled with a stress on what you believe you have achieved. So, as in life, be realistic but don't undersell yourself! This can be in the form of:

a conservative closing statement that reviews succinctly what has been attempted, what has been learned, and what new questions have been raised. (1990: 56)

Wolcott's helpful suggestion is, in my view, somewhat undermined by his use of the adjective 'conservative'. Beware of employing so much caution that you bore the reader! If you can effectively show why you have been stimulated, then you are much more likely to stimulate your audience.

Stimulation requires an active imagination. And, in science, it is theory which feeds the imagination.

Theory has been extensively discussed in the first three parts of this volume. Here I want to suggest a practical sense of theorizing which can help in writing an effective final chapter.

Theorizing as Thinking Through Data

21.5 An imaginative conclusion will move on from the careful description and analysis of your earlier chapters to a stimulating but critical view of the overall implications of your research. Without this, your research may amount to no more than a set of descriptions of data achieved by some mechanical use of a method.

Since much qualitative research works inductively, generating and testing hypotheses during data analysis, your final chapter is often the best place to present theoretical linkages and speculations. As Pertti Alasuutari comments, in qualitative data analysis:

> One preferably starts directly from empirical examples, develops the questions by discussing them, and gradually leads the reader into interpretations of the material and to more general implications of the results. If one feels like discussing and constructing them, the best position for grand theoretical models is *in the final page*. (1995: 183, my emphasis)

Grounded theory is a term used to describe a way of inducing theoretically based generalizations from qualitative data. However, it is crucial that, if grounded theory is your 'thing', you use it imaginatively rather than as a label to dress up a largely pedestrian study (see Charmaz, 2006).

As I argue in Chapter 16, some grounded theory studies fall short of imagination. This possibility is recognized in a leading text on grounded theory:

> It is entirely possible to complete a grounded theory study, or any study, yet not produce findings that are significant. If the researcher simply follows the grounded theory procedures/canons without imagination or insight into what the data are reflecting – because he or she fails to see what they are really saying except in terms of trivial or well-known phenomena – then the published findings can be judged as failing on this criterion [i.e. of being significant]. (Strauss and Corbin, 1990: 256)

The final chapter is likely to be the place where your examiners will discover whether your theoretical pretensions are, as implied by Strauss and Corbin, merely mechanical. But, if theory must never be mere window-dressing, this does not mean that theory is ultimately more important than research. Theory without data is empty; data without theory say nothing.

This reciprocal relationship between theory and data is well captured by Coffey and Atkinson:

> Data are there to think with and to think about ... We should bring to them the full range of intellectual resources, derived from theoretical perspectives, substantive traditions, research literature and other sources ... [this means] that methods of data collection and data analysis do not make sense when treated in an intellectual vacuum and divorced from more general and fundamental disciplinary frameworks. (1996: 153)

The problem is that you may become so immersed in your highly specific research topic that you are ill-prepared to step back and to think about what Coffey and Atkinson call 'more general and fundamental disciplinary frameworks'. You can give your research this broader perspective by forcing yourself to think about how what you have discovered may relate to broader issues than your original research topic. In this way, a very narrow topic may be related to much broader social processes. As we saw in Chapter 16, this was how Mary Douglas's anthropological study of an African tribe took us from a very narrow issue (how the Lele perceive the pangolin) to a very broad social process (how societies respond to anomalous entities).

In this way, argue Coffey and Atkinson: 'qualitative data, analyzed with close attention to detail, understood in terms of their internal patterns and forms, should be used to develop theoretical ideas about social processes and cultural forms that have relevance *beyond these data themselves*' (1996: 163, my emphasis).

 ■ **Attempt Exercise 21.2** ■

Writing for Audiences

21.6 A continuing message of this book is that, like any form of writing, writing a research report should always be framed for particular audiences. Drawing on this insight, many of my PhD students have organized their concluding chapters in terms of the different audiences who might be interested in their research.

Take the case of Moira Kelly's research on how her respondents describe the death of a spouse (discussed in Chapter 3). Her concluding chapter describes what her findings imply for four different audiences: methodologists, theorists, people with a substantive interest in the sociology of health and illness, and health policy makers.

One useful exercise to get you thinking about how to proceed in this way is simply to list all the possible audiences for your research. When I used this exercise recently with students doing business PhDs at the Helsinki School of Economics, the following audiences were noted:

- disciplinary (e.g. management, organization studies, marketing)

- methodological (e.g. case study researchers, interviewers)

- practitioners (e.g. managers, entrepreneurs, marketers)
- the general public (e.g. clients, consumers, politicians).

Such a list of your likely audiences should give you a good idea of how you could structure an effective concluding chapter. But don't just guess what will most interest your audiences! Show your findings to groups drawn from each audience and find out what is relevant to them (see Chapter 27 for further discussion of audiences for research).

■ Attempt Exercise 21.3 ■

Why Your Final Chapter Can Be Fun

21.7 It may surprise you to think that writing your concluding chapter can be fun. Having struggled to reach the end of your data chapters, you may already be exhausted and tempted to try to get away with a short concluding summary. After all, you feel, what more can I add?

I have good news for you! Until your final chapter, you have had to be highly disciplined. Not only have you had to stick to the point, you also (I hope) have had to stick closely to your data. Your only respite has been your footnotes. Used properly, footnotes are the place for asides and barbed comments (never the place for references).

But, if footnotes can be fun, so can your concluding chapter. For this is the place where caution temporarily should go out of the window and lateral thinking should rule. Here is the place to make broader links, eschewing the narrow focus found in the rest of your thesis. Here 'off-the-wall' comments ('from left field' as they say in baseball) are not only allowable but welcome. At last, perhaps, here is a space for you to reveal your true colours – providing that you recognize that such self-expression has always to be recipient designed for an audience.

■ LINK ■

For a comparison of the concluding chapters of 45 PhD dissertations, go to:

www.computing.dcu.ie/~nmcmahon/essays/planning_a_thesis.html

Concluding Remarks

21.8 Let me make an obvious point: when you have finished your final chapter, it is time to submit your thesis. Yes I know research reports can always be improved and the beauty of word processing is that the mechanical aspects of revision are quite simple. But how long do you want to stay a student? Providing your supervisor is supportive, isn't it better to submit right now? Even if your examiners require changes, at least your rewrites will have a pragmatic focus.

Being a perfectionist sounds like a nice identity. As Howard Becker has commented:

> Getting it out the door is not the only thing people value. A lot of important work in a lot of fields has been done with little regard for whether it ever got out the door. Scholars and artists, especially, believe that if they wait long enough they may find a more comprehensive and logical way to say what they think. (1986: 123)

However, Becker also makes us aware that rewriting can be the alibi for the persistent waverer. By contrast, he tells us:

> I like to get it out the door. Although I like to rewrite and tinker with organization and wording, I soon either put work aside as not ready to be written or get it into a form to go out the door. (1986: 124)

After a long period of study, do you really want to 'put work aside'? Follow your supervisor's advice (providing (s)he is not a ditherer!) and get your work 'out the door'!

KEY POINTS

You should never write a summary as your concluding chapter. Instead, your final chapter must help the reader to decide what to make of your dissertation. This should explain:

- the relation between the work done, the original research questions, previous work discussed in the literature review chapter, and any new work appearing since the study began

- anything you would do differently now

- implications for policy and practice

- further research that might follow from your findings, methods or concepts

- the limitations of your own study.

Above all, your final chapter should stimulate your readers by:

- showing how theories have helped you think through your data

- addressing each of the audiences who might be interested in your work.

■ ■ Further Reading ■

Estelle Phillips and Derek Pugh's *How To Get a PhD* (fourth edition, Open University Press, 2005: Ch. 6) is the best British account of the practical issues involved in concluding a research dissertation. On using theory to develop your conclusions, see:

Kathy Charmaz's *Constructing Grounded Theory* (Sage, 2006: Ch. 6); Pertti Alasuutari's *Researching Culture: Qualitative Method and Cultural Studies* (Sage, 1995: Ch. 13); Jennifer Mason's *Qualitative Researching* (Sage, 1996: Ch. 7); Amanda Coffey and Paul Atkinson's *Making Sense of Qualitative Data* (Sage, 1996: Ch. 6).

 ■ **Exercise 21.1**

Get into the habit of keeping files on each of the issues below (taken from Table 21.1):

- the relation between your present work and your original research questions

- anything you would do differently now

- implications for policy and practice

- further research that might follow from your findings, methods or concepts

- the limitations of your own study.

At regular intervals, attempt to write a summary of what you can currently say about each of these issues.

 ■ **Exercise 21.2**

As this chapter has argued:

> Data are there to think with and to think about ... [this means] that methods of data collection and data analysis do not make sense when treated in an intellectual vacuum and divorced from more general and fundamental disciplinary frameworks. (Coffey and Atkinson, 1996: 153)

Find one or two recent journal articles which you think are important and show why they are relevant to your dissertation.

 ■ **Exercise 21.3**

Make a list of the different audiences who might be interested in your research (e.g. disciplinary, methodological, practitioners, general public).

Now work out how you could write a final chapter which framed the contribution of your research for each of these audiences.

Part Five
Getting Support

Contents

Writing a research dissertation can be a lonely activity. In Part Five, I address ways of getting support for your work. Chapter 22 discusses your relationship with your supervisor. In Chapter 23, I examine how to get feedback about your research from the wider community.

Making Good Use of Your Supervisor

Chapter Objectives

By the end of this chapter you will be able to:

- Recognize the problems that can happen in supervision and know how to overcome them.

- Know what to expect from your supervisor.

- Know what your supervisor expects from you.

Introduction

22.1 Over the past 30 years, around 30 students have completed their PhDs under my supervision. I don't know the exact number because the hard disk on my PC crashed not long ago and I lost my CV (a lesson to all of us about the need to back up files!).

I am sure that some students have been happier than others about my supervision. Equally, the enjoyment I derived from the supervision experience varied. In the best cases, the student's work would so stimulate me that I seemed to come up with lots of bright ideas and sparks would fly. On other occasions, I felt quite stupid, bereft of good ideas – maybe, I have to admit, even a little bored.

I like to think that the quality of my supervisions improved over the years as I became more experienced and also more selective about which students I chose to supervise. Towards the end of my career, I simply refused to take on anybody who I had not supervised for their MA. That way, I could ensure that my new PhD students had already learned the way I liked (them) to work.

Now my supervisions are limited to one-off meetings during my PhD workshops in Scandinavian, French, Sri Lankan and Tanzanian universities with business, sociology, social policy and community medicine students. The students simply send me a brief summary of their research and a few questions which I try to answer. I hope to stimulate them but, of course, a lot will depend on whether any new ideas will work (or even be appropriate) in their home university and discipline.

In this chapter, I want to put my experience to work for you.

The chapter is organized in the following sections:

- supervision horror stories (it may be good to frighten you at the start!)

- student and supervisor expectations

- early stages of supervision

- later stages of supervision

- standards of good practice.

Supervision Horror Stories

22.2 The British academic and novelist Malcolm Bradbury (1988) has written about 'the three-meeting supervisor'. The first meeting is when this character informs you about which topic you will study. Three years pass before the next meeting which happens when you deliver your dissertation. The third and final meeting takes place after a telephone call from your supervisor to tell you that he has lost your thesis!

Of course, this story has a farcical element. However, like all good farce, there is an element of truth in it. Back in the 1960s, PhD supervision in many British universities had something of this feel about it – as my own experience as a student demonstrates.

Unfortunately, even today, all is not sweetness and light in the supervision stakes. In Table 22.1 you will find a few horror stories adapted from the 'Higher Education' section of *The Guardian*, a British newspaper, between 2001 and 2003.

I hope that these horror stories do not accord with even the slightest aspect of your own experience. If you are just starting out, let me reassure you that, at least at the present time, such happenings are exceptional, not least because supervisors are usually better trained and are monitored by their departments. Such stories do, however, underline an important point: when writing a dissertation, a bad outcome usually indicates bad supervision.

TIP

Claire Maxwell has suggested some key questions to ask a prospective supervisor:

- **How will you be able to support me if your area of expertise is not fully related to my own research?**

- **How many students have you supervised?**

- **How do you see your role as supervisor?**

- **What can I expect, e.g. likely number of supervisions in my first year? (quoted by Churchill and Sanders, 2007: 35)**

TABLE 22.1 Supervision horror stories

- Everything that could possibly have gone wrong, has gone wrong. My supervisor was a bully and I quarrelled with him. We eventually fell out over working arrangements: I was chastised for arriving late in the mornings, though I often worked till 9 p.m. I began to suffer from anxiety and depression. I took time off, which only made matters worse
- I was within sight of finishing my PhD when my supervisor changed universities. I was isolated and left to plough on alone with my research. Not that I now saw much less of my supervisor. We had not been on speaking terms for some time and I can't even remember the last time we had a supervision
- Our department has a very high staff turnover, with most professors leaving in a year or two. I went through three supervisors, each one worse than the last. After my second supervisor left, during my third year, I got someone who knew nothing about my research area. All three supervisors have tried to steer my research towards a topic that they were personally interested in. With each change, there were miscommunications and political manoeuvring to ensure they would not be blamed for lack of progress on my part
- My supervisor encouraged me to undertake teaching responsibilities, and I ended up leading some of his courses. Off the record, he was sympathetic to my heavy teaching load, but during progress committee meetings he would blame me for too much time spent preparing lectures when I should have been concentrating on research
- My worst experience, and the one that caused me to leave the university, was a personal one. I got engaged and my supervisor said I could return home to get married if I handed in a first draft of my thesis by April. But then my supervisor changed and my next one refused to give me a leave of absence. I was told the decision was 'in my best interests'
- I told my supervisor I wanted to complain about his supervision, only to be told: 'You can make a complaint but you won't have a future in science'
- The department's idea was, if you are not brilliant, get out
- My experience has taught me that most academics have forgotten what it is like to wonder if one would ever actually do research, or to wonder just how research is done, or to not appreciate how large a contribution needs to be so as to be judged original and how one may go about doing it
- My supervisor restricted his written comments to 'super', 'well done' and 'perhaps re-work this paragraph'

Source: adapted from *The Guardian, Higher Education*, 25 September 2001, 23 October 2001, 18 March 2003

Later we will consider standards of good practice. But first let us consider what students and supervisors expect of each other.

Student and Supervisor Expectations

22.3 Estelle Phillips chose as her PhD topic 'the PhD as a learning process'. Some of her findings are reported in Phillips and Pugh (1994). Although her data were obtained in the UK, I have no reason to think that they do not, in general terms, apply elsewhere.

TABLE 22.2 Students' expectations of supervisors

- To supervise
- To read work well in advance
- To be available when needed
- To be friendly, open and supportive
- To be constructively critical
- To have a good knowledge of the student's research area
- To be interested/excited by the topic
- To help the student get a good job afterwards

Source: adapted from Pugh and Phillips, 1994: Ch. 11

TABLE 22.3 Supervisors' expectations of students

- To work independently
- To not usually submit first drafts
- To be available for 'regular' meetings
- To be honest about their progress
- To follow advice
- To be excited about their work
- To be able to surprise the supervisor
- To be fun to be with

Source: adapted from Pugh and Phillips, 1994: Ch. 8

Table 22.2 sets out Phillips's findings about the expectations of PhD students. All the student expectations shown in the table seem quite reasonable to me. If you do not feel that your supervisor is meeting such expectations, it is worth raising your concerns at an early stage.

However, you should also know that your supervisor will have certain expectations about you. A good guide to how the land lies in this area is found in Table 22.3.

I suspect that Table 22.3 will contain some items that you may never have thought about. But, yes, it is true that supervisors expect you to be fun to be with. Most want to be stimulated by and, indeed, to learn from their students.

━━━━━━━━━━━━━━━ LINK ━━━━━━━━━━━━━━━

For a discussion of what to expect from your supervisor go to:

www.city.ac.uk/resstud/dps/research_student_supervision_agreement.doc

Such expectations may, of course, be quite different from your experience. I now consider how your expectations can be converted into (good) practice.

The Early Stages

22.4 The first few months of working towards a PhD are crucial. If you fail to make a good start, it may be very difficult to retrieve the situation at a later point. Here are some points to think about:

- *Choosing a supervisor.* Ideally, you should choose someone whose approach and interests gel with your own. This may be someone whose work you have read or, better still, whose courses you have taken. Alternatively, try to get a look at completed dissertations supervised by this person. Try to avoid simply being allocated a supervisor. Also try to establish beforehand whether your potential supervisor is planning any long trips abroad or other career moves.

- *Do you need joint supervision?* Where your work covers more than one area, it can make sense to have two supervisors. However, tread warily! Not infrequently, joint supervision means that each supervisor will assume that the other is taking care of you. So make sure that there is planning so that you don't fall between the cracks.

- *Combining the PhD with being an RA or a TA.* Sometimes you will be expected to do some research for your supervisor or teaching within your department. If so, again make sure that there is a clear agreement about the extent of this work and the support that you can expect.

- *Getting early direction.* In the early stages, you should expect a lot of support. You should not be fobbed off with a reading list and an appointment in three months' time! Instead, you might expect weekly meetings, based on small tasks, to build your confidence and give you a sense of direction.

- *Being informed.* Right at the start of your studies, you should expect to be properly inducted with regard to your department's research training programme and to your rights and responsibilities as a student.

TIP

It helps to think about how you can use a supervision session most effectively. For instance, work out beforehand what you hope to get out of it and make sure you clarify what is expected before your next supervision (further details on this are provided by Churchill and Sanders, 2007: 183).

The Later Stages

22.5 After the first crucial three to six months, your supervisor should gradually wean you from total dependence. As you become more confident and independent, your supervisor should encourage you to believe that you know more about your topic than (s)he does. At these later stages, the following issues become important:

- *Shaping your writing in a professional manner.* Your supervisor should help you move your style of writing to the kind expected in the journals in your field. For instance, this may mean encouraging you to cut down the kind of tedious literature reviews you wrote as an undergraduate and to use concepts 'economically'. A few concepts (even just one) applied to your data are generally much more productive than data analysis that is all over the place.

- *Self-confidence.* To be economical in this way, you need self-confidence, and this is what your supervisor should provide. Where appropriate, you should also be told that your work is 'up to standard' for the degree you are seeking.

- *Setting deadlines.* Deadlines and targets can be a source of neurosis for students. However, without them, I guarantee you will be lost. Therefore, at the end of each supervision, you should expect to set a reasonable target and agree a date by which it can be reached.

- *Working with other students.* You should not be confined to your relationship with your supervisor. Expect to be advised about relevant conferences and websites. You will also meet other students during your research training. Find out which ones have similar topics to yours or are working with similar concepts and/or data. Then organize discussions with them. Even better, ask your supervisor to set up data sessions with other students that (s)he is supervising.

- *Learning 'tricks'.* Based on a long career of supervision, the American ethnographer Howard Becker (1998) has suggested a number of useful 'tricks' that supervisors can employ for your benefit. As he puts it: 'a trick is a specific operation that shows a way around some common difficulty, suggests a procedure that solves relatively easily what would otherwise seem an intractable and persistent problem' (1998: 4). (For some of these tricks, try Exercise 22.1.)

- *Advising on publications.* Towards the later stages of your work, your supervisor should be a good source of advice about which journals are appropriate for submission of some of your work and about how to organize your presentation for such a setting (see Chapter 26).

- *Giving you a 'mock' viva.* Finally, it is entirely reasonable to expect PhD supervisors to provide a practice dry run for the oral examination (see Chapter 25).

Much of the support that your supervisor can give you should be facilitated by an institutional structure within your department which encourages good practice. I conclude this chapter by discussing such practice.

Standards of Good Practice

22.6 As a research student, you have a right to expect the following institutional structures. Although different formats will apply in different disciplines and countries, what follows seems to me to be a minimum requirement.

- An induction session in which research training is explained and you get to meet new and existing research students

- A graduate committee with an identified and accessible chairperson.

- A handbook of expected practice for the supervision and training of research students. This handbook should set out training requirements and the rights and responsibilities of research students. It should also explain what to do if you want to change supervisors or if you have a problem that you cannot sort out between you.

- Written memos to be agreed after each supervision.

- Annual reports agreed between supervisor and student. These to be submitted for review by the graduate committee of your department.

■ LINK ■

For a discussion of how drawing up a 'contract' can be a basis for supervision, go to:

www.lancs.ac.uk/celt/celtweb/files/SimonFelton.pdf

Concluding Remarks

22.7 The number of students registered for courses involving a research dissertation has increased hugely over the past few decades. One good consequence of this has been that supervision has increasingly become recognized as a professional skill which requires proper training and monitoring.

Of course, getting a PhD, or even an MA, should never be achieved via any methods resembling factory mass production. I hope that there will always be a place for inspiration and lateral thinking. But such features of intellectual achievement should not be a substitute for an institutional structure that offers proper student support and guidance. Let us hope that Bradbury's three-meeting supervisor is a thing of the past!

- Some students have terrible experiences of supervision. By understanding what produced these 'horror stories', you can try to avoid them happening in your case.

- It is not unreasonable to have a set of clear expectations about the support and advice which your supervisor can offer (and to know what to do if these expectations are not met).

- Supervisors have a set of expectations about you too. Know what they are and try to meet them.

- Your department should have structures of training and of monitoring supervision which offer you the support you need.

■ ■ Further Reading ■

Howard S. Becker's book *Tricks of the Trade* (University of Chicago Press, 1998) is a beautifully written account of a lifetime of helping research students to think critically. It is appropriate for both MA and PhD students. For PhD students, Phillips and Pugh's *How To Get a PhD* (fourth edition, Open University Press, 2005) is a goldmine of practical advice. Another useful guide is Churchill and Sanders's, *Getting Your PhD* (Sage, 2007: especially Ch. 15).

■ Exercise 22.1

Here are a few activities which you might ask your supervisor to think about doing with you (adapted from Becker, 1998):

1 Offering a snap characterization of your work which you can, if you wish, deny and thereby be helped to get a better understanding of what you *are* doing.

2 Challenging any generalization that you come up with by asking 'Or else what?' You will then probably find that something you thought impossible (about your topic) happens all the time.

3 Cutting through purely theoretical characterizations of your work by giving you a limited task which asks you to begin from one situation or datum and then to theorize through it.

|23|

Getting Feedback

Chapter Objectives

By the end of this chapter, you will be able to:

- Understand the importance of feedback on your work.

- Recognize and organize opportunities for feedback.

- Understand the nature and importance of shaping your work with an audience in mind.

Introduction

23.1 Analysing research data and writing up our findings are never solitary activities – although this is certainly how they can seem as we labour in front of our PC screen in the small hours. In practice, researching involves entering a series of social relationships. These include supervisor with supervisee; student with student; student with members of the wider academic community; and student researcher with research subjects in the **field**.

As we saw in the previous chapter, such relationships need not just be viewed as potential or real sources of 'trouble'. Instead, they can and should be treated as important sources of insight into how well we are practising our research skills. Effective feedback is an essential resource for effective research. As two psychologists have put it:

> Adults learn best in situations where they can practise and receive feedback, in a controlled, non-threatening environment. So a good principle to aim for is: no procedure, technique, skill, etc., which is relevant for your thesis project should be exercised by you there for the first time. (Phillips and Pugh, 1994: 52)

Non-threatening feedback can also work if your writing seems to have dried up. 'Writer's block' is something we all experience from time to time. So don't despair.

If you can't face feedback, I have found that a complete break for a week or two usually works (for more discussion of writer's block, including solutions, see Ward, 2002: 96–100).

In this chapter, I will discuss three means of obtaining feedback on your research:

- writing draft papers

- giving oral presentations

- reporting back to the people you study.

Writing

23.2 Delivering papers on agreed topics at regular intervals to your supervisor is the standard university method of working towards a final piece of assessed research. Constructive feedback from your supervisor can encourage you to scale new heights. By contrast, where that feedback is minimal or even destructive, your whole enterprise may be threatened.

So, if your supervisor is very critical of a paper you have submitted, you should expect to be told how you can improve your work and to be offered practical suggestions rather than woolly generalities. For instance, being told to think 'more critically' or to 'be more rigorous' is unlikely to be helpful. By contrast, specific advice about a new topic or a different way of pursuing one of your existing topics should give you some useful impetus (see Chapter 22).

But your supervisor is not the only person who can give you useful feedback on your work. Your fellow students, particularly those working in similar areas, should be delighted to provide feedback. In return, they will learn about related work and have the opportunity to test their ideas out on you.

Sometimes you will need to take the initiative to form such a student support group. Sometimes, as I do with my own research students, your supervisor will organize workshops for students working on similar topics or using similar methods to present and discuss their data. In either case, you will gain the opportunity to test out preliminary ideas in a non-threatening environment.

Writing for your peers or speaking to them is wonderful practice at getting the correct level for your thesis. The great temptation in writing up what may be your first piece of serious research is to try to achieve an exalted level of technical language in order to impress your supervisor. Unfortunately, this attempt often leads to clumsy jargon which clouds your real line of argument and confuses your readers.

In discussing writing a thesis, Wolcott wisely addresses this issue of the level at which you write:

> Write for your peers. Pitch the level of discussion to an audience of readers who do *not* know what you are talking about. Write your dissertation with fellow graduate students in mind, not your learned committee members. Address your subsequent studies to the many who do not know, not the few who do. (1990: 47)

Contrary to appearances, Wolcott's injunction 'write for your peers' is *not* a cop-out. For many researchers, the most difficult thing to do is to write with such clarity that their work can be understood and enjoyed by non-specialists. Indeed, for some researchers, the hardest thing to grasp is that writing should always be tailored for as big an audience as possible. This means thinking about what that audience may know already and expect from you. Naturally, the same applies to oral presentations.

| TIP |

Writing can also include creating your own *website*. This helps to give your work a public profile and make contact with research participants or other stakeholders (see Phelps et al., 2007: 123–5).

LINK

For information about creating a website, go to:

http:/www.sagepub.co.uk/phelps

 ■ **Attempt Exercise 23.1**

Speaking

23.3
Take every opportunity to present your research at any setting that arises from an informal meeting of fellow students, to interested laypersons, to a scientific conference in your field. Watch out for 'calls for papers' and regularly inspect the sites where they are posted.

When you speak, tailor what you say for your audience. Early on in my academic career, I was invited to talk about my research at a seminar at another university. I had already grasped the need to tailor my remarks to a particular audience and so had prepared two different talks on my research. One was highly specialist, the other was non-technical. Unfortunately, on that day, I had misjudged my audience and brought with me what turned out to be the 'wrong' talk. Faced with a heavyweight group of specialists, I was insufficiently experienced to improvise and was forced to present the 'Mickey Mouse' version of my research!

I still cringe when I think of this experience. However, although I failed embarrassingly on this occasion, I had at least been partially correct in my method: I had attempted to prepare a talk with an audience in mind (see Cryer, 1996: 133). Just as we design our ordinary conversation for particular recipients (children, colleagues, etc.) so **recipient design** should always go into your oral presentations. As Gary Marx comments:

> Try to remember who you are talking to, and the differential stake you and your audience have in your topic. Gear your talk to your audience. (1997: 107)

Following Marx, you will clearly want to give different kinds of talks to experts in your field, to participants in your research or to general but non-specialist academic audiences. For each audience, you should choose a particular focus (e.g. theory, method, substance) and an appropriate vocabulary (see Strauss and Corbin, 1990: 226–9).

However, such recipient design is insufficient. Many have had the experience of speakers who only have time to get through a small part of their material or who overrun and then use up the time for questions. Good time management is a quality possessed by effective speakers. If you think you will not have the confidence to improvise to beat the clock, then it is wise to try out your talk beforehand with a watch nearby.

The usual experience is that it takes far longer to get through your material than you expect. So take the minimum of material in one file and, if necessary, bring a 'comfort blanket' of additional material in another file to use in the unlikely event that you need it. Bear in mind the wise advice below if time runs out:

> If you find that you are running out of time, do not speed up. The best approach is normally to abort the presentation of your findings … and move straight to your conclusion. (Watts and White, 2000: 445)

Finally, never read out a talk (2000: 444). I know having your full script is a source of comfort. As Gary Marx puts it:

> The fact that you get only one chance with a live audience may engender anxiety and the written word is a safety net. But it has a pre-determined, even stultifying quality, which denies the fluid and interactive nature of live presentations. (1997: 107)

But think back to all those boring talks you have attended in which the speaker had his head buried in his script. Do you really want to inflict that on your audience? More positively: 'You will never know what verbal riffs lie buried in your consciousness if you always cling to the security of the page' (1997: 107). Instead, try to present your points through uncluttered visual aids (PowerPoint slides, overhead projector transparencies). Where you need to provide extensive material (e.g. long transcripts or tables), then distribute handouts.

Above all, try to grab your audience's attention at the outset. There are many tactics you can use at the start of your talk:

- Begin with a puzzle, as in a detective novel.

- Start with an interesting data extract.

- Start with a personal anecdote about how you became interested in your topic.

- If you are not the first speaker, try to relate what you have to say to what has gone before.

- Tell an apposite witty story (but only if this comes naturally!).

Finally, remember that both you and your audience need to get something out of your talk. Avoid the temptation just to give talks based on finished chapters approved by your supervisor. If the chapter is really finished, what will you gain from audience feedback? A much better strategy is to send such a chapter to a journal (see Chapter 26).

Instead, try to use early work or working papers. Here the responses of your audience may well help you to see a way ahead. As Watts and White suggest:

> in giving ... conference papers from your project ... present incomplete work. In this way, you can seek guidance from your audience and receive stimulus for thinking about the next stage of your work ... In your paper you can direct the discussion towards particular issues on which you would like other people's opinions by drawing attention to them. (2000: 443)

 Attempt Exercise 23.2

Let me now illustrate these suggestions by some examples.

The Art of Presenting Research

23.4 You will have gathered already that, in my view, even the most astounding research can sound dull if not properly presented. Unfortunately, this does not mean that poor research can be retrieved if you are a witty and effective speaker because you will eventually be found out! But effective presentation of good research should be your aim.

To flesh out the bare bones of my argument, I have taken extracts from my reports on presentations by research students completing their first year in my own department. Naturally, to protect the innocent, I have given these students false names.

Each student was allowed up to 15 minutes to make a presentation to their fellow students on their progress during their first year and their plans for further work. A further 10–15 minutes were allowed for questions.

Just as we tend to preface 'bad' news by 'good' news when giving information in everyday life, let me begin by some reports of 'good' practice. Below are some extracts from my reports.

Good practice

23.4.1 Pat's talk was lively and clear, making good use of overhead transparencies. She responded well to questions. This was a well-focused presentation, lively and interesting. The handouts were helpful and the video data were fascinating.

Derek gave a lively and relatively clear talk, making good use of his overheads. He spoke with some humour, gave an 'agenda' to his audience and explained the difficulties of his project.

This was highly professional with good use of overheads and handouts. She used her limited time well, managing to accommodate her talk to the 15 minutes available. Her answers to questions were most effective, giving me the impression that she is already in control of her topic.

This was a well-focused presentation, lively and interesting. Sasha's answers to questions were good. Overall, I felt this was an excellent presentation based upon a piece of highly professional research. My views seem to be shared by the students present, one of whom remarked that she hoped her own work would be up to this standard in a year or two's time. Congratulations are due to Sasha and her supervisor.

This was a well-focused presentation, lively and interesting and improvised rather than read. The audience's attention was held throughout. Ray's answers to questions were thoughtful and helpful. In particular, he was able to establish a dialogue with students from a range of backgrounds and was at home responding to theoretical and practical issues. I especially liked Ray's attempt to derive methodological issues from the data analysis. There were time problems from which Ray will have learned something. Overall, I felt this was an excellent presentation based upon a piece of highly professional research.

Summary

The following qualities impressed me in these presentations:

- liveliness
- not reading out a prepared text
- recipient design for the audience
- clarity
- effective visual aids
- humour
- explaining your agenda
- not minimizing difficulties

- good time management

- good response to questions.

Now for the 'bad' news!

Bad practice

23.4.2 John was hampered by lack of preparation. His extempore presentation may have confused the audience by introducing too many topics and using too many examples which were not fully explained. His habit of turning his back on the audience to address the (empty) blackboard was unfortunate and, I am afraid, added to the impression of a non-user-friendly talk. This is disappointing given John's breadth of reading and excellent understanding. I think the only solution is to work harder on trying to relate his concerns to the interests and knowledge of particular audiences.

This was an interesting presentation. However, Bruce made things a little difficult for his audience by offering no initial agenda, by not using overheads and by having only one copy of some data extracts. He also ran into time problems which better planning could have obviated. This presentation will have given him the opportunity in future talks to think through his objectives and to offer more user-friendly methods.

This was probably too specialized for a mixed audience, although Larry responded clearly to questions. The talk came to life when Larry departed from his script and gave an example (about record production) which brought to life the abstract concepts he was using. I strongly suggest that, in future, for such an audience, he uses more overheads and then talks around them, using such helpful examples.

Summary

The following qualities concerned me in this group of presentations:

- lack of preparation

- too much material

- not looking at the audience

- lack of recipient design

- no agenda

- no visual aids

- poor time planning.

Most presentations fell between these extremes. I will conclude with some 'mixed' examples.

Mixed practice

23.4.3 Maurice gave a clear presentation using handouts and overheads. His delivery was good and appropriately recipient designed. My only suggestion is that he should try to type overheads and put less material on each sheet.

Stan had taken the trouble to prepare handouts. However, it was disappointing that, perhaps because of time limitations, he did not have time to analyse the data provided. I would also have preferred him not to read out a paper. It is important to practise the art of talking using only a few props, like overheads, if you want to keep the audience's attention. Nonetheless, Stan's talk was well organized and timed and he offered interesting responses to questions, showing a pleasing ability to admit when he was unsure about a point.

As in an earlier talk, this was very professional, combining good overheads with helpful illustrations from video and audiotape. My only suggestion is that it might be helpful to give more guidance to the audience about the issues to look for before offering data.

Mary gave a confident, well-prepared talk based on a handout. She responded well to questions. My only suggestion is that, in future, she works more on integrating any handout with her talk so that her audience are not confused about what they should be attending to at any one time.

Yoko had thoughtfully prepared overheads but these were not as clearly related to her talk as they might have been. Although it is always very difficult to speak in one's second language, it is difficult to keep the audience's attention when a paper is read. In my view, it is worth Yoko practising at giving presentations simply by talking around her overheads. One way to do this would be to focus on the nice examples of texts and images that she presented and to pull out her analytic and methodological points from them rather than to attempt to read a rather abstract paper.

Julia gave an engaging, lively presentation which held her audience throughout. I liked her explanation of the personal reasons behind her research and admired her ability to speak without notes. Her overheads were useful. Some minor suggestions for future talks: remember to avoid turning away from the audience to look at the screen; think about using other information sources as well as overheads (handouts of definitions would have been useful); try out a talk beforehand so as to avoid time problems.

This was an interesting talk which carefully explained the issues involved for a non-specialist audience. Jane's account of how her interest in the topic 'coalesced' was very useful as were her overhead transparencies (although, in future, she should note that these can be most effectively used by covering up parts of each slide until she gets on to them). She ran into some time difficulties and this is also something to watch in future. Overall, a good account of a fascinating topic.

Luigi made a good attempt to explain a difficult topic to a non-specialist audience. I particularly liked his account of his intellectual and personal background. In future, he will need to pay more attention to explaining his concepts and to time constraints.

Summary

The following were the 'good' and 'bad' news about these presentations:

- using visual aids *but* these are poorly prepared
- well organized *but* reading out a prepared text
- giving examples of data *but* not explaining what to look for
- using handouts *but* not integrating them in the talk
- explaining the background *but* not explaining the concepts
- using overheads *but* turning away to look at them or having too much material on the screen.

Good and bad presentations

23.4.4 Take your oral presentations as seriously as you do your writing. Speak to your audience with clarity, logic, vigour, and examples that will grab them. (Marx, 1997: 107)

In Table 23.1 I set out what we have learnt about making an effective oral presentation of your research.

TABLE 23.1 Giving a talk: problems and solutions

Problem	Solution
Losing your audience	Recipient design
Overrunning	Don't prepare too much material
Boring your audience	Use visual aids: don't read out a talk

> **TIP**
>
> Giving a talk is one way of *networking,* allowing you to make links with people both inside and outside your own department or university (see Churchill and Sanders, 2007: 95–104).

Feedback from the People You Study

23.5

The bottom line for practitioners is always, 'So what?' A qualitative researcher's efforts to convey nonjudgmental objectivity is likely to be perceived instead as a typical academic cop-out. (Wolcott, 1990: 59)

Not least among the people who can offer you feedback are the persons you have studied. Let me give you an example from my research on HIV-test counselling (Silverman, 1997). In order to address practitioners' 'So what?' question, I held many workshops for AIDS counsellors – including many who had not participated in the study. To give some idea of the extent of this 'feedback', between 1989 and 1994 I ran four workshops on the research for counsellors in London (two at hospitals, one at Goldsmiths College and one at The Royal Society of Medicine), as well as three workshops in Australian centres, three in Trinidad and Tobago, and one each in the USA, Finland and Sweden. In addition, each participating centre was given a detailed report of our findings.

At these workshops, we did not shield behind a posture of scientific neutrality. But neither did we seek to instruct counsellors about their presumed 'failings'. Instead, we spoke about the ways in which our data showed that all communication formats and techniques had mixed consequences. We then invited our audience to discuss, in the light of their own priorities and resources, the implications for their practice. Moreover, when asked, we were not afraid to suggest possible practical options.

In my judgement, these meetings were successful, not least because our detailed transcripts showed features of counselling of which the practitioners themselves were often unaware. Often such features revealed how these people were cleverer than they had realized in following their own theoretical precepts and achieving their desired goals.

However, less experienced researchers may be more hesitant to offer feedback to practitioners and organizations. In this case, Wolcott (1990) offers the three ideas set out in Table 23.2.

TABLE 23.2 Giving feedback to service providers

1 Ask for the kind of additional information required for you to make a recommendation (e.g. what exactly is the organization trying to accomplish?)
2 Identify seeming paradoxes in the pursuit of goals (e.g. doctors who encourage their patients to communicate and to make choices may be the most autocratic)
3 Identify alternatives to current practices and offer to assess these

Source: Wolcott, 1990: 60

Of course, not all qualitative research is concerned with service providers such as organizations or professional practitioners. What kind of feedback is possible when you are studying non-work-related activities?

It is important that you try to offer feedback to all parties that are under study. So, if your target is, say, the activities of counsellors or doctors, then you have not finished your task without offering some degree of feedback to their clients or patients. One way to do this is to utilize already existing networks, for example patients' or community groups. So during my work on paediatric clinics in the early 1980s, I spoke to parents' groups at heart and diabetic clinics. For instance, I used my clinic data to show mothers of diabetic adolescents that their feelings of inadequacy were common and probably inevitable given the guilt-provoking character of diabetic control and the usual rebelliousness of teenagers.

Where it is difficult to identity such community groups, you may well find that participants in a study welcome receiving their own transcript of relevant data. For instance, a transcript of your own medical interview may work as a useful reminder of what the doctor said. And a transcript of a life-history interview may give a respondent a tangible autobiographical record.

Obviously, you can learn from such feedback to participants. But, in what sense if at all, can feedback be used to validate your research findings?

Some writers are very gung-ho about the use of feedback as a validation exercise. For instance, Reason and Rowan (1981) criticize researchers who are fearful of 'contaminating their data with the experience of the subject'. On the contrary, they argue, good research goes back to the subjects with the tentative results, and refines them in the light of the subjects' reactions.

This is just what Michael Bloor (1978; 1983) attempted in his research on doctors' decision making. Bloor (1978) discusses three procedures which attempt respondent validation:

1 The researcher seeks to predict members' classifications in actual situations of their use (see Frake, 1964).

2 The researcher prepares hypothetical cases and predicts respondents' responses to them (see also Frake, 1964).

3 The researcher provides respondents with a research report and records their reactions to it.

In his study of doctors' decision making in tonsillectomy cases, Bloor used method 3. However, he had reservations about his surgeons' reactions to his report. It was not clear that they were very interested in findings that were not focused on their day-to-day concerns. Bloor's worries have been very effectively taken up by Fielding and Fielding (1986) (respondent validation is also criticized by Bryman, 1988: 78–9). The Fieldings concede that subjects being studied may have additional knowledge, especially about the context of their actions. However, they conclude:

there is no reason to assume that members have privileged status as commentators on their actions ... such feedback cannot be taken as direct validation or refutation of the observer's inferences. Rather such processes of so-called 'validation' should be treated as yet another source of data and insight. (1986: 43)

I can only add that, if feedback is a highly problematic way of validating research, this does *not* mean that it should be ignored as a way of maintaining contact with subjects in the field. However, this issue should not be *confused* with the validation of research findings.

As Bloor points out, the problematic research status of this activity need not mean that attempts at respondent validation have *no* value. They do generate further data which, while not validating the research report, often suggests interesting paths for further analysis (Bloor, 1983: 172).

Concluding Remarks

23.6
Why does feedback matter? There are two reasons why student researchers write papers and give talks:

- to pass some internal assessment
- to get feedback on their work.

Unfortunately, in our assessment-obsessed university culture, students tend to forget that feedback from peers and advanced scholars serves both normative and instrumental ends.

In a normative sense, offering material for feedback recognizes the community of scholars to which scientific work aspires. Instrumentally, such feedback will undoubtedly help improve your thesis. If you have long-term academic ambitions, it will also help you to improve your teaching skills and, perhaps, to plant the seeds of future journal articles!

So never think of this as 'mere' presentation or the 'boring' bit that has to be got through in order to get your degree. If we cannot use our research to engage others in dialogue, maybe we are in the wrong business!

KEY POINTS

Effective feedback is an essential resource for effective research. This chapter has discussed two means of obtaining feedback on your research:

- by writing draft papers
- by giving oral presentations.

Writing should always be tailored for as big an audience as possible, and this means thinking about what that audience may know already and expect from you. So get feedback from fellow students as well as your supervisor and think about setting up your own website.

Attempt to give a talk on your research before you write a final version for your thesis. In this talk, avoid losing your audience (recipient design your presentation); set a time limit and never overrun; and use visual aids to avoid boring your audience.

Harry Wolcott's little book *Writing Up Qualitative Research* (third edition, Sage, 2009) covers feedback as well as many other practical matters. Pat Cryer's *The Research Student's Guide to Success* (third edition, Open University Press, 2006: Ch. 13) and the chapter by Watts and White in Dawn Burton's edited book *Research Training for Social Scientists* (Sage, 2000: 437–55) discuss giving presentations on your work. Phelps, Fisher and Ellis's *Organizing and Managing Your Research* (Sage, 2007: 263–8) provides very useful advice on using software in your presentations. Gary Marx's paper 'Of methods and manners for aspiring sociologists: 37 moral imperatives' (*The American Sociologist*, Spring 1997: 102–25) is a lively and extremely helpful guide for the apprentice researcher.

 ■ **Exercise 23.1** ■

Select two articles in your area of research from two different journals or books. Work out the audience(s) at which the journal or book is aimed by reading the journal's 'instructions to contributors' or a book's introductory editorial chapter. Then go through the steps below:

1 In what way does each article attempt to reach its appropriate audience(s)?

2 How successful is it in doing so?

3 How could it be improved to appeal more to its target audience(s)?

 ■ **Exercise 23.2** ■

Get invited to give a talk on your research and make sure that somebody attends who is prepared to give you good feedback. Plan the talk to reach the audience (e.g. students, staff, laypeople or a mixture). Having given your talk, ask the attending person for feedback on the success of your talk. Then consider how you could have improved the talk to appeal more to its target audience.

Part Six
Review

Contents

This part of the book contains just one chapter. It sums up many of the themes discussed in this work by seeking to describe how to do 'effective' qualitative research.

24

Effective Qualitative Research

┌─── **Chapter Objectives** ───────────────────────────┐

This chapter offers an opportunity to revise the main themes of this book.

└──┘

Introduction _____

24.1 In this chapter, I want to pull together the different threads that have run through this book. Throughout, I have encouraged you to distinguish relatively easy activities from the really tough ones and to concentrate your efforts on the latter. For instance, writing a literature review should be relatively easy for any graduate student (see Chapter 18). Equally, obtaining your data does not need to be too difficult if you follow some of my suggestions in Chapters 13–16.

By contrast, the really tough issues tend to concern data analysis. This area is discussed in detail in Part Three of this book. In this short chapter, I want to provide a snapshot of the issues involved in the form of four rules to encourage effective qualitative research. Here are the rules:

- Keep it simple
- Take advantage of using qualitative data
- Avoid drowning in data
- Avoid 'journalistic' questions and answers.

I will now review each rule in turn. But one word of warning: none of us can escape our intellectual biography. I have been influenced in more ways than I can realize by my training and experience as (one kind of) a sociologist. Therefore, if any of my rules look a little odd in the light of your own discipline, please discuss it further with your supervisor. Even if you differ, at least you will have a point of departure!

Keep It Simple

24.2 In Chapter 6, I identified a 'kitchen sink' mentality. Kitchen-sinkers attempt to study very broad problems, using many concepts and methods as well as large sets of data. Unfortunately, such a wide-ranging approach is unlikely to impress examiners and often will prevent you finishing your study.

In doing student research, simplicity is not a drawback but a necessity. Here are some ways to keep it simple:

- Narrow down your research problem (Chapter 6 offers a number of ways to do this).

- Use one **model** only (e.g. positivist, emotionalist or constructionist).

- Use **concepts** which fit your model.

- Avoid multiple methods or, if you must use them, make sure they fit your model and research problem.

- Analyse a small dataset (you can always add comparative data later – if you have time).

- Recognize that the comparative method can be used within a small dataset.

Take Advantage of Using Qualitative Data

24.3 Sometimes students elect to use qualitative methods because (they feel) they are not very good at statistics. This is not unreasonable (assuming they are right). However, qualitative methods are not appropriate for every research problem. In Chapter 2, I reviewed a number of student research projects which could more effectively be researched using quantitative rather than qualitative methods. The former approach could focus on the relation between a set of **variables**, and employ **reliable**, standardized **operational definitions** of the variables studied. It could also work effectively with large datasets to establish correlations between these variables.

I showed how it is possible to transform such projects into workable qualitative research studies, for instance by avoiding the language of 'variables' and studying if participants themselves use concepts like 'effectiveness', when and how they do so and with what local consequences. These are interesting research issues but they take us on a very different path to that envisaged by the original formulation of the research problem.

Considerations of this nature suggest that, if we want to do qualitative research, there are a set of strategies to *avoid*:

- Beginning with variables that you wish to relate.

- Beginning with problems that are already defined by members of society (e.g. social or administrative problems).

- Making assumptions about where things take place (e.g. is 'efficiency' a state of mind, a set of behaviours or a common-sense category employed in many different ways?).

- Searching for explanations: 'why' questions are usually best answered by quantitative methods.

- Working with **normative** assumptions (e.g. what is 'effective' communication?) and with prior versions of policy outputs.

However, we do not need to be entirely negative. Taking advantage of qualitative data means using some or all of the following strategies:

- Asking 'how', 'what' and 'when' and delaying (or avoiding) 'why' questions.

- Wherever possible (and it usually is possible) working with **naturally occurring data** (see Chapter 8).

- Studying the categories actually employed by participants (and when and how they are used – and with what effect).

- Studying what is unremarkable, the routine and the 'ordinary'.

- Recognizing the interconnectedness of categories and of activities so that we always study how each is laminated upon another (see Chapter 4).

Avoid Drowning in Data

24.4 A continuing argument of this book is that, if you delay your data analysis until your final year of study, you are courting disaster. By contrast, I have suggested:

- Start data analysis from day 1; if you have no data, then work with other people's data or use other publicly available material, e.g. texts of all kinds (see Chapter 13).

- One case is usually enough, providing you use internal comparisons (see Chapter 9); delay other cases and then try to sample theoretically.

- Keep to small targets; recognize that the student researcher is usually an apprentice and that learning from your mistakes is a key to success.

- Write above your PC the following motto: 'The point of qualitative research is to say a lot about a little'!

Avoid Journalism

24.5 Journalism is a trade which, like any other, has good and bad features. In suggesting that you should avoid journalism, I do not mean to disparage what journalists do; I simply wish to underline that qualitative research should not be the same thing as journalism.

Given the daily nature of most newspapers, journalists tend to focus on unusual, out of the ordinary events which often involve 'celebrities'. When they describe public rather than private issues, the journalistic focus, quite understandably, is on social problems as generally conceived, e.g. the economy, health policy, international relations.

My message to student researchers is: let journalists get on with what they do best. Your job is somewhat different. Now is the time to display the skills which you have learnt through years of training. As an apprentice qualitative researcher, your research will differ from most journalism in the following ways:

- You will formulate a problem in a particular way, e.g. you will not begin from a social problem but will often seek to study something that is quite unremarkable, even 'obvious' to participants.

- Your data analysis will not rely on identifying gripping or spectacular stories; instead it will reveal the various ways in which apparently 'obvious' phenomena are put together.

- You will not rush to conclusions even when you have some compelling instances; instead, you will carefully sift all the evidence, actively seeking out **deviant cases**.

- You will employ the analytical resources of your discipline, working with your data in the context of a coherent **model** and set of concepts.

- You will unashamedly theorize about situations and events, but this will not serve as mere window-dressing (see Chapters 7 and 16); instead you will theorize with your data and build new theories.

 ■ Attempt Exercise 24.1 ■

Concluding Remarks

24.6
This book has been written to offer you practical ways to cope with some of the doubts that affect most novice qualitative researchers. Apart from what I can offer, I suggest that you turn to your fellow students. If you do so, I guarantee that nearly all of them will have been through many of the same doubts about their research and their capacity to do it.

If you remain worried that you do not have enough data, my message has been that you probably have too may! If you believe that your work is not particularly original, I ask: 'Who is?' Just turning to some of the more pedestrian journal articles in your field should convince you of my argument.

As I suggest in Chapter 5, success in student qualitative research can be achieved by demonstrating that you are a 'professional'. We all know that professions contain people with varying capacities. So the bar you face is really quite low. However, I hope you will aspire to something higher!

┌─ **KEY POINTS** ┌

Effective qualitative research can be undertaken on the basis of following these four rules:

- Keep it simple.

- Take advantage of what qualitative data can offer.

- Avoid drowning in data.

- Avoid 'journalistic' questions and answers.

■ ■ Further Reading ■

In my book *A Very Short, Fairly Interesting, Reasonably Cheap Book about Qualitative Research* (Sage, 2007), I expand on many of the themes contained in this chapter.

 ■ Exercise 24.1 ■

Select any qualitative research report in your field. Now proceed as follows:

1   Apply to it the four rules discussed in this chapter.

2   Consider how well the report measures up in relation to each rule.

3   How could the research be improved?

4   Do any of the rules need to be modified or overturned in the light of your example?

Part Seven
The Aftermath

Contents

The four chapters in Part Seven consider the aftermath of a finished research project. Depending on the level of your work, this may involve an oral examination, the possibility of getting a publication and, perhaps, getting a job. Whatever its level, a good research report is always for particular audiences.

25

Surviving an Oral Examination

By the end of this chapter, you will be able to:

- **Be reassured that truly horrific PhD orals are very rare.**

- **Take practical steps to prepare for your oral.**

- **Know how to function effectively at the oral.**

Introduction

25.1 When you have finished a BA or an MA thesis, your task is done. Your research paper will now be marked but its grading will be out of your hands. However, if you are working for a PhD, one further task may await you – your oral examination or 'viva'. Here you will be expected to 'defend' your dissertation, and your performance will have an impact on the outcome. For instance, in Britain, your dissertation may pass but you may be required to retake your viva if your performance is weak.

How this viva is conducted will vary between different universities and countries. In Britain, a specialist external examiner will be appointed from outside your university and will take the lead in questioning you. Further questions will come from an internal examiner who may be rather less of a specialist in your area.

In other countries, many more academics may be able to question you. In the Nordic countries, for instance, an 'opponent' will be appointed from outside your university to interrogate you. The viva will be a public affair with members of the audience able to ask questions.

In Scandinavia, your faculty committee are usually passive observers of the dialogue between opponent and candidate. By contrast, in North America, you will face a faculty committee, all of whom may ask you questions. The character of this dialogue can vary considerably, as an American text points out:

> **The defense ranges from a congenial ritual in which the student publicly presents his or her findings to an assemblage of receptive 'colleagues', to a more excruciating**

examination of the quality of the dissertation and grilling of the candidate by an unsympathetic faculty committee. (Rudestam and Newton, 1992: 142)

To use Rudestam and Newton's word, what can a 'grilling' look like? In this chapter, I set out to prepare you for a PhD oral examination, reviewing the mechanics of the oral and its possible outcomes (including the subsequent revisions to your thesis that your examiners may require.

This chapter seeks to offer sensible reassurance. As I will later demonstrate, the viva is not usually quite as awful as you may suspect. However, to prepare you for the worst, I begin with some 'horror' stories.

Viva Horror Stories

25.2 One student reported a common fear about an impending viva: 'When I went into that room, I was scared – what if they ask me something I do not know, what if they said: this a PhD, you have got to be joking.' Such fears are normal; terrible experiences are much rarer. Rowena Murray (2003: 2) provides four examples of pretty nasty vivas:

- A nine-hour viva.
- Aggressive examiners who seem to want to break down the candidate.
- The candidate forgetting everything she knew ('blank mind syndrome').
- Examiner(s) deciding that you have made a serious error; but this is based on a misunderstanding about what you have said and you don't have the confidence to correct them.

I have a horror story of my own to add. Back in the 1960s, I felt confident about submitting my thesis because of the praise it had received from my PhD supervisors. I was totally unprepared when the external examiner was very critical of what I had written. Indeed, I later learned that it was only my strong defence at the viva that saved me from being failed! Fortunately, the external gave me several pages of suggestions and I managed to put together a revised version which was passed 12 months later.

By now, you may be thoroughly scared. But take comfort. Supervision is much better monitored nowadays and is usually much more effective than the example of the three-meeting supervisor described in Chapter 22. There are also a number of practical steps you can take beforehand to prepare for your examination.

Preparing for Your Oral

25.3 Examiners need time to read your dissertation. They also have busy diaries. So you will probably have from one to three months between submission of your dissertation and your oral examination. How should you spend this time?

TABLE 25.1   Preparing for a PhD oral examination

- Revise your thesis, particularly the concluding chapter
- Prepare a list of points you want to get across
- Be ready to explain and to defend any changes to your original research question
- Read up recent work in your field
- Find out about your external/internal examiners' work
- Practise with others in a mock viva

In the immediate weeks after submission, with the viva some way away, you deserve some time off after your exertions – although a break is usually an unavailable luxury to students in full-time employment. However, as your viva approaches, some preparation is very useful. This preparation can take a number of forms, as set out in Table 25.1.

> **TIP**
>
> **Phillips and Pugh (1994) suggest that summarizing in a sentence each page of your finished thesis can be a very effective way of revising your thesis so that you will be fully in touch with it on the big day. You should then use this summary as a basis for deciding which points you want to try to get across at the examination.**

Now is a good time to research your examiners' own work. Reading their latest papers may well inform you about the likely slant of their questions and, perhaps, allow you to look for any links between your work and theirs – although you should first consult your supervisor about whether this is appropriate.

 ■ **Attempt Exercise 25.1** ▬▬▬▬▬▬

Finally, try to find some fellow students or some friendly faculty members prepared to simulate an oral examination.

Doing the Oral

25.4 Remember that, as a result of your research, you are now a specialist. This probably means that you now know more about your topic than your examiners. As Kjell Rudestam and Rae Newton put it:

> In the best of cases, the oral defense is an opportunity to think about and articulate the implications of your study [for] your own discipline and to be challenged by your committee to claim your right to sit among them as an acknowledged expert in your field of study. (1992: 142)

Being 'an acknowledged expert' is not a licence to wallow in jargon. On the contrary, part of one's expertise is the ability to explain your work in a straightforward way and to make links with the work of others.

So, at the viva, be ready to summarize your main research problem, the contribution of your research and how you would do anything differently. Remember that the oral examination is not a test of memory. So you will be allowed to refer to the text of your thesis as necessary.

 ■ **Attempt Exercise 25.2**

In order to add more substance to these points, in Section 25.7 I have given some details of a Swedish PhD dissertation that I examined a few years ago. While the questions I asked, as opponent, were of course tied to that particular dissertation, I believe that they give you some flavour of the kind of concerns, both specific and general, that examiners raise at PhD vivas.

As Clive Seale (personal correspondence) has pointed out, the skills you need at an oral examination are not dissimilar to those you need at a job interview (see Chapter 28). In both situations, it helps to be fairly assertive while respecting the knowledge and experience of your interviewer. Table 25.2 offers some tips for your oral along these lines.

TABLE 25.2 Tips for the oral examination

- Always say if you have not understood a question; if so, ask for more clarification
- Avoid one-word or one-sentence answers even if the question is a 'closed' one. Use the questions as opportunities to get your point across by making links between the questions and the things you want to say
- Avoid overlong answers which drift far from the original question
- After a sentence or two, ask if you are on the right track and if your examiners want to know more
- Refer to the list of points you want to get across when your examiners ask whether there is anything they have not covered
- Ask your supervisor to make notes of questions and answers. This will be of considerable use if you have to revise your thesis and/or intend to publish any of it

Source: adapted in part from Seale, personal correspondence

■ LINK ■

For information and brief advice on PhD oral examinations in UK universities, go to:

http://port.igrs.sas.ac.uk/viva.htm

Outcomes

25.5 In most British universities, the possible outcomes of a PhD viva are as follows (see also Phillips and Pugh, 1994: 142–5):

- the immediate award of the PhD – often subject to certain minor corrections or amendments

- the requirement that you put right some weaknesses identified in writing by the examiners (the 'yes, but ...' result, as Phillips and Pugh, 1994: 143 put it) and a given time period (up to two years) to do this

- a pass on the dissertation but a fail on the viva, with an opportunity to resit the latter after a period of up to a year

- the examiners deem your dissertation inadequate and cannot see any way in which it can be successfully revised but offer you the lower award of an MPhil degree

- an outright fail with no possibility of resubmission and no offer of any lower degree.

Despite your worst fears, an outright fail is rare. This is less to do with the goodwill of your examiners than with the fact that your supervisors are unlikely to recommend submission unless they believe that your work has a reasonable chance of passing – although the recent punitive policy of the British Economic and Social Research Council on departments whose funded students take more than four years to submit may change this.

If you are passed, remember to ask for advice about what parts of your thesis might be publishable, how you should revise or shorten them, and which journals might be the best place to submit them. Now go out and celebrate!

Revising Your Thesis after the Oral

25.6 In Britain, it is common practice for examiners to require some rewriting of your thesis before they will pass it. After discussion with your supervisor, they will allow you a certain period to undertake such revision – normally between 6 and 18 months.

Following Seale (personal correspondence), I suggest some tips to follow when you are revising a thesis for re-examination:

- Make a list of the main criticisms.

- Make sure your revisions address all of these criticisms.

- Resubmit your thesis together with a separate sheet of paper identifying what you understand the criticisms to have been, how you have addressed them, and the page numbers where this has been done.

A Case Study

25.7 An example of an actual PhD oral may be helpful. Vesa Leppanen completed his thesis at the Department of Sociology at Lund University in Sweden. I was appointed his opponent because Vesa's work was related to mine analytically (we both use **conversation analysis**, CA) and substantively (we both had studied communication between healthcare professionals and patients).

A brief summary of the dissertation

25.7.1 Vesa had researched encounters between Swedish district nurses and their elderly patients. These encounters may take place in the patient's home or at a clinic. Their primary clinical purpose is to perform routine tasks like measuring blood pressure or giving injections. Naturally, in the course of these encounters, other matters arise – from the patient raising a problem to the nurse giving advice. A sample of 32 consultations provided just over 10 hours of videotaped and transcribed nurse–patient interaction – half at primary care centres, half in patients' homes. Standard CA notation was used on the audio. Non-verbal activities were reported by descriptions placed immediately above the place in the transcript where they occurred.

Four principal topics were studied:

- how tests and treatments were discussed

- patients' presentations of their concerns

- how nurses delivered test results to patients

- advice-giving about health behaviours.

The dissertation concluded with a summary of the research findings, a practical recommendation that such data are highly appropriate in training nurses (and many other practitioners) and some general implications for future research. Its call for the study of apparently non-problematic research settings and data is a useful reminder that, when studying the world around us, we should seek to discover the extraordinary in the ordinary (Silverman, 2007: Ch.1).

My questions

25.7.2

- What do you see as the main contribution of your research?

- Would you do anything differently now?

- Chapter 4 on tests and treatments reads as very 'descriptive' based on one extended case. Would you agree? How could it be improved?

- On p. 88, you explain that this chapter serves as a background to the other three data chapters. But can you say anything more, e.g. do you ever meet resistance to tests? Do nurses ever have to work at getting permission?

Several detailed questions on the data analysis follow. Now come some more general points:

- Your data are equally drawn from home and clinic. Why did you decide not to systematically compare these different environments? Don't clinic and home provide very different resources? (I mention one of my past PhDs, by Maura Hunt, who had looked at the problems that community nurses may face in beginning their work in the patient's home, as well as the work of Anssi Peräkylä on doctors' use of X-rays and scans in the clinic to 'prove' diagnoses to patients.)

- Your use of the video material. The only detailed treatment is on pp. 213–18 where you use the video to show how the nurse underlines advice by abandoning other tasks, gazing at the patient and waving a pill bottle. Why is there relatively little use of the video data elsewhere? (I discuss various possible uses of the video data that might have strengthened the dissertation.)

- Have you ever given feedback to the nurses you studied? If not, why not?

- Your only practical conclusion is about the relevance of this kind of detailed research for professional training. I entirely agree about this, but isn't there more that you can say?

- Your discussion of the analytic implications of your research is not very specific. How does your work advance other well-known (named) studies and findings?

My concluding remarks

25.7.3 This is a fascinating, detailed and orderly study of great analytic interest. I learned a lot from reading it. It is also an exemplary case from which nurses and beginning researchers could learn a great deal about the value of the analytic mentality of CA.

The highlights for me were:

1 Various parts of Chapter 5 First, the most detailed treatment on institutional data about the positioning and functioning of the question: 'How are you?' Second, the discussion about how patients achieve recipiency for the statement of their concerns.

2 Parts of Chapter 7. In particular, nurses finding the right position to deliver advice.

3 An unusually lively methods (or procedures) chapter. This provides a nice natural history of your research and a lovely account of the ethnographic work that preceded it.

4 Throughout, I liked your non-partisan spirit and open-mindedness, particularly towards the judicious combination of CA and **ethnography** (e.g. p. 44).

Of course, as you show, bad news is usually delayed. So, in this case too. But I really have only two reservations. The first is your somewhat limited use of your video data. The second is your underplaying of the practical relevance of your research.

But, in the context of such a well-crafted dissertation, these are quibbles. I eagerly encourage you to turn parts of your thesis into journal articles. In particular:

• Your excellent summary and critique of much nursing research (pp. 21–7) is highly relevant in a field riddled by crude positivism and emotionalism.

• Your account of patients' skills in positioning their statement of their concerns is highly original and publishable (pp. 110–28). Perhaps it could be combined with your comparison (pp. 130–1) with Jefferson on everyday trouble-telling, or perhaps the latter could be a separate article.

• Parts of Chapter 7 where you compare your findings with other (named) research on advice-giving and advice-reception are also highly publishable.

The outcome

25.7.4 I am pleased to say Vesa was awarded his PhD by his local committee. When I last heard, Dr Leppanen had a teaching position at a Swedish university and his supervisor, Professor Ann-Mari Sellerberg, had obtained a substantial research grant for the two of them to study telephone counselling by community nurses.

General implications

25.7.5

1 My two first questions are pretty standard for PhD vivas, namely: 'What do you see as the main contribution of your research?' and 'Would you do anything differently now?' It pays to prepare your answers to such questions!

2 Prepare for constructive criticism of your analysis, e.g. 'Chapter 4 on tests and treatments reads as very "descriptive" based on one extended case. Would you agree?' This is a nice example of a question where a one-word answer would have been inappropriate. The right strategy here might be to agree in part but point to counter-evidence elsewhere.

3   Prepare to defend your methods and selection of cases, e.g. 'Your data are equally drawn from home and clinic. Why did you decide not to systematically compare these different environments?' If possible, explain the advantages of not making such a comparison.

4   Be ready to discuss further the contribution of your research to your discipline and (where relevant) to practitioners and policy makers.

5   Expect your examiners to offer advice about which parts of your thesis may be publishable (see my concluding remarks).

Concluding Remarks

25.8 Although the prospect of a PhD oral is intimidating, horror stories are actually quite rare. Use your revision period to prepare a list of points you want to get across at the examination. Now is also the time to find out about your examiners' own published work. In addition, try to get some practice with others in a mock viva.

At the oral examination, always say if you have not understood a question and, if so, ask for more clarification. Avoid one-word or one-sentence answers even if the question is a 'closed' one. Use the questions as opportunities to get your point across by making links between the questions and the things you want to say. But avoid overlong answers which drift far from the original question. Finally, refer to the list of points you want to get across when your examiners ask whether there is anything they have not covered.

It is also a good idea to ask your supervisor to make notes of questions and answers. This will be of considerable use if you have to revise your thesis and/or intend to publish any of it.

KEY POINTS

There are many ways to prepare for your oral. You can:

- Revise your thesis, particularly the concluding chapter.

- Prepare a list of points you want to get across.

- Be ready to explain and to defend any changes to your original research question.

- Read up recent work in your field.

- Find out about your external/internal examiners' work.

- Practise with others in a mock viva.

(Continued)

(Continued)

At the oral itself:

- Always say if you have not understood a question; if so, ask for more clarification.

- Avoid one-word or one-sentence answers even if the question is a 'closed' one. Use the questions as opportunities to get your point across by making links between the questions and the things you want to say.

- Avoid overlong answers which drift far from the original question.

- Ask if you are on the right track and if your examiners want to know more.

■ ■ Further Reading ■

The most useful guides to preparing for oral examinations are: Pat Cryer's *The Research Student's Guide to Success* (third edition, Open University Press, 2006: Ch. 24); Estelle Phillips and Derek Pugh's *How To Get a PhD* (fourth edition, Open University Press, 2005: Ch. 10); and Harriet Churchill and Teela Sanders's *Getting Your PhD* (Sage, 2007: Ch. 10).

 ■ Exercise 25.1

To find out about your examiners' own published work, read at least one book or journal article by each of them. As you read, make note about the following points:

1 What model of social research (see Chapter 2) is being used? How far does it differ or complement your own? What useful lessons can you learn from these differences or similarities?

2 Are there any theoretical developments, methodological innovations or substantive findings that relate to your own work? If so, how can you bring these out in the oral? If not, how can you demonstrate respect for your examiner's approach while standing up for your own?

3 Examine the writing style in this material. How different is it from your own? What can you learn from these differences (or similarities)? For example, do these simply reflect the differing demands of (say) a scholarly journal and a research dissertation, or are there basic differences of temperament and outlook?

 ■ Exercise 25.2

When you have completed your revision, ask your supervisor or a couple of your fellow students who are familiar with your research to give you a mock oral examination. Following Table 25.2 and using your prepared list of points that you want to get across, try out your skills in answering their questions.

26

Getting Published

┌─── **Chapter Objectives** ┐

By the end of this chapter, you will be able to:

- Recognize the realistic publishing opportunities for your work.

- Think about the appropriate place to submit your research.

- Work out how to turn your research into something more appropriate for a journal.

- Understand how journal editors and reviewers make decisions about which papers to publish.

- Treat a decision of 'revise' and 'resubmit' as a golden opportunity.

Introduction

26.1 When you have finished your research study, you usually want its readership to extend beyond your supervisor and examiners. Don't expect that any more than a handful of people will borrow it from your university library. So, if you want your work to be disseminated, you must publish it.

Publishing your research is work. It will take a good deal of effort, time, and patience. It may take you well over one year to publish a manuscript in a refereed journal. The revisions may at times become tedious and far less exciting than the data collection and writing of initial drafts. Reviewers and editors may ask you to change your work significantly and, by the end, your original idea from the first draft may be barely recognizable in the published manuscript. Why then, you might ask, should anyone subject himself or herself to this process?

The simple answer is that you don't have to publish. Most MA dissertations never go beyond their examiners. Moreover, a considerable number of PhD students complete their dissertations and never publish anything. However, you have to realize the consequences of this choice. Without publications, your job opportunities will most likely be limited.

The discouraging news is that, in these competitive times, it is unlikely that an MA or even a PhD will get you a university post. Certainly, a good reference from your supervisor and other examiners will help. And any teaching experience you have gained is also a plus mark if you are seeking a regular academic post. However, if you have not yet made it into print, faced with people with PhDs and several publications, you may not even make it on to the shortlist – at least at prestigious institutions.

Obviously, your desire to publish is only the first part of the battle. In what follows, I discuss four key practical matters:

- the backstage politics to publishing

- the strategic choices available to you

- understanding the kinds of paper that appeal to the editors of academic journals

- knowing how to write an effective journal article.

The Backstage Politics of Publishing

26.2 In an ideal world, the peer-refereed system of publishing would allow for scholarly writing to be judged purely on the basis of its merits. And for the most part, that is precisely what happens. Yet it would be naive not to acknowledge the presence of other extraneous influences in the world of publishing. A good discussion of such factors is offered in Frank E. Hagan's 'The essentials of research methods in criminal justice and criminology' (2005: 10–11). Hagan reviews three fascinating, but somewhat disheartening, articles that point to the backstage politics of publishing. The first is Robert Merton's (1968) essay on 'The Matthew effect in science'. Merton's use of the term was inspired by the following biblical passage: 'For unto everyone that hath shall be given, and he shall have abundance: but from him that hath not shall be taken away that which he hath' (Matthew 13: 11–12).

In the context of publishing, the Matthew effect implies that previously published authors, especially those who do not challenge canonical views of their discipline, are more likely to be published again. In Merton's words:

> **The Matthew effect consists in the accruing of greater increments of recognition for particular scientific contributions to scientists of considerable repute and the withholding of such recognition from scientists who have not yet made their mark. (1986: 58)**

Hagan notes that the Matthew effect was tested by Michael Mahoney (1977), who asked 75 reviewers of a psychology journal to evaluate five different versions of a fictitious article. The five versions (a) supported pure behaviourism, (b) negated behaviourism, (c) offered no findings, and (d) and (e) reported mixed results. Of the five versions, the one that agreed with the basic tenets of behaviourism (i.e. did not challenge an established doctrine) was accepted by all the assigned reviewers. On the other hand, the version challenging behaviourism was rejected and highly criticized for its methodology. According to Hagan, in a similar study by Douglas Peters and Stephen Ceci (1982), the researchers took 12 previously published articles and resubmitted them to the same journals where they had appeared two years earlier. The titles were changed and the names of the authors and their universities were altered, the latter being done to reflect less prestigious institutions. Three of the resubmissions were recognized, but eight of the remaining nine were rejected. While the study itself was published, one of the authors nearly lost tenure because of it (Hagan, 2005: 10).

Though such events may be isolated and your work may very well be judged on its own merits, practicality and realism dictate that novice authors maintain their associations with their senior mentors to the extent possible. Specifically, it is good practice to establish your publication record by co-authoring papers with a senior scholar in your field. Eventually, your work will be recognized by editors on its own terms, but until then, try to bask in someone else's reflected glory.

Similarly, institutional affiliation seems to play a role in reviewers' evaluations. Therefore, if you are likely to acquire a job in an institution that is less prestigious than the one from which you will receive your PhD, try to earn your first few publications while you are still at your PhD university. That way, you can use that institution's name for your journal submission.

Strategic Choices

26.3 There are three sets of issues here: the medium of publication (usually a book or journal article), the particular outlet chosen (publisher or journal) and the kinds of material that obtain publication. Each of these issues is discussed below.

Books

26.3.1 You may have plans to publish your PhD as a book. But don't count on it! PhDs can be written for a tiny audience – effectively composed of your supervisor, committee or examiners. Before a publisher will even consider publication, they will usually want to know how you plan to revise your thesis to reach a wider audience.

The other thing is that publishers in the new millennium are not actually standing in line to publish (even revised) PhDs. Unless you can find a kind university press, you will discover that publishers are driven by the commercial need to find books that will sell upwards of 5,000 copies. And the sad fact is that even a good research monograph will be unlikely to sell more than 1,000 – an amount that probably will mean that its publisher will actually lose money.

In 1990, it was this situation that made Harry Wolcott (1990) write about how difficult it can be to get your PhD published in entirety. A decade or more later, things are still tougher. Most social science publishers will now only rarely publish research monographs – even by established scholars. So, for most researchers, the answer is to be realistic! Pick out a promising data chapter and rewrite it for a journal.

Choosing a journal

26.3.2 The moral of this story is to plan ahead. So, if your supervisor likes, say, one of your data chapters, discuss with her whether it might not be worth sending it to a journal.

Of course, it is important to find the journal which is likely to be most sympathetic to what you have to say because its audience shares your interests and its editorial policy is favourable to your kind of ideas and/or data.

For example, qualitative researchers should be cautious about journals that expect papers to be written in the standard form of introduction, methods, results and discussion. As Pertti Alasuutari (1995: 180–1) points out, this format is likely to be inappropriate to non-quantitative, inductive studies. Again, not all qualitative journals have the same policy about legitimate approaches and/or adequate datasets. For instance, a paper submitted by one of my students was unexpectedly turned down on the grounds that 'it did not have a big enough dataset'.

So find the right journal. Seek guidance from established academics and look at recent editions of journals they mention. Look out for statements of policy printed in most journals, and note changes of editor and of editorial policy.

Responding to editors' decisions

26.3.3 Once you have submitted, don't be discouraged by a rejection. Most journal articles are rejected or returned with a request for substantial revision. So treat the outcome as a learning experience. Be prepared for challenging comments, and don't expect others to be surprised by requests for revision ('They said what?', Churchill and Sanders, 2007: 90). Wendy Hulko's attempts to publish her dissertation (which used grounded theory) are documented next.

> ### STUDENT EXAMPLES
>
> ### Sometimes Numbers Matter
>
> I used grounded theory methodology for my doctoral research on the relationships between the experiences of older people with dementia and the intersections of 'race', class, ethnicity and gender. My estimated sample size was 12 older people with dementia and their significant others and, through theoretical sampling, I planned to ensure that participants ranged from multiply marginalized to multiply privileged on the basis of their class, gender, 'race' and ethnicity. In order to demonstrate trustworthiness, I used a range of data collection methods (interviews, participant

observation, photography, focus groups), kept a reflexive journal, engaged in both member checking and peer debriefing, used purposive sampling, created an audit trail, and undertook persistent observation.

Believing that I had achieved theoretical saturation, I stopped recruiting participants once I had a diverse sample of eight older people with dementia, with whom I had spent a considerable amount of time over the course of three individual interviews (person with dementia), two to three group observation sessions (person with dementia, his/her significant others, other members of his/her social world), and one joint focus group (persons with dementia and their significant others). Nevertheless, the sample size became the big issue when it came to publishing my research. Moreover, I found that the complexity of grounded theory research does not lend itself well to the 'slicing the salami' approach to publishing.

I had thought I could publish an article on each of the three categories of my grounded theory, yet was unable to parcel them off in this way, as the theoretical complexity became lost, which made the sample size more problematic for the audience. I could not understand the amount of attention being placed on the small n when this was clearly a qualitative study that had met the trustworthiness criteria – the standards for judging qualitative research. In the end, I realized that focusing on the eight older people with dementia with whom I had spent more than 75 hours over a nine-month period of data collection and data analysis was not doing my study sufficient justice, as far as editors and peer reviewers were concerned. I felt that I needed to count the number of data collection points (43), include the more than 50 additional people who participated in the study through the participant observation sessions (and signed consent forms and/or photo release forms), and then distinguish between my primary sample of eight and my secondary sample of 50+. In a sense, this meant playing the numbers game and representing the research differently than I had in my theoretically complex and methodologically dense PhD thesis. However, I did manage to find a way to do so that was honest and did not misrepresent the qualitative nature of the study; for example, I presented the findings (categories or themes) in a purely qualitative fashion (see Hulko, in press), so as to avoid producing a 'quasi-quantitative' representation of qualitative research. [Wendy Hulko, Public Health Sciences, Toronto]

Wendy refused to be discouraged after her paper was initially rejected. She eventually realized that, in return for a submission, you are very likely to get a set of (often detailed) referees' comments upon which you can base a revised submission.

TIP

Treat referees' comments as gold dust. However biased you might think they are, they inform you, in practical detail, of the external audience outside (what may be) your cosy relationship with your supervisor. So now you can see what might be required to make your way in the academic world. If your resubmission is not much better received, you probably have only yourself to blame.

Recognizing the format for a journal article _____

26.3.4 Above all, bear in mind that journal articles (usually around 6,000 words) are often much shorter than data chapters from a PhD. This can make things very difficult for you since, in a shorter space, you must fill in your audience about the overall orientation of your research. So, in writing a journal article, you must, at one and the same time, be highly focused but also provide a proper context.

Easier said than done! How do you write a paper that is likely to be published? And how do you cope with such strict word limits? Don't you need more rather than fewer words to explain the context of your research?

There are four quick solutions to these dilemmas (further advice is provided by Phelps et al., 2007: 276):

- Select a topic which will be the most intriguing to readers of this journal.

- Ensure that this topic can be handled with a limited number of data extracts.

- Provide the appropriate context for your work: for instance, your audience will not need to be reminded about the basic assumptions of research in their area.

- Stick rigidly to the point throughout.

The rest of this chapter will expand upon this advice. Later I will discuss how to focus a journal article within the required word length. Such focus, of course, requires that you have a good sense of what journal editors are looking for. So now I will look in more detail at the criteria used by academic journals to make their decisions.

What Journals Are Looking For _____

26.4 The policy of academic journals may vary by their focus, discipline or audience. As I have already noted, many quantitatively oriented journals expect their articles to have a standard format which assumes that all research has an initial hypothesis and that some form of random sampling will be employed. Equally, journals that seek to appeal to practitioners and other non-specialists will be particularly interested in looking for papers that set out to have this wider appeal.

Despite this degree of variation, my experience suggests that there are several criteria that recur in referees' comments in the kind of qualitative journals to which you might submit a paper. These criteria are set out in Table 26.1.

Table 26.1 indicates what to do if you want your submitted piece to have a reasonable chance of success. It, therefore, implies a series of 'don'ts':

- Don't cite models or approaches if they are mere window-dressing.

- Don't vary the format; announce a clear structure at the start and stick to it.

TABLE 26.1   Evaluation of qualitative articles

1   Goodness of fit between the model chosen and what is actually delivered
2   Internal coherence
3   Showing something 'new' when compared to past work
4   Speaking to the interests of the journal's target audience
5   Clear presentation

Source: adapted from Loseke and Cahill, 2004

- Don't forget that your paper should contribute to an ongoing conversation of scholars in your area.

- Don't defend approaches already familiar to readers of the journal.

Reviewers' Comments

26.5 As well as these general points, it is also useful to have advance warning of the specific kind of criticisms that reviewers make about the submissions they see. Since other people may be quite sensitive about showing you the critical reviews they have received, I have set out below extracts from some of my (usually anonymous) reviews during the past few years. Naturally, I've tried to delete any references that might identify the paper or the author. No doubt I am still going to make myself very unpopular by giving these examples!

To help you follow these comments, I have grouped them as 'good news' and 'bad news'. Each section contains portions of comments about many papers.

Good news

26.5.1

- A fascinating topic with some nice data.

- This is an interesting paper, using theoretically generated analysis on a practically relevant topic.

- This paper deals with an important issue. As presently written, it is highly accessible to practitioners and patients.

- The paper is based on an apparently well-transcribed piece of data.

- The data chosen are very manageable.

- This is a carefully done study and brings out some important practical issues.

- This is a highly ambitious methodological paper. Its claim to originality, I take it, is that several different methods can be combined to shed more light on a text than any one alone. There is considerable insight in the way in which these methods are used.

- This paper discusses some potentially interesting data. It uses an approach which, I presume, will be relatively unfamiliar to readers of the journal. Quite correctly, therefore, the author(s) take up a fair bit of space explaining the approach used.

Bad news

26.5.2 I have grouped these 'bad news' comments under several headings.

Over-Ambition

- I think it currently tries to do too much.

- Unfortunately, the abstract promises much more than is ever delivered.

- So many issues are raised that it is difficult for any to be developed properly. Each would make a separate paper. Given so many issues, it is not surprising that the data analysis is rather thin and not really linked to the literature review.

Over-Generality

- The broad-brush approach adopted here I found frustrating. There is no attempt to ground the argument in a piece of data.

Unanalytic

- For the most part, the observations on the data strike me as commonsensical. To develop this paper further, much more use needs to be made of the vast literature on this subject based on transcripts of this kind.

- The final sentence of the abstract is trite and unnewsworthy.

- The analysis of data only begins more than halfway through the paper and is very thin.

- It hardly analyses its data at all and should be rejected.

- The paper works by assertion. For instance, it simply isn't always the case that [X follows Y].

- Unfortunately, the data analysis is very thin indeed, barely rising above descriptions which are sometimes banal.

Inconsistency

- Methodologically, the approach does not fit the issues that the author wants to address.

Methodological failings

- I found the citation of 'cases' less than convincing. While space constraints always limit the number of data extracts one can use, the paper fails to give any sense that **deviant cases** were analysed and that prior assumptions were in any way tested by the data.

Lack of orginality

- The paper discusses a contentious methodological issue. It is also an issue that has been discussed in a mountain of publications over the last 10 years. Therefore, it is particularly hard to say anything fresh about the topic.

Lack of clarity

- I am unclear about the relevance of the approach used; the presence of several traditional assumptions which sit uneasily with it; and the issue of practical relevance.
- I don't understand the first sentence of the abstract.

Lack of recipient design

- The section on theory is, I feel, inappropriate. Readers who know about this already will be bored, and readers who do not will not want to cope with a theoretical discussion before they get to the data. Much better, then, to introduce the required elements of theory in the course of the data analysis.
- You may lose your international audience by going straight into issues relating to one small country.

I hope that my present readers will not be intimidated by these comments. Please treat them as providing guidance about practices best avoided. However, I try never to be merely negative. Below are some suggestions I have made to authors.

26.5.3 Suggestions

- I would like the paper to be revised to become sharper in focus and to take account of other relevant work.
- You need an introduction setting out the *general* themes. Then an early data extract would whet the reader's appetite.

- I suggest that you submit your revised draft to a native English speaker. Currently, there are multiple infelicities.

- If space allowed, the analysis would also benefit from comparison with one more case.

- The present conclusion combines analytic *descriptions* of the findings and practical recommendations. Instead, I would like to see the practical conclusions separated and the paper's analytic *contribution* clarified.

It may be the case that my own reviewing methods are idiosyncratic and even unfair! If so, I hope you never come across me as a reviewer! However, every reviewer is likely to attend to the word limits of the journal. I now turn to the art of writing a short journal article.

How To Write a Short Journal Article _____

26.6
As already noted, most journals nowadays cap papers at around 6,000 words. Yet no doubt you want to context your research – and you have so many data and so many findings. How can you present your research in such a small frame?

There are three ways to shorten a paper:

- Stick rigidly to the point (e.g. one topic, one case, one theory, one model, one method).

- If you are working within an existing approach or model, don't waste time defending it (reinventing the wheel).

- Consider whether you need all your footnotes. Surely if they are not worthy of being in your main text, you do not need them at all? At this level, you should not need extensive footnotes to demonstrate your academic respectability.

By shortening your paper through such techniques, you can create space to enlarge on what matters. For example:

- focusing on a topic that will intrigue readers of this journal (e.g. one relating to a recent debate)

- demonstrating credibility by combining intensive and extensive methods (e.g. short data extracts and simple tabulations)

- writing a conclusion that displays lateral thinking, for instance by relating your substantive account to a broader area.

Finally, if your paper is still too long, consider splitting it up into different topics appropriate for several journals. Working the same material in a number of different ways is what Gary Marx has called **leverage**. Marx's idea is discussed in the following chapter.

■ Attempt Exercise 26.1

Concluding Remarks

26.7 Publications are good for academic careers. They also can provide an outlet for your key data chapters as well as for beloved draft chapters that you decided were too peripheral to be included in the final version of your thesis.

Getting published depends upon making a number of strategic choices (e.g. book or journal article; which journal to select). There are several ways of improving your chance of getting your paper accepted by a journal. First, 'decide on what you wish to focus. What is your theoretical story?' (Strauss and Corbin, 1990: 246). Second, you need to ask yourself:

> **Do I need this detail in order to maximize the clarity of the analytic discussion, and/or to achieve maximum substantive understanding? (1990: 247)**

Remember that your audience is both bigger than and very different from the small audience for your thesis. So ruthlessly strip out inappropriate references and material and recontext your work. As Harry Wolcott (1990: 51) puts it, when writing a journal article, 'dedissertationalize' your work. Don't expect to get your paper accepted as is. Make use of the referees' comments as helpful encouragements to rewrite a better article!

Finally, you should try to write a compelling argument. Jay Gubrium (personal communication) has suggested that many qualitative data are 'inherently' interesting. Take advantage of this and use the interest that the reader may have in your material to your advantage. Tease, entice and puzzle your readers.

■ LINKS ■

For brief practical advice on publishing qualitative research in management, go to:

http://division.aomonline.org/rm/pratt_files/pratt.htm

For education research, go to:

www.aera.net/uploadedFiles/Publications/Journals/Educational_Researcher/3408/02ERv34n8_Klingner.pdf

For nursing research, go to:

http://findarticles.com/p/articles/mi_m0FSL/is_/ai_81161396

┌─────┐ KEY POINTS ┌─────

There are at least five ways of improving your chances of getting a paper accepted by a journal:

- Find a focus.

- Avoid too much detail.

- Redefine your audience.

- Expect an initial rejection and make use of referees' comments in a second submission.

- Make a compelling case.

■ ■ Further Reading ■

Useful sources on this topic are: Donna Loseke and Spenser Cahill's chapter 'Publishing qualitative manuscripts' in Seale, Gobo, Gubrium and Silverman's (eds) *Qualitative Research Practice* (Sage, 2004); Harry Wolcott's little book *Writing Up Qualitative Research* (second edition, Sage, 2001: Ch. 7); and Nigel Gilbert's chapter 'Writing about social research' in Gilbert's (ed.) *Researching Social Life* (third edition, Sage, 2008, Ch. 21).

 ## ■ Exercise 26.1 ■

Nigel Gilbert (2008) suggests choosing a journal article written by someone else and writing a review of it as if you were the referee. If you need guidance on what to look for, use some of the 'good news' and 'bad news' lines of approach found in this chapter.

Now ask your supervisor to read your review. Use the feedback you get to:

1 Think critically about how you might publish your own work.

2 Invite your supervisor to ask book review editors to send books to you for review in journals (this is one way to get a first step on the publications ladder!).

|27|

Audiences

┌─── **Chapter Objectives** ┌─────

By the end of this chapter you will be able to:

- **Recognize the range of different audiences for social science research.**

- **Know what is involved in tailoring your work to meet audience expectations.**

Introduction

27.1 As I suggested in the previous chapter, getting published is all about designing your writing for a particular audience. In this way, we attempt to tailor our writing for the likely sense-making priorities of our audience. As Amanda Coffey and Paul Atkinson put it:

> Reading is an active process, and no text can have a completely fixed meaning ... when we write – and hence inscribe certain preferred interpretations in our books, dissertations and papers – we do so with an implied audience of readers. (1996: 118)

In this sense, fellow academics are only one of several potential audiences, including policy makers, practitioners and laypeople. Each group will only want to hear about your work if it relates to their needs. These four audiences and their likely expectations are set out in Table 27.1.

The expectations of academic audiences about both written work and oral presentations have already been discussed at length in this book. However, the range of other audiences shown in Table 27.1 may tend to induce despair about the amount of work required to meet their separate expectations and needs. However, there is a simple, easy-to-follow message: good communication requires focus and yet more focus.

The trick is to combine a recognition of the expectations and needs of such audiences with our own active shaping of our materials. The good news is that a little practice may make you adept at working the same material in a range of different ways. In this context, Gary Marx's concept of 'leverage' is very useful. As he puts it:

TABLE 27.1   Audiences and their expectations

Audience	Expectation
Academic colleagues	Theoretical, factual, or methodological insights
Policy makers	Practical information relevant to current policy issues
Practitioners	A theoretical framework for understanding clients better; factual information; practical suggestions for better procedures; reform of existing practices
Lay audiences	New facts; ideas for reform of current practices or policies; guidelines for how to manage better or get better service from practitioners or institutions; assurances that others share their own experience of particular problems in life

Source: adapted from Strauss and Corbin, 1990: 242–3

> Try to leverage your work. The sociological equivalent of a bases-loaded homerun is to take material prepared for a class lecture, deliver it at a professional meeting, publish it in a refereed journal, have it reprinted in an edited collection, use it in a book you write, publish foreign versions and a more popular version and have the work inform a documentary. (1997: 115)

 ■ **Attempt Exercise 27.1**

Marx reminds us of the range of audiences that await the qualitative researcher. In the rest of this chapter, I consider the three non-academic audiences listed in Table 27.1: policy makers, practitioners and lay audiences. How do you fashion what Marx calls 'a popular version' for such audiences?

The Policy-Making Audience

27.2 The idea that social research might influence public policy provides an inspiration for many young social scientists. In most English-speaking countries, the sad truth is that things have never worked in this way.

■ LINK ■

For a recent newspaper article that comments upon this sad truth, go to:

http://www.guardian.co.uk/commentisfree/2008/aug/19/labour

Qualitative research has rarely had much appeal to civil servants and administrators geared to focus on numbers and the 'bottom line'. The one possible exception,

Erving Goffman's (1961) account of the dehumanizing consequences of 'total institutions' in his book *Asylums*, appears merely to have legitimated the cost-cutting frenzy known as 'community care'.

Moreover, it is arguable that number-crunching researchers have fared little better. As Roger Hadley (1987: 100) has pointed out, 'not being heard' is the common experience of Anglo-American social researchers who attempt to influence public policy. Among the reasons for this, Hadley suggests, is that:

> **Research is often commissioned to buy time in the face of public scandal or criticism. This means that: 'the customer's motives for commissioning a research project may not necessarily be directly related to an interest in the topic concerned'. (1987: 101)**

The time lag between commissioning a study and receiving a report may mean that the customer's interests have shifted. Academic researchers who produce unpalatable conclusions can be written off as 'unrealistic' (1987: 102).

Of course, fashions change. At the time of writing, there is some evidence that public bodies may be starting to take qualitative research more seriously. **Focus groups** in particular seem to be 'the flavour of the month', mainly, I think, because they are relatively cheap and quick and give nice 'sound-bites' for politicians and advertisers. However, such changes in fashion do little to affect the natural tendency of policy makers to redefine the meaning of research 'findings'.

I should also add that we often don't help ourselves when we want to influence policy makers.

Our communication failures include:

- putting more effort into collecting data than into analysing their implications

- not being prepared to context what we say in current policy debates while being ready to tell people things they don't want to hear

- not thinking through new or innovative approaches to policy problems based on our research (see Duncan, 2005: 11).

However, as Bloor (2004) has noted, the policy community is not the sole audience for social research.

The Practitioner Audience

> The real opportunities for sociological influence lie closer to the coalface than they do to head office ... [they] lie in relations with practitioners, not with the managers of practice. (Bloor, 2004: 318)

27.3 Taking the example of the sociology of health and illness, Michael Bloor argues that practitioners rather than policy makers are the most reliable and eager audience for social research:

> Sociologists who have conducted research on sociological aspects of health and medicine ... have long been aware that there is a role for sociologists as participants in debates on public policy, but that there are also other audiences for social research, notably audiences of patients and practitioners (clinicians, nurses and other professionals). (2004: 307)

Bloor suggests that qualitative social researchers have a twofold advantage in influencing practitioners. First, they can build upon their research relationships with practitioners in order to discuss practical implications. As he puts it:

> In respect of practitioners who are research subjects, qualitative researchers can call upon their pre-existing research relationships with their research subjects as a resource for ensuring an attentive and even sympathetic response to their research findings. A close personal and working relationship, based on lengthy social contact and built up over weeks and months, is likely to ensure that, not only will practitioner research subjects have a particular interest in the findings (because of the identity of the researcher as much as a particular interest in the research topic), but also practitioner research subjects may be willing to devote an unusual amount of time and effort to discussions of the findings. (2004: 320–1)

Second, even if you have no research relationship with them, the detail and transparency of some qualitative data have an appeal to many practitioners:

> the qualitative researcher has the advantage that the research methods allow rich descriptions of everyday practice which allow practitioner audiences imaginatively to juxtapose their own everyday practices with the research description. There is therefore an opportunity for practitioners to make evaluative judgments about their own practices and experiment with the adoption of new approaches described in the research findings. (2004: 321)

Bloor's argument resonates with my own recent experience with AIDS counsellors. Like most practitioners, counsellors will be suspicious that outside researchers intend to be judgemental. It helps to reassure them that you do not believe in any normative, decontextualized theory of *good* communication. For further discussion of how to approach such practitioner audiences, see Silverman (2006: 349–76; 2007: 85–118).

The Lay Audience

27.4 There are at least four reasons why qualitative researchers may become involved in reporting back to lay audiences:

1 to answer questions asked by your respondents
2 to 'check' provisional findings

3   to provide 'feedback' to organizations and relevant groups

4   to provide information for the media.

Points 1 and 2 have been considered in Chapter 23. In particular, you should refer to Section 23.5 on feedback as a validation exercise for point 2.

Feedback to lay audiences is usually set up because of your own desire to 'give something back' to the general public. The format should vary according to whether your audience are members of an established organization or simply a group of people with similar interests or concerns.

As an example, following my own research on hospital clinics for children, I gave a talk to the parents' association at one of the hospitals I had studied. In this talk, following Table 27.1, I discussed new facts from my research about doctor–parent communication. I also examined the implications of my findings for reform of current hospital practices. Subsequently, I was invited to write a short piece on my research for the newsletter of a British organization called the Patients' Association. In this article, I covered much the same ground as well as adding guidelines for how to manage better or get better service from hospitals that treat sick children. Finally, I spoke at a meeting of parents of children with diabetes. My aim here was to stress what my research had revealed about the painful dilemmas experienced by such parents. In this way, I sought to assure them that others share their own experience and that there is no need for them to reproach themselves.

It is most unlikely, however, that you will be able to reach a general audience through the mass media. Nearly all social science goes unreported by such media. Needless to say, this is even more true of student research.

However, perhaps your research has provided you with a story that you want to tell to the general public. How should you go about this?

Perhaps a journalist approaches you after a talk you have given. More likely, a media contact will begin after you have studied the kind of topics covered by broadcast programmes and by particular journalists and approached the 'right' person.

For example, when my book on communication in hospital clinics was published (Silverman, 1987), I rang the medical correspondent of a national newspaper. He was very interested in some of my findings and, by the next day, I had a reporter at my house.

At this point, I panicked! I started to worry that the reporter might sensationalize my research and, thereby, upset the medical staff who had supported it. To try to avoid this, I got the reporter to agree for me to tape-record her interview and for me to have a sight of her copy before it was published.

My cautiousness had an unforeseen and unfortunate consequence. The 'story' that followed ended up being so bland that it was never printed.

This experience highlights the dilemma that researchers have in seeking to get their work more widely known. The cautious way in which researchers are taught to write about their findings runs up against the media's need to pull in audiences with sensational stories. So it is always a question of balance between the media's sense of what is 'newsworthy' and your own desire for an accurate, unsensationalized account of your research.

TIP

Green and Thorogood (2004) suggest it is worth calculating a 'Fog Index' when you try to write for non-specialists. You calculate this by:

- working out the average number of words in each sentence

- adding the percentage of words of three or more syllables to this

- multiplying by 0.4.

Then 'as a rule of thumb, if the result of the Fog Index is more than 12, general readers may find the text difficult' (2004: 227–8).

Concluding Remarks

27.5 It is appropriate that, towards the end of this book, we are reflecting on 'audiences'. Too often, qualitative research is written up in an intellectual and social vacuum in which one writes for just oneself or, at best, for one supervisor. Sometimes, this partial approach can succeed in getting you the degree you require. More frequently, in the absence of actual or imagined audiences, it will lead to writer's block and consequent failure to complete.

In the final analysis, if you want to succeed in your research and beyond, you will have to be responsive to the various audiences who might be prepared to listen to what you have to say. As in so many other aspects of life, people who complain about the 'cruel world' are often the very people who disdain the occasionally difficult but generally rewarding business of listening to what others are saying.

KEY POINTS

Communication should always be designed for a particular audience:

- Academic colleagues will expect theoretical, factual, or methodological insight.

- Policy makers will want practical information relevant to current policy issues.

- Practitioners will expect a theoretical framework for understanding clients better; factual information; practical suggestions for better procedures; reform of existing practices.

- The general public wants new facts; ideas for reform of current practices or policies; guidelines for how to manage better or get better service from practitioners or institutions; and assurances that others share their own experience of particular problems in life.

If you want to communicate effectively, you must focus upon your audience's concerns and recipient design your output accordingly.

Anselm Strauss and Juliet Corbin's *Basics of Qualitative Research* (third edition, Sage, 2008: Ch. 13) covers both written and oral presentations of your research for different audiences. Gary Marx's paper 'Of methods and manners for aspiring sociologists: 37 moral imperatives' (*The American Sociologist*, Spring 1997: 102–25) is a lively and extremely helpful guide for the apprentice researcher desiring to make links with a range of audiences. Roger Hadley's chapter 'Publish and be ignored: proselytise and be damnned' in G.C. Wenger's (ed.) *The Research Relationship: Practice and Politics in Social Policy Research* (Allen & Unwin, 1987: 98–110) is a lively account of the pitfalls of trying to reach a policy audience. Practitioner audiences are very well discussed in Michael Bloor's chapter 'Addressing social problems through qualitative research' in Silverman's (ed.) *Qualitative Research: Theory, Method and Practice* (second edition, Sage, 2004).

■ Exercise 27.1

Refer back to Gary Marx's comments, cited in this chapter, about 'leveraging' your work. Now take any chapter of your dissertation and outline how you might write it up for as many as possible of the following audiences:

1   a specialist academic journal

2   a non-specialist social science audience

3   policy makers

4   practitioners

5   the general public.

Now try out these different versions with their intended audiences.

|28|

Finding a Job

Chapter Objectives

By the end of this chapter, you will be able to:

• Work out ways of getting on a shortlist.

• Devise strategies that improve how you present yourself at job interviews.

• Respond appropriately to job offers and rejections.

Introduction

28.1 Another, more forbidding, audience awaits most of us: the employer. There are three stages in finding a job:

1 learning about appropriate vacancies

2 getting on a shortlist

3 succeeding at a job interview.

In this final chapter, I will deal with each stage in turn.

Learning about Vacancies

28.2 There are two main information channels about jobs: formal and informal. The formal channels consist of websites, job advertisements in the general press and in more specialist, professional publications, as well as the job markets that may be set up at career fairs and meetings of professional associations. For instance, the annual meetings of the American Sociological Association provide a venue for university employers to meet potential recruits.

━━━━━━━━━━━━ LINK ━━━━━━━━━━━━

For academic jobs in the UK, go to:

http://www.timeshighereducation.co.uk/jobs_home.asp?navCode 84

The informal channels work through the guidance and information you can get from people on 'the inside'. Here the most likely contacts will be your supervisor(s) and, perhaps, the academics who examined your thesis.

Whatever channels you use, it is worth making an inventory of the skills you possess and then relating them to the skills demanded by likely employers. This should be done well before you complete your degree so that you can seek to give yourself the best chances on the job market.

Your research should have given you the useful qualities of being able to express yourself clearly, to work independently and to meet deadlines. It will also have probably provided you with substantive knowledge of a particular area relevant to university and non-university employers.

Other kinds of marketable skills that you can pick up during your university courses are:

- Information technology skills
- knowledge of basic statistical packages
- teaching experience
- administrative skills (for instance, gained by serving as a student representative).

So plan for the future: find out where the job openings are and gain the skills that will be most likely to fit you for them.

━━━━━━━━━━━━ LINK ━━━━━━━━━━━━

To help you to think about what jobs to apply for, go to:

http://www.phdjobs.com/how-to-identify-the-job-that-best-suits-you/

 ■ **Attempt Exercise 28.1** ━━━━━━━━━━━━━━━

Getting on a Shortlist _____

28.3
Of course, before you get a job interview, you have to be short-listed. My experience as candidate and selector tells me that there are several things that may tilt the balance in your favour. For instance:

- Write a curriculum vitae that embodies the capacity for logical, organized thought that your employer will be looking for. Spelling mistakes and hasty corrections are complete 'no-nos'! Don't undersell yourself. Recipient design your CV for different employers, having worked out which features are most likely to interest a particular employer.

- Choose referees that cover the different aspects of your life in which a particular employer is likely to be interested. Try to ensure that you are getting the 'right kind' of references. At interview, try to elicit information about how helpful your references were and/or ask referees if you can have sight of an old reference they wrote for you. If a possible referee does not seem highly enthusiastic about agreeing to write a reference for you, find somebody else.

- Always write an accompanying letter with your CV in which you explain why your experience is right for this job and your provisional thoughts about what fresh ideas you can bring to the tasks involved.

Shortlisting committees will generally assess your application in terms of agreed criteria. For instance, many years ago, I was asked to write a report for a university making a senior academic appointment in the field of medical sociology. I used the following criteria in my assessment of the candidates:

1 breadth of interests

2 quality of published work

3 research productivity

4 international research contacts

5 overall standing as a sociologist.

I then attached a letter grade to these criteria for each candidate.

This gives you an idea of some of the criteria that selectors may use when they scan your CV. Of course, how they will use these criteria is an open question. As my own research on selection interviews suggests, such criteria generally operate to rationalize decisions that are already made rather than to cause these decisions (Silverman and Jones, 1976).

The Job Interview

28.4

Job selection interviews are one of the most intimidating experiences that we have to go through. Part of the reason for this is that we know that employers will treat our answers as a way of evaluating our qualities. This is, of course, very different from question–answer sequences in ordinary conversation where no such hidden agenda may be present.

For instance, as Graham Button (1992) points out, in ordinary conversation, where an answerer seems to have misunderstood a question, the questioner will repair the understanding. This is shown in Extract 28.1:

Extract 28.1 [Button,1992]

Mandy: There should be 'bout twuny or so people
Tina: I hope- will Chris be coming?
Mandy: If she can: [: get
Tina: [No you ninny Christo<u>pher</u>

Button (1992) compares this extract with data from a job interview for the post of head of an arts faculty in an English comprehensive (or high) school. Extract 28.2 occurs during this interview:

Extract 28.2 [IV = interviewer, IE = interviewee; Button, 1992, adapted)

IV: Huhrm (.) What sort of sty::le do you see (.)
      yourself as- as a le::ader of- of (.) a- a team of
      teach<u>ers</u>.
      (0.5)
IE: D'you mean how w'd I get other people to do it.
      (1.5)
IE: Well er:: (0.5) I think there are two ways of approaching tea::m teaching

Although, as Button suggests, IV's question is hearable as about person management, IE chooses to hear it as about a teaching style ('team teaching') and the selectors do not take up the opportunity he gives them to correct him. Later, however, the selectors noted that the candidate's answer 'does not answer the question'.

As Button points out, unlike the Mandy Tina extract, where Tina corrected Mandy's understanding of her question:

> the interviewers never undertook this sort of correction on occasions where under-
> standing problems may have been possibly relevant. Interviewers not only did not
> start to speak at first possible places where a transfer of speakership could be
> coordinated [e.g. pause (1.5) in Extract 28.2 – but note that IV might have nodded
> at this point], they neither, without request from the candidate, intervened in the
> course of an answer. (1992: 217)

Button's data make clear that you can expect few favours at job interviews. Preparation and planning will help you to present yourself in the best light. Some ideas about what such preparation can involve are set out in Table 28.1.

As at your university oral examination, your job interview is the time to sell yourself while respecting the knowledge and experience of your assessors. So refer back to Table 28.1 and follow the tips there about self-presentation.

Concluding Remarks

28.5
As with policy makers, selection committees have their own agendas. For instance, in the shortlisting example discussed earlier, the appointing committee chose not to follow my advice.

TABLE 28.1 Getting through job interviews

- *Research.* Find out what the job entails in order to relate your own experience to the duties involved. Check the employer's website and talk to anybody listed on the job advertisement
- *Rehearsal.* Compose half a dozen sentences to cover: how your background fits the job description; why you want to work here; and what you hope to be doing in 5 years time. Practise these out loud so they are easy to say
- *Interview.* Goldilocks found the porridge either too hot or too cold. By contrast, don't say too much in any answer but ask the panel if you have covered what they wanted. If you are worried about saying too little ('drying up'), use a written note of some key sentences as a prompt
- *Afterwards.* Before accepting a job, negotiate the terms and conditions. If you are turned down, don't take it personally: there is always a lottery element in any appointment and you will have gained experience for your next interview

Source: adapted from Bradby, 2003

Nonetheless, this is a game that has to be played and which can be played well or badly. So go to it!

KEY POINTS

There are two main information channels about jobs:

- formal channels (websites, job advertisements and job markets)

- informal channels which work through the guidance and information you can get from people on 'the inside'.

Whatever channels you use, make an inventory of the skills you possess and then relate them to the skills demanded by likely employers.

To improve your chances of getting a job, you should:

- Write a model curriculum vitae showing logical, organized thought.

- Redesign your CV for the needs of different employers.

- Choose referees that cover the different aspects of your life in which a particular employer is likely to be interested.

- Try to ensure that you are getting the 'right kind' of references.

- Always write an accompanying letter with your CV geared to what you can bring to this particular opening.

- Prepare yourself for the job interview and check with the selectors before making any one answer very long.

Harriet Churchill and Teela Sanders's *Getting Your PhD* (Sage, 2007: 122–6) offers sound advice on searching for both academic and non-academic jobs. For research on job selection interviews, see David Silverman and Jill Jones's *Organizational Work: The Language of Grading/The Grading of Language*, Collier-Macmillan, 1976) and Graham Button's chapter 'Answers as interactional products: two sequential practices used in job interviews' in Drew and Heritage's (eds) *Talk at Work* (Cambridge University Press, 1992: 212–34).

 ■ **Exercise 28.1**

Collect weblinks or job advertisements for positions that interest you. Now make a list of the skills you possess and then relate them to the skills demanded by likely employers.

Appendix: Simplified Transcription Symbols

[	C2: quite a [while Mo: [yea	Left brackets indicate the point at which a current speaker's talk is overlapped by another's talk.
=	W: that I'm aware of = C: =Yes. Would you confirm that?	Equal signs, one at the end of a line and one at the beginning, indicate no gap between the two lines.
(.4)	Yes (.2) yeah	Numbers in parentheses indicate elapsed time in silence in tenths of a second.
(.)	to get (.) treatment	A dot in parentheses indicates a tiny gap, probably no more than one-tenth of a second.
_____	What's *up*?	Underscoring indicates some form of stress, via pitch and/or amplitude.
::	O: *kay?*	Colons indicate prolongation of the immediately prior sound. The length of the row of colons indicates the length of the prolongation.
WORD	I've got ENOUGH TO WORRY ABOUT	Capitals, except at the beginnings of lines, indicate especially loud sounds relative to the surrounding talk.
.hhhh	I feel that (.2) .hhh	A row of h's prefixed by a dot indicates an inbreath; without a dot, an outbreath. The length of the row of h's indicates the length of the in- or outbreath.
( )	future risks and ( ) and life ( )	Empty parentheses indicate the transcriber's inability to hear what was said.
(word)	Would you see (there) anything positive	Parenthesized words are possible hearings.

(( ))	confirm that ((continues))	Double parentheses contain author's descriptions rather than transcriptions.
. , ?	What do you think?	Indicate speaker's intonation (. = falling intonation; , = flat or slightly rising intonation)
>	> What do you think?	Indicates data later discussed

Glossary

Adjacency pairs   Consecutive actions which are grouped in pairs and constrain what the next speaker may do (e.g. questions and answers).

Anecdotalism   Found where research reports appear to tell entertaining stories or anecdotes but fail to convince the reader of their scientific credibility.

Analytic induction   The equivalent to the statistical testing of quantitative associations to see if they are greater than might be expected at random (random error). Using AI, the researcher examines a case, and, where appropriate, redefines the phenomenon and reformulates a hypothesis until a universal relationship is shown (Fielding, 1988: 7–8).

CAQDAS   Computer-assisted qualitative data analysis software.

Case study   Research based on the study of a limited number of naturally occurring settings.

Coding   Putting data into theoretically defined categories in order to analyse them.

Chicago School   A form of sociological ethnography usually assumed to originate in the 1920s when students at the University of Chicago were instructed to put down their theory textbooks and to get out on to the streets of their city and use their eyes and ears. It led to a series of studies of the social organization of the city and of the daily life of various occupational groups.

Cognitive anthropology   Attempts to understand the structures that organize how people perceive the world. This leads to the production of ethnographies, or conceptually derived descriptions, of whole cultures, focused on how people communicate.

Concepts	Clearly specified ideas deriving from a particular *model*.
Constructionism	A model which encourages researchers to focus upon how phenomena come to be what they are through the close study of interaction in different contexts. It is opposed to *naturalism* and *emotionalism*.
Content analysis	Involves establishing categories and systematic linkages between them, and then counting the number of instances when those categories are used in a particular item of text.
Contextual sensitivity	Involves the recognition that apparently uniform social institutions (e.g. 'tribes', 'families', 'crime') take on different meanings in different contexts.
Continuer	An utterance which signals to a listener that what they have just said has been understood and that they should now continue (see *conversation analysis*).
Control group	A group not given some stimulus provided to another group; a control group is used for comparative purposes.
Conversation analysis (CA)	A qualitative approach based on an attempt to describe people's methods for producing orderly talk-in-interaction. It derives from the work of Harvey Sacks (1992).
Credibility	The extent to which any research claim has been shown to be based on evidence.
Culture	A common set of beliefs, values and behaviours.
Deviant case analysis	In qualitative research, involves testing provisional hypotheses by 'negative' or 'discrepant' cases until all the data can be incorporated in your explanation.
Discourse analysis	The study of 'the way versions of the world, of society, events, and inner psychological worlds are produced in discourse' (Potter, 2004: 202).
Emotionalism	A model of social research in which the primary issue is to generate data which give an authentic insight into people's experiences. Emotionalists tend to favour open-ended interviews (see Gubrium and Holstein, 1997).
Empirical	Based on evidence through observation or experiment.

Empiricism	An approach which believes that evidence about the world does not depend upon *models* or *concepts* (see *positivism*).
Ethics	Guidelines or principles relating to good professional practice.
Ethnography	Puts together two different words: 'ethno' means 'folk', while 'graph' derives from 'writing'. Ethnography refers, then, to social scientific writing about particular folks.
Ethnomethodology	The study of folk – or *members'* – methods. It seeks to describe the methods that persons use in doing social life. Ethnomethodology is not a methodology but a theoretical *model*.
Field	The setting or place where *ethnographic* research takes place.
Fieldnotes	Records of observations and speech fragments arising from the field.
Focus groups	Group discussions usually based upon stimuli (topics, visual aids) provided by the researcher.
Formal theories	Theories which relate findings from one setting to many situations or settings (see Glaser and Strauss, 1967).
Frame	Using the metaphor of a picture frame, Goffman (1974) applies this term to reference how people treat what is currently relevant and irrelevant. Such treatment defines the frame through which a setting is constituted.
Gatekeeper	Someone who is able to grant or refuse access to the *field*.
Genealogical	Following Foucault (1977; 1979), the study of the ways in which *discourses* have been structured at different historical points.
Generalizability	The extent to which a finding in one setting can be applied more generally.
Grand theory	A term used by Mills (1959) to describe highly abstract speculation which has little or no use in research.
Grounded theory	A theory which involves three stages: an initial attempt to develop categories which illuminate the data; an attempt to 'saturate' these categories with many appropriate cases in

order to demonstrate their relevance; and the attempt to develop these categories into more general analytic frameworks with relevance outside the setting.

Hermeneutics An approach concerned with interpretation (originally derived from the study of biblical texts).

Hyphenated phenomena A concept which refers to the way in which apparently stable social phenomena (a 'tribe' or a 'family') take on different meanings in different contexts. Thus a-family-as-seen-by-the-oldest-child takes on a different meaning than a family-as-seen-by-the-youngest (see *constructionism*).

Hypothesis A testable proposition often based on an educated guess.

Idiom A term used by Gubrium and Holstein (1997) to describe a set of analytical preferences for particular concepts, styles of research and ways of writing (see *model*).

Inductive Based on the study of particular cases rather than just derived from a theory.

Interactionism A theory, commonly used in qualitative sociological research, which assumes that our behaviour and perceptions derive from processes of interaction with other people.

Intervening variable A *variable* which is influenced by a prior factor and goes on to influence another. Commonly used in quantitative research to work out which statistical association may be spurious.

Interview society A term used by Atkinson and Silverman (1997) to point out the ways in which interviews have become a central medium for understanding who we are.

Laboratory study A method used in quantitative research in which subjects are placed in an artificial environment and their responses to various stimuli are measured.

Leverage Used by Marx (1997) to describe ways of finding multiple publishing outlets for one piece of research.

Low-inference descriptors Recording observations 'in terms that are as concrete as possible, including verbatim accounts of what people say, for example, rather than researchers' reconstructions of the general sense of what a person said, which would allow

researchers' personal perspectives to influence the reporting'
(Seale, 1999: 148) (see *reliability*).

Member
Used by Garfinkel (1967) to refer to participants in
society. It is a shorthand term for 'collectivity member'
(see *ethnomethodology*).

**Membership
categorization
device**
A collection of categories (e.g. baby, mommy, father = family;
male, female = gender) and some rules about how to
apply these categories.

Methodology
Refers to the choices we make about appropriate *models*,
cases to study, methods of data gathering, forms of data
analysis, etc., in planning and executing a research study.

Methods
Specific research techniques. These include quantitative
techniques, like statistical correlations, as well as techniques
like observation, interviewing and audio-recording.

Models
Provide an overall framework for how we look at reality.
They tell us what reality is like and the basic elements it
contains ('ontology') and what is the nature and status of
knowledge ('epistemology'). See also *idioms*.

Narratives
The organization of stories (e.g. beginning, middle and end;
plots and characters) which make stories meaningful or coherent in a form appropriate to the needs of a particular occasion.

Naturalism
A model of research which seeks to minimize presupposi-
tions in order to witness subjects' worlds in their own terms
(Gubrium and Holstein, 1997).

**Naturally
occurring data**
Data which derive from situations which exist independently
of the researcher's intervention.

Normative
Pertaining to a norm or value; prescriptive.

**Operational
definitions**
Working definitions which allow the measurement of
some *variable* within quantitative research.

Paradigm
A conceptual framework (see *model*).

Paradigmatic
A term used in structuralism to indicate a polar set of
concepts or activities where the presence of one denies the
existence of the other (e.g. a red traffic light).

Participant observation	A method that assumes that, in order to understand the world 'first hand', you must participate yourself rather than just observe at a distance. This method was championed by the early anthropologists but is shared by some ethnographers.
Positivism	A model of the research process which treats 'social facts' as existing independently of the activities of both participants and researchers. For positivists, the aim is to generate data which are valid and reliable, independently of the research setting.
Postmodernism	A contemporary approach which questions or seeks to deconstruct both accepted concepts (e.g. the 'subject' and the 'field') and scientific method. Postmodernism is both an analytical model and a way of describing contemporary society as a pastiche of insecure and changing elements.
Preference organization	A concept derived from *conversation analysis* which suggests that recipients of actions recognize a preference for what they should do next.
Recipient design	Work that is designed for a particular audience (the term derives from *conversation analysis* where it is used to describe how all actions are implicitly designed in this way).
Reflexivity	A term deriving from *ethnomethodology* where it is used to describe the self-organizing character of all interaction so that any action provides for its own context. Mistakenly used to refer to self-questioning by a researcher.
Relativism	A value position where we resist taking a position because we believe that, since everything is relative to its particular context, it should not be criticized.
Reliability	'The degree of consistency with which instances are assigned to the same category by different observers or by the same observer on different occasions' (Hammersley, 1992: 67) (see *validity*).
Respondent validation	Involves taking one's findings back to the subjects being studied. Where these people verify one's findings, it is argued, one can be more confident of their validity.
Researcher-provoked data	Data which are actively created and, therefore, would not exist apart from the researcher's intervention (e.g. interviews, focus groups).

Rewriting of history	A term used by Garfinkel (1967) to refer to the way in which any account retrospectively finds reasons for any past event.
Romanticism	An approach taken from nineteenth-century thought in which authenticity is attached to personal experiences (see *emotionalism*).
Sample, sampling	A statistical procedure for finding cases to study. Sampling has two functions: it allows you to feel confident about the representativeness of your sample, and such representativeness allows you to make broader inferences.
Semiotics	The study of signs (from speech, to fashion, to Morse code).
Social constructionism	See *constructionism*.
Social structure	A term used in sociology and anthropology to describe the institutional arrangements of a particular society or group (e.g. family and class structures).
Social survey	A quantitative method involving the study of large numbers of people, often through the use of questionnaires.
Structuralism	A *model* used in anthropology which aims to show how single cases relate to general social forms. Structural anthropologists draw upon French social and linguistic theory of the early twentieth century, notably Ferdinand de Saussure and Emile Durkheim. They view behaviour as the expression of a 'society' which works as a 'hidden hand' constraining and forming human action.
Subculture	A set of beliefs, values and behaviours shared by a particular group.
Substantive theory	A theory about a particular situation or group. Can be used to develop *formal theory*.
Syntagmatic	A term used within *semiotics* to denote the order in which related elements occur (e.g. how colours follow one another in traffic lights).
Textual data	Documents and/or images which have become recorded without the intervention of a researcher (e.g. through an interview).

Theories	Ideas which arrange sets of concepts to define and explain some phenomenon.
Thick description	A term from anthropology and *ethnography* used to describe research reports which analyse the multiple levels of meaning in any situation (see Geertz, 1973).
Triangulation	The comparison of different kinds of data (e.g. quantitative and qualitative) and different methods (e.g. observation and interviews) to see whether they corroborate one another.
Turn-taking	The sequential organization of speech acts (see *conversation analysis*).
Validity	'The extent to which an account accurately represents the social phenomena to which it refers' (Hammersley, 1990: 57). Researchers respond to validity concerns by describing 'the warrant for their inferences' (Fielding and Fielding, 1986: 12) (see *reliability*).
Variables	Factors which are isolated from one another in order to measure their relationship; usually described in quantitative research.

References

Acourt, P. (1997) 'Progress, utopia and intellectual practice: arguments for the resurrection of the future'. Unpublished PhD thesis, University of London, Goldsmiths College.

Alasuutari, P. (1995) *Researching Culture: Qualitative Method and Cultural Studies*. London: Sage.

Antaki, C. and Rapley, M. (1996) '"Quality of life" talk: the liberal paradox of psychological testing'. *Discourse and Society*, 7 (3), 293–316.

Arber, S. (1993) 'The research process'. In N. Gilbert (ed.), *Researching Social Life* (pp. 62–80). London: Sage.

Arditti, J.A. and Few, A.L. (2006) 'Mothers' reentry into family life following incarceration'. *Criminal Justice Policy Review*, 17 (1), 103–23.

Armstrong, D., Gosling, A., Weinman, J. and Marteau, T. (1997) 'The place of interrater reliability in qualitative research: an empirical study'. *Sociology*, 31 (3), 597–606.

Atkinson, J.M. (1978) *Discovering Suicide*. London: Macmillan.

Atkinson, J.M. and Heritage, J.C. (eds) (1984) *Structures of Social Action*. Cambridge: Cambridge University Press.

Atkinson, P. (1992) 'The ethnography of a medical setting: reading, writing and rhetoric'. *Qualitative Health Research*, 2 (4), 451–74.

Atkinson, P. and Coffey, A. (2004) 'Analysing documentary realities'. In D. Silverman (ed.), *Qualitative Research*, 2nd edn (pp. 56–75). London: Sage.

Atkinson, P. and Silverman, D. (1997) 'Kundera's immortality: the interview society and the invention of self'. *Qualitative Inquiry*, 3 (3), 324–45.

Avis, M., Bond, M. and Arthur, A. (1997) 'Questioning patient satisfaction: an empirical investigation in two outpatient clinics'. *Social Science and Medicine*, 44 (1), 85–92.

Back, L. (2004) 'Politics, research and understanding'. In C. Seale, G. Gobo, J.F. Gubrium and D. Silverman (eds), *Qualitative Research Practice* (pp. 261–75). London: Sage.

Baker, C. (2002) 'Ethnomethodological analysis of interviews'. In J. Gubrium and J. Holstein (eds), *Handbook of Interview Research* (pp. 777–96). Thousand Oaks, CA: Sage.

Baker, C. and Keogh, J. (1995) 'Accounting for achievement in parent–teacher interviews', *Human Studies*, 18 (2/3), 263–300.

Baker, P. (2006) *Using Corpora in Discourse Analysis*. London: Continuum.

Barbour, R. (2007) *Introducing Qualitative Research*. London: Sage.

Barker, M. (2003) 'Assessing the "quality" in qualitative research: the case of text–audience relations'. *European Journal of Communication*, 18 (3), 315–35.

Barthes, R. (1973) *Mythologies*. London: Paladin.

Baruch, G. (1981) 'Moral tales: parents' stories of encounters with the health profession'. *Sociology of Health and Illness*, 3 (3), 275–96.

Becker, H. (1963) *Outsiders: Studies in the Sociology of Deviance*. New York: Free Press.

Becker, H. (1967) 'Whose side are we on?' *Social Problems*, 14 (3), 239–47.

Becker, H. (1986) *Writing for Social Scientists*. Chicago: University of Chicago Press.

Becker, H. (1998) *Tricks of the Trade: How To Think about Your Research While Doing It*. Chicago and London: University of Chicago Press.

Becker, H.S. (2004) 'Comment on Kevin D. Haggerty, "Ethics creep: governing social science research in the name of ethics"'. *Qualitative Sociology*, 27 (4), 415–16.

Becker, H. and Geer, B. (1960) 'Participant observation: the analysis of qualitative field data'. In R. Adams and J. Preiss (eds), *Human Organization Research: Field Relation and Techniques*. Homewood, IL: Dorsey.

Bell, J. (1993) *Doing Your Research Project*, 2nd edn. Buckingham: Open University Press.

Berelson, B. (1952) *Content Analysis in Communicative Research*. New York: Free Press.

Bergmann, J. (1992) 'Veiled morality: notes on discretion in psychiatry'. In P. Drew and J. Heritage (eds), *Talk at Work* (pp. 137–62). Cambridge: Cambridge University Press.

Blaikie, N. (1993) *Approaches to Social Enquiry*. Cambridge: Polity.

Bloor, M. (1978) 'On the analysis of observational data: a discussion of the worth and uses of inductive techniques and respondent validation'. *Sociology*, 12 (3), 545–57.

Bloor, M. (1983) 'Notes on member validation'. In R. Emerson (ed.), *Contemporary Field Research: A Collection of Readings*. Boston: Little, Brown.

Bloor, M. (1997) 'Addressing social problems through qualitative research'. In D. Silverman (ed.), *Qualitative Research: Theory, Method and Practice* (pp. 221–38). London: Sage.

Bloor, M. (2004) 'Addressing social problems through qualitative research'. In D. Silverman (ed.), *Qualitative Research: Theory, Method and Practice*, 2nd edn (pp. 304–23). London: Sage.

Blumer, H. (1969) *Symbolic Interactionism*. Englewood Cliffs, NJ: Prentice Hall.

Boden, D. and Zimmerman, D.H. (eds) (1991) *Talk and Social Structure: Studies in Ethno Methodology and Conversation Analysis* (pp. 44–71). Cambridge: Polity.

Bosk, C. (2004) 'The ethnographer and the IRB: comment on Kevin D. Haggerty, "Ethics creep: governing social science research in the name of ethics"'. *Qualitative Sociology*, 27 (4), 417–20.

Bosk, C.L. and De Vries, R.G. (2004) 'Bureaucracies of mass deception: institutional review boards and the ethics of ethnographic research'. *The Annals of the American Academy of Political and Social Science*, 595, 249–63.

Bradbury, M. (1988) *Unsent Letters*. London: Andre Deutsch.

Bradby, H. (2002) 'Getting through employment interviews'. *Network*, 84, 20–1.

British Research Councils (1996) *Priorities News*, Spring. Swindon: ESRC, http://www.pparc.ac.uk/home_old.asp.

Brown, J.R. (2000) 'Privatizing the university'. *Science*, 290 (5497), 1701.

Brown, P. and Levinson, S. (1987) *Politeness: Some Universals in Language Usage*. Cambridge: Cambridge University Press.

Bryman, A. (1988) *Quantity and Quality in Social Research*. London: Unwin Hyman.

Buchanan, D.R. (1992) 'An uneasy alliance: combining qualitative and quantitative research methods'. *Health Education & Behavior*, 19 (1), 117–35.

Bulmer, M. (1984) *The Chicago School of Sociology*. Chicago: Chicago University Press.

Burton, D. (ed.) (2000) *Research Training for Social Scientists*. London: Sage.

Button, G. (1992) 'Answers as interactional products: two sequential practices used in job interviews'. In P. Drew and J.C. Heritage (eds), *Talk at Work* (pp. 212–34). Cambridge: Cambridge University Press.

Byrne, P. and Long, B. (1976) *Doctors Talking to Patients*. London: HMSO.

Chapman, G. (1987) 'Talk, text and discourse: nurses' talk in a therapeutic community'. Unpublished PhD thesis, University of London, Goldsmiths College.

Charmaz, K. (2006) *Constructing Grounded Theory: A Practical Guide through Qualitative Analysis*. London: Sage.

Christians, C. (2005) 'Ethics and politics in qualitative research'. In N. Denzin and Y. Lincoln (eds), *Handbook of Qualitative Research*, 3rd edn (pp. 139–64). Thousand Oaks, CA: Sage.

Churchill, H. and Sanders, T. (2007) *Getting Your PhD: A Practical Insider's Guide*. London: Sage.

Cicourel, A. (1968) *The Social Organization of Juvenile Justice*. New York: Wiley.

Clavarino, A., Najman, J. and Silverman, D. (1995) 'Assessing the quality of qualitative data'. *Qualitative Inquiry*, 1 (2), 223–42.

Clifford, J. and Marcus, G. (eds) (1986) *Writing Culture: The Poetics and Politics of Ethnography*. Berkeley, CA: University of California Press.

Cochrane, J. (2004) *Between You and I: A Little Book of Bad English*. Naperville, IL: Sourcebooks.

Coffey, A. and Atkinson, P. (1996) *Making Sense of Qualitative Data*. London: Sage.

Cohen, S. (1980) *Folk Devils and Moral Panics: The Creation of the Mods and Rockers*. Oxford: Martin Robertson.

Cohen, S. and Young, J. (1973) *The Manufacture of News*. London: Constable.

Cornwell, J. (1981) *Hard Earned Lives*. London: Tavistock.

Crothers, C. (1991) 'The internal structure of sociology departments: the role of graduate students and other groups'. *Teaching Sociology*, 19, 333–43.

Cryer, P. (1996) *The Research Student's Guide to Success*. Buckingham: Open University Press.

Cryer, P. (2006) *The Research Student's Guide to Success*, 3rd edn. Buckingham: Open University Press.

Curtis, S., Gesler, W., Smith, G. and Washburn, S. (2000) 'Approaches to sampling and case selection in qualitative research: examples in the geography of health'. *Social Science and Medicine*, 50, 1000–14.

Czarniawska, B. (2007) *Shadowing and Other Techniques for Doing Fieldwork in Modern Societies*. Malmo: Liber.

Dalton, M. (1959) *Men Who Manage*. New York: Wiley.

Davies, S. and Guppy, N. (1997) 'Field of study, school selectivity, and student inequalities in higher education'. *Social Forces*, 75, 1417–38.

Delamont, S. and Atkinson, P. (2001) 'Doctoring uncertainty: mastering craft knowledge'. *Social Studies of Science*, 31 (1): 87–107.

Deming, A.H. (1998) 'Science and poetry: a view from the divide'. *Creative Nonfiction*, 11, 11–29.

Denzin, N.K. (1993) 'Rhetoric and society'. *The American Sociologist*, 24, 135–46.

Denzin, N. (1994) 'The art and practice of interpretation'. In N. Denzin and Y. Lincoln (eds), *Handbook of Qualitative Research* (pp. 500–15). Thousand Oaks, CA: Sage.

Denzin, N. (2000) 'The practice and politics of interpretation'. In N. Denzin and Y. Lincoln (eds), *Handbook of Qualitative Research*, 2nd edn (pp. 897–922). Thousand Oaks, CA: Sage.

Denzin, N. and Lincoln, Y. (eds) (1994) *Handbook of Qualitative Research*. Thousand Oaks, CA: Sage.

Denzin, N. and Lincoln, Y. (eds) (2000) *Handbook of Qualitative Research*, 2nd edn. Thousand Oaks, CA: Sage.

Denzin, N. and Lincoln, Y. (eds) (2005) *Handbook of Qualitative Research*, 3rd edn. London: Sage.

Dingwall, R. and Murray, T. (1983) 'Categorization in accident departments: "good" patients, "bad" patients and children'. *Sociology of Health and Illness*, 5 (12), 121–48.

Douglas, M. (1975) 'Self-evidence'. In M. Douglas, *Implicit Meanings* (pp. 276–318). London: Routledge.

Drew, P. (2001) 'Spotlight on the patient'. *Text*, 21 (1/2), 261–8.

Drew, P. and Heritage, J.C. (1992) 'Analysing talk at work: an introduction'. In P. Drew and J.C. Heritage (eds), *Talk at Work* (pp. 3–65). Cambridge: Cambridge University Press.

Duncan, S. (2005) 'Towards evidence-inspired policy-making'. *Social Sciences*, ESRC, 61, 10–11.

Durkheim, E. (1951) *Suicide*. New York: Free Press.

Durkin, T. (1997) 'Using computers in strategic qualitative research'. In G. Miller and R. Dingwall (eds), *Context and Method in Qualitative Research* (pp. 92–105). London: Sage.

Emerson, R.M., Fretz, R.I. and Shaw, L.L. (1995) *Writing Ethnographic Fieldnotes*. Chicago: University of Chicago Press.

Emmison, M. and Smith, P. (2000) *Researching the Visual*. London: Sage.

Engebretson, J. (1996) 'Urban healers: an experiential description of American healing touch groups'. *Qualitative Health Research*, 6 (4), 526–41.

Eriksson, P. and Kovalainen, A. (2008) *Qualitative Methods in Business Research*. London: Sage.

Fairclough, N. (1992) *Discourse and Social Change*. Cambridge: Polity Press.

Fielding, N. (1982) 'Observational research on the National Front'. In M. Bulmer (ed.), *Social Research Ethics: An Examination of the Merits of Covert Participant Observation*. London: Macmillan.

Fielding, N. and Fielding, J. (1986) *Linking Data*. London: Sage.

Fielding, N. and Lee, R. (eds) (1991) *Using Computers in Qualitative Research*. Newbury Park, CA: Sage.

Fisher, M. (1997) *Qualitative Computing: Using Software for Qualitative Data Analysis*. Aldershot: Ashgate.

Flick, U. (2007) *Designing Qualitative Research*. London: Sage.

Flyvbjerg, B. (2004) 'Five misunderstandings about case-study research'. In C. Seale, G. Gobo, J. Gubrium and D. Silverman (eds), *Qualitative Research Practice* (pp. 420–34). London: Sage.

Forrest, B. (2001) 'The wedge at work: how intelligent design creationism is wedging its way into cultural and academic mainstream'. In R.T. Penncock (ed.), *Intelligent Design Creationism and Its Critics: Philosophical, Theological and Scientific Perspectives* (pp. 5–53). Cambridge, MA: MIT Press.

Foucault, M. (1973) *The Order of Things: An Archeology of Human Sciences*. New York: Vintage.

Foucault, M. (1977) *Discipline and Punish*. Harmondsworth: Penguin.

Foucault, M. (1979) *The History of Sexuality*, Vol. 1. Harmondsworth: Penguin.

Frake, C. (1964) 'Notes on queries in ethnography'. *American Anthropologist*, 66, 132–45.

Fraser, M. (1995) 'The history of the child: 1905–1989'. PhD thesis, University of London, Goldsmiths College.

Frazier, C., Bishop, D., Lanza-Kaduce, L. and Marvasti, A. (1999) 'Juveniles in criminal court: past and current research from Florida'. *Quinnipiac Law Review*, 18 (3), 573–96.

Freebody, P. (2003) *Qualitative Research in Education*. London: Sage.

Garfinkel, H. (1967) *Studies in Ethnomethodology*. Oxford: Polity.

Geertz, C. (1973) *The Interpretation of Cultures*. London: Fontana.

Gilbert, N. (2008) 'Writing about social research'. In N. Gilbert (ed.), *Researching Social Life*, 3rd edn (pp. 328–44). London: Sage.

Gilbert, N. (ed.) (2008) *Researching Social Life*, 3rd edn. London: Sage.

Gilbert, N. and Mulkay, M. (1983) 'In search of the action'. In N. Gilbert and P. Abell (eds), *Accounts and Action*. Aldershot: Gower.

Glaser, B. and Strauss, A. (1964) 'The social loss of dying patients'. *American Journal of Nursing*, 64 (6), 119–21.

Glaser, B. and Strauss, A. (1967) *The Discovery of Grounded Theory*. Chicago: Aldine.

Glaser, B. and Strauss, A. (1968) *Time for Dying*. Chicago: Aldine.

Glassner, B. and Loughlin, J. (1987) *Drugs in Adolescent Worlds: Burnouts to Straights*. New York: St Martin's.

Gobo, G. (2008) *Doing Ethnography*. London: Sage.

Goffman, E. (1959) *The Presentation of Self in Everyday Life*. New York: Doubleday Anchor.

Goffman, E. (1961) *Asylums*. New York: Doubleday Anchor.

Goffman, E. (1974) *Frame Analysis*. New York: Harper and Row.

Gorton, W.A. (2006) *Karl Popper and the Social Sciences*. New York: SUNY.

Gouldner, A. (1954) *Patterns of Industrial Bureaucracy*. Glencoe, IL: Free Press.

Green, J. and Thorogood, N. (2004) *Qualitative Methods for Health Research*. London: Sage.

Guba, E. and Lincoln, Y. (1994) 'Competing paradigms in qualitative research'. In N. Denzin and Y. Lincoln (eds), *Handbook of Qualitative Research* (pp 105–117). Thousand Oaks: Sage.

Gubrium, J. (1988) *Analyzing Field Reality*. Newbury Park, CA: Sage.

Gubrium, J. (1992) *Out of Control: Family Therapy and Domestic Disorder*. London: Sage.

Gubrium, J. (1993) *Living and Dying in Murray Manor*. New York: St Martin's Press.

Gubrium, J. (1997) *Living and Dying in Murray Manor*. Charlottesville, VA: University Press of Virginia.

Gubrium, J. and Buckholdt, D. (1982) *Describing Care: Image and Practice in Rehabilitation*. Cambridge, MA: Oelschlager, Gunn and Hain.

Gubrium, J. and Holstein, J. (1987) 'The private image: experiential location and method in family studies'. *Journal of Marriage and the Family*, 49, 773–86.

Gubrium, J. and Holstein, J. (1995) 'Qualitative inquiry and the deprivatization of experience'. *Qualitative Inquiry*, 1 (2), 204–22.

Gubrium, J. and Holstein, J. (1997) *The New Language of Qualitative Method*. New York: Oxford University Press.

Gubrium, J. and Holstein, J. (ed) (2002) *Handbook of Interview Research*. Thousand Oaks: Sage.

Gubrium, J. and Holstein, J. (2009) *Analyzing Narrative Reality*. Thousand Oaks, CA: Sage.

Hadley, R. (1987) 'Publish and be ignored: proselytise and be damned'. In G.C. Wenger (ed.), *The Research Relationship: Practice and Politics in Social Policy Research* (pp. 98–110). London: Allen and Unwin.

Hagan, F.E. (2005) *The Essentials of Research Methods in Criminal Justice and Criminology*. Boston: Pearson Education.

Haggerty, K.D. (2004) 'Ethics creep: governing social science research in the name of ethics'. *Qualitative Sociology*, 27 (4), 391–414.

Hahn, C. (2008) *Doing Qualitative Research Using Your Computer: A Practical Guide*. London: Sage.

Hamburg, P. (2004) 'The new censorship: institutional review boards'. *Supreme Court Review*, 271–354.

Hammersley, M. (1990) *Reading Ethnographic Research: A Critical Guide*. London: Longmans.

Hammersley, M. (1992) *What's Wrong with Ethnography? Methodological Explorations*. London: Routledge.

Hammersley, M. (2008) *Questioning Qualitative Inquiry: Critical Essays*. London: Sage.

Hammersley, M. and Atkinson, P. (1983) *Ethnography: Principles in Practice*. London: Tavistock.

Hammersley, M. and Atkinson, P. (2007) *Ethnography: Principles in Practice*, 3rd edn. London: Tavistock.

Handy, C. and Aitken, A. (1994) 'The organisation of the primary school'. In A. Pollard and J. Bourne (eds), *Teaching and Learning in the Primary School* (pp. 239–49). London: Routledge.

Hart, C. (1998) *Doing a Literature Review: Releasing the Social Science Imagination*. London: Sage.

Hart, C. (2001) *Doing a Literature Search*. London: Sage.

Heath, C. (2004) 'Analysing face-to-face interaction: video and the visual and the material'. In D. Silverman (ed.), *Qualitative Research: Theory, Method and Practice*, 2nd edn (pp. 265–81). London: Sage.

Heath, C. and Luff, P. (2000) *Technology in Action*. Cambridge: Cambridge University Press.

Heaton, J.M. (1979) 'Theory in psychotherapy'. In N. Bolton (ed.), *Philosophical Problems in Psychology* (pp. 179–98). London: Methuen.

Heise, D. (1988) 'Computer analysis of cultural structures'. *Social Science Computer Review*, 6, 183–96.

Heritage, J. (1984) *Garfinkel and Ethnomethodology*. Cambridge: Polity.

Heritage, J. and Sefi, S. (1992) 'Dilemmas of advice: aspects of the delivery and reception of advice in interactions between health visitors and first time mothers'. In P. Drew and J. Heritage (eds), *Talk at Work* (pp. 359–417). Cambridge: Cambridge University Press.

Hesse-Biber, S. and Dupuis, P. (1995) 'Hypothesis testing in computer-aided qualitative data analysis'. In U. Kelle (ed.), *Computer Aided Qualitative Data Analysis: Theory, Methods and Practice* (pp. 129–35). London: Sage.

Hickey, T. (2005) *Taking Sides: Clashing Views in Crime and Criminology*. Columbus, OH: McGraw-Hill.

Hickey, T. (2006) *Taking Sides: Clashing Views on Crime and Criminology*, 7th edn. Dubuque, IA: McGraw-Hill.

Hill, C.E. et al. (1988) *Therapist Techniques and Client Outcomes*. London: Sage.

Himes, A.C. (2003) 'A formula for successful grant writing: four proven keys'. *Academic Leader*, 19 (3), 4, 8.

Hindess, B. (1973) *The Use of Official Statistics in Sociology*. London: Macmillan.

Holstein, J.A. (1992) 'Producing people: descriptive practice in human service work'. *Current Research on Occupations and Professions*, 7, 23–9.

Holstein, J. and Gubrium, J. (1995) *The Active Interview*. Thousand Oaks, CA: Sage.

Holstein, J. and Gubrium, J. (eds) (2008) *Handbook of Constructionist Research*. New York: Guilford.

Horner, C. (2007) *The Politically Incorrect Guide to Global Warming and Environmentalism*. Washington, DC: Regnery.

Hornsby-Smith, M. (1993) 'Gaining access'. In N. Gilbert (ed.), *Researching Social Life* (pp. 52–67). London: Sage.

Houtkoop-Steenstra, H. (1991) 'Opening sequences in Dutch telephone conversations'. In D. Boden and D.H. Zimmerman (eds), *Talk and Social Structure: Studies in Ethnomethodology and Conversation Analysis* (pp. 232–50). Cambridge: Polity.

Huberman, A.M. and Miles, M.B. (1994) 'Data management and analysis methods'. In N. Denzin and Y. Lincoln (eds), *Handbook of Qualitative Research* (pp. 413–27). Thousand Oaks, CA: Sage.

Hughes, E.C. (1984) *The Sociological Eye*. New Brunswick, NJ: Transaction.

Hulko, W. (in press) 'From "not a big deal" to "hellish": the experiences of older people with dementia'. *Journal of Aging Studies*.

Humphreys, L. (1970) *Tearoom Trade: Impersonal Sex in Public Places*. Chicago: Aldine.

Hyland, K. (2002) 'Directives: arguments and engagements in academic writing'. *Applied Linguistics*, 23 (2), 215–39.

Irurita, V. (1996) 'Hidden dimensions revealed: progressive grounded theory study of quality care in the hospital'. *Qualitative Health Research*, 6 (3), 331–49.

Isaac, A. (1998) *African American Students' Guide to Surviving Graduate School*. Thousand Oaks, CA: Sage.

Israel, M. and Hay, I. (2006) *Research Ethics for Social Scientists*. London: Sage.

Järviluoma, H., Moisala, P. and Vilkko, A. (2004) *Gender and Qualitative Methods*. London: Sage.

Jefferson, G. (1984) 'On stepwise transition from talk about a trouble to inappropriately next-positioned matters'. In J.M. Atkinson and J.C. Heritage (eds) *Structures of Social Action: Studies of Conversation Analysis* (pp 191–222). Cambridge: Cambridge University Press.

Jeffery, R. (1979) 'Normal rubbish: deviant patients in casualty departments'. *Sociology of Health and Illness*, 1 (1), 90–107.

Jenkings, K.N. Woodward, R. and Winter, T. (2008) 'The emergent production of analysis in photo elicitation: pictures of Military identity'. *Forum Qualitative Social Research* (Volume 9): No. 3 Art. 30.

Jones, J.H. (1981) *Bad Blood*. New York: Free Press.

Kafka, F. (1961) 'Investigations of a dog'. In *Metamorphosis and Other Stories*. Harmondsworth: Penguin.

Kelle, U. (ed.) (1995) *Computer Aided Qualitative Data Analysis: Theory, Methods and Practice*. London: Sage.

Kelle, U. (2004) 'Computer assisted qualitative data analysis'. In C. Seale, G. Gobo, J.F. Gubrium and D. Silverman (eds), *Qualitative Research Practice* (pp. 473–89). London: Sage.

Kelle, U. and Laurie, H. (1995) 'Computer use in qualitative research and issues of validity'. In U. Kelle (ed.), *Computer Aided Qualitative Data Analysis: Theory, Methods and Practice* (pp. 12–28). London: Sage.

Kelly, M. (1998) 'Writing a research proposal'. In C. Seale (ed.), *Researching Society and Culture* (pp. 111–22). London: Sage.

Kelly, M. (2004) 'Research design and proposals'. In C. Seale (ed.), *Researching Society and Culture*, 2nd edn (pp. 129–42). London: Sage.

Kendall, G. and Wickham, G. (1998) *Using Foucault's Methods*. London: Sage.

Kirk, J. and Miller, M. (1986) *Reliability and Validity in Qualitative Research*. London: Sage.

Kitzinger, C. and Wilkinson, S. (1997) 'Validating women's experience? Dilemmas in feminist research'. *Feminism and Psychology*, 7 (4), 566–74.

Konecki, K. (2005) 'Wizualne wyobrazenia. Główne strategie badawcze w socjologii wizualnej a metodologia teorii ugruntowanej'. *Przegląd Socjologii Jakosciowej*, I (1), Pobrany Miesiac 10, Rok 2007.

Konecki, K. (2008) 'Touching and gesture exchange as an element of emotional bond construction: application of visual sociology in the research on interaction between humans and animals'. *FQS Forum on Qualitative Research*, Vol. 9, No. 3, Art. 33. http://www.qualitativesociologyreview.org/PL/Volume1/PSJ_1_1_Konecki.pdf.

Koppel, R., Cohen, A. and Abaluck, B. (2003) 'Physicians' perceptions of medication error using differing research methods'. Paper presented at the meeting of the European Sociological Association (Qualitative Methods Group), Murcia, Spain.

Kuhn, T.S. (1970) *The Structure of Scientific Revolutions*, 2nd edn. Chicago: University of Chicago Press.

Kuhn, T. (1996) *The Structure of Scientific Revolutions*. Chicago: University of Chicago Press.

Kvale, S. (2007) *Doing Interviews*. London: Sage.

Lee, R.M. and Fielding, N.G. (1995) 'Users' experiences of qualitative data analysis software'. In U. Kelle (ed.), *Computer Aided Qualitative Data Analysis: Theory, Methods and Practice* (pp. 29–140). London: Sage.

Lewins, A. and Silver, C. (2007) *Using Software in Qualitative Research: A Step-by-Step Guide*. London: Sage.

Lincoln, Y. and Guba, E. (2000) 'Paradigmatic controversies: contradictions and emerging influences'. In N. Denzin and Y. Lincoln (eds), *Handbook of Qualitative Research*, 2nd edn (pp. 162–88). Thousand Oaks, CA: Sage.

Lincoln, Y.S. and Denzin, N. (1994) 'The fifth moment'. In N. Denzin and Y.S. Lincoln (eds), *Handbook of Qualitative Research* (pp. 575–86). Thousand Oaks, CA: Sage.

Lindström, A. (1994) 'Identification and recognition in Swedish telephone conversation openings'. *Language in Society*, 23 (2), 231–52.

Lipset, S.M., Trow, M. and Coleman, J. (1962) *Union Democracy*. Garden City, NY: Anchor Doubleday.

Livingston, E. (1987) *Making Sense of Ethnomethodology*. London: Routledge.

Loseke, D. (1989) 'Creating clients: social problems' work in a shelter for battered women' *Perspectives on Social Problems*, 1, 173–93.

Loseke, D. and Cahill, S. (2004) 'Publishing qualitative manuscripts: lessons learned'. In C. Seale, G. Gobo, J.F. Gubrium and D. Silverman (eds), *Qualitative Research Practice* (pp. 576–91). London: Sage.

Lynch, M. (1984) *Art and Artifact in Laboratory Science*. London: Routledge.

Madison, S. (2005) *Critical Ethnography: Methods, Ethics, and Performance*. Thousand Oaks, CA: Sage.

Mahoney, M.J. (1977) 'Publication prejudices: an experimental study of confirmatory bias in the peer review system'. *Cognitive Therapy and Research*, 1, 161–75.

Malinowski, B. (1922) *Argonauts of the Western Pacific*. London: Routledge.

Marsh, C. (1982) *The Survey Method*. London: Allen and Unwin.

Marshall, C. and Rossman, G. (1989). *Designing Qualitative Research*. London: Sage.

Marvasti, A. (2003a) *Qualitative Research in Sociology*. London: Sage.

Marvasti, A. (2003b) *Being Homeless: Textual and Narrative Constructions*. Lanham, VA: Lexington Books.

Marvasti, A. (2004) *Qualitative Research in Sociology*. Thousand Oaks, CA: Sage.

Marx, G. (1997) 'Of methods and manners for aspiring sociologists: 37 moral Imperatives'. *The American Sociologist*, 102–25.

Mason, J. (1996) *Qualitative Researching*. London: Sage.

Mason, J. (2002) *Qualitative Researching*, 2nd edn. London: Sage.

Maynard, D.W. (1991) 'Interaction and asymmetry in clinical discourse'. *American Journal of Sociology*, 97 (2), 448–95.

McKeganey, N. and Bloor, M. (1991) 'Spotting the invisible man: the influence of male gender on fieldwork relations'. *British Journal of Sociology*, 42 (2), 195–210.

McLeod, J. (1994) *Doing Counselling Research*. London: Sage.

Mehan, H. (1979) *Learning Lessons: Social Organization in the Classroom*. Cambridge, MA: Harvard University Press.

Mercer, K. (1990) 'Powellism as a political discourse'. Unpublished PhD thesis, University of London, Goldsmiths College.

Mergenthaler, E. (1996) 'Emotion-abstraction patterns in verbatim protocols: a new way of describing psychotherapeutic process'. *Journal of Consulting and Clinical Psychology*, 64 (6), 1306–15.

Merton, R.K. (1968) 'The Matthew effect in science' *Science*, 159, 56–63.

Miall, D.S. (ed.) (1990) *Humanities and the Computer: New Directions*. Oxford: Clarendon.

Miles, M. and Huberman, A. (1984) *Qualitative Data Analysis*. London: Sage.

Miles, M. and Huberman, A. (1994) *Qualitative Data Analysis*, 2nd edn. London: Sage.

Miller, G. and Silverman, D. (1995) 'Troubles talk and counseling discourse: a comparative study', *The Sociological Quarterly*, 36 (4), 725–47.

Miller, J. and Glassner, B. (1997) 'The "inside" and the "outside": finding realities in interviews'. In D. Silverman (ed.), *Qualitative Research* (pp. 99–112). London: Sage.

Miller, J. and Glassner, B. (2004) 'The inside and the outside: finding realities in interviews'. In D. Silverman (ed.), *Qualitative Research: Theory, Method and Practice*, 2nd edn (pp. 125–39). London: Sage.

Miller, R. and Bor, R. (1988) *AIDS: A Guide to Clinical Counselling*. London: Science Press.

Miller, S., Nelson, M. and Moore, M. (1998) 'Caught in the paradigm gap: qualitative researchers' lived experience and the politics of epistemology'. *American Educational Research Journal*, 35 (3), 377–416.

Mills, C.W. (1959) *The Sociological Imagination*. New York: Oxford University Press.

Mitchell, J.C. (1983) 'Case and situational analysis'. *Sociological Review*, 31 (2), 187–211.

Moerman, M. (1974) 'Accomplishing ethnicity'. In R. Turner (ed.), *Ethnomethodology* (pp. 34–68). Harmondsworth: Penguin.

Moisander, J. and Valtonen, A. (2006) *Qualitative Marketing Research: A Cultural Approach*. London: Sage.

Monk, R. (1991) *Ludwig Wittgenstein: Duty of Genius*. Harmondsworth: Penguin.

Morley, D. (1992) *Television, Audiences and Cultural Studies*. London: Routledge.

Morse, J.M. (1994) 'Designing funded qualitative research'. In N. Denzin and Y. Lincoln (eds), *Handbook of Qualitative Research* (pp. 220–35). Thousand Oaks, CA: Sage.

Mulkay, M. (1984) 'The ultimate compliment: a sociological analysis of ceremonial discourse'. *Sociology*, 18, 531–49.

Murcott, A. (1997) 'The PhD: some informal notes'. Unpublished paper, School of Health and Social Care, South Bank University, London.

Murray, R. (2003) 'Survive your viva'. *Guardian Education*, 16 September.

Myers, M. and Avison, D. (2002) *Qualitative Research in Information Systems*. London: Sage.

Nelson, C. (2003) 'Can E.T. phone home? The brave new world of university surveillance'. *Academe*, 89, 30–5.

Neubauer, B. (2005) *The Write-Brain Workbook: 366 Exercises to Liberate Your Writing*. Cincinnati, OH: F & W .

Nish, W.W. (2007) 'Professors' pet peeves: how to receive a less than enthusiastic letter of recommendation'. Retrieved 4 November 2007 from Hanover College Psychology Department's Graduate School Planning website at http://psych.hanover.edu/gradschoolplanning.html.

Noaks, L. and Wincup, E. (2004) *Criminological Research*. London: Sage.

Noble, W. (2006) *Noble's Book of Writing Blunders and How To Avoid Them*. Cincinnati, OH: Writer's Digest Books.

O'Brien, M. (1993) 'Social research and sociology'. In N. Gilbert (ed.), *Researching Social Life* (pp. 1–17). London: Sage.

O Dochartaigh, N. (2007) *Internet Research Skills*. London: Sage.

Penslar, R.L. (2007) *IRB Guidebook*. Retrieved 15 October 2007 from the US Department of Health and Human Services at http://www.hhs.gov/ohrp/irb/irb_guidebook.htm.

Peräkylä, A. (1989) 'Appealing to the experience of the patient in the care of the dying'. *Sociology of Health and Illness*, 11 (2), 117–34.

Peräkylä, A. (1995) *AIDS Counselling*. Cambridge: Cambridge University Press.

Peräkylä, A. (2004) 'Reliability and validity in research based upon transcripts'. In D. Silverman (ed.), *Qualitative Research: Theory, Method and Practice*, 2nd edn (pp. 282–303). London: Sage.

Peters, D.P. and Ceci, S.J. (1982) 'Peer-review practices of psychological journals: the fate of published articles, submitted again'. *The Behavioral and Brain Sciences*,1982, 187–95.

Peters, R. (1997) *Getting What You Came For: The Smart Student's Guide to Earning an MA or PhD*, rev. edn. New York: Farrar, Straus, and Giroux.

Phelps, R., Fisher, K. and Ellis, A. (2007) *Organizing and Managing Your Research: A Practical Guide for Postgraduates*. London: Sage.

Phillips, E. and Pugh, D. (1994) *How To Get a PhD*, 2nd edn. Buckingham: Open University Press.

Plutzer, E. (1991) 'The Protestant ethic and the spirit of academia: an essay on graduate education' *Teaching Sociology*, 19, 302–7.

Popper, K. (1959) *The Logic of Scientific Discovery*. New York: Basic.

Popper, K. (1963) *Conjectures and Refutations: The Growth of Scientific Knowledge*. London: Routledge.

Potter, J. (2002) 'Two kinds of natural'. *Discourse Studies*, 4 (4), 539–42.

Potter, J. (2004) 'Discourse analysis as a way of analysing naturally-occurring talk'. In D. Silverman (ed.), *Qualitative Research: Theory, Method and Practice*, 2nd edn (pp. 200–21). London: Sage.

Potter, J. and Wetherell, M. (1987) *Discourse and Social Psychology: Beyond Attitudes and Behaviour*. London: Sage.

Potter, J. and Wetherell, M. (1994) 'Analysing discourse'. In A. Bryman and R.G. Burgess (eds), *Analysing Qualitative Data* (pp. 47–66). London: Routledge.

Potter, S. (ed.) (2002) *Doing Postgraduate Research*. London: Sage.

Propp, V.I. (1968) *Morphology of the Folktale*, 2nd rev. edn. L.A. ed. Wagner. Austin, TX: University of Texas Press.

Psathas, G. (1990) *Interaction Competence*. Washington, DC: University Press of America.

Punch, K. (1998) *Introduction to Social Research: Quantitative and Qualitative Approaches*. London: Sage.

Punch, K. (2006) *Developing Effective Research Proposals*, 2nd edn. London: Sage.

Punch, M. (1986) *The Politics and Ethics of Fieldwork*. Beverly Hills, CA: Sage.

Punch, M. (1994) '*Politics and Ethics in Fieldwork*'. In N. Denzin and Y. Lincoln (eds), *Handbook of Qualitative Research* (pp. 83–97). Thousand Oaks, CA: Sage.

Pursley-Crotteau, S. and Stern, P. (1996) 'Creating a new life: dimensions of temperance in perinatal cocaine crack users'. *Qualitative Health Research*, 6 (3), 350–67.

Radcliffe-Brown, A.R. (1948) *The Andaman Islanders*. Glencoe, IL: Free Press.

Rapley, T. (2004) 'Interviews'. In C. Seale, G. Gobo, J.F. Gubrium and D. Silverman (eds), *Qualitative Research Practice* (pp. 15–33). London: Sage.

Reason, P. and Rowan, J. (1981) *Human Inquiry: A Sourcebook of New Paradigm Research*. Chichester: Wiley.

Reid, A.O. (1992) 'Computer management strategies for text data'. In B.F. Crabtree and W.L. Miller (eds), *Doing Qualitative Research* (pp. 125–45). Newbury Park, CA: Sage.

Richards, L. and Richards, T. (1994) 'Using computers in qualitative analysis'. In N. Denzin and Y. Lincoln (eds), *Handbook of Qualitative Research* (pp. 445–62). Newbury Park, CA: Sage.

Richardson, L. (1990) *Writing Strategies: Researching Diverse Audiences*. Newbury Park, CA: Sage.

Richardson, L. (1992) 'The consequences of poetic representation'. In C. Ellis and M. Flaherty (eds), *Investigating Subjectivity* (pp. 125–37). Thousand Oaks, CA: Sage.

Richardson, L. (2000) 'Writing: a method of inquiry'. In N. Denzin and Y. Lincoln (eds), *Handbook of Qualitative Research*, 2nd edn (pp. 923–48). Thousand Oaks, CA: Sage.

Riessman, C.K. (1993) *Narrative Analysis*. Newbury Park, CA: Sage.

Riessman, C. (2005) 'Exporting ethics: a narrative about narrative research in South India'. *Health* (special Issue on Informed Consent, Ethics and Narrative), 9 (4), 473–90.

Riessman, C.K. (2008) *Narrative Methods for the Human Sciences*. Thousand Oaks, CA: Sage.

Rose, G. (2007) *Visual Methodologies*. London: Sage.

Rosenau, P.M. (1992) *Postmodernism and the Social Sciences: Insights, Inroads, and Intrusions*. Princeton, NJ: Princeton University Press.

Rudestam, K. and Newton, R. (1992) *Surviving your Dissertation*. Newbury Park, CA: Sage.

Ryen, A. (2004) 'Ethical issues'. In C. Seale, G. Gobo, J.F. Gubrium and D. Silverman (eds), *Qualitative Research Practice*. London: Sage.

Sacks, H. (1974) 'On the analysability of stories by children'. In R. Turner (ed.), *Ethnomethodology*. Harmondsworth: Penguin.

Sacks, H. (1984a) 'On doing "being ordinary"'. In J.M. Atkinson and J. Heritage (eds), *Structures of Social Action: Studies in Conversation Analysis* (pp. 513–29). Cambridge: Cambridge University Press.

Sacks, H. (1984b) 'Notes on methodology'. In J.M. Atkinson and J. Heritage (eds), *Structures of Social Action: Studies in Conversation Analysis* (pp. 21–7). Cambridge: Cambridge University Press.

Sacks, H. (1992) *Lectures on Conversation*, Vols 1–2. Oxford: Blackwell.

Sacks, H., Schegloff, E.A. and Jefferson, G. (1974) 'A simplest systematics for the organization of turn-taking in conversation'. *Language*, 50 (4), 696–735.

Saukko, P. (2003) *Doing Research in Cultural Studies*. London: Sage.

Schegloff, E. (1986) 'The routine as achievement'. *Human Studies*, 9, 111–51.

Schegloff, E. (1991) 'Reflections on talk and social structure'. In D. Boden and D. Zimmerman (eds), *Talk and Social Structure: Studies in Ethnomethodology and Conversation Analysis* (pp. 44–70). Cambridge: Polity.

Schneider, A. (1998) 'Harvard faces the aftermath of a graduate student's suicide'. *Chronicle of Higher Education*, 23 October.

Schreiber, R. (1996) '(Re)defining my self: women's process of recovery from depression'. *Qualitative Health Research*, 6 (4), 469–91.

Schwartz, H. and Jacobs, J. (1979) *Qualitative Sociology: A Method to the Madness*. New York: Free Press.

Seale, C. (1996) 'Living alone towards the end of life'. *Ageing and Society*, 16, 75–91.

Seale, C. (1999) *The Quality of Qualitative Research*. London: Sage.

Seale, C. (ed.) (2004) *Researching Society and Culture*, 2nd edn. London: Sage.

Seale, C. (2006) 'Gender accommodation in online cancer support groups'. *Health*, 10 (3), 345–60.

Seale, C. and Charteris-Black, J. (2009) 'Keyword analysis'. In I.L. Bourgeault, R. DeVries and R. Dingwall (eds), *Handbook of Qualitative Health Research*. London: Sage.

Seale, C. and Kelly, M. (1997) 'A comparison of hospice and hospital care for people who die: views of the surviving spouse'. *Palliative Medicine*, Vol. 11 (2): 93–100.

Seale, C., Charteris-Black, J. and Ziebland, S. (2006) 'Gender, cancer experience and internet use: a comparative keyword analysis of interviews and online cancer support groups'. *Social Science and Medicine*, 62 (10), 2577–90.

Seale, C., Gobo, G., Gubrium, J.F. and Silverman, D. (eds) (2004) *Qualitative Research Practice*. London: Sage.

Seldin, P. (2004) *The Teaching Portfolio: A Practical Guide to Improved Performance and Promotion/Tenure Decisions*. Bolton, MA: Anchor.

Sharples, M., Davison, L., Thomas, G. and Rudman, P. (2003) 'Children as photographers: an analysis of children's photographic behaviour and intentions at three age levels'. *Visual Communication*, 2 (3), 303–30.

Shaw, I. and Gould, N. (2002) *Qualitative Research in Social Work*. London: Sage.

Shea, C. (2000) 'Don't talk to humans: the crack down on social science research'. *Lingua Franca*, 10 (6).

Silverman, D. (1968a) 'Clerical ideologies: a research note'. *British Journal of Sociology*, XIX (3): 326–333.

Silverman (1968b) 'Formal organizations or industrial sociology: towards a social action analysis of organizations'. *Sociology*, 2: 221–38.

Silverman, D. (1970) *The Theory of Organizations*. London: Heinemann Educational Books.

Silverman, D. (1981) 'The child as a social object: Down's syndrome children in a paediatric cardiology clinic'. *Sociology of Health and Illness*, 3 (3), 254–74.

Silverman, D. (1983) 'The clinical subject: adolescents in a cleft palate clinic'. *Sociology of Health and Illness*, 5 (3), 253–74.

Silverman, D. (1984) 'Going private: ceremonial forms in a private oncology clinic'. *Sociology*, 18, 191–202.

Silverman, D. (1985) *Qualitative Methodology and Sociology: Describing the Social World*. Aldershot: Gower.

Silverman, D. (1987) *Communication and Medical Practice: Social Relations in the Clinic*. London: Sage.

Silverman, D. (1989) 'Making sense of a precipice: constituting identity in an HIV clinic'. In P. Aggleton, G. Hart and P. Davies (eds), *AIDS: Social Representations, Social Practices*. Lewes: Falmer.

Silverman, D. (1990) 'The social organization of HIV counselling'. In P. Aggleton, G. Hart and P. Davies (eds), *AIDS: Individual, Cultural and Policy Perspectives* (pp. 191–211). Lewes: Falmer.

Silverman, D. (1993) *Interpreting Qualitative Data* (First Edition), London: Sage.

Silverman, D. (1997) *Discourses of Counselling: HIV Counselling as Social Interaction*. London: Sage.

Silverman, D. (1998) *Harvey Sacks: Social Science and Conversation Analysis*. Cambridge: Polity.

Silverman, D. (2001) *Interpreting Qualitative Data: Methods for Analysing Text, Talk and Interaction*, 2nd edn. London: Sage.

Silverman, D. (2004a) 'Analysing conversation'. In C. Seale (ed.), *Researching Society and Culture*, 2nd edn (pp. 261–74) London: Sage.

Silverman, D. (ed.) (2004b) *Qualitative Research: Theory, Method and Practice*, 2nd edn. London: Sage.

Silverman, D. (2006) *Interpreting Qualitative Data*, 3rd edn. London: Sage.

Silverman, D. (2007) *A Very Short, Fairly Interesting, Reasonably Cheap Book about Qualitative Research*. London: Sage.

Silverman, D. and Bloor, M. (1989) 'Patient-centred medicine: some sociological observations on its constitution, penetration and cultural assonance'. In G.L. Albrecht (ed.), *Advances in Medical Sociology* (pp. 3–26). Greenwich, CT: JAI.

Silverman, D. and Gubrium, J. (1994) 'Competing strategies for analyzing the contexts of social interaction'. *Sociological Inquiry*, 64 (2), 179–98.

Silverman, D. and Jones, J. (1976) *Organizational Work: The Language of Grading/the Grading of Language*. London: Collier-Macmillan.

Silverman, D., Baker, C. and Keogh, J. (1997) 'Advice-giving and advice-reception in parent–teacher interviews'. In I. Hutchby and J. Moran-Ellis (eds), *Children and Social Competence* (pp. 220–40). London: Falmer.

Singleton, R., Straits, B., Straits, M. and McAllister, R. (1988) *Approaches to Social Research*. Oxford: Oxford University Press.

Small, S.A. (1995) 'Action-oriented research: models and methods'. *Journal of Marriage and Family*, 57 (4), 941–55.

Smith, J.K. and Heshusius, L. (1986) 'Closing down the conversation: the end of the qualitative–quantitative debate among educational enquirers'. *Educational Researcher*, 15, 4–12.

Sontag, S. (1979) *Illness as Metaphor*. Harmondsworth: Penguin.

Speer, S. (2002) '"Natural" and "contrived" data: a sustainable distinction?', *Discourse Studies*, 4 (4), 511–25.

Spencer, L., Ritchle, J., Lewis, J. and Dillon, J. (2003) *Quality in Qualitative Evaluation: A Framework for Assessing Research Evidence*. London: Government Chief Social Researcher's Office.

Spradley, J.P. (1979) *The Ethnographic Interview*. New York: Holt, Rinehart and Winston.

Stake, R. (2000) 'Case studies'. In N. Denzin and Y. Lincoln (eds), *Handbook of Qualitative Research*, 2nd edn (pp. 435–54). Thousand Oaks, CA: Sage.

Stimson, G. (1986) 'Place and space in sociological fieldwork'. *Sociological Review*, 34 (3), 641–56.

Strauss, A. and Corbin, J. (1990) *Basics of Qualitative Research*. Newbury Park, CA: Sage.

Strauss, A. and Corbin, J. (1994) 'Grounded theory methodology: an overview'. In N. Denzin and Y. Lincoln (eds), *Handbook of Qualitative Research* (pp. 262–72). Thousand Oaks, CA: Sage.

Strauss, A. and Corbin, J. (2008) *Basics of Qualitative Research*, 3rd edn. London: Sage.

Strong, P. (1979) *The Ceremonial Order of the Clinic*. London: Routledge.

Suchman, L. (1987) *Plans and Situated Actions: The Problem of Human–Machine Communication*. Cambridge: Cambridge University Press.

Sudnow, D. (1968a) *Passing On: The Social Organization of Dying*. Englewood Cliffs, NJ: Prentice Hall.

Sudnow, D. (1968b) 'Normal crimes'. In E. Rubington and M. Weinberg (eds), *Deviance: The Interactionist Perspective*. New York: Macmillan.

Ten Have, P. (1998) *Doing Conversation Analysis: A Practical Guide*. London: Sage.

Tenner, E. (2004) 'The pitfalls of academic mentorships'. *Chronicle Review*, 50 (49), B7.

Turner, R. (1989) 'Deconstructing the field'. In J.F. Gubrium and D. Silverman (eds), *The Politics of Field Research* (pp. 30–48). London: Sage.

US Department of Health and Human Services (2005) Code of federal regulations. Title 45: Public welfare (§46.102d). Retrieved 4 November 2005, from http://www.hhs.gov/ohrp/humansubjects/guidance/45cfr46.htm#46.102.

Valero, Y.F. (2001) 'Departmental factors affecting time-to-degree and completion rates of doctoral students at one land-grant research institution'. *Journal of Higher Education*, 72 (3), 341–67.

Van de Werfhorst, H.G. and Andersen, R. (2005) 'Social background, credential inflation and educational strategies'. *Acta Sociologica*, 48 (4), 321–40.

Vandiver, M., Giacopassi, D.J. and Gathje, P.R. (2002) '"I hope someone murders your mother!": an exploration of extreme support for the death penalty'. *Deviant Behavior*, 23, 385–415.

Van Maanen, J. (1988) *Tales of the Field*. Chicago: University of Chicago Press.

Venkatash, S. (2008) *Gang Leader for a Day*. London: Allen Lane.

Walsh, D. (1998) 'Doing ethnography'. In C. Seale (ed.), *Researching Society and Culture* (pp. 225–38). London: Sage.

Ward, A. (2002) 'The writing process'. In S. Potter (ed.), *Doing Postgraduate Research* (pp. 71–116). London: Sage.

Warren, A. (1988) *Gender Issues in Field Research*. Newbury Park, CA: Sage.

Warren, A. and Rasmussen, P. (1977) 'Sex and gender in fieldwork research'. *Urban Life*, 6, 359–69.

Watts, H.D. and White, P. (2000) 'Presentation skills'. In D. Burton (ed.), *Research Training for Social Scientists*. London: Sage.

Webb, B. and Stimson, G. (1976) 'People's accounts of medical encounters'. In M. Wadsworth (ed.), *Everyday Medical Life*. London: Martin Robertson.

Weber, M. (1946) 'Science as a vocation'. In H. Gerth and C.W. Mills (eds), *From Max Weber*. New York: Oxford University Press.

Weber, M. (1949) *Methodology of the Social Sciences*. New York: Free Press.

Weinberg, M.S. (1994) 'The nudist management of respectability'. In P. Kollock and J. O'Brien (eds), *The Production of Reality: Essays and Readings in Social Psychology* (pp. 392–401). Thousand Oaks, CA: Pine Forge.

Whyte, W.F. (1949) 'The social structure of the restaurant'. *American Journal of Sociology*, 54, 302–10.

Whyte, W.F. (1993) *Street Corner Society* (Fourth revised edition). Chicago: University of Chicago Press.

Wield, D. (2002) 'Planning and organizing a research project'. In S. Potter (ed.), *Doing Postgraduate Research* (pp. 35–70). London: Sage.

Wilkinson, S. (2004) 'Focus group research'. In D. Silverman (ed.), *Qualitative Research: Theory, Method and Practice*, 2nd edn (pp. 177–99). London: Sage.

Wilkinson, S. and Kitzinger, C. (2000) 'Thinking differently about thinking positive: a discursive approach to cancer patients' talk'. *Social Science and Medicine*, 50, 797–811.

Wittgenstein, L. (1980) *Culture and Value*. Trans, P. Winch. Oxford: Blackwell.

Wolcott, H. (1990) *Writing Up Qualitative Research*. Newbury Park, CA: Sage.

Wolcott, H. (2001) *Writing Up Qualitative Research*, 2nd edn. Thousand Oaks, CA: Sage.

Wolcott, H. (2009) *Writing Up Qualitative Research*, 3rd edn. London: Sage.

Wolfe, A. (1990) 'Books vs. articles: two ways of publishing sociology'. *Sociological Forum*, 5 (3), 477–89.

Yagoda, B. (2007) *When You Catch an Adjective, Kill It: The Parts of Speech, for Better and/or Worse*. New York: Broadway.

Author Index

Subject Index